Antitrust Abuse in the New Economy

Antitrust Abuse in the New Economy

The Microsoft Case

Richard L. Gordon
The Pennsylvania State University

Edward Elgar
Cheltenham, UK • Northampton, MA, USA

Published by
Edward Elgar Publishing Limited
Glensanda House
Montpellier Parade
Cheltenham
Glos GL50 1UA
UK

Edward Elgar Publishing, Inc.
136 West Street
Suite 202
Northampton
Massachusetts 01060
USA

A catalogue record for this book
is available from the British Library

Library of Congress Cataloguing in Publication Data
Gordon, Richard L., 1934–
    Antitrust abuse in the new economy : the Microsoft case / Richard L. Gordon.
        p. cm.
    1. United States—Trials, litigation, etc. 2. Microsoft Corporation—Trials, litigation etc. 3. Antitrust law—United States. 4. Restraint of trade—United States. 5. Computer software industry—Law and legislation—United States. I. Title.

KF228.U55 G67 2002
343.73'0721—dc21   2002021984

ISBN 1 84064 928 3

Printed and bound in Great Britain by Biddles Ltd, *www.biddles.co.uk*

Table of Contents

Preface

On November 5, 1999, Judge Thomas Penfield Jackson's "Findings of Fact" in U.S. et al. v. Microsoft was issued. My then passive interest in the case inspired a downloading of the Findings. I found them disturbing. The Findings confirmed the assertions of case opponents that the charges too narrowly focused on competition between Microsoft and one then emerging, then independent, software firm, Netscape.

Given these concerns, I began what became extensive downloading of further material. I started with the testimony of the expert economists and the main statements by the attorneys for both sides. Eventually, more testimony was examined, and the government's exhibits were viewed. Quickly, I decided that the widely disseminated view that a brilliant government case had overwhelmed an inept Microsoft defense was at best incomplete. The more I delved, the more deficiencies emerged. Checking government charges against the exhibits indicated that the assertions were totally unsubstantiated and government misrepresentation was rampant.

Clearly, the favorable journalistic interpretation of the government's case is correct in the narrow sense that the government succeeded almost completely in persuading Judge Jackson. My objection is that this victory was attained in undesirable ways, specified in Chapter 1. The case was developed in a fashion inconsistent with how an antitrust case should be conducted.

Antitrust law is concerned with the functioning of the market economy. Proper enforcement requires understanding and use of the relevant economics. This is widely recognized by employing expert economists and citation of the economics literature.

As this book documents, the government's case consists entirely of nasty sounding internal memorandums from Microsoft and complaints from people disgruntled with Microsoft. The economics starts and finishes with terse statements of principles. The government's economic experts rely almost entirely on the documents and complaints to evaluate the case. Their reference to either the economics literature or other evidence is almost nonexistent.

In contrast, Microsoft presented a systematic economic analysis of the case and forcefully indicated the absence of such analysis in the government's case. Thus, once one rejects the legal and journalistic criterion that winning is what matters, the case is one in which unsound government arguments won over a much more coherent, more valid Microsoft defense.

This neglected problem seemed worthy of documentation. Curiously, the subsequent flood of commentaries on the case only reinforced my interest. Even case opponents failed to note the case's weaknesses and Microsoft's demonstration of these defects. Some critics seemed to concede the relevance of the various courtroom tricks at which the government apparently far outdid Microsoft.

Here, the effort is primarily to review the critical supporting economic principles and apply them to the case. Microsoft relied on terse statements of the theory and extensive empirical evidence. Whatever the wisdom in the courtroom, this limitation is inconsistent with the goals of this book. To demonstrate the weakness of the economics, the relevant theory needs note. A second goal is to document the reliance on anecdotes and apparent bad appearances and the absence of adequate supporting analysis.

This effort is an unplanned extension of my four decades of exploration of another area of government intervention, energy. Typically of academic energy economists, I developed repugnance at government activity in the sector. Eventually, I became aware that specialists in other areas of government action had similar objections to the conduct of policy. Indeed, no government regulation is exempt from devastating criticism from the economists specializing in the subject. However, many economists are reluctant to generalize from this experience.

Around the middle 1980s, my growing concerns inspired examination of the supposedly extremist ideological writings of strong advocates of free-market economics. Particular attention was given the Chicago and Austrian approaches.

This inspired producing a book (Gordon 1994) arguing that opposition to regulation was widespread among economists. The bulk of the book was devoted to examples that started with antitrust and ended with public ownership of land. With all that presented, I then argued that free-market proponents, especially of the Chicago and Austrian types, were simply particularly forceful expositors of beliefs widely supported by economists. As generalists, these free-market advocates were unaware how damning was the applied analysis.

My 1994 treatment of antitrust managed to stress issues central to the Microsoft case. One section summed up the problems of measuring the intensity of competition. The next part stressed the drawback of claims that competitive tactics, particularly predation, were an effective way to limit competition. The concentration reflected the emphasis given to predation in the economic literature. Since the case involved tying and exclusive dealing, a look at the germane literature became appropriate. It proved thin and critical of the fascination in antitrust enforcement over the use of tying.

My earlier discussion of antitrust concluded with review of the laws. That sketch, in turn, ended by noting that Dominick Armentano's (1990) call for abolition of antitrust was only an alternative interpretation of familiar criticisms of antitrust. Others, notably Robert Bork (1978) and Richard Posner (1976), viewed the defects in implementation as remediable by altering the focus of enforcement. Armentano countered that the defects were too deep-seated to remedy with anything short of repeal.

How best to identify competition and inefficient competitive practices are the issues of the Microsoft case. Therefore, this book expands on my earlier writings on these questions and applies the material to the case.

Since so many commentators on the case advised one side or the other, confessions of involvement or noninvolvement are routine. This need to disclose has unfortunate aspects examined in Chapter 6. For present purposes, the critical point is that while I have interacted with many of those involved on both sides, that involvement covered energy matters totally unrelated to the case.

Chapter 1 Introduction: The Case and Its Critics

With enormous publicity (discussed in Chapter 6), the Microsoft Corporation was charged on May 18, 1998, tried (between October 18, 1998 and June 26, 1999), and convicted (on April 3, 2000) as a monopolist that abused its monopoly power. The suit was a joint prosecution by the Antitrust Division of the U.S. Department of Justice (DOJ) and nineteen state Attorneys General of two cases. The cases are U.S. v. Microsoft Corporation (98-1232) and State of New York *ex rel.* Attorney General Eliot Spitzer, *et al.*, versus Microsoft Corporation (98-1233). These plaintiffs are called here "the government." Moreover, Microsoft countersued the states.

The government saw Microsoft as possessing monopoly power so obvious that it needed little appraisal (see Heilemann 2000, 302 and 309). The government concentrated on Microsoft's business practices. These were allegedly designed only to preserve the monopoly by illegal methods. Microsoft countered both phases of the charge. The company disputed the assertion of monopoly and the evidence presented to support that contention. Similarly, it challenged the veracity of the allegations about its tactics.

The Microsoft case, thus, is an effort to brand the Microsoft Corporation as a vicious monopolist such as Standard Oil of New Jersey in the early twentieth century. The Standard Oil analogy cuts both ways. Part of the massive revaluation of past policies is work arguing that Standard Oil was a force for progress, not evil. The Microsoft case was the first major antitrust case for many years. Presumably, the primary influence was the nature of the Clinton administration's appointments in the antitrust field. The administration's appointees were far more favorable to vigorous use of the antitrust than their predecessors in the Reagan and Bush administrations.

The antitrust case against Microsoft is in several ways a pioneering action but also in several other ways a reprise of familiar antitrust debates. The case critically depends on new, controversial concepts in economics. However, the government barely explained and never evaluated these concepts.

As documented in Chapter 6, the case is about the Internet, and both sides presented their arguments on the Internet. The underlying material is much more freely available than in past cases. More conventional communications mediums also vigorously reported on the case; the coverage seems unusually heavy for a antitrust case. No prior case seems to have generated so many journalistic books or so extensive rapid scholarly reaction (see Chapter 6).

The concerns relate to old problems arising in a new industry. The key old side of the case is that it represents governmental acceptance of the complaints of aggrieved competitors. Adoption of the arguments seems to include acquisition of these competitors' animosity towards Microsoft.

As the literature on the case makes clear, the case germinated from the dudgeon of Microsoft's rivals. Chief among them were Netscape, Sun Microsystems, and Oracle, but probably also including America Online, IBM, and Apple Computer. Executives from all these firms except Oracle served as government witnesses in the case.

However, it was the alleged harm to Netscape that was the bulk of the case. Microsoft allegedly fatally damaged the purportedly poor, innocent, striving newcomer. Microsoft was charged with seeking to undermine by illegal tactics Netscape's position as the leading provider of Internet browsers, the programs used to connect computers with the Internet.

Netscape was incorporated in April 1994, released the "beta" version of its Netscape Navigator program on October 13, 1994, and the final version on December 15, 1994 (Barksdale 1999, 30-33). (The beta version is standard software industry terminology for a version made available for consumer testing before final release. Alpha refers to versions too imperfect to release.) Eventually, Netscape Navigator evolved into Netscape Communicator. This book follows the participants in and commentators on the case in using the original name throughout.

Netscape's Marc Andreessen had bragged that Netscape Navigator would become a "middleware" platform hosting software that could run with every operating system. Andreessen was a cofounder and vice president for technology of Netscape. He was still in his twenties and came to Netscape from the University of Illinois where he headed a group that developed a pioneering browser called Mosaic. His platform would make Microsoft's operating system, Windows, irrelevant. An operating system is the program that provides essential organizational instructions to personal computers. Windows is the leading operating system used for personal computers. The programs that undertake practical operations such as word processing are termed applications. Microsoft then undertook allegedly illegal acts solely to end the threat. The response was developing and aggressively promoting a rival browser, Internet Explorer.

As Microsoft counters, America Online (AOL) purchased Netscape with stock worth $4.3 billion when the sale was announced in November 1998 and $10 billion when the deal was completed in 1999. Microsoft naturally uses that sale to show that no harm arose. The government counters that the sale was despite the damage. In particular, the government's case centers on the middleware threat. Allegedly, this was Microsoft's sole concern, and, while Netscape survives, the challenge does not. That this argument is defective is a central argument of this book.

The case involves struggles among at least three firms with leading roles in a part of the computer sector. In addition to Microsoft and Netscape, Sun Microsystems, a specialist in larger computers called servers, was challenging Microsoft through offering a new computer language Java and by proposing the network-computer alternative to the personal computer. That alternative would have consumers employ a simpler machine that was linked to one of Sun's servers. The server would provide material presently stored on a personal computer. Conversely, as was inadequately noted in the case, upgrades in both Intel processors and Windows were creating challenges to Sun in the server realm (see Muglia 1999).[1] Microsoft acted to counter the challenges. In choosing among the combatants, the government argued that Microsoft was the firm with monopoly power and thus deserving of rebuke.

As commentaries on the case note (e.g., McKenzie 2000b, 199-204 and Liebowitz and Margolis 1999, 248), the aggrieved companies hired consultants to prepare an antiMicrosoft argument reflecting their ire. The government accepted these complaints and launched the case. These government officials also adopted indignation of these rivals. Indeed, the government used James Barksdale, then the president and chief executive officer of Netscape, as its first witness. Barksdale's testimony was an overview of the Netscape aspects of the case. He made every one of the government's points. Economists were enlisted. The journalistic coverage was favorable to the government. Finally, Judge Thomas Penfield Jackson, who tried the case, accepted the gist of the case, again particularly including wrath.

The June 28, 2001 Circuit Court of Appeals decision in the case gave considerable attention to Judge Jackson's views and his willingness to share them with journalists. The Circuit Court rejected several important decisions by Jackson. These reversals (and the upholding of other findings) arose from a reasoned approach lacking in the government and Jackson treatments. That decision, however, had considerable drawbacks. These involve reticence fully to confront the errors of economic appraisal made by Jackson.

Post-trial commentary was similarly divided. Some endorsed the government's view. Others saw the case as another example of how antitrust

---

[1] As with several direct testimonies in the case, this was not dated. However, these were released at the time of courtroom appearance so the year of issue can be and was inferred.

laws are used to limit competition. To be sure, the strongest advocates of minimum government such as Milton Friedman, the leading proponents of Austrian economics, and, as discussed in Chapter 6, several libertarian think tanks vigorously criticized the case. This reflected long-standing skepticism about antitrust.

However, before and after, other skeptics about public policy were more divided. As discussed here, the most critical example was one of the government's expert economists, Franklin M. Fisher of the Massachusetts Institute of Technology (MIT). His prior writings were critical of concepts that he accepted during the case. The other expert, Frederick Warren-Boulton, was a former Antitrust Division economist now in private consulting. He is best known for specialized work on vertical integration, rather than for broad commentaries on antitrust. Two other important supporters of the case were former law school professor and circuit court judge Robert Bork and University of Chicago economics professor Dennis Carlton (Heilemann 2000, 280-82; also see Carlton and Waldman 1998 and 2000).

The full acceptance and employment of the reproof of interested parties are disturbing. Such arguments should be and usually are viewed skeptically at least by academic economists and judges. Advocates of public policy that aids business characteristically produce frantic, often indignant cries for action. U.S. oil producers and coal producers everywhere complained about unfair competition from imported oil. Farmers assert that middlemen deprive them of a fair living. Small business decries competition from chains. Skeptics about the Microsoft case see the government once again agreeing to respond to accusations from competitors. The striking difference is that these rivals are themselves strong, thriving firms.

Too little attention was given to the legitimacy of all this ire. The issue is whether the case was economically valid. The economic attack on antitrust centers on this issue. Posner's (1976) and Bork's (1978) widely cited critiques of antitrust insist that the sole focus be economic efficiency. While suggestions of other goals exist, the alternatives are, to the extent they can be defined, inappropriate public-policy guides. Antitrust, moreover, is likely to prove an unsatisfactory means to these alternate ends.

Economics, for example, recognizes that another concern is the distribution of results among different people. This acknowledgement, however, starts with caveats about the absence of consensus on the appropriate sharing mechanisms. Economics can add important warnings. The first is about the difficulties of measuring distributional effects of individual polices. The second is caution that rarely can regulations confine impacts to whomever someone wants to favor. Price controls tend initially to aid rich and poor alike. (The poor are ultimately hurt because the rich are better able to evade.) These problems then imply drawbacks to attaining goals other than efficiency.

Economics also warns that efficiency attainment is itself tricky. The Lipsey-Lancaster (1956) concept of the second best warns that in an inefficiency-ridden economy, eliminating only one departure from the theoretic ideal need not be desirable. Buchanan ([1969] 1999) presents a more general argument adding in the difficulties of appraisal when markets are in disequilibrium.

All this leaves the Posner-Bork proposal the least worst. Implementation requires a maximum effort to utilize the germane economics carefully and thoroughly to establish an antitrust charge. A classic statement in the literature was an observation by Judge Charles Wyzanski in the United Shoe Machinery case. He warned that continuation of antitrust powers depended on assurance that they were not abused. The caveat arose because the laws give sweeping powers while economics warns of the problems of evaluation. The zeal to win at any cost that characterized the Microsoft case seems a blatant failure to heed Wyzanki's warning,

Most journalistic observers characteristically failed to recognize the economic issues. As is typical of journalism, gladiatorial skill was emphasized over difficult technical arguments. Stress was on supposedly unsatisfactory deposition testimony by Microsoft chairman Bill Gates and other Microsoft executives, botched courtroom demonstrations, and alleged but nonexistent inconsistencies in the testimony of Richard L. Schmalensee also of MIT, the expert economist for Microsoft.

This book views the case as ill conducted and ill advised. Both the form and substance are unsatisfactory. The government's argument is incomplete, incoherent, and inconsistent. The government drowned the court in details to create an impression of illegal behavior. Surface appearances dominated.

The parts were never shaped into a coherent demonstration of anticompetitive behavior that systematically presented and developed properly the long chain of reasoning supporting the breakup of Microsoft. Examination suggests that the avoidance reflects an underlying weakness. While Microsoft clearly saw those deficiencies, its defense also overemphasized the details. This excess probably was necessary because so much needed response. I could not avoid extensive review but separated it from the analysis.

The case is a disturbing combination of unsatisfactory economic arguments and clever efforts to exploit every real or fabricated Microsoft misstep. Antipathy went deeper than appropriate. The government and its expert economists substitute anger for economic analysis. Apparently, this caused the government and its expert economists to feel that presentation of the analytic and factual bases for the charges was unnecessary.

The government relies predominantly upon the documents and testimony in the case. The core is material from Microsoft and its critics asserting Microsoft's fear of a Netscape platform threat and a desire to respond by developing a successful alternative. Stress was on a few often-cited colorful statements by Microsoft employees. However, the government systematically employed distortions to advance its case. These damaging quotations prove hearsay, taken out of context, or insignificant. Even so, these quotations fail to substantiate the government case; often indeed, even the cited material undermines the case. Based solely on categorical, unsubstantiated declarations by Fisher and Warren-Boulton, the government leaps to conclude that illegal means were employed to attain Microsoft's goals.

Given that these problems are so evident, this raises questions about the care with which the government economists examined the material. Nevertheless, in a paper coauthored with Daniel Rubinfeld, Fisher contended, "The overwhelming flood of statements from Microsoft's executives and other employees does not leave much ambiguity as to what was happening in this case (2000a, 94)."

Schmalensee's testimony explicitly notes about the government economists, "where I would expect to see objective analysis based on quantitative data, I see nothing but unsupported–and unanalyzed–assertions" (par. 325, 164). Schmalensee (paras. 325-8, 164-5) expands.

This concern was expressed often in the case. In response to pretrial complaints by Microsoft, the government's opening arguments (October 19, 1998, a.m.) included a lengthy effort to defend the use of such documents. However, the opening arguments of Microsoft (October 20, 1998) reiterate the complaint. Microsoft's Proposed Findings of Fact (mfof) (paras. 119-21, 53-4) contains even more forceful statements (see Chapter 6). The case record amply confirms Schmalensee's reproach.

Considerable effort also was devoted to creating the appearance of incompetence or worse in Microsoft witnesses. In the most verifiable instance, the attack on Schmalensee, faults were invented to distract attention from the strength of his arguments. Much time was then spent unsuccessfully asking Microsoft representatives to confirm the government's interpretation.

Incessant assertion was made that only anticompetitive motives prevailed. Microsoft's position in operating systems is always described as a monopoly. Every Microsoft action is only to end middleware competition.

Clearly, the government side strongly believed in the case and convinced many others. Critics consider the case weak and that Microsoft was being punished for being so vigorously competitive. The operating-system monopoly charge is questionable; the assertion that only the middleware threat mattered is false.

The matters of substance and their implications are given the expected alternative explanations by each side. The government case was based on controversial economic principles that are asserted without proof. The government ignores the existence of a massive literature skeptical of its arguments. Analytic issues arise in the treatments of not only the market power of Microsoft, but also of the tactics it used to promote Internet Explorer. Classic relevant-market questions occur.

To this is added the particularly undeveloped assertion that the existence of a large stock of software, termed the applications barrier to entry, was the source of Microsoft's market position. This stress is the key unusual feature of the case. This employs a network-externality concept widely discussed in an economics literature ignored in the case. Examination would have shown the theory lacked practical relevance.

Moreover, the bulk of the limited analytic argument that the government presented arises in response to the analysis developed for Microsoft by Schmalensee. To be sure, Schmalensee's presentation of theory was terse and, in the network-externality case, confined to a short assertion. That appraisal was correct but undocumented. While that may be appropriate for the courtroom, it does not meet the needs of formal economic review. Thus, this book seeks to examine the relevant theoretic background.

Facing Schmalensee's presentation of criticisms, the government responds with unsubstantiated, vituperative denials. Whatever the limits of the Circuit Court of Appeals decision reviewing the case, that review well illustrates the usual practice of citing articles from the economics and the economically-informed legal literature.

Five to ten times as much effort was devoted to Microsoft's tactics as to the monopoly issue. The government presented neither its own coherent development of the accusation nor a satisfactory response to the Microsoft defense. This deficiency arose although Fisher presented material stressing the importance of proving monopoly. A discrepancy between terse but mostly solid presentations of the basic principles and failure explicitly to utilize them in evaluating the case is a chronic problem with Fisher's contribution.

These principles warrant summary here. (In this and other cases, the danger of distortion by condensation was outweighed by the need for more concise presentation.) Fisher begins by delineating the issues that he was asked to treat. The first is whether Microsoft has monopoly power. The others are three different names for misuse of monopoly–anti-competitive conduct generally, anti-competitive conduct in "markets" other than for operating systems, and unreasonable restraints of trade. He explains at length that anticompetitive actions can only succeed if monopoly exists. He includes the caveat:

Certain conduct (e.g., non-predatory price competition or product improvements) is so important to the competitive process, and the potential costs of interference are so high, that it is considered competitive (and not anti-competitive) even where it results in securing or maintaining a monopoly (par. 10, 4).

However, in his treatment of Microsoft, he invariably rejects by fiat suggestions that its actions are such legitimate competitive responses.

By the end of the trial, Fisher had presented and advocated at least two mutually inconsistent theories of Microsoft's monopoly, and the government had accepted both. One involved monopoly without maximizing short-run profits; the other argued that short-run profits were maximized. Whether this included the value of Internet Explorer was ignored.

That inconsistency is modest compared to that between the two theories presented in the trial and the theory presented to justify splitting Microsoft into separate operating systems and applications companies.

The government claimed that Microsoft's monopoly arose because of the large number of programs available for Windows. The Microsoft defense was that only a few basic programs matter. The case for break-up tacitly accepts Microsoft's view. The rationale for dividing the company is that the separate division would be more likely to make versions of the Office word processing, spreadsheet, and related programs package for the rival Linux operating system. This Linux version then would make that system a stronger competitor to Microsoft. This means, as Microsoft claimed, that a few programs are critical.

The treatments of the tactics issues are problematic in several ways. The government adopted an inappropriate framework, and every subsequent participant in the case including Microsoft itself has responded mechanically to that framework. The basic difficulty is that the issue is the vigor of Microsoft's effort to compete in Internet browsers. The government asserts that the actions were inefficient. Distinguishing excess is inherently difficult, and the proofs in the case are nonexistent.

The government designed arguments that combine dubious elements that too conveniently and too neatly resolve the issues. No economic analyses appear of why Microsoft is guilty of either monopoly or the anticompetitive actions. No evidence is provided that anyone was ruined or that customers suffered. Fisher conjectures that Microsoft's monopoly discouraged countless innovators who would have greatly improved the technology.

The government relies on Fisher's belief that preserving the Windows monopoly from a Netscape/Java platform threat is the sole explanation for everything. Fisher stresses the predatory nature of Microsoft's acts. Fisher denies that any other threats are relevant. At times, he even denigrates the Netscape/Java threat (see Chapter 9). His sole basis is documentary material generated in the case. These deficiencies reflect the underlying implausibility of the case.

Fisher devised arguments indicating ruin of Netscape was not essential. For proof, he relies on mention of the concept of raising rivals' costs. However, as I frequently reiterate in later chapters, he never explains the concept or its severe drawbacks. This is a grave defect because the case against Microsoft depends entirely on proving that the actions inefficiently raised rivals' costs. Moreover, the government also made other charges. These were tying, exclusive dealing, and monopolizing browsers.

To strengthen the case, several separate disputes between Microsoft and other firms were considered. However, noting other threats is inconsistent with the central case. The government uses them to suggest a pattern of aggressive behavior by Microsoft. The existence of so many challenges undermines the basic premise that only a middleware threat matters. The weaknesses of the examples undermine their value to the government. In no instance is evidence clear. In most cases, what is involved is a dispute between Microsoft and a company (Intel, IBM, and Sun Microsystems) capable of holding its own.

In short, Microsoft was correctly portrayed as an aggressive competitor that wanted to win and exhorted itself to do so. This does not matter unless Microsoft caused harm to consumers. Evidence of such harm was absent. This was the inevitable consequence of resort to the impossible-to-verify raising rivals' cost charge. In contrast, clear evidence appears of the consumer benefits of Microsoft's actions.

It remained for post-trial analyses by economists dubious about the case to initiate discussion of the comparative merits of the case. To date, those who support the case have failed to mount a comparably analytic rebuttal. The evaluation presented here suggests this reflects the absence of analytic support.

While Microsoft responded to these charges, Microsoft's conviction means that its response failed in the critical task of persuading Judge Jackson. As critics, including at least one Judge on Circuit Court of Appeals, complained during the oral arguments, Jackson only makes a series of declarations. Most accept the government's assertions.[2] Jackson never mentions, let alone rejects, the Microsoft arguments. Neither citations nor commentaries indicate why the government assertion is preferable. Jackson swallows the government's case and ignores the devastating criticism from Microsoft.

---

[2] The transcript for the Court of Appeals does not identify the individual judges. Reynolds (2001) makes a similar point and cites others who had done so.

Auletta (2001) attributes the verdict to the government's success at making credibility the central issue. However, Auletta is unaware that the attacks obscured failure to prove the economic assertions.

The Schmalensee observation and many by the Microsoft attorneys indicate an awareness of the problems. The attorneys placed everything relevant on the record. This book cannot resolve this failure. Written transcripts do not capture whatever bad interactions took place, and appraising moods is not economic analysis.

This book, therefore, critically examines the government's economic arguments, the Microsoft response, and what economic analysis indicates about the issues. Treatment of the supporting economics and using them to organize the case clarifies exactly why the case is so problematic. For review of the Microsoft case, the minimum appropriate literature reviews are of the material on predation, other tactics for securing monopoly, and network externalities.

The primary objective is more fully to document several critical economic defects in the government's case. This is an approach absent from the prior literature on the case, vast as it is. Curiously, given the volume of this material generated, no one has fully analyzed the government case and Microsoft's response. Prior critics were more selective about concepts. Important underlying economic issues at best were treated too tersely. In sum, prior commentators were concerned only with an overview. I share interest in the broad picture but want to go farther. This extension tells much about the limit of applied economics and its treatment by the courts.

To be sure, much of what appears here repeats prior work. Many of the conclusions reached here were written down after what seemed a sudden new insight. Ultimately similar arguments were found in the case records, subsequent commentary, or an earlier draft. The discussion here, however, is fuller than prior ones.

The stress on economics involves grave concerns about the proper role of economic expertise. Microsoft and Schmalensee properly complain that the government's expert economists presented conclusions beyond their competence. To make matters worse, the government cites these opinions as the basis for critical conclusions. This may in part be due to a limitation imposed on witness numbers. Schmalensee too treats material outside his expertise. In particular, he, Fisher, and Warren-Boulton are the presenters of conflicting data on Netscape Navigator's market share. Schmalensee lessens the drawbacks of testimony on this area by reference to the input of a specialist in survey data. This still does not eliminate the problem that an inordinate amount of time was devoted to arguing about these almost certainly unsatisfactory data. This book largely ignores this debate.

A disturbing aspect of the stress on documents is its blatant selectivity. Single sentences are quoted without regard for the context, the timing, the plausibility, the meaning, or the qualifications of the writer. When examined, the material never supports the main government arguments.

The discussion in subsequent chapters starts with a survey of the economic background. Then attention turns to the case. Chapter 2 reviews the evolution of economic analysis of monopoly and of attitudes towards public policy to control monopoly. Chapter 3 sketches the problems of identifying monopoly.

The discussion of the case shows that the government adopted a widely used, but also heavily criticized, method of defining a relevant market and viewing market shares. Schmalensee's defense of Microsoft builds on the standard censure of a structural approach. Moreover, Fisher's sketch of the theory in his direct testimony also presents the essence of such attacks, which he had often expressed in prior writings. On the basis of industry statements, Fisher, nevertheless, accepts the structural model proposed by the government.

The economics of predation and other tactics are examined in Chapter 4. The debate over network effects is treated in Chapter 5. Neither side surveyed this theory. Schmalensee's statements only (correctly) summarized the literature. However, a critique including software examples (Liebowitz and Margolis 1999) was issued during the trial. The book devastatingly attacks both the theories justifying concern and the assertions that important practical examples prevail.

The treatment of the case itself starts in Chapter 6 with a review of the issues and how they were handled in the case. Chapter 7 then presents the debate over Microsoft's monopoly power. Chapter 8 turns to examination of the theoretic aspects of competition with Netscape Navigator and the other rivalries treated. Chapter 9 examines the evidence presented in alleged support of the case. This division was adopted to lessen severe expositional problems. The government's discussion is dominated by presentation of detailed reviews of Microsoft actions. These prove empty. However, demonstration of the defects requires examination of minutia. That treatment is necessary for completeness but not necessarily for every reader's edification. Therefore, the separation.

Chapter 10 reports the decisions at the district and circuit court level and deals with the broader implications of the case. Chapter 11 presents a summary and conclusions.

Chapter 2 Modern Economics and the Microsoft Case

The case sought to alter the thinking of economists and policymakers about monopoly. Therefore, this chapter reviews what economists have argued on monopoly and its control. Review starts with the 1930s. At that time, consideration of competition policy developed into a more formal branch of economics called industrial organization. The discussion tries to convey how the process evolved into the twenty-first century. The literature distinguishes between the basic problem of appraising monopoly power and the further issue of the role in monopolizing of various business tactics. Work on tactics arose mainly in response to concepts arising in antitrust and other policy disputes. The writings show that at best these tactics sometimes are effective and harmful.

The industrial-organization literature includes many theories of possible market behavior and extensive debates over their implications. Much effort was made to examine experience to determine what problems arose, what role–if any–public policy has, and how well public policy has worked. The present treatment necessarily is selective since this book is shorter than a standard treatment of the issues. Stress is on the widely recognized pitfalls that the government ignored in the Microsoft case. These are the theoretic and empirical problems in identifying a monopoly and determining whether a firm's practices are inefficient.

Before starting, some generalizations seem desirable. The more important relate to the inherent limitations of economic analysis. As I have argued previously (1994), economic theory is an invaluable aid to empirical analysis but cannot predict the outcome of any actual situation. Anyone familiar with logical analysis knows that, if enough assumptions are adopted, anything can be proved. Economic theory has, in fact, encompassed so many possibilities that anything is possible in principle.

As also seems inadequately recognized, however, the difficulties of empirical analysis force economists to made judgments about which interpretation is most plausible. The facts usually are sufficiently unclear that different equally skilled analysts can reach widely conflicting conclusions. For example, it is a commonplace that formal statistical studies of economic phenomena have inherent drawbacks. The design, accuracy, and extent of data are always insufficient. The classic identification problem precludes conclusive results. Only the outcomes of market developments are observed. Limitations prevail with the techniques used to move backward to the underlying demand, supply, and public-policy forces that produced the outcomes. What is called observational equivalence often, perhaps almost always, arises. This term denotes a situation in which the competing models of behavior all predict the actual outcome. The Microsoft case abounds with examples.

The response to these difficulties is to adopt, consciously or unconsciously, an overall outlook on policy. This viewpoint reflects perceptions about the nature of markets and governments. The attitudes arise from the effects of both theoretical writings and observation of reality.

These outlooks range greatly. However, I contended previously (1994) that the proposition Stigler (1959, 1965) expounded that economists prefer markets to government accurately describes the situation. Enthusiasm for massive government action constitutes heterodox economics. As I also noted, this viewpoint can be and is implemented in many different ways.

In dealing with the Microsoft case, the key differences are attitudes towards antitrust. As discussed later in this chapter, the dominant viewpoint is that monopoly is difficult to detect and reform and antitrust enforcement is defective. The central concern is over a tendency towards inappropriate actions, very often to protect an inefficient firm from competition. The range of reform proposals goes from better administration to abolition.

However, views on antitrust are irrelevant here. The primary requirement is that an antitrust case should involve development of a coherent economic analysis. As contended in Chapter 1, this is an obvious deficiency of the case. Moreover the danger of using antitrust to perpetuate or even increase inefficiency, as noted, is widespread and characterizes the case.

A second less critical governing principle here is that economics is better viewed as evolutionary than revolutionary. Concern over monopoly, for example, goes back at least to Adam Smith. (Some critics, notably Schumpeter (1954), insist that Adam Smith only synthesized previously developed ideas. However, Smith is easily obtained; his alleged inspirations are not. Therefore, Smith is the most convenient starting point.)

The classical position on monopoly was that, while firms obviously wanted it, it was difficult to maintain at least without government support. This classical position never secured full practical implementation and long endured analytic criticism. How visions of competition fared from the middle nineteenth century to 1929 involves controversy. The essence is that a weakening arose, but the support remained strong. Some observers accuse

John Stuart Mill of introducing fatal concessions to intervention. Others date the critical changes as late as the 1930s.

Conversely, the literature on the rise of U.S. antitrust laws (Thorelli 1955, Letwin 1965) stresses that economists saw no need for the laws because the world was naturally competitive. Concern over monopoly was one basis for advocacy of socialism. The U.S. decision to create government programs to control monopoly appears to have arisen from purely political considerations. Economists of the time still maintained a classical position. Subsequently, the confidence weakened only to revive with massive policy failures in the 1970s.

This chapter provides an overview of these developments. The treatment begins with rise of heterodox theories of the monopoly problem, notes the effort by Edward Mason to promote sounder analyses, and turns to work at the University of Chicago stressing defects of attacks on monopoly. Then, the new theories and their critics are examined.

From Means to Mason: The Rise of Industrial Organization Economics

The great depression produced a giant blame game. Many aspects of the economy were considered as the source of woe. These included the financial sector, public-utility holding companies, agriculture, and monopoly. More broadly, whatever was previously believed, one effect of the great depression was weakening the faith in the market economy.

This involved efforts of heterodox economists, particularly Gardiner Means (1939), to develop new views of monopoly. Means engaged in data mining that he believed justified the conclusion that monopoly was a pervasive problem that was correctable by public policy. Means developed the influential practice of calculating the market shares of large companies. He calculated the share of the four, eight, twelve, and twenty largest firms in Census industry groups. The resort to group totals was to preserve the secrecy of individual-firm data. The key problems are that Census industries do not comprise well-defined markets and economic theory indicates that market-share data are insufficient to determine the vigor of competition (see Chapter 3). Nevertheless, the legacy of these calculations persists in antitrust. It was a central issue in the Microsoft case.

On the policy side, writers other than Means made proposals for many forms of correction. This inspired a variety of efforts to control business practices. These included efforts greatly to increase antitrust enforcement. In addition, direct regulation of public utilities and financial institutions and government ownership were tried.

Within economics, the challenges inspired many others to examine monopoly questions. Many of these critics were (and still are) also unorthodox. However, the most influential effort was that of Edward S. Mason at Harvard University to apply standard economics to the problem. The deficiencies of Means's analyses were a major impetus. Reexamination for this book of Mason's writings made clearer than ever that his core contribution was insistence that assertions about market situations be soundly grounded in economic principles. To this day, industrial-organization economics is the implementation of that guideline.

Mason produced a few articles outlining his concepts, so few, in fact, that they only comprised about half of the anthology of his main writings (Mason 1957). (One section covers the role of large firms; another, antitrust; other sections treat wage-price flexibility problems and raw materials.) More importantly, he encouraged graduate students to undertake detailed empirical studies of charges of monopoly in major industries.

Obviously, this work too reflected the limitations of theory and verification. Nevertheless, the work inspired a less alarmist approach to monopoly. A major component was work reestablishing optimism about competition and pessimism about the ability of antitrust enforcers correctly to identify correctable monopolies.

However, two of Mason's students moved from their case studies to further work that tried to provide an analytic and empirical basis to justify the 1930s concern over monopoly. Bain was particularly critical. In a series of articles, a book on optimum firm size, and the first systematic text on industrial organization (1949, 1956, 1968), he presented the case for radical action against monopoly. This amounts to a theoretic support of Means's arguments. Another Mason student, Carl Kaysen, in collaboration with Harvard Law School professor Donald Turner (1959), reiterated the argument for radical action. They called for breaking up firms in industries in which a few firms had high market shares. This latter work not only builds on Bain, but was incorporated into Bain's later writings.

Other Harvard products were more skeptical of such arguments and more conscious of the problems of government intervention. This skepticism ultimately proved more influential.

One element of Bain was arguing, particularly in his pioneering textbook, that analysts consider structure, conduct, and performance (the outcome of structure and conduct). This is often linked to Mason's discussions of structure and performance. However, Mason stressed the difficulties of neat categorization; Bain seemed to advocate a rigid framework. Several later writers, notably the contributors to Adams's long-lived collection of case studies, built on Bain rotely employing this framework.

This, reflecting the influence of Thomas Kuhn's book (1970) on scientific progress, is often termed a paradigm. However, the divisions are too artificial and restrictive. As Mason suggested, the issues do not neatly fall into the categories. More critically, as discussed below, the approach assumes a greater ability than exists of using theory to appraise markets. Moreover, since the method merely proposes the form in which familiar points are presented, it does not seem to produce the breakthroughs that comprise a paradigm as defined by Kuhn.

In any case, what is most important about the Harvard work is in inspiring the widespread practice of careful study of markets grounded in economic theory. As suggested, Bain's framework and policy proposals were neither the standard views of Mason's students nor the only outlook in economics.

The Increase of Skepticism: Chicago and Others

Given its adherence to a more classical view of economics, by the 1950s, the University of Chicago became a major center of work in the realm. A remarkable group of scholars dealt with a broad range of conceptual and empirical issues about competition and its regulation. This group included lawyers interested in economics as well as economists. The Chicago involvement ranged widely. Many of the leaders–e.g., Stigler, Coase, and Posner–ended, but did not begin, their academic careers at Chicago. Others–such as McGee, Demsetz, and Bork–did most of their work elsewhere.

The work included rethinking of the problems of evaluating structure and conduct. The material challenged the premise that monopoly was widespread. Efforts were made to show the problems of reliance on market shares. The endeavor extended to detailed analysis of the various tactics alleged to further monopoly. The discussions treated among other things the issues of predation, tying, price maintenance, and advertising. The arguments tended to stress the benefits of unregulated markets. While such a stress has many critics, it is consistent with the tradition of economics.

Nevertheless, many find it desirable to stress that the market orientation is stronger at the University of Chicago. In particular, one major figure in the effort, law school professor (and now U.S. Circuit Court Judge) Richard Posner (1979), argued that this Chicago work was a substantial challenge to the otherwise universally accepted Harvard (i.e., Bain-Kaysen) position. Both admirers of and antagonists to the Chicago viewpoint accepted Posner's version. McGee (1988) and Stigler (1988) contrast with Adams (1990), Scherer and Ross (1990), and Tirole (1988).

Both sides find the vision convenient. In particular, Posner's objective was to prove that Chicago had undermined defective old ideas. Others took this as proof of reckless abandonment of old wisdom. I see it as advancing the effort to show the defects of the alarmists' views of the 1930s. Chicago was important, but not unique, in this process.

The policy disasters of the 1970s made many economists rethink their positions. Suddenly, the classical viewpoint and its anti-intervention supplements received increased respect (recall Chapter 1). Support of free-market economics enjoyed a resurgence. Much, such as most attacks on regulatory policies, was independent of any special economic outlook. However, respect for Chicago grew.

The particularly anti-intervention arguments of the "Austrians" also received increased support (see Vaughn 1994). The main Austrian figures, von Mises and Hayek, differ from the Chicago approach in stressing broad issues such as the feasibility of planning. Chicago efforts typically treat specific issues such as predation. These concerns thus moved the process started by Mason back towards a viewpoint more sympathetic to the free-market outlook of nineteenth-century economists.

One element of this change was increased attention to arguments that governments cannot be trusted to regulate competition. After 112 years, U.S. antitrust remains a changing, contentious practice. A wide range of opinions prevails. Some claim that antitrust discipline sharpens the behavior of U.S. firms and makes them stronger competitors. At the other extreme, it is contended that the laws have a pernicious influence that can be eliminated only by repeal. The vast literature suggests that the assertions of strong benefits are conjectures that ignore or at least minimize faults recognized in examinations of practice (e.g., Shenefield and Stelzer (1998, esp. 128-30)). The most extensive Chicago discussions, Bork (1978) and Posner (1976), stressed these problems but argued that better enforcement could remedy the defect. Stigler (1966) was more skeptical.

Other observers have insisted that this is naive advice. Governments have neither the competence nor the motivation for the task. Classic anti-intervention arguments centering on the difficulties in determining what comprises efficiency and on the pressures to ignore efficiency are employed. The flaws were intrinsic, and antitrust laws should be abolished.

Dominick Armentano (1990) is clearly the principal figure here. In the face of persistent neglect, he persevered in making his case that the record suggested that antitrust on balance harmed competition and would never stop doing so. The argument consisted of reviewing the cases typically examined in studies on antitrust and reaching standard conclusions about the cases. His unusual step is arguing that these errors are neither minor nor correctable.

McChesney and Shughart (1995) edited an anthology providing further development of the case for abolishing antitrust. Among the points made was that belief that antitrust could be transformed into a procompetitive policy was inconsistent with Chicago views. Failure of repeated reform efforts was treated in Chicago writings of a sign that the policy would never work well. The critics argued that Chicago should have applied the point to antitrust. Americans who consider themselves Austrian economists are severe critics of antitrust. (See also Graglia 1999, cited in the Microsoft appeal reply brief.)

Posner is correct, however, that various economists and lawyers who identified themselves with the University of Chicago led in developing economics focused on stressing the strength of actual competition and the weakness of government regulation. Briefly, the "Chicago" efforts developed the case for the continued validity of the traditional presumption by economists that competition prevails despite efforts to suppress it. Even when narrowly conceived (in defining both who and what are included), many separate threads are involved. First is the theme (quite well anticipated by Adelman in his antitrust work in the 1940s and 1950s) that benefit to competition, not to competitors, was the relevant concern. Bork's (1978) and Posner's (1976) books on antitrust stress this point.

A second point is that the measurement of monopoly power is difficult. McGee and Demsetz made important contributions. Their work was a systematic attack on a structural approach. A major target was Bain's earlier assertions that leading firms were larger than necessary to attain efficient size and could be broken up without producing inefficiency.

Third, the approach skeptically examined charges that certain tactics were important anticompetitive devices. These include predatory pricing (McGee), vertical integration (Bork, McGee and Bassett), vertical restraints (Mathewson and Winter), and retail price maintenance (Telser). McGee both extended the theoretic concerns about predatory pricing and presented evidence that the case against Standard Oil was invalid.

A subsequent effort by Harvard Law School professors Philip Areeda and Donald Turner (1975) to clarify the law on predatory prices produced a torrent of commentary. Its essence was that the Areeda and Turner test was too lenient on predators. These commentaries inspired many responses. Areeda and Turner themselves responded to the earliest critics. McGee (1980), Easterbrook (1981), and others contended that the proposed alternatives had severe implementation problems. These drawbacks made the alternatives less workable than Areeda and Turner (see Chapter 4).

Chicago work began with recognition that antitrust enforcement regularly identified and sought condemnation of business practices that seemed restrictive. However, such conclusions relied on surface appearances. No attention was given the absence of economic analysis. The Chicago approach stressed providing and testing such analyses. The lesson is critical to treating the Microsoft case. The clearest defect is that the meaning of the criticized actions is never analyzed, even badly.

What matters here is providing a fair treatment of the Chicago approach. As typical commentaries on Posner stress, one major element was undermining reliance on simple market-share measures of monopoly. As Chapter 3 argues, this thrust is simultaneously less startling and less challenged than any other aspect of the Chicago approach. Bain's structure, performance, conduct methodology is recognition of the limitations of a purely structural approach. The critical difference is in the weight assigned, often only tacitly, to the warnings. Chicago was a prime source of caveats that the drawbacks were inadequately recognized.

A second key aspect of the Chicago approach was that just noted of scrutinizing claims about techniques that allegedly promoted monopoly. Skepticism about these claims was not unique to Chicago, but Chicago pursued the effort far more vigorously and effectively than elsewhere.

A third element of the Chicago approach was to insist on empirical tests of claims of problems and the ability of public policy to resolve them. This is a continuation by other means of the practice Mason initiated of encouraging empirical analyses. The Harvard studies were less uniformly antiregulation than the Chicago ones but hardly ringing endorsements of intervention. This book is in the Harvard tradition of a detailed discussion that is based on study of an antitrust case but reaches conclusions that are clearly anti-intervention. I consider myself a neoclassical economist reaching Chicago and Austrian conclusions. Here I could be accused of being more Austrian than Chicago.

The New Industrial Economics

The 1980s involved the rise of work whose practitioners termed the new industrial organization. Examination shows that initially the only really new thing was the proliferation of many much more formal models of all the issues. All the problems treated were familiar ones. This new industrial organization considers an enormous variety of assumptions and produced a profusion of models dealing more explicitly with a range of questions about firm and industry behavior. Many interventionist models arose.

Different explanations exist about the motivations and implications of these efforts. One force was simply the growing pressure to develop more formal models. For what were primarily theoretic considerations, the work focused on the myriad way monopoly power might be utilized. Market failure proved more suited than government failure to the mathematical pyrotechnics by which bright theorists prove they are worthy of appointment to the economics faculties of leading universities.

The revival of game-theory models of oligopoly seems clearly motivated by a desire to theorize without concern for practical implications. Before and after the development of the models, it was clear that the oligopoly problem was the quintessence of a subject in which anything was possible in theory. Game-theory models of oligopoly lessen certainty about outcomes and what affects them. Among other things, game theory is unable to establish the presumption in prior work that collusion among oligopolists is likely.

In any case, these oligopoly models lack even marginal relevance to the Microsoft case. Models in which firms can undertake strategic behavior to harm rivals are more germane. Chapter 4 explores this further.

Moreover, too many people, including economists, are intimidated by progovernment rhetoric with which they are inundated. They become reluctant to accept strong criticisms of intervention. These influences interact. Too many theoretical economists lack interest in and, therefore, understanding of markets. This reinforces the natural tendency to believe that what one produces is useful.

It is unclear to what extent the developers had a clear objective of challenging the growing optimism about free markets. What is clearer is the diversity of opinions among them about the relevance of their work. By themselves, the new theories, as with all theories, provided only new potentially testable hypotheses about competition.

Some insist that these are realistic models that can and should be applied in public policy. They consider the work a needed corrective to the vigorously anti-intervention models that had dominated antitrust. In particular, some stress that the theory produced a post-Chicago outlook to correct the alleged naiveté of the Chicago outlook. However, the efforts at best challenged only the theoretic basis of Chicago skepticism about the efficacy of anticompetitive tactics.

Others recognize the new industrial organization as untested concepts whose relevance remains to be shown. The critics feel that these theorists have no sense (and possibly no concern) about which assumptions are best employed in policy analysis. This theory can be, has been, and should be considered a way to extend the ability to analyze actual conditions. I believe these models support the prior skepticism because the arguments so often require the presence of peculiar, difficult to observe conditions.

In the late 1980s, numerous books emerged dealing with this new theory. First was an advanced textbook review by Jean Tirole (1988); second was a *Handbook* edited by Schmalensee with Willig (1989) containing review articles by leading participants. The chapters' authors in Schmalensee and Willig differed in their treatment of relevance. Some saw that new action was needed; others recognized the lack of evidence of relevance. Others such as Spulber (1989), Krouse (1990), and Shy (1995) produced advanced texts. Numerous more standard industrial organization texts incorporated the material. Examples included Scherer and Ross (1990), Carlton and Perloff (1994), and McGee (1988). The first was a new version of the long-established leader in the field. The second was a major new effort. The third was explicitly a Chicago approach.

Reexamination of these and other works strengthened concern that new industrial organization only provides elaborate examination of familiar complex issues. The greater complexity, if anything, increases doubts about practical relevance.

The effort to revitalize the monopolistic-tactics concept is the aspect critical to the Microsoft case. Chapter 4 develops the argument that these models only increase the possibility in theory that such tactics will work. Some of the enthusiasts of new industrial organization assert that this work undermines the Chicago approach (Ordover and Saloner 1989, 590-92). However, empirical support remains nonexistent, and the Microsoft case reinforced the doubts.

However, as Chapter 5 indicates, eventually the new issue of network industries emerged. These were cases where the consumers interacted and the need existed for a technology that facilitated this interaction. An anecdote that the standard typewriter keyboard layout was inefficient inspired theorizing about the ability of markets correctly to select the most efficient technology. This produced an outpouring of theoretical analyses showing such inefficiency could arise. Then skepticism arose.

As suggested in Chapter 1, the Microsoft case is a mixture of pre-Chicago and post-Chicago approaches. The old-fashioned stress on high shares of a "relevant" market is justified by reference to the network-externality argument. A liberal dose of new and old visions of the power of anticompetitive weapons appears.

Other issues are at least lurking. Windows is a durable good, a differentiated product, and a product of regularly changing design. Concerns arose over the vertical relationship between Windows and Internet browsers. While the primary case was that Internet Explorer was a device to protect the Windows monopoly, Fisher suggested that Microsoft sought to leverage the Windows monopoly into an Internet monopoly. The charges include use of price discrimination.

The Critics

Vigorous criticism of new industrial economics is extensive. A widely criticized failure of new industrial organization is not undertaking the third critical phase of Chicago economics, empirical tests. Again, the ability to prove anything by changing assumptions is critical. The enthusiasm about new models of market tactics is not justified by evidence that these models are any more applicable than those criticized in Chicago work. Indeed, what might be termed a post-post-Chicago response emerged from delving into the empirical relevance of these post-Chicago models.

At least three major reviews of Schmalensee and Willig expressed skepticism. Fisher (1991) produced one of the three. The other critiques were by Klevorick (1991) and Peltzman (1991). Fisher's critique, moreover, is not his only work skeptical of concepts he used in the Microsoft case. Schmalensee cites two; others exist. The most important is that in another landmark case against IBM, a much-admired but also much-hated dominant firm, Fisher was the principal economist for the defense. In the trial, Schmalensee (par. 175, 87) quotes arguments against structural measures in a book Fisher coauthored with McGowan and Greenwood (1983) on the IBM case.

Fisher's critique of Schmalensee and Willig includes complaints about theories that make anything possible and are not readily testable. He noted that the applicability of the theory had not been proven (205). He adds that part of the problem is inadequate testing. Yet, he notes skepticism about our ability to measure market power (or "even know what the right measure is") (216). He also sets up five rules for industrial organization–the absence of organizing principles, that theory can prove anything, stripped-down models often are inapplicable, theorists are casual about "what constitutes verification," and much empirical work lacks a sound theoretic base.

Fisher makes many further remarks. Of particular note is an entire section "Relating to Antitrust" (220-3). In it, he repeats concerns about the problems of market definition, the absence of simple relationships between structure and performance, and measuring profits but notes that theory shows the importance of considering barriers to entry (221). He then reflects that the theory raises possibilities of "what *might* happen" and a sentence later "*could* be anticompetitive" (his emphasis, 222). He warns that "detailed examination of the context of the case" is needed to settle the issue (222). He adds, "Modern theory, by merely showing that a variety of things *can* happen, is likely to stimulate plaintiff's imagination" (222 emphasis in original).

These and similar writings are radically inconsistent with Fisher's testimony in the Microsoft case. Indeed, his professional writings support the arguments against prosecuting Microsoft. Fisher has recognized, but only cursorily responded, to the problem (see Chapter 6).

The critical problem with post-Chicago theory is its taxonomic character. The theory at best can only indicate the conditions under which an outcome will occur. Similarly, the models then can only delineate the situations in which the result is inefficient. The debate among economists about post-Chicago analysis reflects familiar disagreement over feasibility. Those who believe that the new theories have important policy implications presume that it is feasible to determine whether a challenged action is effective and inefficient. The objection is that such determination is not practicable.

Two post-trial articles reiterate this concern about post-Chicago economics in very different ways. Herbert Hovenkamp, the author of a prominent antitrust law text, tries to reconcile the problems with post-Chicago analysis with what he views as a desirable correction of the Chicago school's undue optimism about the natural vigor of competition (2001). He displays the standard hope of those favorable to a post-Chicago approach that the problems can be overcome. Since he is less specific than commentators examined in Chapters 8 and 10, the only further point to make is that he claims about the Microsoft case "relatively little about it is 'post-Chicago'" (2001, 304). The assertion is remarkable since he cites literature presenting contrary views.

Coate and Fischer (2001), in contrast, believe that the information requirement of post-Chicago theory cannot be met in practice. They use Supreme Court decisions defining standards for expert testimony as their focus; they argue that post-Chicago models cannot satisfy these criteria. Fisher's testimony in the Microsoft case is such a tempting target that, although Microsoft did not accuse failure to meet the guidelines, Coate and Fischer argue such a deficiency occurred. Chapter 8 reviews their critique.

The Microsoft case gives no comfort to the advocates of application. The government often notes post-Chicago concepts of network industries and raising rivals' costs. However, they prove empty slogans. The theorists admit that quantitative evidence is needed to prove that the criteria of inefficiency prevail. In the absence of any data, the government ignored the requirement. Incessant assertion of applicability replaced the quantitative evaluation necessary to prove possible bad effects actually arose.

The next three chapters here deal first with general principles of appraising whether a firm possesses monopoly power. The bulk of the case uses standard arguments. Attention then turns to the economics of competitive tactics. Finally, the government employed an unconventional explanation of why Microsoft possessed a monopoly. It was alleged that the established position of Microsoft created insurmountable barriers to entry. As neither side noted, this argument drew upon a newer branch of new industrial organization. Understanding the limits of the theory helps understand the weakness of the case. Conversely, the case reinforces concerns about the relevance of the theory.

Chapter 3 Determinants of Monopoly in Theory and Practice

Neither theory nor practice gives clear principles for evaluating the extent of monopoly. The search for simple, readily calculated indicators has shown that they do not exist. More critically, this difficulty has long-standing, widespread recognition.

In examining these issues, the central questions are whether monopoly is widespread and, if so, what public policies, if any, can counteract such monopoly. Advocates exist of the view that monopoly is both unimportant and uncorrectable. Others see at least some importance and controllability. Nevertheless, a clear tendency to increased skepticism about intervention appears in formal writings on the subject.

Mason's pioneering work in establishing industrial organization involved warning about the limitations of a purely structural approach. For example, in his 1957 introduction to the antitrust section of his collected articles after a review of the critical issues, he observed, "We cannot, therefore, afford to abandon behavioral tests in favor of a purely structural concept of competition" (1957, 328). More critically, Bain is the classic case of recognizing that more than structure matters but still using a structural approach. He undertook studies that convinced him that the drawbacks of a structural approach were unimportant in practice.

The Chicago approach is a major effort to reduce or perhaps eliminate such confidence. The basic premise is that competitive forces are so powerful that nothing but government intervention can preserve monopoly. The tradition associated with and in many ways established by Adam Smith is that competition, while resisted by firms, tends to emerge and governments are more likely to thwart than to encourage that emergence. Conversely, skepticism exists about the ability and willingness of governments to identify and correct monopoly.

A large part of the criticism involves extending the theory to emphasize more fully the problems of identifying an undesirable monopoly. The theoretic requirements for ascertaining monopoly worthy of correction are more stringent than the structural tests advocated by proponents of radical restructuring. In particular, proof requires far more evidence than can be secured.

All criticisms express the same concerns. Existing competitive pressures can come from firms other than those producing identical products. Substitutes often exist, but their impact is variable. Thus, questions arise about what to include as competition and how to include it. Another consideration is freedom of entry. Firms may be constrained by recognition that others can easily enter the industry if monopolistic output restriction is attempted. Bain pioneered the development of limit-price models that treat how best to respond to entry threats. Yet another problem is possible conflicts between economies of scale and atomistic competition. Economists as diverse as McGee (1988) and Williamson (1968) stress the often real conflict between optimum size and maintaining large numbers of actual competitors.

A much noted practical consideration is measurement. It is routinely observed in the literature that the industry classifications used for government statistics correspond badly with economic concepts of markets. A more fundamental problem is that accounting conventions violate economic principles and, therefore, do not measure profits in an economically valid fashion. For example, accounting data are not adjusted for inflation as economic measures should be, and standard accounting procedures for depreciation do not produce economically correct numbers. Work by Fisher, McGowan, and Greenwood (1983) codified this long-known but previously neglected proposition.

Finally, even if a market is properly defined, the implications of a given structure are unclear. Oligopoly theory cannot even predict what will happen in the two-firm case conventionally treated. All these ambiguities limit the ability to identify correctable inefficient market structures.

Werden, a Department of Justice economist, presented (1992) a review of how his agency tried to implement the relevant-market concept. His treatment begins with recognition of the criticisms in the literature of a structural approach (125-7). His history provides extensive material on the difficulties associated with a structural approach.

Actually, a purely structural approach is now a myth. Even in antitrust enforcement, behavior and conduct measures are used to defend structural assertions. With the rejection of the Means-Bain-Kaysen-Turner view of widespread obvious monopoly, the government must always prove by viewing conduct and performance measures that the structure is correctly specified. This was clearly true in the Microsoft case (see Chapter 7).

While much could be reviewed, the emphasis here is on writings concerned with the defects of a structural approach. Particular attention is given to the approach of Landes and Posner and the economists who commented on them. This exchange's intrinsic interest is accentuated here because Schmalensee was one of those commentators. Note also is taken of McGee's work including his contribution to a symposium in which Chicago economists debated believers in a structural approach. Another consideration is that the Microsoft case involved debates over whether shares or amounts were more important. The economics are clear-cut but still merit attention. This discussion comes first because of its relevance to the debate over antimonopoly policy.

The only truly satisfactory use of market shares is to refute charges of monopoly. Energy economics, for example, is another case in which product-line and geographic lines are unclear. A common explicit or implicit strategy is to note that even using the narrowest reasonable definition indicates strong competition.

A Note on Relatives and Absolutes in Economics

The Microsoft case involved among other things questions about whether market share or market size was relevant. The policy implications of shares and size are well discussed in the industrial organization literature. Reviewing that treatment helps clarify the debates in the case. A critical contributor was M. A. Adelman.[1] In work that started with supermarkets (relating to the antitrust case against the then prominent A&P supermarket chain) (1959) and carried over into his many years of work on oil, he stressed the different purposes that share and size measures meet. It is share that is more relevant to the existence of monopoly power. Monopoly power, after all, means strength compared to rivals. With all its defects, market share is clearly the more relevant indicator of comparative strength. Similarly, Lerner's celebrated monopoly ratio measures excess profits at the margin relative to price.

However, economic payoffs always involve the absolute numbers. Investments of any type involve an amount expended to secure additional incomes. McGee's, Landes and Posner's, and Schmalensee's treatments of identifying policy-relevant monopoly, for example, include both a relative impact and absolute component. The existence of power depends on relative position. The importance of the power depends on the absolute size of the firm as well as its relative power. An antitrust prosecution ideally is an investment in reduced exercise of monopoly power. The costs of prosecution do not differ greatly with firm size. Thus, the biggest payoffs

---

[1] The argument was developed in his Ph. D. thesis; his 1959 book was a revision of that thesis; several earlier articles made the main points.

come in correction of big monopolies, i.e., those with a strong position in a big market.

Adelman raises a different point. The two industries on which he has concentrated, retail trade and petroleum, share the characteristics of numerous firms competing in very large markets. The large market size makes it possible to recover large individual-firm investments. Chain stores could profitably invest in securing lower-cost merchandize through both more sophisticated purchasing practices and, if necessary, stimulating new competition. The firm could itself enter the supplying area, directly finance an entrant, or encourage financing by offering a long-term contract.

Assessing Monopoly

As suggested, monopoly is a much-debated issue, and rethinking in economics has caused return to earlier views that competition is hard to restrain. The changes were documented in several ways. A major effort to alter thinking was a conference in the early 1970s. There skeptics about the importance of monopoly and the validity of structural tests, particularly Demsetz and McGee, confronted defenders, particularly Scherer and Weiss (Goldschmid, Mann, and Weston 1974).

Demsetz's theme is the conflict between those who think only government aid can sustain monopoly and those who contend that monopoly power is durable without aid. The latter he terms self-sufficient (164-5). Since the role of government in promoting monopoly is undisputed among economists, Demsetz devotes almost all his attention to criticizing self-sufficient monopoly. He stresses defects in the demonstration that high profits arise when the leading firms have high market shares. Part of that criticism includes recognition that accounting profits are defective measures for economic analysis (167, 175). He (174) also is skeptical about entry barriers because the standard explanation of needing capital and funding of advertising is unconvincing. A promising entrant should be able to finance both. He suggests a more interesting barrier is the skills due to experience. His apparent point is that the advantages may be inherent and intervention cannot and should not attempt correction.

McGee's contribution covers these issues but stresses the problems of properly defining and measuring economies of scale. That was the basis for his challenge to the proposition that large firms were so obviously above minimum efficient size that they could be broken up painlessly. This builds on a recurrent theme in his writings (1971, 1988) that, with economies of scale and differences in efficiency of firms, moving from pure monopoly to pure competition could raise costs so much the prices would rise.

His other writings also stress that market share, Lerner ratio, and profitability measures are all relative. To justify action, the absolute amount of damage must be measured. The usual textbook measure is deadweight loss, and he suggests its employment. This is strictly speaking incorrect. A vast literature (see Varian 1992 and Willig 1976) indicates that deadweight loss is only an approximation of the impossible-to-compute true loss measure. (The problem is that the deadweight loss measure ignores the loss of purchasing power, the income effect, from a price rise.)

For present purposes, Landes and Posner (1981) and the resulting commentary, especially by Schmalensee are of particular relevance. First, Landes and Posner seek explicitly to demonstrate the drawbacks of stressing shares in relevant markets. Second, they present a method of appraisal that Fisher echoed (without acknowledgement) in his Microsoft case testimony. Third, Schmalensee made amendments that anticipate his contributions to the case. (Schmalensee provided the first of four discussions; the others are ignored here as not adding to understanding of issues in the Microsoft case.)

Landes and Posner focus on the relationship between formal economic measures of market power and market shares. They start with recognition that these concepts cannot be applied because of lack of the needed data (943). Their justification is that the analysis shows what must be considered in evaluating monopoly.

They stress Abba Lerner's monopoly ratio and its relationship to elasticity of demand. Lerner's ratio is the excess of price over marginal cost divided by price. The standard analysis involves combining the ratio, the equilibrium condition that marginal revenue (MR) equals marginal cost (MC), and the relationship between marginal revenue and elasticity.

The standard proof of the relationship of marginal revenue to elasticity, with R as revenues, P as price, Q as quantity, and E as elasticity, is:

$$R \equiv PQ; \frac{dR}{dQ} = P\frac{dQ}{dQ} + Q\frac{dP}{dQ} = P + Q\frac{dP}{dQ}$$

$$= P + Q\frac{P}{P}\frac{dP}{dQ} = P\left[1 + \frac{Q}{P}\frac{dP}{dQ}\right] = P\left[1 + \frac{1}{E}\right]$$

A critical implication is that inelastic demand (algebraically greater than minus one) means negative marginal revenue. This means that lowering output raises revenues (and, if costs exist, also lowering costs). Revenues are maximized with an elasticity of one. Where costs exist, the profit-maximizing output is lower than the revenue-maximizing output. Reducing output below the revenue-maximizing level initially raises profits because the cost reductions outweigh the revenue rise. However, at a point (namely when the marginal costs reach parity with marginal revenue), further output reduction lowers profit. Thus, an elasticity greater than minus one is inconsistent with profit maximization. This demonstration is needed because the proposition was mishandled in the case.

$$\text{If } E > -1; \frac{1}{E} < -1; 1 + (1/E) < 0$$

Then writing the Lerner ratio, substituting marginal revenue for marginal cost, and using the formula relating marginal revenue to elasticity yields:

$$\frac{P-MC}{P} = \frac{P-MR}{P} = \frac{P-P[1+1/E]}{P} = 1-1-\frac{1}{E} = -\frac{1}{E}$$

Landes and Posner present an extension to the case of a dominant firm (985-6). Using their notation, superscripts differentiate demand (d) from supply (s) and subscripts distinguish among the market (m), the dominant firm (i), and the fringe (j). The start is that by definition the dominant firm produces the difference between total demand and fringe output. The first step is to differentiate the dominant firm's output with respect to price. Then a series of steps are taken to relate the elasticity of demand faced by that dominant firm to market demand elasticity, the elasticity of fringe supply, and market share.

The first step is to multiply both sides by the ratio of price to the dominant firm's sales. This means the left-hand term becomes the elasticity of demand faced by the dominant firm. To translate further the right-hand side, the first term is multiplied by the ratio of market demand to itself, and the second term is multiplied by the ratio of fringe output to itself. The first term then becomes the elasticity of market demand times the ratio of total consumption to dominant-firm output. The second term becomes the elasticity of fringe supply times the ratio of fringe supply to dominant-firm supply. Then, the market share values S_i and S_j are defined and related to each other. This gives the final formula in which the dominant firm's elasticity is related to market demand elasticity, fringe supply elasticity, and market share.

$$\frac{\partial Q_i^d}{\partial P} = \frac{\partial Q_m^d}{\partial P} - \frac{\partial Q_j^s}{\partial P}$$

$$E_i^d = \frac{\partial Q_i^d}{\partial P}\frac{P}{Q_i^d} = \frac{\partial Q_m^d}{\partial P}\frac{P}{Q_i^d} - \frac{\partial Q_j^s}{\partial P}\frac{P}{Q_i^d}$$

$$= \frac{\partial Q_m^d}{\partial P}\frac{P}{Q_i^d}\frac{Q_m^d}{Q_m^d} - \frac{\partial Q_j^s}{\partial P}\frac{P}{Q_i^d}\frac{Q_j^s}{Q_j^s} = E_m^d\frac{Q_m^d}{Q_i^d} - E_j^s\frac{Q_j^s}{Q_i^d}$$

$$\frac{Q_i^d}{Q_m^d} \equiv S_i; \frac{Q_j^d}{Q_m^d} \equiv S_j = 1 - S_i;$$

$$\frac{Q_j^s}{Q_i^d}\frac{Q_m^d}{Q_m^d} = \frac{Q_j^s}{Q_m^d}\frac{Q_m^d}{Q_i^d} = \frac{S_j}{S_i} = \frac{1 - S_i}{S_i}$$

$$E_i^d = \frac{E_m^d}{S_i} - E_j^s\left(\frac{1 - S_i}{S_i}\right)$$

Having presented their formula, Landes and Posner examine the implications. They start with verbal discussion of how the formula demonstrates that more than market share matters. They add that this requires greater consideration of substitutes in production and consumption and ease of entry (945-51). They then note (951-2) that because of imperfect cooperation monopoly power will be lower for cartels and oligopolies.

The remainder of the article discusses various further considerations. A critical one is adding a deadweight loss criterion of absolute importance (952-8). They deal briefly and inconclusively with the problems of defining a relevant market (960-63). Criteria are proposed for determining the geographic extent of the market (963-72). The use of the approach to estimate the effect of mergers is examined (972-4). The application to estimating damages follows (974-5) and then recognition that the apparatus is inapplicable to cases when public policy creates a monopoly (975-6).

They conclude that the law is moving towards recognition of the need for a broader evaluation criterion (976-83).

Schmalensee's 1982 comments make important extensions. First, he argues (1790) that only important market power matters. He contends that a firm's size is more important than share because it better reflects the deadweight loss (1791-2). He warns of the problems arising in considering that the single-product firm to which Landes and Posner's model applies is a textbook fiction (1792-3). Consideration of the probable durability of market power is urged (1793-6). His advice (1796) is that, even if no long-run power exists, act if short-run power and industry dynamics justify. The point is that the long run may be too long. This seems difficult to make operational. The Microsoft case involves debates over evaluation horizons. He raises concerns about the workability of the model with oligopoly or imperfect substitutes (1796-8).

Anticipating the Microsoft case, he warns that the relevant market may not be readily defined (1798-1800). He raises further problems in applying the Landes-Posner measures (1800-804). Reflecting then new work by Fisher, he warns of problems of inferring economic implications from standard accounting data (1805-6). However, he ended with the assertion that, nevertheless, persistent high profits were a concern. Just what he meant is unclear. He can be correct only if believed that the measurement problems could be overcome. The only reason this matters is that a fuss was made in the trial about this statement about profitability.

He ends with discussion of the relevance of price discrimination and predation. He notes that market power is required to discriminate or predate. However, no simple relationship exists between predation and discrimination and the degree of market power (1806-7). Therefore, the antitrust implications are unclear.

In sum, this work suggests the difficulties in identifying monopolies worthy of public-policy response.

Chapter 4 Predation, Tying, Vertical Squeezes, and Other Competitive Tactics

As noted, a major aspect of the Chicago approach is showing the theoretic and empirical drawbacks of arguments that predation and other business practices promote monopoly. Then the key post-Chicago work tried to weaken these conclusions. These efforts have already inspired refutation.

The Microsoft case is implicitly based on these newer post-Chicago theories of competitive behavior. In particular, the government and its consultants are fascinated by Salop's concept of raising rivals' costs. All this ignores the controversy over the practical relevance of post-Chicago theory or for that matter of any theory of predation.

This chapter deals with these issues.[1] It starts with a review of the overall problems with tactical arguments. Then predation and its new-industrial-organization cousins, nonpredatory practices such as raising rivals' costs that also harm competitors, are examined. Then views on tying, leverage, and essential facilities are presented.

Four Monopoly Profits and Other Problems of Competitive Tactics

As suggested in Chapter 2, arguments that certain tactics assist monopoly originated outside economics. A major impetus was anger by business executives about losing out to rivals. Ultimately economists examined the theoretic and empirical basis of these charges. The usual outcome of ambiguity in theory and questionable empirical relevance arose. However, the results are stronger than usual. Many of the concerns prove implausible.

Predatory pricing, strategic pricing, and similar tactics affecting competition among firms are by far the most extensively studied and surveyed type of competitive tactics. Much writing, including mine, talks of hardly anything else. The discussions in the Microsoft case of tying, choke points, and essential facilities inspired attention to the relevant literature. It proved quite thin.

---

[1] This discussion builds on several prior writings.

Predatory pricing has the unique status among competitive tactics of being defined as automatically inefficient. The implications of other tactics are ambiguous. This is a key issue in the Microsoft case. Guilt depends on the inefficiency of tactics that are not predation as traditionally defined. Chapter 8 argues that the government failed even to state, let alone to prove, this proposition.

A fundamental limit on any theory of supporting tactics is imposed by basic monopoly theory. One incomplete shorthand is that monopoly power is finite and this restricts the use of tactics. A fuller view of monopoly is that its outcome depends critically upon whether or not price discrimination is possible. Without discrimination, monopoly profit is produced by restricting output below the competitive level. This lowers welfare by eliminating production more valuable than the resources needed to produce it. However, methods of price discrimination exist that allow higher profits than without discrimination and do not restrict output.

The key is a system of pricing in which the last unit each customer purchases is sold for the price a competitive firm would charge. One approach is to charge a fee to allow unlimited purchases at the competitive price. Another is a sliding price scale so that each successive unit or block of purchases sold at a lower price than the prior one. In the initial fee case, that fee is the monopoly profit. With a sliding scale, the monopoly profits are from the higher prices on the initial units sold.

Another variety of discrimination has the price differ among customers but each customer pays the same price for every unit purchased. As an enormous literature (see Varian 1989) shows, the net effect on welfare then depends upon the prevailing market conditions.

Many models of tactics suggest that they facilitate discrimination. The validity of such suggestions can be challenged. However, if correct, they raise the public-policy difficulty that the result may be welfare increasing. Schmalensee raised this point in oral testimony in the case (see Chapter 8).

Another concern is what Telser (1966) termed the deep-pockets concept. He noted that a critical further dubious assumption was that the predator had deep pockets, a superior access to financing. This assumes that monopoly profits are a particularly good way to finance the creation of new monopolies and that the threatened rivals both have fewer alternative internal revenue sources and lack the ability to secure outside financing. This idea certainly is popular with businessmen. Barksdale of Netscape presented it in his testimony in the Microsoft case. These assumptions are questionable in general and silly, given the support available to Netscape, in the Microsoft case.

The assertion conflicts with the efficient-market principle that good opportunities can be financed in the marketplace. The essence of criticisms such as Telser's is that the efficient-market concept is practically applicable. In addition, more than one monopolist might view a situation. One deep pocket might defeat another. Again the case is illustrative. Newcomers such as American Online and Netscape secured substantial financing from venture capitalists. In the AOL case, it became so strong that it could and did become Netscape's deep pocket. In short, the traditional approach of asking whether monopoly is possible remains central. As discussed below, the ability to use existing monopoly to create a new monopoly is possible only under special circumstances.

Predation I: The Chicago Critique

Bad economic concepts, particularly if they justify intervention, often defy refutation for decades or even centuries. Predation is another prime example. Predation is selling below cost, presumably to bankrupt rivals. The concept arose from the cries of firms losing to competitors. The frequency of charges necessitated economic analyses. Economic theory stresses that successful predation is unlikely and, moreover, can benefit the predator only by preserving or creating a monopoly. Case law in predation supports these points. Therefore, adequate proof in a predation case requires at least demonstration of both monopoly and a clearly predatory act.

Allegations are widespread that selling below cost or otherwise sacrificing profits to drive out customers is a sensible strategy. The alleged payoff is that once the rivals are gone, prices can be raised sharply to secure substantial profits. As much work has shown, this is questionable reasoning.

An enormous literature exists considering the theory and practice of predation and its detection. Theory suggests predation has severe drawbacks as a tactic. The modern literature dates back to John McGee's 1958 article. Prior to that, predation was a largely hidden subject. The issue rises in at least two contexts, antitrust economics and "dumping" in international trade. Discussion here stresses the antitrust side. The substantial literature on dumping makes the same points. Both literatures stress the role of losing firms in making the charge.

In my graduate-school class work (1956-8), the oral tradition was that the difficulty of permanent elimination of competition made the concept dubious. The price rises invite the revival of departed firms. McGee extended the basis for skepticism. He noted that predation is very expensive to the predator. It has to undertake the massive below-cost sales that depress the price. Recoupment would be very difficult.

More critically, his reexamination of the usual example of successful predation, Standard Oil, suggested that the tactic for preempting rivals was attractive buyouts, not predation. This inspired various efforts to examine whether other examples of predation existed. This endeavor has persisted and thus includes responses to subsequent treatments of predation. Most work reinforced McGee's conclusions. The endeavor, however, unearthed a few cases in which predation might have been tried and a dispute of McGee's findings.

Koller (1971) undertook a broad survey of predation charges and found them unwarranted. Subsequently, Liebeler (1986) examined more recent cases. His article sketches each case found and considers whether they met all the criteria of guilt set by the U.S. Supreme Court. He judged that at most one case met these criteria.

Burns argued that American Tobacco might have engaged in predatory behavior. Granitz and Klein (1996) (cited and criticized in Lott 1999) argued that McGee had neglected more subtle predatory aspects of Standard Oil behavior. Nevertheless, the basic point remained valid. It is still questionable that predation is a widely employed practice.

In 1999, Lott, a veteran observer of the debates over competition, undertook to test the validity of contemporary predation theory. He concentrated on selected aspects of the debate. His book tersely but effectively examines the logic of traditional and new theories, offers extensions, and tests the applicability of different theories. This simultaneously supports his doubts about the relevance of predation and shows how difficult it is to test for it. Nominally, his concern was newer theories, but his coverage was more general. Indeed, it appears that a major unstated implication is that tests of predation are independent of the theoretic model selected.

His survey of theory treats the essence of the older and the newer theories, the (lack of) empirical support, and the most recent antitrust applications, mainly a case about price cutting in cigarettes (Brown and Williamson) and the ongoing Microsoft case. Brown and Williamson, Lott notes, was affirmation that good prospects for success must be proved in a predation case.

He then develops and tests a model of what is needed to ensure predatory activity by private firms. He relies on a simple, ingenious proposition that, for predation to be a sensible strategy, managers must be rewarded, rather than punished, for temporary losses. He argues that this is true for the new models of predation but leaves implicit that the same test applies to old theories. As he clearly indicates, many problems hindered the test. A small number of firms have been the subject of a court case alleging predation. Many of these are privately held. Even for the publicly held companies, the data are inadequate for full direct tests of behavior. Moreover, legal barriers to takeovers arose after the predation cases, and thus Lott must rely on other indicators that management is protected.

Given the many deficiencies in the data, he employs numerous statistical models to determine whether firms involved in predation provide the managerial incentives needed. He finds that the data do not support the premise that predators clearly are protected from takeover and rewarded for predation. In his main models, he analyzes whether engaging in predation enhances executive compensation, whether firms accused of predation differ from other firms in possessing characteristics that lessen removal of management, and conversely whether engaging in predation affects management turnover. Significant effects of predation prove absent.

In addition, he melds predation theory with economic theories of politics to suggest government-owned enterprises have greater incentive to predate than do profit-maximizing private firms. He then tries to test this view by crossing the artificial line between antitrust and regulation of international trade. The best possible test is whether firms owned by foreign governments are singled out for dumping charges. He is well aware that dumping investigations use looser standards for selecting and evaluating.

With these caveats, he proceeds to develop various variants of a statistical model of the initiation and confirmation of dumping charges. His conclusions here start out claiming vindication of the hypothesis that nonmarket economies predate but eventually retreat to the more tenable position that importing countries act as if nonmarket economies are a greater threat.

Finally, to show the sensitivity of the new theory to assumptions, he discusses situations in which the victim may have better information than the predators. This produces an extension of predation theory that emphasizes options for the "victims." The victims in a potentially predatory situation necessarily possess better information than the presumed predator on some critical matters, namely their own situation. Such knowledge allows the managers to profit from speculating in the stocks of the predator. He considers examples, the absence of legal prohibitions of the practice, and a short, fairly simple development of the underlying theory.

Sappington and Sidak (2000) in their review of the book curiously argue that Lott succeeded better at his international trade analysis. This seems the reverse of the truth. The essence of Lott's argument is the difficulty of implementing a statistical verification of the ability to predate. With that premise, the lack of statistical support affirms his skepticism.

Predation II: Areeda and Turner Search for Clarification

In the *Harvard Law Review*, Areeda and Turner (1975) initiated a new round of debate. While sharing doubts about the true importance of predation, they decided that the courts needed guidance for dealing with predation cases that would inevitably arise. Thus, a workable practical measure of the existence of predation was required. They noted that the correct economic criterion was price below marginal cost, but marginal cost data were not available. They proposed looking at average variable costs as a proxy.

The argument has at least three defects that make the rule too restrictive. First, as the evolution of predation law in the courts indicates, the rule provides an incomplete appraisal. Before acting, other factors should be considered, notably the evidence about the alleged predators' intentions, the probability of success, and whether damage occurred (see Liebeler, 1986 and Lott, 1999).

Second, economic theory more generally states the profit-maximizing condition as the equality between marginal cost and marginal benefit. It is recognized that marginal benefits can include more than the revenues from the sale considered. Additional sales can be generated from other products or future sales of the same product. The sale allows production and, where learning by doing is involved, is an investment in lowering production costs.

Third, average costs are meaningful only for the simplified textbook concept of the single-product firm. For the multiproduct firms that actually exist, the contribution to cost recovery of any one product depends on the relative strength of its demand. An infinite number of shares in revenues among the products can attain the underlying requirement that the firm does not lose money. Thus, natural gas is jointly produced with crude oil, but its importance in cost recovery differs radically. At one extreme, the gas is a waste to burn up. At the other, it can contribute more to revenues than does crude oil. Similar problems arise with determining the contribution to Windows revenue of adding Explorer.

Their rules, nevertheless, were viewed as too streamlined by several prominent economists. Scherer (1976a, 1976b), Williamson (1977, 1979), Baumol (1977), Joskow and Klevorick (1979), and Ordover and Willig (1981a, 1981b) proposed more complex but supposedly more realistic rules. Baumol wanted consideration of the duration of prices. Joskow and Klevorick proposed more detailed reviews. Ordover and Willig wanted consideration of whether innovations were predatory.

As Chapter 2 noted, many further articles were written trying to interpret this debate. Areeda and Turner replied to Scherer (1976) and to Williamson (1977). McGee (1980) returned with an article concluding that the extensions were worse than the Areeda-Turner rules. McGee's treatment deliberately ignores the complications noted here. In these circumstances, the cost test won by default. Other contributions included one by

Easterbrook (1981) that Schmalensee cited in his Microsoft case testimony (par. 531, 274).

Salop (1981) organized a conference at the Federal Trade Commission at which papers and transcribed discussions treated both sides of the argument. Included were one incarnation of the Ordover and Willig paper and a discussion that attacked their approach as dangerously chilling to competition.

Nevertheless, as often noted outside the case and ignored within, the Ordover and Willig test lives as the Microsoft case. As discussed in Chapter 8, Fisher adopted a criterion of damage close to that proposed by Ordover and Willig (1981a, 9). They dealt with the problem of predatory quality, a better, more expensive product at the same price and treated specifically innovations with systems.

Ironically, one of the best criticisms of the fascination with predation appears in a 1988 article by Fisher commenting on the Matsushita case, a landmark in establishing stringent requirements for finding predation. He vividly notes at length about the mythological character of predation charges. He refers to a seeming morality play "often without much sound basis in fact or economic analysis." He adds, "One of the most persistent of antitrust fairy tales is that of predation, with the predator in the role of the wicked witch. Predation can and sometimes does occur, but far less often than is alleged." The article is then organized as treatment of three "myths." They are that the only concern is selling below cost, deep pockets matter, and price differences to different customers imply predatory pricing in the low-cost market.

All this shows that traditional concepts of predation are inapplicable to the Microsoft case. Neither a ruined competitor nor a price that could be raised is involved. Schmalensee complains that the government's case does not clearly satisfy the prevailing legal criteria (par. 534, 276 and paras. 567-70, 292-4). By the end of the trial, the government had abandoned traditional predation analysis (see Chapter 8).

All the defects of the Areeda-Turner rule, nevertheless, matter in the case. In particular, the proofs of damages are nonexistent. A central issue in the case is whether Microsoft's browser-pricing policies are justifiable by the incomes generated from increased sales of Windows and other products. Finally, the case is all about whether jointness really exists.

Predation III: Post-Chicago and Its Critics

The 1970s debates over Areeda-Turner proved not to end the story. New industrial economics contains models in which competitors act to restrain rivals by damages that do not cause ruin. The latest round of efforts consists of analytic and empirical efforts to refute these new models. The basic problem is that these new models only show that under some circumstances the tactics can produce inefficient outcomes. Views on relevance split over beliefs about the ability to determine in practice whether the sufficient conditions prevail.

Both those convinced that markets work better than governments and their opponents can find support. The pro-market types view these models as showing that no matter how complicated the analysis gets it does not build a convincing case for intervention. None of the complications clearly unearths problems that are even possibly correctable. Interventionists, however, see these extensions as raising clearly relevant issues.

On the critical side, my colleague Andrew N. Kleit, often with various coauthors, has presented critiques of many aspects of the debate. He has considered predation theory (Boudreaux and Kleit 1996a, 1996b), raising rivals' costs (Coate and Kleit 1994), resale price maintenance (Kleit 1993), and several classic antitrust cases often believed to justify concern over raising rivals' cost or other competitive techniques. His targets include Terminal Railroad (Reiffen and Kleit 1990), computer reservation services (Kleit 1992), *Lorain Journal* (Lopatka and Kleit 1995), Otter Tail Power (Kleit and Michaels 1994), and most recently Interstate Circuit (Butz and Kleit 2001). All are cases often cited as ones in which post-Chicago analyses are germane. Kleit and his collaborators argue this misconstrues the cases.

In contrast, Bolton, Brodley, and Riordan (2000) insist that predatory pricing is a relevant problem in antitrust. This involves belief that predation is important and that courts can appraise its existence. They believe that the new theories are persuasive and the empirical evidence suggests that predation sometimes arises. They are aware that the validity of the charge differs from case to case. They believe, however, that the courts are capable of appraising each situation. Thus, they propose principles of evaluation that can be implemented. These criteria are thoroughly neglected in the Microsoft case. Therefore, presentation here of these norms is in Chapter 8 as part of the critique of the government's case. The article is another indicator of how subjective appraisals can differ. Clearly, the authors reject the concerns of prior writers about the inability of courts adequately to consider economic arguments. The Microsoft case indicates insuperable difficulties is employing these concepts in antitrust.

What is clear is that the most these new models can do is establish when a given tactic produces inefficient results. For reasons already suggested, the model Salop and Scheffman introduced in 1983 and more fully developed in 1987 is the most interesting effort. The work presents a model based on traditional concepts of maximizing behavior. The model specifies the existence of a critical input.

The basic 1987 model starts with the optimizing decision of a potential predator. These are to obey Lerner's optimality condition for a monopolist plus a new optimality condition for the input price. The next step is showing that the critical condition for increased profitability is a rise in the price of the monopolized good greater than that of average costs. It is then demonstrated that the effects on price, fringe output and profits, and welfare depend on the circumstances. What is critical for the welfare rise is that the predator be the lower cost producer charging a price above marginal cost. Given all that needs determination, the model seems a frailer basis for policy than Salop appears to believe.

Coate and Kleit (1994) specify several specific failings of the model. The starting point is that, in many cases, the rise in rivals' costs requires paying the suppliers of inputs to restrict output. This generally makes the strategy more expensive (75-7). Coate and Kleit then examine a case presented by Krattenmaker and Salop (1986) to show how high these costs can be. In particular, compensation must be given to those who restricted output and those who would have entered in response to the higher input prices. The higher price of the good using the input increases the willingness to pay for the input. Transaction costs and bilateral bargaining costs also arise (77-80). Thus, the strategy has greater difficulty than the Salop and Scheffman article recognized.

Coate and Kleit show problems with other models of raising rivals' costs and conclude by noting the lack of empirical support. In particular, Ordover and Saloner (1989) listed three antitrust cases as examples of raising rivals' costs. Coate and Kleit (86-8) present reasons why each example is unsatisfactory. Kleit's other work, as noted, treats other cases used as examples of raising rivals' costs and finds these other cases also fail to support the hypothesis.

Tying, Bundling, Leverage, and Essential Facilities: Antitrust versus Economics

While many articles exist about strategic pricing, little is available on other practices with which antitrust is concerned. Most discussions arise in two interrelated areas, vertical relations and price discrimination. The vertical-control literature deals among other things with efficiency problems in the relationship between a manufacturer and a reseller. Whatever the market structure, problems may arise in assuring that the reseller operates efficiently. Chicago economics included considerable work on how restrictions on resale prices and exclusivity requirements could promote efficiency. With monopoly and the ability of the reseller to vary the proportion in which the monopolized good is used comes the problem of eliminating the inefficient input pattern produced by that monopoly. Vertical integration is one solution; a discriminatory pricing method is another. Thus, consideration of vertical ties leads into also treating discrimination.

Typically, surveys of the literature separate the discrimination issues from the vertical control issues. This is true in Schmalensee and Willig (where Varian (1989) treats discrimination including that by tying and Katz (1989) treats vertical relations), Tirole (1988), Carlton and Perloff (1994), and McGee (1988). The chief exception is Scherer and Ross (1990) who treat tying for discrimination within their vertical-control chapter.

The economic literature on tying is thin. The critical contribution is the Whinston (1990) analysis of the circumstances under which tying could facilitate extending monopoly. Katz (709), Tirole (334-5), and Carlton and Perloff (467) note the existence of the work in the first two cases in its draft version. Only Katz tries to explain it. Whinston (2001) used his analysis to evaluate the Microsoft case and recognized that the evidence in the case is insufficient to meet his criteria for monopoly-creating tying.

Whinston's modeling (1990) is another example of post-Chicago taxonomy. His preliminary comments indicate that tying can aid a monopolist by causing a rival to exit but the welfare effects are ambiguous (839). His cases include ones in which tying is undesirable as well as desirable to the monopolist. The proofs all involve brute force calculation of the profitability of alternative situations.

His starting case is of "no commitment." This means that the firm offers the two products separately as well as a bundle. This produces no effect because the optimum price of the bundle is the sum of the optimum stand-alone price (842-3). This proves true if the firm offers the bundle and separately sells the monopolized product (A). However, the result when only the bundle and the product not monopolized (B_1) are sold is the same as when the bundle is sold, namely a reduction of the profits of the rival seller of the unmonopolized good (843-6). However, the welfare effects are unclear.

His treatment of "heterogeneous consumer preferences" (imperfect substitution) indicates that the rival may not always be harmed. In dealing with complementary products, he similarly shows the efficacy of tying depends upon the circumstances and the welfare implications are still unclear. Thus, introducing economies of scale and oligopoly into Posner's case of use in fixed proportions does not eliminate the irrelevance of tying. The departure of the rival in the other good lowers sales of A. Tying aids the tying firm in the further cases of competing against an inferior rival producer of A or when the other product with a rival supplier has alternative uses. A bundle and independent offer of B_1 can cause exit of the rival and increased sales of B_1.

The Microsoft case inspired efforts to expand the theory and to refute that expansion. The expansion is Carlton and Waldman (1998, 2000). The response is Hylton and Salinger (2001). Carlton dutifully notes his role as Sun's expert in its suit against Microsoft. Hylton and Salinger similarly indicate research support from Microsoft.

Carlton and Waldman deal with two cases of tying. In the first, the monopolist faces a potential entrant in the monopolized good and has one existing rival for a complementary good. That rival produces a higher quality good at the same marginal costs as the monopoly. Competition is conceived as a Bertrand (price-setting) game. The second considers using tying to extend the original monopoly into a new market.

The analysis again involves appraising the profitability of different strategies. In these models, the outcome varies with conditions, and Carlton and Waldman derive the sufficient conditions for profitable ties. Again, the welfare implications of a profitable tie are uncertain.

The penultimate section of Carlton and Waldman deals with antitrust by noting the practical limits of the theory. They warn of the error of confusing theoretical possibility with empirical demonstration. Given the danger of banning desirable actions, they suggest that the existence of plausible benefits of tying should override tying charges. This is close to the earlier Circuit Court ruling that Judge Jackson tried to circumvent. More critically, it is a variant on the skeptical reviews of post-Chicago theory.

Hylton and Salinger (2001) indirectly confirm the view that tying is a legal concept belatedly treated by economics. They distinguish among classical, Chicago, and post-Chicago phases of the debate (7). They start with a review of case law and then turn to the underlying economics. While their treatment of Chicago and post-Chicago cites relevant economic writings, none are provided for the classical approach in either the discussion of cases (8-11) or the sketch (27-8) in the review of economics.

The most important part of Hylton and Salinger is the review (39-50) of Whinston (1990) and Carlton and Waldman (1998, 50-51). An extensive effort is made to explain Whinston; Carlton and Waldman are treated more cursorily. Hylton and Salinger see the need actually to eliminate rivals, the high cost, and the failure to compare with other tactics as critical points (49-50). The basic problem that harm is only a possible outcome is treated only by noting a firm "might have an incentive" to tie (49). The remainder of the article discusses why, as a result, severe problems arise in implementing post-Chicago theories. This is overkill since the theories convey their practical limitations.

The government covered all possibilities in attacking Microsoft. It tossed in an exclusive dealing charge, the only one rejected by Judge Jackson. Economists commenting on the case helpfully cited a post-Chicago effort (Rasmusen, Ramseyer, and Wiley, 1991) to prove exclusive dealing can be an effective strategy. The model assumes firms have textbook u-shaped cost curves that produce a minimum efficient scale that is greater than the demands of one customer but less than total market demand. The model is another case of a possible bad result that, as the authors admit at the outset, depends critically on the inability of consumers to communicate. The model seems actually to assume that both consumers and potential competitors are unaware of the consequences of an exclusive-dealing contract. The cost assumptions adopted are ones that usually produce pure competition. That should preclude success at buying the right to monopolize.

The essential-facilities doctrine receives even less attention. The one treatment in the books examined is a brief mention in the foreign country antitrust section of a chapter of Scherer and Ross on antitrust policies toward structures (487). That discussion uses the alternative term "bottleneck facilities" that are "essential" and not easily duplicated. More importantly, the manuscript version of the leading reference on the subject (Reiffen and Kleit 1990) is cited without noting that the work argues that the essential-facility concept is empty. They point out that an essential facility is simply an upstream monopoly and a policy of nondiscriminatory sales to all is optimal in the case where no substitution is possible. Terminal Railroad, in fact, employed a policy of free access at uniform prices.

The above has shown that the new models of competitive tactics only define the conditions under which different tactics produce inefficient outcomes. For these tactics to be prevalent, the required conditions must be present and visible to business executives. A further, even more difficult, problem is whether an antitrust agency and its economists can develop and present to a court a satisfactory determination of whether a given business action truly promotes monopoly. Some enthusiasts of the theory believe that the effort required for such a determination is manageable. Others object. Several considerations influence the views. First is attitudes about the robustness of the theory. Second is appraisal of the empirical evidence. Third is the view of what governments can accomplish.

Chapter 5 QWERTY: Threat or Fable, Towards the Applications Barrier to Entry

The competitive advantage of an established position based on a specific technology became a concern of economic analysis only in the late 1980s. The stimulus was allegations in popular writings of mistaken choices of technology. This inspired development of models of technology displacement. The theory reflects the prior complaint that it proves that anything is possible. Nevertheless, this theory served as tacit rationale for the applications barrier to entry.

This chapter deals with the practical and theoretic basis for the arguments. The empirical support consists of dubious anecdotes. The nominal basis for the theory is an assertion that the currently standard QWERTY layout of a typewriter keyboard was clearly inefficient and persisted only by inertia. This inspired a search for more examples and supporting theory.

Many sought to develop theories of technological choice. Two economists, Stan J. Liebowitz and Stephen E. Margolis (here LM), were suspicious of the empirical evidence, tested it further, and then examined the theoretical work.

David, Arthur, QWERTY, the Network Externality, and the Fable of the Keys

In the formal economics literature, the concern about inefficient choice of technology started with David's 1985 article on typewriter keyboards. David contended that the standard QWERTY arrangement of typewriters was designed to slow down users of the primitive early typewriters. Inertia maintained the design despite the existence of a demonstrably better arrangement. However, no documentation was produced. The argument, nevertheless, was widely repeated by economists.

Eventually many models were developed to explain how inefficient choice could occur. Brian Arthur apparently was the pioneer, but by the time his work was published other, better, analyses such as Katz and Shapiro (1985, 1986) had appeared. (David cites a 1983 draft of what appears to be the 1989 Arthur article.) These other pioneers indeed were more persistent contributors than Arthur.

Actually, literature reviews indicate a concern with the problem long before Arthur. Economides maintains an online bibliography on network effects that printed out as 73 pages. Examination indicates that far more than technology choice is involved. In particular, public utilities, particularly electricity and telephones, are network industries. Therefore, much on the theoretic and applied literature of public utilities appears in the bibliography. Conversely, a few basic articles receive the most frequent citations in the literature.

Arthur presented a model in which once a convention such as the design of a typewriter keyboard is adopted it can become so entrenched that even an obviously superior alternative will be precluded from displacing the incumbent. Arthur added to QWERTY the preference for internal combustion in cars and for light-water over gas-cooled nuclear reactors.

Before these theoretic exercises had ceased, LM (1990) entered the debate with their debunking of the case against QWERTY. They extended their work to evaluate other claims and skeptically to view the theory. All this was brought together in 1999 in a book that summarized prior theoretical and empirical work, did work on competition in computer software, and made comments on the Microsoft case. (A second edition in 2001 added only more comments on the case.)

LM were struck by the inadequacy of the proofs that QWERTY was inferior. David relied on assertions that a U.S. Navy report, which he had not seen, proved the superiority of the Dvorak layout. LM also were skeptical of David's analytic conclusions. They managed to unearth the actual study. It proved to have been supervised by August Dvorak, the inventor of the alternative layout, and methodologically unsound. Other studies that they found suggested that the original choice of layout was more efficient than David believed. Moreover, QWERTY emerged originally from competition among rival typewriter manufacturers to provide better layouts. Thus, the major example of the inappropriate technology furor proves a loser's rationalization, the historical defect of interventionist arguments.

The results appeared as the lead article of the April 1990 issue of the *Journal of Law and Economics* with the title "The Fable of the Keys." The title was designed jocularly to relate their work to prior refutations of market inefficiency. In 1973, Stephen N. S. Cheung had used the title "The Fable of the Bees: An Economic Investigation." The first half of the title was that of Mandeville's eighteenth century book about selfinterest. The

Cheung article tested J. E. Meade's assertions about the inability of markets to ensure the optimal provision of apple tree pollination by bees. Cheung found that apple growers did contract with beekeepers for pollination services. Cheung also found that the reciprocal problem postulated by Meade of inadequate access of bees to trees was nonexistent.

LM argued that they had added to the contributions of Cheung and also of Ronald Coase (1988) who showed that, contrary to a standard example, private groups successfully provided lighthouses. LM were correct, but perhaps not as they hoped. As with the lighthouses and bees, the QWERTY myth lived on. Therefore, as noted, LM went on to examine other cases and the emerging supporting theory.

Their book starts with a reprint of the fable and later treats previously reported work dealing with two other widely mentioned alleged errors in choice of technology. LM show that neither the Sony beta format for video tape recorders nor the Apple Macintosh operating system was markedly superior to its rival. Then LM treat the metric system, Japan's planning agency–MITI, and the FORTRAN computer language. LM also present extensive examination of the principal application programs used in desktop computers. Here, the same history emerges. Leadership radically changes as better programs emerge, and the best program wins.

Betas, it turns out, had no advantage. The winning VHS alternative had the same performance and greater capacity. When introduced, the Macintosh operating system so strained then available computer capacity that PCs using DOS, the first Microsoft operating system, were faster. As computers caught up, Microsoft went on to Windows, a reasonable approximation of the Macintosh operating system. Here LM are too kind to Apple. Its operating system always has been easier to use, but many drawbacks prevailed. The Macintosh was not superior to PCs in every respect; Apple seemed to seek a price premium; the company at times was so badly adrift that its survival was in doubt. Similarly, LM found FORTRAN was less durable than contended. The metric system does not produce great advantages. MITI was fallible.

The software tests are by far the largest part of the book. LM successively review Windows, office suites, spreadsheets, word processors, personal finance, desktop publishing, web browsers, and online services. They show the tendency of magazine review ratings and market shares to correspond and for programs to lose ground when their performance lagged those of rivals.

They only mention (1996) light-water reactors, an example that is particularly familiar to me. It also is invalid. Arthur had swallowed the assertions of two MIT nuclear engineers that the failure of nuclear power was due to the wrong choice of reactor design. This assertion ignores the many other problems that arose, the continued preference for the light-water approach, and the fiasco encountered by the company attempting to commercialize the supposedly superior gas-cooled reactor. Its demonstration plant (Fort St. Vrain in Colorado) failed to operate regularly. Orders for commercial-sized units were cancelled.

LM's appraisal of the theory is deliberately much simpler than standard work on the subject. They produced the usual conclusion that the existence of a lock-in depends critically on the circumstances. The theory, for example, allows too much as well as too little displacement of established technology. In particular, LM recognize that the status quo imposes transition costs. However, this does not preclude the profitable coexistence of a rival. Their conclusion then is that bad choice of technology is a concept of which no convincing practical examples exist and about which the theoretical justification is unsatisfactory.

Their theoretical discussion examines the different ways the time path of decision making may matter. They (1999, 57) indicate that a combination of unlimited economies of scale and neglect of foresight is required to produce bad choices. Both assumptions are sufficiently inappropriate to constitute fatal flaws in the theory.

They turn to the impacts of the incentives to the owner of the best technology and its customers to invest in securing dominance. As LM argue (57-8), the economic definition of technical superiority, a higher payoff, creates impetus for the owner to undertake and win a contest. This is the obvious implication of the application of foresight. Their empirical work shows that the evidence supports their presumption.

In dealing explicitly with the issues of externalities, they introduce an analysis showing that at least with increasing costs the owner of a network can profit from promoting efficiency and will do so. Arthur, moreover, seems to have committed the classic error of confusing technical progress with the effects of increasing scale at a given time. (This matters because it is the scale effect that produces natural monopoly.) LM go on to point out that software reproduction is not the only supply cost and these other costs probably rise with scale.

Another model explores how consumer preferences and their interaction in the marketplace affect choices among technologies. They examine the consequences of alternative assumptions. Ultimately, they reach a case in which skewed assumptions do produce a lock-in and then show that their earlier argument about incentives of the owner of the superior technology to attract customers applies. The lock-in can be reversed.

However, they again seem overly polite in dealing with the fundamental problem that the dependence model relies on a long chain of improbable assumptions to prove that bad choices sometimes can be made. In addition, the usual government-failure arguments apply. As the Microsoft case makes clear, governments are unlikely accurately to identify and correct bad choices.

Two leading developers of the theory, Michael Katz and Carl Shapiro clearly stated the point. They closed a survey article (1994, 1 12-13) on network effects by noting the applicability to policy response of classic anti-intervention arguments. First, they recognize that private actions can internalize the externalities. Second, governments are likely to stress the status quo over efficiency. Third, governments lack the knowledge to determine the most efficient action.

This is an implicit reminder that the literature has treated an externality problem without explicit consideration of Coase's (1960) argument that, if bargaining costs are sufficiently low, private mechanisms can efficiently internalize the externality. (LM apply this principle to the Microsoft case but leave the broader implications implicit. However, their analysis is equivalent to the attainment of internalization by private actions.) An important element of recalling Coase is to recognize his warning that both a private and a public solution may be imperfect and the choice between them is unclear.

The literature on network externalities has become enormous. Review of leading examples confirmed the Liebowitz and Margolis conclusions. Katz and Shapiro and Farrell and Saloner are among the more persistent contributors.

Katz and Shapiro's first effort (1985) stresses, as would much subsequent work, attaining compatibility among network standards. Also characteristically, the results consist of sufficient conditions and possibilities for inadequate or excessive coordination. Thus, they start by characterizing behavior with or without compatibility. This leads to the conclusion that complete compatibility increases total output. This, in turn, inspires tacitly Coasean concern over mechanisms to attain compatibility. They determine that side payments may not attain efficiency, set principles for industry standards, and show that unilateral efforts to attain convertibility will be excessive or inadequate depending upon the circumstances.

Their second effort (1986) turned to the adoption of new technologies. Here they deal with the various inefficiencies that necessarily result from a conventional private market without a mechanism to internalize the network externalities. They consider one internalization mechanism, the existence of a sponsor for the technology. They raise concerns that that sponsor will ignore impacts on rival technologies and overdo. A clear problem is that if only the inferior technology is sponsored, it may win. They then derive the case that even with sponsorship of both technologies the wrong technology may win because of response to a temporary cost advantage.

Eventually, they reach the point that the sponsor of the superior technology would have an incentive to subsidize adoption in the period of cost disadvantage (840). They note that traditional predation analysis would mistake such subsidy for predation. In short, buried in their extensive review of possibilities and their references to Arthur and David is recognition that an efficient method of externalization exists. They provided the basis for the LM conclusions but failed to recognize how much they have undermined the case.

Another pioneering article by Farrell and Saloner (1986) concentrates on optimality conditions for a market solution. They too eventually introduce an incentive pricing scheme as an internalization scheme and reiterate the problem of conflict with the Areeda-Turner rules. In short, even before Arthur actually got his article published, the literature had indicated that the standard mechanisms for internalization might be available. While they may not admit it, the other theorists incorporated the possibility of efficient private internalization.

As LM's concluding appendixes discuss, these arguments are no longer mere academic arguments. They are major elements in the Microsoft case. LM use their analysis to conclude that the case against Microsoft is unfounded. They have particular fun pointing out the role in the case of advocates of network-externalities concerns. They again probably did not go far enough. Key writers made an analysis similar to LM's part of their work but did not give it enough attention. Neglect of Coase in 1985 or 2001 is an incredible hiatus.

Thus, this form of post-Chicago theory not only has the standard characteristic that incorrect decisions are only a possible outcome, but features that make that result doubtful. Reliance on the inability to recognize and finance a good investment is required and that is never a satisfactory basis. It certainly was not in the Microsoft case. Thus, the core of the case was based on ignoring the theory and particularly its questionable practical relevance.

Chapter 6 Introduction to the Case

As indicated, the remainder of this book seeks to present and evaluate the case developed. To attain this goal, much information must be managed. Attention must be given the points raised, who raised them, where they were presented, and how they were raised. These considerations interact. Aside from the expert economists, the witnesses were chosen because of knowledge about some aspect of the case. Why they participated is clearer after the case is outlined. As argued here, some choices made by both sides, particularly but not exclusively of witnesses, seem questionable.

The treatment of the case is divided into four parts. This chapter describes the case with stress on the defects in its conduct. Chapter 7 treats the operating-system monopoly, Chapter 8, the conceptual problems with the attack on Microsoft tactics, and Chapter 9, the deficiencies of the supporting evidence about these tactics.

This chapter starts with a summary of the substance of the case. The discussion is made independent of how the contentions were presented. Then presentation is examined. A sketch is given of who participated and how the material is available. This chapter moves to illustrations of how the government used irrelevant material to discredit Microsoft. Then, observations are made about what this suggests about the desirability of antitrust laws.

The Basic Case

As noted, the case has a narrow focus. Microsoft was one of the suppliers of the operating system for the line of personal commuters IBM introduced in 1981. These computers were intended to respond to the challenge posed by emerging producers of microcomputers, most notably Apple. Apple responded in 1984 by introducing a new line of computers, the Macintosh, using a radically different graphical type of operating system. Previously, users had to master codes denoting the tasks to be undertaken; instructions were typed in. With the Macintosh, a pointing device called a mouse is employed to lock into locations on the computer screen where needed information appears. Clicking a button on the mouse then instituted an action. Apple adapted this technology from work at Xerox, which was unwilling to market the ideas. Microsoft responded in 1985 by developing its own graphical system called Windows (mfof par. 25, 12).

In a graphical system, what is seen initially on a computer screen is called the desktop. Various objects reside on the desktop. Those that can be clicked immediately to initiate an action are termed icons. More complex objects called folders contain multiple items.

With the emergence of the Internet, programs called browsers are needed for access. A hot new venture called Netscape arose in April 1994 to provide such a browser, Netscape Navigator. Navigator secured great success. Microsoft decided that the Internet was so important that the company must make a browser a feature provided with Windows. The timing of that decision is disputed by the two sides, see Chapter 9. Microsoft contends its decision antedated the creation of Netscape. The government comes close to claiming the decision was made a few weeks before Internet Explorer was introduced. That browser, Internet Explorer, was marketed in August 1995 with Microsoft's popular Windows program and in June 1998 integrated into Windows 98 (mfof par. 27, 13).

The government argues that ultimately Netscape Navigator using Sun Microsystems's Java language would serve as a platform on which programs would be written and end the applications barrier to entry. Therefore, Microsoft engaged in illegal efforts to prevent the emergence of this Navigator/Java platform. The concern is that Microsoft sought to harm not Netscape Navigator, but only the Netscape/Java platform. As might be suspected, this specification of a narrower objective allows the government to assert damage despite Netscape's healthy status. Moreover, as a result, Microsoft's actions allegedly violate the antitrust laws in four ways.

The illegality arises because Microsoft had a monopoly and used inappropriate ways to protect that monopoly. Microsoft retorts that it responded to broad competitive challenges by competing vigorously and fairly to secure wide acceptance of Internet Explorer. A major drawback of the case is the observational equivalence between the behavior charged by the government and fair vigorous competition. In addition, the basic claims made are invalid.

In practice, the government tried and succeeded in persuading the District and Circuit Court judges that the monopoly was too obvious to merit detailed discussion (see Chapter 7). Conversely, the charge of illegal defense of monopoly was divided into many parts. A major consequence of this strategy is that what proves a simple argument requires extensive criticism. The charge against Microsoft is that it bought customers at too high a price. The government presents extensive evidence of buying use of Internet Explorer but never shows that the price is too high. These parts comprise the bulk of the case. This separation and elaboration encouraged indignation about the appearances of the acts. This diverted attention from the need conclusively to prove that the result was a successful illegal effort to thwart the emergence of a Netscape/Java platform. The consequence here is the need to devote considerable effort to the defects of each detail.

The monopoly is that of Windows in the computer industry. The government asserted that the relevant market was Intel-compatible personal computers. In this market, Microsoft allegedly had an impenetrable monopoly. This monopoly was attributed to the existence of 70,000 programs for Windows. This overwhelming difference between Windows and other operating systems allegedly created an "applications barrier to entry."

The illegal-response charge is based on the claim that monopolist Microsoft improperly created and promoted Internet Explorer solely to eliminate the Netscape/Java threat. The illegality started with making Explorer a component of Windows and providing Explorer free to others, particularly users of earlier versions of Windows and to Apple users. Combining programs is common in the computer industry. Therefore, the government sought to assert the effort involved undertaking unusual actions inspired by the desire to end the platform threat.

Another major element of the illegality case is that Microsoft widely engaged in foreclosing practices. As argued in Chapter 8, these practices amount to buying users for Internet Explorer. Again, the issue is one of illegal harm. Chapter 8 stresses that, as the government recognized, the Microsoft behavior radically differed from the usual model of predation. These differences create severe problems for proving the case. In neither economics nor antitrust is promotion undesirable. The issue is whether this support took predatory or other "anticompetitive" (i.e., inefficient) forms. The peculiarities of the Microsoft case are ones that cause severe problems in establishing illegality.

An additional complication was that the 1998-2000 trial was the successor to an earlier one relating to restrictions on Microsoft's behavior relating to tying products. The District of Columbia Circuit Court of Appeals had overturned a District Court order by Jackson to prevent the bundling of Explorer into Windows 95. The decision was based on the inadequacy of proof to justify the action. Provision of proof might have produced a prohibition. That decision, nevertheless, stressed the difficulties in assessing the validity of the inclusion because of "the undesirability of having courts oversee product design."[1]

---

[1] The decision was downloaded from the Microsoft web site in a form that lost page and paragraph number.

The main restriction employed by Microsoft was requiring computer manufacturers (original equipment manufacturers or OEMs) to display an Explorer icon at initial start-up. That supposedly greatly encouraged installation of Internet Explorer. As discussed in Chapter 9, the indirect effects of other controls on OEMs were portrayed as more harmful than the requirement of icon display. The controls, in fact, precluded neither display of a Netscape Navigator icon nor even making Netscape Navigator the default browser.

Deals were made with others that provided Explorer without charge and assistance from Microsoft for agreeing to favor Explorer over Netscape Navigator. Efforts were directed at online services (OLSs), providers of Internet access (Internet service providers, ISPs) or content (Internet content providers, ICPs), independent software vendors (ISVs), and Apple Computer. Judge Jackson called the Internet service providers Internet access providers (IAPs). OLSs differ from the ISPs by providing content disseminated only to subscribers. A special incentive was creation of folders on the Windows desktop that contained links to firms agreeing to favor Internet Explorer. The government views these actions as an illegal and fatally debilitating blow to Navigator as a platform. Thus, these transactions are further indicators of illegal protection of a monopoly. The view here is that these are simply the efforts of a new competitor to gain a foothold.

Additional charges were raised. The dealings with Apple allegedly also involved trying to suppress the development of a program called QuickTime. Another firm called RealNetworks was also pressured (although this received little attention). Similarly, Microsoft was accused of undermining programming efforts at Intel and of producing a form of Java designed to sabotage the ability of Java to compete with Windows. Finally, assertions were made of efforts to intimidate IBM and Compaq. The Compaq charge relates to efforts to enforce the terms of the Windows licensing agreement. The IBM assertions involved alleged pressures to rely more heavily on Microsoft software.

These further charges are clearly designed to show that the rivalry with Netscape is part of a tendency by Microsoft to act aggressively. This causes many problems. A classic concern over antitrust, as noted, is that it often is misused to protect competitors from more efficient rivals. Clearly, those most highly suspicious of antitrust quickly concluded that the Microsoft case was another example. A private suit by Netscape may have been preferable. It remains unclear whether the treatment of other Microsoft actions is more than a minimum effort to meet concerns that the government is giving free legal services to Netscape.

The broadening also creates internal inconsistency in the case. The relating of multiple threats is inconsistent with the central theme that the

Netscape/Java hazard is unique. The treatment of other challenges to Microsoft stresses that these rivalries provide resistance and ignores that the cumulative effect might severely restrain Microsoft.

Finally, the substance of these additional charges is dubious. In every instance treated in the case, bitter enemies of Microsoft present their grievances, and Microsoft responds. (Some animus was corporate; other, personal.) Both sides should be suspect. Even if resolution were possible, the charges would still be overblown. Each involved failed pressure, a participant able to resist Microsoft, or both. The one case in which Microsoft may have had success, Intel, is the one in which the other firm had the most power to resist. As the government tried to ignore, Intel is as indispensable to Microsoft as Microsoft is to Intel.

Other questionable efforts arose in treating the central issue of the Netscape/Java platform. One has received so much attention that it needs introduction here and further treatment in Chapter 9. The government's charge of predatory intent starts with allegations about a meeting on June 21, 1995 between Microsoft and Netscape. A memorandum completed right after the meeting by Netscape's Marc Andreessen asserted that the proposals were for a division of the market between Microsoft and Netscape (GX 33). This memorandum was immediately sent to the Department of Justice. In the case, the offer was represented as a proposal for illegal market sharing.

All the government's arguments in the case prove too closely tailored to the peculiarities of the situation. The critical one was of concentration on platform competition. This ignores that the reality of the platform peril was unclear and, even if the danger were real, its termination is not readily verified. Moreover, if the threat were that great, nothing short of a Standard-Oil type buyout would inoculate Microsoft from its effects. The vision does, however, justify reliance on loose criteria of acceptable evidence.

This is only part of the problem. The government needed conclusively to establish the existence of a Microsoft monopoly and the inefficiency of its tactics. Neither was done. Finally, the government case engages in an excess of balancing acts.

The government case involves a long chain of reasoning:

1. The relevant market is Intel-compatible personal computers.
2. Microsoft is a monopolist in that market.
3. The monopoly stems from an applications barrier to competition.
4. Servers, smaller devices, and similar alternatives are not competition for the personal computers.
5. Extant operating systems such as Unix, Linux, Be, and Apple are not competitive threats.

6. However, the promise that Netscape Navigator using Java might become a competitive platform was a credible threat.
7. The start of the pressure was a "naked market sharing" offer to Netscape on June 21, 1995.
8. To initiate a campaign of pressure on the Netscape/Java platform, Microsoft's response was a browser strategy involving developing Internet Explorer, eventually designing it as an integral part of Windows, including it with all shipments of Windows, and not charging extra for the browser. (This assertion ignores that Internet Explorer was introduced a few weeks after the meeting with Netscape.)
9. This strategy is explicable only by a desire to kill the platform threat to Microsoft's monopoly. No other explanation for creating Internet Explorer is credible. The most important rejected alternative was that Microsoft was concerned with the need for more competition in the browser market.
10. This was an illegal tie-in, exclusive dealing, and predation.
11. The first major element of the campaign was unreasonable restrictions on OEMs.
12. Another unreasonable effort was the dealing with American Online (AOL) and other OLSs and ISPs.
13. Microsoft unduly pressured Apple to adopt Explorer.
14. Overly generous deals were made with ICPs.
15. The campaign is merely the most obvious of numerous Microsoft abuses. It also:
    a. Threatened Apple if it continued producing QuickTime for Windows,
    b. Threatened an Intel software development,
    c. Threatened RealNetworks,
    d. Produced a "polluted" version of Java,
    e. Threatened IBM and Compaq.
16. The attack on the Netscape/Java platform succeeded.
17. That success harmed consumers.

The government thus presents very strong charges against Microsoft. Failure to provide support, as noted, is the concern here. The chain of reasoning is totally defective. The arguments are invalid and badly presented.

In their "direct testimonies" (the trial term for the written statements), the government's expert economists fail badly, and the government does no better. The germane economic theory is ignored. No statement is made of what comprises satisfactory proof. Proof is absent. Total reliance is on memorandums and the charges of rivals.

The Components of the Case: Two Phases, Limited Witnesses, Written Testimony, Many Documents

Evaluation is complicated because both the substance and its presentation are convoluted. These complexities involve the content and form of the evidence, how and by whom it was presented, its availability, and the many efforts within and outside the trial to evaluate the information. Properly to explain the case, it is necessary to steer the reader through the morass.

As anyone ever exposed to a major lawsuit will recognize, the case involved sweeping up a vast amount of material. The exhibits presenting this information are the most problematic evidence. The government's case centers on these documents. The exhibits, however, are indigestible; I skimmed all those posted by the government and sampled Microsoft's.

Redaction and failure to post are only the initial difficulties. Many exhibits fail to indicate their author. The exhibits differ wildly in nature and relevance. Neither inspection nor reliance on citations by the attorneys is a completely reliable filtering device. What seems innocuous on skimming may prove to provide a phrase some diligent researcher for the legal teams found useful. The citations may overlook contradictory material that somehow fell into the record.

The government exhibit list starts with exhibit 1 and ends with exhibit 2,519. The list shows only exhibit number, which (of two) computer procedure was used for display, and file size. Citations are scattered through the Findings of Facts, but the nature of the material is not always made clear. Many numbers are skipped. Plowing through the Findings of Fact showed that many of the missing numbers belonged to exhibits kept secret. Even so, what left is formidable. About 955 are listed.

More than 50 of the entries contain only descriptions of exhibits, mostly articles. These undisplayed articles include several that are important to the case. Most critically, the practice was followed for all but one of the articles about Gates alleged to be evidence of predatory intent. Similarly, the government posted only the most accessible of Schmalensee's articles that supposedly were inconsistent with his testimony in the case. Moreover, while his testimony in other cases is reproduced, it is limited to the portions that the government contends are contradictory.

Many memorandums were collected from Microsoft, Netscape, and other companies. The companies involved included participants in the disputes treated in the case, those from the sectors in which Microsoft was accused of excessive promotion of Internet Explorer, and even some computer users.

The government emphasized Microsoft documents. They were by far the largest component. These ranged from presentations of basic points to inconsequential remarks. Something was provided on each element of the government's case. Duplication is frequent. Over 50 Netscape memorandums reporting lost of business were viewed. In them is the frequent use of predation or other terms suggesting antitrust violations.

However, much more was shown. Numerous contracts are part of the public record. Material circulated as part of business operations was included; examples include guidelines to OEMs for installing Windows and even the license statements that appear when programs are installed. A block of exhibits consists of depositions. Magazine articles are included. There are also handwritten notes, hard copies of many slide presentations by executives of Microsoft and other companies, data compilations, many meaningless stills from videotape demonstrations, and at least one resume.

A great deal of amateur economic analysis appeared and received solemn treatment. The worst aspect of this is the heavy reliance of the government on market appraisals by executives of Microsoft and its rivals.

The Microsoft exhibit list provides short descriptions of each available exhibit; moreover, the exhibits are grouped by their day of introduction. However, the posting is incomplete; downloading must be done a page at a time; the results are not always legible.

The central, successful role of this documentation is the most chilling element of the case. Even if accurate and complete, documents only convey that part of the justification that was foreseen and someone cared to write down. Not only might other motivations have existed, but it is unwise to brand as predatory actions taken in the anticipation of benefits because the decision makers cannot specify precisely in advance.

The use of documents, in fact, is perverse. Key factual issues such as the importance of the writer, the timing of writing, and the content require only literacy to appraise. Fathoming motivation may be impossible; it certainly is not an aspect of economic expertise. However, statements of objectives were the dominant interest.

Moreover, in several critical cases, checking the documents indicates misrepresentation. Indiscreet phrases are cited while ignoring that the substance is innocuous. At other times, the quotation omits critical further information. Another device is to collect material suggestive of a conspiracy and treat it as conclusive proof.

Many people were deposed, interrogated under oath, before the trial; a block of exhibits consists of excerpts from depositions. No pretrial statements of courtroom witnesses were posted. This precludes checking courtroom challenges of the prior testimony. Each side drew on a different source of data on trends in browser usage. While both sides undoubtedly prepared press releases, only those from Microsoft are included in an Internet archive.

The trial then involved weaving this material together to meet the attorneys' legal goal of convincing the judge. This objective can be and was far different from presenting and refuting a logically tight argument that Microsoft was a predatory monopolist. The case suggests that creating an appearance sufficed. Demonstrating that a surface impression succeeded and that the underlying case is dubious is the focus of this book.

The attorneys naturally get the first and last words. The courtroom proceedings started with case summaries by both sides (on October 18 and 19, 1998). At the end of the trial (September 21, 1999), the case was recapitulated. As it turned out, several sets of last words emerged. The process divided the decision into three steps—a finding of fact, conclusions of law, and, after guilt was found, a remedy. The first presented what the judge claimed he ascertained. The statement in the case engendered considerable controversy discussed in Chapter 10. The conclusions of law indicated the legal consequences of the facts, and the remedy did something. At each stage, each side submitted their proposals for the statement. Oral arguments followed. Then the judge decided.

The two proposed findings of fact, the judge's actual findings of fact and conclusions of law, and the circuit court's decisions are the critical legal statements. The attorneys' proposed findings are by far the most extensive presentations of the cases. Similarly, Jackson's most substantial effort was his findings of fact. These documents are Plaintiffs' Joint Proposed Findings of Fact (August 10, 1999) (774 pages) (gfof), Defendant Microsoft Corporation's Revised Proposed Findings of Fact (September 10, 1999) (at least 675 pages) (mfof), and Jackson's Findings of Fact (November 5, 1999) (207 pages) (cfof). Further oral observations were made on February 22 and May 24, 2000. The later proposed conclusions of law, remedy proposals, appeals briefs, and rebuttals from the attorneys added nothing to the understanding of the underlying issues.

Judge Jackson's Findings of Fact presented categorical undocumented statements about what arguments in the case were accepted. He provided no citations even of the few case documents that he quoted. The origins of his arguments were ignored. No literature was cited. These findings agreed that a monopoly existed and that Microsoft acted illegally to preserve that monopoly. Even silly government arguments were accepted. However, he decided to reject one of the government's charges (see Chapter 10).

The case was appealed. This produced another pair of briefs, oral arguments, and another court decision. The oral hearings by the Circuit

Court of Appeals and the court's decision provided another view of the issues. The hearings evoked considerable hostility by some judges to the government's arguments. The opinion that emerged in June 2001 muted the hostility and excessively limited what was rejected. Chapter 10 argues that the restraint left standing economically defective conclusions.

Following the initial statements, witnesses were used to support this material. Participation in the first phase of the case was limited to 12 witnesses for each side. The "direct testimony" consisted (with one exception) of written statements. The oral presentation started with cross-examination. That cross-examination comprised the bulk of the oral testimony. Since cross-examination is fault finding, the worst aspects of each witness dominated the record. In the rebuttal stage, each side was allowed three witnesses, but the direct testimony was oral.

The Other Witnesses

Treatment of the contributions of the witnesses is another tricky task. My original intent was only to read both the direct and oral testimony of the economists, and the attorneys' statements. As my curiosity increased, so did what I examined. I have reviewed all the direct testimony and the oral testimony of all but four of the witnesses.[2] Even a minimally adequate summary of the contentions is inordinately long. The following review of witnesses tries to suggest the weight each side gave to different issues and identify testimonies of relevance. The noneconomists are identified and the essence of their statements is noted.

The initial 12 government witnesses consisted of one each concerned with six claims of improper Microsoft actions, four on software design, and the two economists. Those treating charges were from Netscape, Sun Microsystems, Apple, Intel, America Online, and Intuit (the developer of Quicken and TurboTax, two popular financial applications). The AOL and Intuit executives made much more limited statements than did the others. The Intel executive worked on software. Two professors of computer science discussed the necessity and desirability of integrating Explorer into Windows. One demonstrated his program to hide Internet Explorer. A computer journalist presented claims about customer objections to the integration of Explorer into Windows. An IBM executive treated browser issues and the difficulties of developing a competitive operating system.

Microsoft chose nine executives. One, Paul Maritz, presented general information and discussion of several of the disputes. He was the only witness responding to the charges about Intel but also made comments on

---

[2] The exclusions were Colburn's and Felten's initial testimonies, Harris, and Farber.

Sun, Apple, and Netscape. James Allchin discussed Internet Explorer. The others (in order of appearance) treated ICPs, ISPs excluding AOL, AOL and secondarily evidence of consumer support for an integrated browser, the negotiations with Netscape, the discussion with Apple about QuickTime, restrictions on OEMs, and the dispute with Sun over Java implementation. Executives from a software company and Compaq presented terse, vapid direct testimony asserting they found Microsoft a fine company.

More fully and chronologically, the witnesses were as follows.

James Barksdale was then the President and chief executive officer of Netscape. He presented a detailed statement that basically reiterated the government's assertion that Netscape was subjected to intense and damaging competitive pressure. However, given his responsibility to Netscape, he also indicated that, nevertheless, Netscape remained viable. Similarly, he initially bragged about how Netscape showed the feasibility of distributing software over the Internet and then complained about being relegated to such Internet distribution.

This statement proves a discussion of all Netscape aspects of the case including recitation of a vast amount of information allegedly communicated by third parties. In the sense that it is replete with conclusions about the underlying economics, it might be considered a third economist's report. He was heavily cross-examined on his charges against Microsoft and his role in initiating the case.

David M. Colburn was Senior Vice President of Business Affairs AOL. He gave a very summary view of AOL's decision to adopt Internet Explorer as its primary Internet browser. He contended that inclusion in a desktop folder in Windows was the crucial reason.

Avadis Tevanian, Jr. was the Senior Vice President for Software Engineering of Apple. He complained about both alleged attempts to limit the development of an Apple program called QuickTime and pressures including threats not to update the Macintosh version of the critical Office suite of programs unless Apple gave Internet Explorer preferential treatment.

Steven McGeady was a software executive of Intel. His testimony relates to Microsoft's objections to Intel's development of software called Native Signal Processing. He claims that the objection was grounded in opposition to competition and that Microsoft threatened to withhold support for a new Inter chip unless Intel stopped developing software that Microsoft considered a competitive threat. He was the sole witness who presented his direct testimony orally.

McGeady also is the sole source for the government's favorite quotation about Microsoft. In the first session at which he testified (November 9, 1999, p.m.), discussion of a meeting between Intel and Microsoft (48-56) led to recollections about statements by Microsoft executive Paul Maritz in a meeting on November 7, 1995 (after the introduction of Internet Explorer):

> There were two phrases that are easy to remember. One was that it was Microsoft's plan to cut off Netscape's air supply, keep them by–(sic) by giving away free browsers, Microsoft was going to keep Netscape from getting off the ground (November 9, 1999, p.m., 53).

The other phrase was "embrace, extend, extinguish" (54). Examination elicited a third quotation "We are going to fight this with both arms" (54).

The first quotation was widely employed as proof of Microsoft's predatory intent. Fisher quotes it twice (par. 125, 57; par. 130, 60). Barksdale cites it three times. (While his testimony preceded McGeady's, the quote appeared in a newspaper article and in McGeady's deposition.) Gfof quotes it 14 times, albeit with six in one paragraph. That paragraph tries to refute Maritz's denial of the quote (par. 91.3.1, 201-2). The bases are that his denial was more equivocal in his deposition than in his trial testimony and that he told people about the plan to provide free browsers.

Heilemann (2000, 303-4) reports that he found a corroborating witness (who stressed that the phrase was meaningless). In contrast, Microsoft found an e-mail to McGeady from Netscape founder Jim Clark recalling a reported use of the air supply remark by Gates in a meeting with Intel chairman Andy Grove. Clark urged McGeady to testify (DX 1807).

Microsoft's response (mfof par. 1399, 630-31) both challenges the legitimacy of the quotation and notes that such bravado was common in the industry. Barksdale, in oral testimony, notes reading that Larry Ellison of Oracle had used the expression (October, 20, 1998, p.m. 59-60; cited mfof par. 1399, 630-31). The transcript (60-61) shows that Barksdale could not recall how he learned that Microsoft had made the air-supply comment.

In fact, the veracity of the remark is inessential. What matters is its invalidity. The remark was made after the introduction of Internet Explorer, was directed at bystanders, and incorrectly described reality. Material the government ignored suggests awareness of both the inevitability of free browsers and the ability of Netscape to survive. The free-browser development was at the heart of Rosen's dealings with Netscape (see Chapter 9). Rosen noted that Netscape had strong financial backing. A Gates memorandum written about the time of the June 21, 1995 meeting with Netscape says "Clients make no money ... Servers will make money." (GX 22) (The government's only use of GX 22 is to quote an in-between sentence, "Netscape is very influential on what happens with Clients.") The

Microsoft attorneys make the stronger case that the free-browser decision was made before Netscape was incorporated (mfof paras. 704-8, 323-5).

Glenn E. Weadock, President of Independent Software Inc. and author of several computer books, reports a survey of users about what they want in software. His small, mostly government-selected sample wants simple software and particularly separate and removable Internet browsers.

John Soyring, Director of Network Computing Software Services, IBM, tersely treated, by assertion, two broad issues, the importance of having enough applications and the separability of a browser. His oral testimony concentrated on why IBM's rival operating system failed.

Warren-Boulton then appeared.

James A. Gosling, Vice President and Chief Scientist Java Software Division of Sun, presented (22-32) his complaints about how Microsoft implemented Java. The bulk of his statement examines the nature and advantages of Java (1-19). Arguments against incorporating a browser in an operating system (19-21) are tossed in.

David J. Farber, Professor of Telecommunications Systems at the University of Pennsylvania, claimed that Explorer did not have to be bundled.

Edward W. Felten, Assistant Professor of Computer Science, Princeton University, discussed how an earlier version of Explorer could be removed and the version bundled with Windows 98 can be hidden. He too argues that separation is possible. This is a prelude to a series of courtroom demonstrations on how to hide Internet Explorer.

William H. Harris, President and Chief Executive Officer of Intuit, complained that he "had" to trade exclusivity for favorable position of the desktop. This is calling a voluntary trade forced; this type of argument proved common.

Fisher then was the last government witness. Schmalensee was the first Microsoft witness. The latter decision was problematic under the ground rules of the case. With oral testimony starting with cross-examination, the government could and did make Schmalensee's initial appearances a continuous effort to discredit the testimony. This was not unique to Schmalensee or even to the government side. Cross-examination seeks to create a bad impression.

Paul Maritz, Group Vice President, Platforms and Applications, presented the most substantial statement by a Microsoft executive. He supplemented Schmalensee on the nature of competition and why a free browser was provided. He concluded with treatment of the disputes with Intel, Apple, and Netscape. Maritz presented the only treatment of the Intel dispute. The last two, however, each were also treated by a separate witness. In the Apple case, the other witness only treated QuickTime; Maritz then provided the sole review of the dispute involving provision of an updated version of Office for the Macintosh. He also treats Java, to which another witness was assigned. He also denied McGeady's assertions.

Dr. James Allchin, Senior Vice President for Personal and Business Systems, provided a descriptive discussion of why Explorer is integrated and can be hidden but not removed (paras. 30-203, 10-36) with responses to other charges. This is Microsoft's principal statement about Internet Explorer. Therefore, it is examined more closely in Chapter 9.

Michael T. Devlin, President of Rational Software Corporation, gave a brief statement that Microsoft is a good company (HTML). (Microsoft provided all the statements in the HTML Internet format. Most also were available as Word documents. HTML means that a Word version is unavailable.)

William Poole, senior director of business development for the personal and business systems group, focused on accords with ICPs including a response to Harris.

Cameron Myhrvold, Vice President Internet Customer Unit, presented the case that Microsoft assisted the ISPs starting by providing a competitor for Netscape. This is a general discussion ignoring AOL. The basic argument is that competition was fostered by providing an alternative to Netscape and making it available to providers that Netscape ignored. He contends that the accords with most ISPs were loose and could be terminated with 60 days' notice (paras. 31-2, 11).

Brad Chase, Vice President of Marketing Personal and Business Systems Division, devoted the first half to a response to the assertions by Colburn of AOL. He notes that promotion on the desktop was a big concern to AOL but not the only reason for choice. He adds that, because Internet Explorer was broken into components, it was better suited to AOL's desire for a browser shell for what would seem an AOL browser. Chase cites indications that Netscape was uncooperative with AOL.

On the favorable placement point, Chase observes that AOL already had secured such placement from the OEMs and would not gain from placement by Microsoft. He adds that Gates shared these doubts and that they ultimately designed a special folder as a compromise form of access through Windows.

Chase's second half starts with yet another discussion of why Explorer is superior and praised as such. He turns to a discussion of customer reaction with the explicit goal to refute Weadock's charge that his sample of users was discontent with the inclusion of Explorer.

John Rose, Senior Vice President and Group General Manager, Enterprise Computing Group of Compaq, talked about his company's good relations with Microsoft (HTML). Given the brevity and banality of the statement, the extensive attacks on Rose (see Chapter 9) in gfof proved surprising. The government had secured material about problems between Compaq and Microsoft about displaying the Internet-Explorer icon and sought to determine the witness's knowledge on the subject. Reading his oral testimony and then rereading the gfof suggested problems typical to the case. Government attorney David Boies questioned Rose extensively about matters about which Rose had no knowledge; among the charges in the gfof then was this lack of knowledge.

Rose apparently is the source of the 70,000 applications assertion raised in the case. The first reference that I detected was a question by Boies (February 17, 1999, p.m., 18) including "what you have referred to as the 70,000 applications that exist for the Windows operating system." Since Boies generally confronted witnesses with material from their prior depositions, the 70,000 may have appeared in Rose's deposition.

Dan Rosen, General Manager New Technology, provided an explanation of Microsoft-Netscape negotiation by the person in charge. The highlights are examined in the section in Chapter 9 on the charges (HTML).

Eric Engstrom, General Manager MSN Internet Access, gave Microsoft's side of the QuickTime issue (HTML).

Joachim Kempin, Senior Vice President International Original Equipment Manufacturer Group and Internet Customer Unit, argued that Microsoft's restrictions are limited and do not preclude use of Navigator. This is explored further in Chapter 9 (HTML).

Robert Muglia, Senior Vice President Applications and Tools, gave a statement of Microsoft's view of the Java issue. He too is cited below because of his elucidation of various issues, particularly on Sun's desire to undermine Microsoft.

In the rebuttal phase, Fisher and Schmalensee reappeared. The government recalled Felten and asked Garry Norris, programming director, networking hardware division and former director software strategy and strategic relations for the personal computer division of IBM, to testify. Microsoft's other witnesses were Colburn of AOL as a hostile witness and Gordon W. Eubanks, the president of yet another company (Oblix) and former head of Semantics, a leading producer of "utility" software (used for dealing with problems such as disk failures and viruses).

Norris asserted that Microsoft threatened to withhold licensing of Windows and offered unfavorable terms unless IBM stopped supporting competing software. Colburn proved unresponsive by denying that he knew enough to resolve the issues. Eubanks argued his experiences validated Microsoft's vision that the market is highly competitive,

The outcome suggests defective selection on both sides. The greatest waste was the government's stress on discrediting the integration of Internet

Explorer. The conclusions are that browsers can be separated and concealed and that some users prefer separate and removable browsers. These results do not seem worth so much effort. The outcomes are predictable. The existence of Netscape Navigator is ample proof a browser can be separate. The issues are peripheral. Hall and Hall (1999, 37) call the effort a waste of time. This is another example of stressing appearances over serious economic arguments.

Four initial government witnesses and Norris in the rebuttal phase each treated an individual battle with Microsoft. This equal weighting is inconsistent with the relative weight these charges received in the gfof and the relative merits of the charges. Plausibility was not helped by letting Barksdale's treatment of the central Netscape issue roam so far from his direct knowledge. To make matters worse, the Sun, Intel, Apple, and IBM (Norris) witnesses also presented mélanges of charges that were inadequately resolved in the trial. Some of that inadequacy came from the difficulties of evaluating who was most plausible; other arose from the barriers the trial rules set to pursuing further information. Moreover, the Sun, Intel, and IBM charges are based on the implausible assertion that Microsoft can successfully bully these companies.

The remaining two (Colburn of AOL and Harris of Intuit) are disappointing. Colburn was incapable in initial and rebuttal testimony to deal with issues raised by Microsoft. Harris is bemoaning the attractiveness of Windows. Finally, Warren-Boulton added little. In short, it could be argued that at least ten of the government witnesses were unnecessary.

The worst defect on the Microsoft side was recalling Colburn. The statements from the two initial outsiders were vacuous, but Eubanks was not. The internal witnesses clearly were chosen to refute specific government witnesses and differed considerably in the extent and quality of their testimonies. More critically, by responding so mechanically to the government, Microsoft also devoted excessive attention to secondary issues.

In particular, the most substantial replies to charges are Chase on AOL, Rosen on Netscape, Allchin on providing Explorer, Engstrom on Apple, and Muglia on Java. Maritz provides a transition between Schmalensee's outsider view of the situation and how Microsoft thought. Even these treatments show flaws. Allchin's terminology obscures the timing of Microsoft's decision to offer a browser. Rosen's description of his dealings with Netscape is too convoluted. Part of this is due to the complexity of the negotiations. Part is writing style. Some may be confusion arising from the pressure to insist that browsers are not separate products. Kempin, Poole, and Myhrvold skim the surface.

Other material, such as that subpoenaed from Microsoft and depositions of people who did not testify in court, was critical. None proved conclusive.

It is undisputed that Microsoft wanted to compete with Netscape. What matters is whether deliberately anticompetitive methods were used. The evidence is at best suggestive. Thus, the government used inferences, predominately by Fisher and Warren-Boulton, to complete its argument. The quality of these inferences is the core of discussions in the next three chapters.

A surprising further conclusion from examination of the material is that veracity is much less important than journalistic accounts (e.g., Heilemann 2000) suggested. Wariness extended often to instinctive efforts to deny embarrassing statements. Never does this matter. Even if the denied remarks were true, they still prove nothing.

The Battle of the Expert Economists

Probably because of the limit on witnesses, the three expert economists tried to present an overview of the case. This tended to involve presentation and evaluation of material on areas far outside their expertise. The most elaborate work beyond economic analysis related to the browser-use data. The direct testimonies explained this material, and much of the oral testimony was devoted to securing further comments.

These efforts were central to the case. In the attorneys' statements, the invariable bases for economic conclusions and the frequent justifications of points in which the economists had no expertise were statements by the economists. Thus, the nature of their contribution needs explanation.

The three experts' testimonies are Direct Testimony of Frederick R. Warren-Boulton (November 18, 1998); Direct Testimony of Franklin M. Fisher (January 5, 1999); and Direct Testimony, Richard L. Schmalensee (January 3, 1999). Fisher is the U.S. government's expert; Warren-Boulton, the states'.

They differ radically in size, organization, and approach. Schmalensee's statement (328 pages of main text, 122 pages of substantive appendixes; 515 total) is by far the largest and, more critically, also by far the best reasoned. His support team at National Economic Research Associates (NERA) produced supporting papers. Schmalensee entwines his theoretic arguments in a review of computer-industry history and current conditions.

He follows an organizational pattern standard for the case of starting with whether Windows is a monopoly and moving to treat at much greater length the issues with Internet Explorer. In his strongest sections, he interweaves economic theory and the evidence from computer industry experience to develop his case. He presents supporting data from many sources, mostly in the literature on the computer industry, to justify his conclusions.

His theorizing is generally terse, and his citation of supporting material is inconsistent. In treating the operating-system monopoly, Schmalensee's only citations on concepts of competition are of Fisher's writings skeptical of a structural approach. Worse, the only citation on network effects is an article asserting relevance to software. Far less than all the available analytic ammunition, such as discussed here in Chapters 3, 4, and 5, was used. In other areas such as predation, the implied essential-facility argument that he detects, and the objectives of antitrust, he provides a good sampling of relevant material.

However, he does correctly convey the state of the relevant theoretic debates and effectively employs the theory as a guide to empirical analysis. His presentation presented a challenge that the government's experts, the government attorneys, Judge Jackson, and the Circuit Court all failed.

Schmalensee's treatment of operating-system monopoly, in particular, is helpful because it forces consideration of the weak initial government case. Chapter 7 argues that the government's effort to respond again subdivides to obscure. Schmalensee indicates the possibility of unexpected developments. The government limits its reply to denigrating each challenge. Their collective impact is ignored.

In contrast, the treatment of browser competition is where the pressure to be comprehensive is more problematic. Three difficulties prevail. The theoretical discussions, while more complete, are more scattered than in the monopoly sections and, in the critical case of defining browser competition, too imprecise. Second, the converse of limited theoretic discussion is the dominant role of information about the creation, promotion, and success of Internet Explorer. Third, this involved venturing beyond his expertise.

The worst example, as noted, is the large amount of the report, including an extensive appendix, devoted to data on browser use. In this regard, Microsoft followed the government in trusting an economist rather than a data-analysis specialist to present the data. Microsoft did retain such a specialist to advise Schmalensee, but that specialist was not asked to testify. To be sure, this provides far more than the terse summary of results given by Fisher and Warren-Boulton and the gfof's disjointed treatment.

As a result of his lack of citations, Judge Jackson does not explain why Schmalensee's alternative is ignored. The Circuit Court, in turn, went through the pretense of evaluating the argument and rejected it for fallacious reasons (see Chapter 10). Whatever his association with Microsoft, Schmalensee made arguments widely held by economists.

Fisher (110 pages) and Warren-Boulton (87 pages) differ from Schmalensee in several ways. The disparity in the size of the three efforts arises from differences in the adequacy of response. Fisher and Warren-Boulton deal with applications to the case by stating conclusions buttressed, if at all, by quotations from the Microsoft documents, industry statements elicited for the case, and the browser-use data employed by the government. The gfof, in turn, frequently uses these assertions as its evidence. Mfof vigorously criticized (par. 125, 56-7). It counted 230 references by Fisher to documents and testimony including 109 from depositions and declarations. Therefore, this book is full of reminders of this practice.

Fisher differs from the other economists and the findings of fact in presenting a discrete discussion of relevant theoretical propositions prior to and separate from his appraisal of the case. Moreover, his introductory section makes statements not reiterated. Thus, in the next two chapters, I try to integrate the material from these different sections.

He provided far more nuanced concepts of competition than he applied to the case but unsatisfactorily treated anticompetitive tactics. Fisher's cursory treatment of competition (paras. 25-39, 9-15) is so conventional that it supports almost any viewpoint including both his and Schmalensee's (see Chapter 7). Fisher's discussion of network effects includes recognition that the barrier can be overcome (paras. 40-45, 15-16). Finally, Fisher's theory proposed a major unwise extension of predation theory. His theoretic section advocates consideration of opportunity costs measured by foregone revenues, in this case from selling Internet Explorer, rather than the conventional production-cost basis (paras. 46-54, 16-19). He also produced a confused treatment of tying (paras. 55-60, 19-22).

Warren-Boulton presents an overly general definition of competition (paras. 26-32, 12-15) and a treatment of network effects (paras. 46-54, 20-4) that comes close to asserting that they can never be overcome.

Among the implications of these peculiarities is that Warren-Boulton and Fisher made more substantial additions in oral testimony than did Schmalensee. By the nature of oral testimony, these comments are summary and scattered. Fisher is emphasized here over Warren-Boulton because Fisher had more to say, presented more of the government's favorite quotations, and made a more vigorous, less restrained attack on Microsoft. The gfof then collects and displays these arguments. The mfof replies.

Schmalensee, as shown in Chapter 1, strongly attacked the reliance on industry statements. In the exchange with Fisher sponsored by the AEI-Brookings Center, David Evans of NERA and Schmalensee, in effect, contend that the government only presented statements that indicate concern over Netscape Navigator and a desire to compete (2000a, 85, 2000b 99). None affirm an intention to adopt predatory measures. They cite the criticism of reliance on such evidence in the book on the IBM case that Fisher coauthored (85).

The response by Fisher and his coauthor Daniel Rubinfeld is that the evidence in Microsoft is far stronger than in the IBM case (2000a, 94). This is a stretch. The discrepancies with Fisher's prior work are much more extensive than Microsoft's attorneys indicated. Examples that I used in Chapter 2 were not mentioned in the case. Hazlett (1999, 46-8) reports that, in a predatory pricing case in cable television, Fisher dismissed as irrelevant statements in the incumbent's memorandums seeking to block entry.

At least three objections arise to the Fisher-Rubinfeld rejoinder. First is that this interpretation can be and is widely disputed. Second, appraising the veracity of witnesses is not economic expertise. It is what litigation does (as a colloquy between Schmalensee and Judge Jackson (June 21, 1999, p.m., 80-1) indicated). Third, what an economist can do is identify and state the relevant theory, know what data are needed to test alternative hypotheses implied by the theory, and conduct such a test. This, however, is what Fisher and Warren-Boulton fail to do.

A further problem with Fisher's testimony was his over-reliance on devices such as a formula that a challenged Microsoft action "doesn't make sense from a business standpoint." The phrase appears nine times in Fisher's direct testimony and often is used in his oral testimony (e.g., par. 116, 52; par. 118, 53; par. 127, 58; par. 133, 63; par. 136, 64; par. 138, 66 and January 7, 1999, a.m., 46-7). In every case, it is a means to assert without proof that the government's case is correct.

Fisher's first use comes with citation of an executive with Apple Computer (par. 116, 52). He adds that the phrase came from a deposition by an Apple executive who said Engstrom attributed the view to Gates. In the trial, Microsoft's attorneys remind Fisher of this origin (January 6, 1999, p.m., 71-3). Thus, hearsay of hearsay on a special case inspired Fisher's catchphrase for the general case. This illustrates Fisher's excessive use of sinister-sounding statements. Schmalensee (par. 579, 297) comments "as if this quote somehow proved something of economic significance."

Another problem is neglect of the literature. Fisher only cites two articles–Areeda and Turner on predation and Salop and Scheffman on raising rivals' costs. The citation of Areeda and Turner is misleading (see Chapter 8), and Salop and Scheffman are left unexplained, a deficiency never remedied. Warren-Boulton only cites a leading law text on antitrust.

Experience with undertaking expert statements indicates that they are crafted in consultation with the attorneys. The latter have the primary responsibility for ensuring that the statement satisfies the requirements of the case. Not coincidentally, the problems with the expert testimony are identical to those with the overall case.

For the remedy phase, DOJ enlisted an almost new set of experts (with new arguments contradictory to those used in the case) to justify breaking up Microsoft as a remedy for its actions. (Felten returned.)

The Resulting Problems

The streamlining had mixed impacts. Neither the limitation on witnesses nor the choices made for witnesses seemed effective. Even if the selection of witnesses had been better than it was, the witness limitation proved problematic. The witnesses, particularly but not exclusively the expert economists, had to present much that would better have come from people with more direct knowledge. The result in any case was indigestible. Mechanically, the biggest problem is separating out the critical material.

Done properly, as they often were not, the written statements had substantial advantages over oral testimony. The statements could be clearer, more detailed, and less disjointed than oral testimony.

The oral testimony examined proved unsatisfactory. The dominance of cross-examination was the main defect. The discussions often weaved. Masses of material were presented to the witnesses for comment that rarely proved constructive.

At best, the result was an "admission" that the material seemed valid. This involved the standard legal device of asking a question that has only one correct answer and then claiming the response proves something. The typical form is "if my premises are correct, does my conclusion follow?"

While both sides used this technique, the gfof overuses such admissions of the obvious to claim weakness in the defense. Conversely, efforts to resist government interpretations were damned as "unreliable."

The process necessarily involves many pauses to ensure that the proper legal procedures are followed. In particular, Microsoft and others successfully contended that the material included trade secrets. Therefore, the public record includes much material indicating "redaction" (censoring) of material. Some of this redaction produces incomprehensibility at least until other material is examined. A critical example is that what OEMs pay for Windows was considered a secret. The lawyers often quarreled over how to work around that secrecy.

Of those examined, the most important oral testimonies were those of Fisher, Warren-Boulton, and Schmalensee. A great deal of critical material came from depositions or documents. Courtroom examination, therefore, was not provided of many people with major influence.

Perhaps naively, it seems that, nevertheless, more oral testimony from more fact witnesses might have better resolved the numerous disputes of fact. At a minimum, several witnesses attained, at least among journalists, the reputation of honest whistle-blowers. Microsoft suggested they were disgruntled employees. Presumably that could have been verified. The unsatisfactory outcome of the recall of Colburn from AOL produced a colloquy about altering the rules to secure better testimony.

Among the many complications are the numerous nearly impossible to resolve conflicts between the prosecution and defense on the interpretation of events and their consequences. The best solution is to ask what the attorneys deliberately evaded–why does it matter? The evasion arose because of the stress on impressions. The germane disputes include the Netscape market-sharing claims and all the allegations about Microsoft actions other than to promote Internet Explorer. Surprisingly, examination of the supporting material often greatly lessens the confusion.

Debates also arose over aspects of the history of the browser battle. Microsoft and the government disagree about when it was decided to create Internet Explorer and when the integration strategy was adopted. Controversy also prevailed about the comparative quality of Explorer and Navigator at different times and about whether the timing of the rise in share of Explorer was consistent with the claim that superior quality was the influence.

Of course, the criticized procedures are standard legal techniques. This is precisely the point. A concern in the critiques of antitrust, particularly the writings of Easterbrook, is that these legal conventions and the limited economic expertise of judges restrict what antitrust reasonably can do.

The Lawyers Summarize

As noted, the proposed findings of fact sum up the arguments, and their overall content is best indicated here. The two sides use radically different approaches. The government's document makes many short assertions followed by supporting material. In most cases, the support is only quotation or description of other people's material. The choices often are forced. Here I extensively appraise the validity of these quotations. Other problems relate to fragmentation, duplication, illogical organization, and calumny. The Microsoft response shows few of these problems.

The government moves through the issues in roughly the order listed above. The only organizational oddity needing mention now is how operating-system competition was handled. The treatment starts by reciting statements supporting the government's theory of monopoly. Examination of criticism comes in a concluding subsection titled "Dean Schmalensee's contrary analysis is unreliable."

This immediately suggests several further serious problems with the gfof. The first is that this resort to pejorative language is endemic. Schmalensee is termed unreliable, not just for the alleged discrepancies evaluated later in this chapter, but merely for disagreeing with the government. Other witnesses and the data used by Schmalensee are similarly characterized.

Another defect is the chopping up of the issues into fine parts. Again multiple drawbacks arise. By only treating the limitations of each little point, the government avoids treatment of the overall effect. Too little attention is given the quality of the quotation. The qualifications of the source are often ignored. The worst problem is use of Fisher and Warren-Boulton as the authorities on questions with no economic content. Less surprising is neglecting the bias of government witnesses. Dubious and inconsistent points are raised.

The process also produced extensive repetition. One blatant example occurs in the section on Microsoft's market share. Separate sections treat past, present, and future conditions. In each, the government quotes on two consecutive pages Fisher's observation that Microsoft's share of the market as defined by the government is over 90 percent (par. 2.1, 28-9). Chapter 9 extensively discusses several more substantial examples. As viewing citations here should indicate, the gfof has the mechanical problem of employment of an intricate paragraph numbering system.

Given all the charges, the Microsoft response (mfof) is mainly a catch-up effort.[3] The problems with the gfof were forcefully indicated. The first complaint was that the gfof is padded by extensive repetition (par. 73, 29). Other criticisms are internal inconsistency, "stunning concessions that undermine the claims," inadequate proof, incorrectly characterizing desirable actions as anticompetitive, and pressing refuted charges. The government relied excessively on "inadmissible hearsay" and "bald assertions by their two economists" (par. 74, 30).

The only inadequately documented charge is of stunning concessions. The supporting material consisted of numerous illustrations of defects. These examples do not always indicate which type of error was involved. Those most closely resembling concessions are narrowing the attack on including Internet Explorer in Windows and the inadequacies of the response to Schmalensee. My examination discloses so many others (see Chapter 9) that the term became my catchphrase.

The mfof critique of the government's economists in the case (paras. 111-29, 49-59) contains charges ranging from ones similar to those made here to the nearly frivolous. The Microsoft statement, in particular (par. 121, 54; par. 127, 58), notes that the government economists relied on documents and testimony, at times making judgment outside their area of competence. It was added (par. 124, 55-6) "Fisher, whose testimony Schmalensee also addressed in detail, offered numerous opinions that were

---

[3] My downloading produced a version three pages shorter than the original; my use of references to paragraph as well as page numbers ensures that the correct material is identified.

based on untested, and therefore unverified, economic theories that appear to have been invented for use in this case." This appraisal mirrors statements that Fisher made to dismiss Microsoft defense arguments but still understates the problems with Fisher.

In what follows, a few attorneys are named. Boies, an attorney in private practice, was hired to serve as the lead government attorney and undertook all the examinations and cross-examinations noted here. While Sullivan & Cromwell–a New York City firm representing Microsoft–had several attorneys handling the witnesses, only a few are mentioned here. Michael Lacovara cross-examined Fisher and Warren-Boulton and led the direct testimony of Schmalensee in the rebuttal phase. Richard J. Urowsky examined Schmalensee during his first appearance. John L. Warden cross-examined Barksdale and presented summary statements.

Two court reporters alternated. Separately paged transcripts were issued for the morning and for the afternoon sessions. (A legal transcript is double spaced with numbered lines and everything in capital letters.)

Legal transcribers are excellent, but imperfect, and oral speech often does not flow smoothly. When editing is not problematic, the speaker can correct. This is not possible with evidence. Therefore, the transcript shows the presentations as interpreted by the transcriber. The speakers' errors and missteps stay. The transcriber can and obviously did introduce errors. Schmalensee's reference to Areeda-Turner was rendered "Rita Turner" (June 21, 1999, p.m., 81). With Eubanks, the transcriber at the first session was provided enough information to record his new company correctly as Oblix. The other stenographer recorded the company as Obelisk.

The Availability and Presentation of Case Material

At least four Internet sites are of interest. Both sides have postings. The presentation is skewed to the Microsoft side. DOJ's is limited to attorneys' statements, depositions from those not among the courtroom witnesses, direct testimony, exhibits from its case, and the Judge's decisions. Microsoft provides all its statements, only selected exhibits and depositions, the transcripts of the entire trial, press releases, third-party material that supports its defense, and links to other supporting material. All three expert economists had associations with consulting firms. Fisher is a principal and officer of Boston-based Charles River Associates (CRA). Schmalensee consults through but has no financial interests in National Economic Research Associates (NERA). The Web sites of both CRA (CRA.com) and NERA (NERA.com) provide material on the case. NERA, however, presents more than CRA. DOJ has posted no supporting material.

The direct testimony often did not provide usable information about the exhibits utilized. The exhibits were initially stamped with an alphanumeric code designation and then given an exhibit number. Some direct testimonies (e.g., Barksdale, Warren-Boulton, and Schmalensee) refer to the original code; the DOJ and Microsoft web sites list by exhibit number.

The accessible record consists of thousands of pages. The most important resides on my hard drive, was transformed into assorted documents to aid evaluation, and often consulted to check a point.

All the available case material was downloaded on the Internet. This was received in various formats and citation here seeks to come as close to correctness as the limitations of the downloading process allows. (This exercise reinforced recognition that the government's case grossly exaggerates the difficulties of using a computer.)

A Note on Computer Formats and Their Implications

Several approaches can be and were used to present material on the Internet. The simplest is the HMTL protocol for Internet files. These are independent of the format of the source. However, the normal way to generate writings is a word-processing program. The leader in this area is Microsoft's Word, but the government and Judge Jackson clung to a preference for the older champion, Word Perfect. Adobe Systems has developed the PDF (portable document format) that exactly reproduces the source document.

The postings in the case shifted among HMTL, word processing, and PDF (with some documents available in two of the three). This produces technical problems. Only PDF always maintains the original pagination. HMTL files typically paginate without regard for the original arrangement; the HMTL form is much shorter than a word-processing document and may print out differently depending on the hardware and software used.

Word-processing programs do not necessarily exactly reproduce the original document. The worst actually occurring case was when the HMTL document provided no means of identifying content. For example, the Microsoft brief to the Circuit Court as available from the Microsoft web site only in HMTL has neither page nor paragraph numbers.

A further consideration is that the attorneys and judges cite paragraph numbers rather than pages. To remedy uncertainty about original page numbers and deal with prior citations of paragraph numbers, paragraph numbers are also cited here.

None of this can eliminate slips by the authors or me. The documents have obvious errors.

The Commentary

A vast amount of directly relevant material outside the case emerged before, during, and after the case. The efforts range widely in size, content, and viewpoint. Much is purely journalistic. At least three book-length journalistic accounts appeared. *The New York Time*s reporters covering the case published a book based on their articles. Articles in the *New Yorker* and *Wired* also became books. Here, the *Wired* article and Auletta's book from his *New Yorker* articles are cited. This follows up numerous articles and the printing of many opinion pieces.

Economist Richard B. McKenzie (2000b) prepared a more analytic review. In contrast to the concentration here on economics in the case, he takes a broader perspective and deals at length with the role of political pressures by firms competing with Microsoft.

Earlier chapters drew upon two books, by Lott and by Liebowitz and Margolis, at least partially motivated by the case. Liebowitz and Margolis, moreover, treat the case. Many scholarly articles and think-tank pieces have appeared. The *American Economic Review* (2000) presented four papers on the case including one by Fisher and one by Schmalensee. *The Journal of Economic Perspectives* (Spring 2001) had a three-article symposium on the case. A check of the Lexis/Nexis database of academic law journals disclosed many articles on the case. The journals specializing on antitrust are outside the Lexis/Nexis universe.

As noted in Chapter 1, the think-tank work is largely opposed to the case. However, the exception, the AEI-Brookings Joint Center for Regulatory Studies, is perhaps the most important source. Robert Litan, a former Department of Justice official and the codirector from Brookings, supports the government; Robert W. Hahn, the codirector from AEI, opposed the case. Each produced numerous commentaries; these were distributed through the center.

The Center was an outlet for others on both sides. A particularly important effort was a short (downloadable) book in which Fisher and Schmalensee (each collaborating with another economist involved in the case) directly debated the issues. Fisher's coauthor was Daniel Rubinfeld of the University of California, the chief antitrust division economist when the case was launched. Schmalensee's co-author was David Evans of NERA. These works were extended for publication elsewhere.

In all forms, these follow-ups illustrate the marked differences in approach. The different versions of Fisher and Rubinfeld and of Schmalensee and Evans move little beyond the case arguments. Fisher and Rubinfeld, particularly in the AEI-Brookings version, only add the additional arguments made in oral testimony to the direct testimony. The expanded version contains most of Fisher's direct testimony and little more. The Evans-Schmalensee efforts relate the arguments to subsequent developments. These efforts all are more useful as guidance to those unfamiliar with the case than the source of important new insights. In particular, the stances are, not only unchanged, but not better presented.

Fisher and Rubinfeld in their AEI-Brookings work present a four-point effort to assuage criticism of the case. They only assert the validity of Fisher's testimony; the proof remains absent. The first three points are essentially a summary of Fisher's basic contentions. The first claim is that the case did not arise because Microsoft was innovative or even a monopolist. The concern was anticompetitive acts that prevented others from innovating (2000b, 4).

Their second contention is "that arguments that the risk of inappropriate antitrust enforcement is excessive in an innovative, dynamic industry ...." ignore the high costs of Microsoft's anticompetitive actions (4). The third point is that the leveraging to promote Internet Explorer was attacked, not just because a browser monopoly was created, but because that monopoly preserved the operating-system monopoly (5).

The last point deals with the charge that harm was not proved. They assert that this is refuted later in the paper, and is in any case irrelevant. The subsequent proof of consumer harm is only a restatement of the reduced-innovation conjecture that Fisher presented in oral testimony.

The first stated reason for irrelevance is the claim that antitrust law does not require such proof. This seems the wrong comment for economists. They are not experts at what the law says. To be sure, widely cited discussions suggest a tendency to neglect consumer damages. Judge Jackson (Conclusions of Law, 7) cites the 1992 Eastman Kodak criterion of "threatens to defeat or forestall the corrective forces of competition."

As economists, Fisher and Rubinfeld should be more concerned about damages or at least the plausibility that damage would arise. Neglect of such prospects is another defect in the government's case.

Their second point indicates that since the damages come after predation succeeds, a demand for proof immunizes predatory practices. This is another way to evade the need to appraise whether damage is likely.

Their last rationale for neglecting proof is "Third, the fact that innovation can bring consumer benefits should not provide a license for innovative firms to engage in anticompetitive acts." However, asserting the possibility of harm is not proof.

A particular problem with the dismissal of proof is that it too neatly evades defects in Fisher's analysis (see Chapter 8). That analysis asserts that payoff has started so that, in this case, proof should be possible.

Other participants included the Independent Institute. Its most notable activities were publishing the Liebowitz and Margolis book and sponsoring an advertisement signed by 220 economists (including me) criticizing the Microsoft and Visa/Master Card antitrust cases. The ad inspired yet another controversy. A *New York Times* reporter covering the Microsoft case chose to file a story, which ran on the front page of the September 18, 1999 Sunday edition indicating that the Independent Institute received financial aid from Microsoft. These funds allegedly were directly used to fund the advertisement. Whatever the exact details of the relationship between Microsoft's financial aid to the Institute and the ad, the signers lent their names solely because of their agreement with the viewpoint expressed.

It was eventually disclosed that the story resulted from efforts by Larry Ellison of Oracle to investigate Microsoft's efforts to secure support. Ellison contended on CNN's Moneyline that the Independent Institute was a Microsoft front organization. The Institute existed long before the case and showed its view of antitrust by publishing a new edition of Armentano.

The Cato Institute has presented commentaries both as Policy Analysis papers and in its magazine *Regulation* (in which I reviewed Liebowitz and Margolis and Lott).

Citizens for a Sound Economy Foundation made a single but useful contribution. It produced an anthology of pro-Microsoft articles (Beckner and Gustafson 2000). This started with six substantial pieces, four by economists, one by a law school dean, and the sixth by a writer for *Byte*, a magazine devoted to computers. This was followed by 30 short pieces mostly by economists and lawyers. The last part consisted of editorials.

The Hudson Institute published a book criticizing point by point Judge Jackson's findings of facts (Reynolds 2001). Reynolds bases his attack on total rejection of the government's case. In particular, Reynolds contends (see Chapter 8) that the platform threat is a totally incorrect explanation of Microsoft's motives. He argues that Microsoft's concern was not erosion by a new entrant into platforms, but a lesser ability to compete because Netscape's success would foreclose opportunities to benefit from the Internet. His view is that the government was siding with an inefficient firm, Netscape. He chooses to counter the government's ardor with his own. Thus, he refers to Netscape as a price gouger.

Many other economists and attorneys made or drafted contributions to scholarly journals. Among the opponents of the case were Elzinger, Crandall, and Economides.[4] Defenders include Scherer, Noll, Salop, and

---

[4] Elzinger is a particularly striking case. He was affiliated with Charles River Associates, but his proMicrosoft material was issued by National Economic Research Associates. He testified as a Microsoft expert in the 2002 retrial.

Carlton. A straddle is taken by Hall and Hall (1999). While they see many defects in the government case, they also believe Microsoft undertook inefficient behavior for which it should be punished. They too see serious drawbacks to breaking up Microsoft and suggest simply fining it, a common reaction.

Heilemann's journalistic review (2000), stresses the suit was the result of successful lobbying by Microsoft's rivals. However, Heilemann and Auletta (2001) also adopt the viewpoint that an arrogant, uncomprehending Microsoft, and particularly Bill Gates, unwisely battled too vigorously against the suit. Heilemann uncritically accepts the government's claim that the expansion of the suit beyond Netscape resulted from new evidence (283, 284). The article is largely an antiMicrosoft diatribe. Heilemann and Auletta show no comprehension of economics.

This literature is far too vast and diffuse to treat comprehensively. I used the material here mainly as sources of evaluations on critical points.

The Side-Issue Problem

The converse of the government's sketchy economics is its extensive efforts to employ damaging language and attacks on the integrity of Microsoft witnesses. This emphasis is another indicator of the weakness of the case. To a large extent, the information needed to evaluate these charges is unavailable. The evaluations relate to impressions that the transcripts are unable to convey. Again appraisal at times involves questions that an economist lacks competence to judge.

Two attacks received the most attention. The first was over Bill Gates's attitude towards the case. The second was the effort to portray Schmalensee as corrupted by Microsoft. Another alleged failing was the purported deficiencies of at least Allchin's efforts to provide a video-taped demonstration about disputed technological questions. The last involves unavailable material of a noneconomic nature and necessarily cannot be treated here.

The available record on Gates consists of transcripts of selected portions inserted into the trial at every possibility. By definition, the aural and visual elements, of which much was made, are lost.

The transcripts show a predictable, repetitious effort to secure confessions and wariness on Gates's part. The critical exchanges relate to material on which the government was trying to place a conspiratorial interpretation that Gates systematically denied. The questions often were asked and answered several times.

Gates sparred over words. For example, a major theme was his recollection of the material that he wrote and received. Gates typically indicated that, while the evidence made his participation evident, he could not recall it. The government seeks to portray Gates as so closely involved that nothing escapes his attention. More fundamentally, the government clearly was looking for answers that could be quoted as "admissions." Then the government used his caution against him. Given the zeal to prosecute, it is possible that Gates lost simply by being deposed. The government would have found some way to discredit whatever he said wherever he said it. Whenever Gates replied uh-huh, he was asked to say yes or no although other witnesses making a similar response were not challenged.

The strangest case was that, at one point (December 15, 1998, a.m., 22-3), when asked whether he typed "high" for the priority given an e-mail, he indicated the computer did. This is technically correct; one clicks a priority setting rather than actually typing the word high. John Rose of Compaq (February 18, 1999, a.m., 70) made almost the same point. He was explaining how he "clicked" to chose a browser. Judge Jackson asked Rose "did you have to type it in?" Rose replied "No, I just clicked. I never typed, your honor." In both cases, this provides a possibly conscious reminder about the questioner's ignorance about computers.

Such wariness was standard in the trial. The Gates statements, for example, are not greatly different from Barksdale's courtroom response to similar questioning.

One area stressed by the government was that Gates was aware of the harm that free browser would do to Netscape. The basis was that Microsoft had studied the business status of Netscape; the study, completed more than a year after the introduction of Internet Explorer, estimated sources of income (GX 100). Gates had made statements to journalists and financial analysts noting that Netscape's dependence on browser revenues was undermined by the rise of free browser. Gates stressed that his statements were replies to inquiries.

The only example available from the Department of Justice, a 1995 *New York Times* column, ends with a long discussion of Netscape. The conclusion was that Netscape faced the pressure Microsoft had endured of inflated stock valuation. Earlier, he said "we thrive on spirited competition from good companies such as Netscape." Still earlier he spoke of the "lack of focus" of the big companies with which he competed early in Microsoft's history (GX 333). The government quotes (from unposted articles) Gates's statements about the vulnerability of Netscape to the rise of free browsers.

The government repeatedly asks Gates whether his strategies were deliberately to harm Netscape. He demurs. He apparently denies that even a rival browser created for other reasons necessarily would hurt Netscape. However, the same reasons that make it irrelevant whether Maritz talked about air supply also invalidate the inferences about Gates.

Heilemann (2000, 291-2, 299) interprets the deposition as "unmitigated disaster" (291). This he attributes to deficiencies of Gates to whom he applies ten derogatory terms from "dour" to "a baby" (290). Heilemann adds "the deposition fairly screamed that the dissembling at the company started at the top." Boies, however, is "patient and persistent." Heilemann adds that Gates indicated that he was guilty only of rudeness to Boies. A later complaint by Gates that he expected questions about competition in software and got asked about pieces of paper leads Heilemann to say Gates "was paranoid, self-pitying, and quite possibly delusional" (299). However, the only example Heilemann presents is the quibble noted about the computer doing the typing.

Clearly, Gates was antagonistic and wary, and Boies was relentlessly trying to make Gates accept the government's allegations. However, what matters here is with all the effort nothing of substance emerged. That the judge succumbed remains a key issue in the case (see Chapter 10).

However, the crux of the attack on Schmalensee is the consistency among his economic appraisals in this case, testimony in other cases, and professional writings. Thus, this is clearly an economic issue appropriate for appraisal here. The clear conclusion emerges that the charges were groundless. Distortion and frivolity abounded.

The effort had at least three parts. Boies distributed through the cross-examination inquiries designed immediately or eventually to discredit Schmalensee. The bulk of the cross-examinations, however, involved unsuccessful efforts to undermine Schmalensee's arguments about the case. The second phase apparently was alerting journalists to resulting problems. The third step was attacks in the findings of fact and other documents.

The groundwork involved asking Schmalensee about four articles and four cases in which the government purported to find discrepancies with his views in the case. Another device was the lawyer's trick of asking whether something, whatever its relevance might be, had been studied. The most bizarre was presenting Schmalensee with Microsoft material that the government contended was data manipulation and asking Schmalensee whether he agreed with the government (see below).

Considering that the challenges drew upon two decades of extensive writings and testimony, some contradictions were likely. The most important of the articles were the *Harvard Law Review* (1982) contribution to a symposium on a paper by Landes and Posner about market power and a summary of that article issued as a NERA publication. Characteristically, the Department of Justice posted the text of the accessible *Harvard Law Review* article but only posted a citation of the NERA piece. An e-mail to David Evans of NERA produced a copy. The original paper and the NERA version present what he testified in the Microsoft case, that market share is an unsatisfactory measure of monopoly power. Schmalensee's writings recognized that market-share approaches were widely employed, sometimes worked, and were defective in many cases.

Heilemann (2000, 303) made inept selection of illustrations of the defects of Schmalensee's testimony. Heilemann uses the wrong example from the *Harvard Law Review* article. Boies used a clumsy statement about the implications of profit rates (January 14, 1999, p.m., 42). Schmalensee concluded the section of the article that recognized Fisher's criticisms of accounting data by stating persistent high profits still were relevant. Boies asked about the consistency with current views. Schmalensee's response to Boies was rambling but not damaging. Moreover, the question was hypothetical. The government never presented profit estimates.

Heilemann's other example is the failure to examine the profitability of Windows (see below). The choices clearly were made because more colorful language was involved. Conversely, his article ignores Warren-Boulton and only mentions Fisher's reputation.

Two other articles were challenged. Schmalensee was confronted (June 24, 1999, p.m., 41) on an article identified only by exhibit number and asked about his endorsement in it of Scherer's rule-of-reason approach to judging predation. (The Web page for the exhibit cites, but does not contain, a 1979 article on the Realemon case.) He replies that this now seems less appealing. What is critical for Boies is that the Scherer approach included consideration of statements of intent. In response to leading questions, Schmalensee makes the obvious reply that good evidence must be respected (43-4). He also shows skepticism about documentary evidence. A final challenged but unposted 1987 article related to barriers to entry.

The most important challenged case involved Caldera, a software supplier. The entrée into discussing the case was its mention by Schmalensee as an example of prior work for Microsoft. No exhibits were provided on the case. A few lines of Schmalensee's oral testimony are the only treatment. He contends that, since the debate was solely over competition in operating systems, the structural approach is appropriate (January 13, 1999, p.m., 29). He in this case missed the stronger point, that it is always the defendant that is harmed by a narrow definition. Acceptance of such a definition is sensibly made when the narrowing still allows a strong defense. Caldera was suing Microsoft. Schmalensee used such an argument when asked about a similar market definition approach in the Bristol case (January 13, 1999, p.m., 5).

The treatment of Schmalensee in the findings of facts consists of several sections devoted entirely to him and scattered additional citations too casual to review. The attacks on his integrity were disbursed among these sections.

The first and most important of the sections (paras. 39-50, 70-107) devoted to Schmalensee is predominantly an internally inconsistent effort to respond to Schmalensee's analysis of the competition faced by Microsoft. However, it begins with two examples of purported contradictions with prior work. The Caldera case is used as an example of using the Intel-compatible-desktop-computer market definition (par. 40.1.1, 70). Selective quotations from the two articles on evaluating market power are used to suggest a nonexistent discrepancy between the articles and his views in the case. Later a sentence is taken from his ease-of-entry article. The quote warns that only actual entry confirms that barriers are low (par. 42.4.1, 82). This tautology is termed another inconsistency.

A brief subsection (par. 174, 332-3) attacks Schmalensee's views on the effects of browser competition. The basis is that he did not examine technological issues, particularly the removability of Internet Explorer from Windows.

A confusing criticism arises later about data availability. It is correctly noted in a discussion of the costs of Internet Explorer (par. 302, 535-6) that Schmalensee (June 24, 1999, 16) saw no data on the revenues expected from Internet Explorer; his comment that such estimates seemed too speculative to use was omitted. Then (par. 303, 537-8) in the midst of excoriating Maritz over inconsistency about the availability of the costs of developing Internet Explorer, the gfof says the availability of cost data refutes uncited Schmalensee testimony.

What makes the charge even stranger is that Schmalensee did claim the unavailability of satisfactory data on the profitability of Windows (January 20, 1999, 46-9) and much fuss was made about this outside the trial (see Heilemann 2000, 303). Heilemann indicates that this created an enduring impression of gullibility. This perhaps was because within the trial Fisher was induced to comment, "I think Professor Schmalensee, with his usual good nature, was rather credulous" (June 1, 1999, 68). This charge, had it been put in gfof, could have been criticized for neglecting Schmalensee's further more critical point that, for reasons Fisher had stressed in prior writings, accounting data are defective measures of profitability.

Another subsection (paras. 3 14-17, 558-63) is an attack on Schmalensee's critique of the predation charge. Again, comparison to other work is only incidental and frivolous; in the middle of this section, he is challenged about his prior adoption of Scherer's concepts for evaluating predation. This is used only to justify the charge "Fourth, Dean Schmalensee's refusal to examine why Microsoft actually undertook its better than free pricing (Schmalensee Dir. ¶¶ 337-338) renders his analysis unreliable" (par. 314.4, 560). The supposed error is that Schmalensee denies that the government had conclusive evidence that Microsoft's sole goal was to end the middleware threat.

The last and longest treatment (paras. 372-82, 673-724) is predominantly a response to Schmalensee's analysis of the success of Internet Explorer. While analytic issues are noted, the bulk of the discussion covers the browser usage and distribution data. Lacking even a seemingly substantial lapse, the government invents them.

More blatantly, the government fabricated and utilized a charge of accepting data manipulation. Boies (January 24, 1999, a.m., 54-7) presented Schmalensee with Microsoft memorandums about altering the questions on a survey of software developers. Gates notes that evidence of support would be helpful. Another executive, Nathan Myhrvold, notes that correct wording is critical. The example cited is concern that the language suggests that a browser is a separate product. The government interprets this as an effort at "manipulating." Schmalensee observed that the Microsoft executive's comment is a natural one for anyone aware of the pitfalls of polling (55). Gfof (par. 376.3, 679) then presents the refusal to accept the government's view and mention of the resulting study as evidence of "the pitfalls of relying on survey data and undermines the reliability of Dean Schmalensee's testimony."

He also is accused of presenting several "misleading" graphs. The defect is alleged failure to make apparent that the data relate to total rather than new users (par. 378, 695-6). Predictably, one charge about five charts is inflated into four subcharges. The basis, equally predictably, is that Fisher thinks the charts are misleading (June 1, 1999, p.m., 44-5). The Microsoft attorneys note that the first challenged chart was described as a stock chart and that Boies later asked Schmalensee whether a stock meant total rather than new users. An assent follows (mfof paras. 424-5, 191-2, correctly citing January 21, 1999, p.m., 48, 57).

The government courtroom attack on Schmalensee added innuendo, understandably omitted from the gfof, that Schmalensee's long and remunerative association with Microsoft distorted his judgment. Boies started his cross-examination of Schmalensee (January 13, 1999, p.m., 18-20) by noting Schmalensee's work as an expert for Microsoft. Boies returned to this issue in later examinations (June 23, 1999, a.m., 42-8). Serving as an expert only means agreement with the client's case. Microsoft had previously more lightly challenged Fisher on similar matters.

This arose despite Schmalensee's testimony in the case about why he could not and did not twist his testimony to fit Microsoft's needs. Thus, he responds to suggestions that he developed his analysis of whether Windows sell at a monopoly price to please Microsoft, "I value my professional reputation" (January 20, 1999, p.m., 42). A fuller statement states his responsibility to give the client an effective presentation of "the facts as I understand it," be honest with the court, and protect his reputation (June 24, 1999, a.m., 68). He tactfully left unsaid the obvious point that, as an experienced witness, he was aware that inquiries such as Boies's were standard.

This indicates that it is the government charges that were unreliable. Microsoft's attorneys nicely epitomized "This is part of a larger stratagem employed by plaintiffs: unable to confront the core of Schmalensee's testimony, and the extensive empirical analysis underlying it, plaintiffs nibble at the fringes and distort Schmalensee's prior work" (par. 78, 31).

In subsequent statements, however, the government asserted that its attack was successful. The final argument (September 21, 1999, a.m., 15) gives a summary statement, presumably later justified by the gfof about why to disregard Schmalensee. A New York State attorney in the case talked of needing only two days to "destroy" Schmalensee (Houck 1999, 5).

As is typical of many widely presented allegations, those against Schmalensee persist after refutation. McKenzie (2000b, 21) describes Schmalensee as "thoroughly embarrassed" by discrepancies between the testimony and prior writings. Liebowitz and Margolis (1999, 263-6), however, recognize that the government's attacks on Schmalensee involved convincing the press to exaggerate minor problems. They realized that Schmalensee developed a strong case that "was ignored in the cross-examination" (and, as it turned out, in the subsequent phases of the trial).

As already suggested, it is Fisher's prior writings that are the most difficult to reconcile with testimony in the case. The primary fault was noted above. His appraisal on Microsoft's market position is inconsistent with earlier writing and the sketch of theory in his direct testimony.

In post-trial work, Fisher (2000) starts with a denial that he switched sides between the cases. He claims Microsoft obviously has a stronger position than did IBM and ignores the inconsistencies between his prior writing and his testimony in the Microsoft case. He never substantiated his conclusions. He introduced his position with his declaration and has not budged. The bulk of Fisher's paper is a summary of his courtroom arguments, again stressing documents.

A footnote indicates that he was not cross-examined on these discrepancies. However, this was a lapse by the Microsoft attorneys that they seemed to regret. Lacovara tried to question Schmalensee (January 21, 1999, p.m., 71-3) about Fisher's writings. The government objected because this should have been done on cross-examination of Fisher, and the court agreed. Schmalensee's direct testimony cites discrepancies between Fisher's prior work and Fisher's testimony in the case. At one point in the trial, Warren-Boulton is reminded that his acceptance of the market-share concept is inconsistent with Fisher's earlier writings (November 19, 1998, a.m., 56).

A Note on the Experts and Expertise

The treatment of Schmalensee suggested a critical point about experts. The idea that ideas are bought is silly since enough different opinions exist that already sympathetic experts can be and are selected. Integrity concerns and the threat of cross-examination are powerful preventives of a perfidious perversion of position.

Such attacks in or out of court have at least two major flaws. The primary is that the direction of causation is reversed. Support is an exercise in voluntary exchange. Scholars devise opinions independently. Sponsors usually seek from among those scholars whose independent work is congenial to the backer.

Corporate support is better viewed as providing a desirable alternative to a government monopoly on research. Indeed since companies rich enough to support research are on both sides of the issue, the process is more competitive than government efforts.

Fudging is difficult in court. Lawyers are thorough to a fault and seek to uncover radical departures from past statements. The second major defect is the (probably deliberately) naive ways different sponsors are treated. Among governments, self-styled public interest groups, and corporations, only the last are deemed biased. If you cannot refute the argument, you attack the sponsors. Denunciations of aegis are always efforts to discredit advocates in a nontechnical fashion. Dealing with the substance is harder but still the only relevant concern.

A further concern is the naiveté of many discussions of policy debates. The economic theory of politics severely criticizes the vision of the disinterested public service. These theories warn that motivation by personal gains of many varieties is as likely in government as in the private sector. In particular, governments adopt positions and allocate funds in fashions supporting those policies. It is scarcely odd that scholars, including me, opposing a government position get support for such research from the private sector. Similarly, those advocating actions that the government proposes are funded. Emphasis on sponsorship evades what really matters. The germane question is how good are the arguments. Judge Jackson seems victim to misunderstanding on this and many other issues. That the Microsoft executives were rich or even that they were arrogant is not the concern. Again, the issue is the adequacy of the case.

Implications

Several things emerge from this material. The most important is that the trial had too narrow a focus. The browser battle is only an example of the many struggles for dominance. Netscape's control over the Internet was a Microsoft concern. The government ignores that Microsoft's efforts had a benefit of challenging Netscape that may or may not have outweighed any effect on Microsoft's position in operating systems.

One interpretation of the case is that the government was thwarting the indisputably procompetitive effects, at least in the short run, of more browser competition in response to much more speculative claims that the entry would preserve an operating-systems monopoly and ultimately lessen competition in browsers. Bittlingmayer's comments on the case note that success at making Navigator the platform for major application would be a new, not necessarily better, dominance (1999, 23). This was not the only rivalry at stake. Sun was simultaneously facing a challenge from Microsoft and seeking to challenge Microsoft.

The trial also makes clear that a large and growing group of actors are involved and they must cooperate even when competing. Rosen noted "today's partner is tomorrow's competitor, and vice-versa, and companies in these industries always distinguish between short and long-term relationships" (par. 49, 17). The traditional types of actors include chipmakers, computer makers, operating-system developers, and applications software developers. The Internet created new participants, the service and content providers. The contributions of each group must be compatible with those of the others. This requires constant interaction.

As the dispute over the infamous June 21, 1995 meeting between Microsoft and Netscape indicated, turf wars can arise over whether Microsoft or an application software company provides the technology. That meeting produced a charge that Microsoft would withhold needed information about interfaces unless Netscape ceased developing a Windows browser (see Chapter 9).

Moreover, companies routinely operate in more than one sector. Intel dominates chips but also provides other hardware and software. IBM and Sun are in hardware, systems and applications software, and chips. Microsoft is in applications as well as operating systems software. Moreover, the entry into browsers is one of many Microsoft decisions to enter popular new areas (see Chapter 8). Microsoft also offers MSN, a rival to AOL, and produces some hardware. Microsoft introduced a game machine in 2001.

Applications-software developers, as illustrated by Intuit, considered the Internet a tool to extend (among other things, by facilitating downloading) their business and thus became Internet content providers. The AOL-Netscape merger is an example of an Internet service provider extending entry into software. The subsequent AOL-Time Warner merger added content and distribution channels. Another point that arises is that the benefits Microsoft offered to those cooperating with it included cooperative advertising. This was something Netscape could readily provide.

Another obvious problem is the inherent nature of attorneys' statements. The tendency is to make every point that might get accepted and to adopt phraseology that accentuates the charges. As noted, when the government appraises criticism such as Schmalensee's testimony, the arguments are not wrong or inadequately substantiated as might be charged in scholarly debates but "unreliable." Microsoft defenses are routinely dismissed as "pretextual." As is often noted later, the result is presentation of material that exceeds the limits of credulity.

A further consideration, as already noted, is the validity of the evidence. It consists almost entirely of selections from internal documents of Microsoft and the other actors and testimony of participants chosen for their hostility to Microsoft. Fisher, Warren-Boulton, and the government fof share this defect. The gfof, as noted, only presents terse assertions documented by quotations supposedly supporting the point. To make matters worse, the source is too often Fisher. In many cases, he is merely reporting what others state or dealing with matters such as computer technology in which he has no expertise. When treating economic issues, he too relies only on documents. Even so, the material often fails to make the intended point. As also already noted, Schmalensee and the Microsoft attorneys complained bitterly about this.

An even more challenging problem is the key role of computer expertise in the case. A simpler side relating to the government's view of final consumers as near idiots only requires asserting the knowledge acquired as a final user. The government was well aware that large organizations are major purchasers that possess and utilize the requisite knowledge. The problem of inordinate inconvenience was evoked to suggest injury to such sophisticates. A parallel juggling act is stress on the dominance of OEM distribution over sales of operating systems directly to final users except when a point can be made by stressing the importance of such final sales.

However, a central issue in the case is the nature of the embedding of Internet Explorer in Windows 98. The government alleges that the combination is both undesirable and easily reversed. The government already lost in the Circuit Court of Appeals on the grounds that the courts are not competent to treat such technical issues. That court originally suggested that a fuller investigation might overcome the problem but in hearing the appeal of the case considered here was not pleased at the treatment. The record amply justifies this.

The government's plausibility is not assisted by the elements of its argument that stress the disadvantages of extra features. Many commentators unfavorable to the case have noted the clear defects of such arguments. A major element of the history of computing is the increase in what computers can store and manipulate. The persistent response is making programs more complicated. The key programs including operating systems increased in size and swallowed up previously separate programs.

This is part of a broader problem that the government's case is bloated. The process recalls W. S. Gilbert's lines given to Pooh-Bah to rationalize his florid description of the imaginary execution of Nanki-Poo in *The Mikado*, "Merely corroborative detail, intended to give artistic verisimilitude to an otherwise bald and unconvincing narrative."

As discussed further in Chapter 8, the charges involve issues that are secondary. In every case, the most that can be said is that the disputes were resolved. Two proposals, those for Microsoft-Netscape cooperation and of Apple-Microsoft cooperation related to QuickTime, were, if made, rejected. The others–IBM, Intel, and "polluting" Java–have dubious implicit premises. The first two cases assume that two very strong companies important to Microsoft can be bullied with impunity. The polluted Java argument is even more clearly dubious. It presumes that computer-programming professionals do not understand what they are doing.

The upshot is that both sides bury in a mass of details the essence of the case. The material, as noted, boils down to the assertions that Microsoft is a monopolist that successfully engaged in predation or other anticompetitive acts. The government case is that its economists agree with these basic contentions. The problem is that the economists do not seriously discuss the underlying economics or provide a careful discussion of their applicability to the case.

Chapter 7 The Treatment of Monopoly in the Case

As suggested, the dispute over whether Microsoft was a monopolist was convoluted in form and substance. The crux is simple and classical. The conflicting visions of competition in the case prove predictable. The government, as often noted already, postulates Microsoft as ruling supreme in the cocoon of the market for Intel-compatible personal computers. Only the Netscape/Java middleware-platform threat matters. Despite the hypothetical nature of that challenge, it is elevated into an opportunity needing government protection. The government's case dismisses by fiat all other threats to Microsoft. However, when convenient to refute a specific defense, the government introduces evidence on the weaknesses of the challenge or of the importance of other rivals.

Microsoft responds that competitive threats are broader than the government recognized and forced Microsoft to refrain from monopolistic behavior. The discussion often drifts into inconsequential debates about form. A critical example is that the government kills structural analysis to save it.

Again the unsatisfactory form of the government's case hinders review. The start is the direct testimony of Fisher and Warren-Boulton. Fisher's statement contains introductory statements of general principles for analyzing monopoly (paras. 25-39, 9-15). A separate examination of the case is presented (paras. 62-78, 22-31); it ignores the prior theoretic principles. Warren-Boulton presents his principles (paras. 26-32, 12-15) as a preliminary to his appraisal of Microsoft's position in operating systems (paras. 33-64, 16-28). Both evaluations consist of categorical statements justified only by quotations from the material gathered for the case. These are Microsoft memorandums and solicited industry statements that no competition exists. The observations fall far short of meeting Fisher's criteria for appraising monopoly, and documents are inadequate support.

The government's case is mostly an elaboration of the Fisher and Warren-Boulton arguments. Fisher and Warren Boulton agree that the relevant market is Intel-compatible personal computers. In that market,

Microsoft has a large share and an applications barrier to entry protects Microsoft from entry. The idea was that a vast number (supposedly 70,000) of applications existed for Windows and any entrant had to ensure that sufficient numbers of applications would follow its introduction of an operating system.

In contrast, Schmalensee (paras. 29-205, 16-101) responded with a comprehensive treatment. He integrates his analytic principles with the applications to the case. The evidence that supports his conceptual points appears immediately after each concept is stated. His sources are much broader than case documents. He employs extensive information on software markets. (Also see oral testimony June 22, 1999, p.m., 52-83.) Therefore, Schmalensee provides a far more satisfactory framework for the competitive analysis than did the government economists.

A basic issue for Schmalensee is the relevance to the case of a structural approach. He dealt extensively with the defects of the government's structural approach; his post-trial work included further comments. He next views the competitive pressures faced by Microsoft. Part of this is the relevance of network effects. The final element is the assertion that Microsoft's policy of low prices, innovation, and heavy investment in assisting software developers indicates that competitive pressures preclude monopoly profits. His treatment of the price of Windows presents estimates that the monopoly price is much higher (about $2,000) than the actual price (under $65) of Windows.

Evidently, this disparity and the resulting challenge were apparent from his pretrial statement. The oral testimonies of Fisher and Warren-Boulton contain material designed to bolster the case. The gfof attempts a more unified case (paras. 39-50, 70-107). This is presented as an attack on Schmalensee and includes disparagement of his integrity denounced in Chapter 6.

In this government response, unconnected arguments are strung together, and, in the standard practice of the gfof, supported by quotations. Thus, the gfof contains incomplete discussions that assert without any analytic or factual support that Schmalensee's approach is invalid. The arguments are dubious, evasive, and inconsistent. By noting in effect that Schmalensee's case is nuanced, the government tries to suggest that it is wrong.

A persistent problem is that many of Microsoft's actions might be taken whether or not it was a monopolist. The government invariably stresses that monopolists would show such behavior and ignores that firms without monopoly also might act similarly. This "consistent with" fallacy arises often.

Post-trial writings provide vital extensions. These involve Fisher, Schmalensee, and several nonparticipants. These diverse sources and radical differences among the treatments produced complex and thus difficult to treat expositions. For present purposes, the dispute is broken into several components. The first is what the expert economists said about the relevant theoretic issues. Stress is on Fisher's conceptual points about monopoly, its detection, and the role of network effects. Then, Fisher's direct testimony presentation of the government's case is reviewed.

Schmalensee's critique is discussed next. This is broken into three parts. The first is an overview. This second is his critique of structural analysis; the discussion extends to post-trial comments by Schmalensee and others. The third is his evaluation of competition in software and operating systems. Following Schmalensee, this treatment ends with his criticisms of the government economists. My emphasis throughout is on the basic arguments; the nature of the evidence cited is only sketched. To allow a unified exposition on the price of Windows, Schmalensee's analysis of the subject and the government's response are treated after examination of the other elements of the government's case.

The government's reply is treated next. The effort has four elements. The first seeks to save the structural argument. The second and most extensive part of the response is a point-by-point effort to show that each threat considered by Schmalensee is not presently strong enough by itself to undermine Windows. The cumulative effect is never treated. In the process, conceptual points on barriers to entry are raised. The treatment of the government's view of barriers to entry is followed here with examination of the meaning of a large and growing stock of Windows applications.

The third aspect is to quarrel about Schmalensee's observations about innovation, interaction with software developers, fear of piracy, and the effects of the installed base. The fourth facet of the reply is the presentation of the two theories of why Microsoft is a monopolist. One is that the restraint still leaves monopoly profits; the other is that the price maximizes short-run profits. As noted above, this last is treated after review of the Schmalensee arguments to which the government responds.

The discussion of Schmalensee's arguments and the government's response starts with a review of the alternative models of Microsoft behavior proposed. Next comes a sketch of the basic economic concepts involved. It is shown that while Fisher always recognized these principles, Warren-Boulton neglected them. Discussion follows of Schmalensee's calculations of the monopoly price of Windows and the government response.

Then the arguments made in the remedy phase are explored. This involves another gross inconsistency in the government's arguments. The (almost) fresh band of experts for the remedy phases adopted, without the appropriate embarrassment, the Microsoft position that a few critical applications are what counts. Thus, breaking up Microsoft was desirable because the applications company would produce Office for Linux and cause Linux to thrive. Suddenly, Linux was no longer the joke Fisher termed it.

Finally, a summary and conclusions appear.

Theory by Fisher, Reactions, and Implications

Fisher provided a solid presentation of the relevant contemporary theory of monopoly. His principles are similar to those discussed in Chapter 3, indeed virtually a précis of Landes and Posner as modified by Schmalensee. However, his applied analysis ignores his guidelines. Fisher leaps from these concepts to implementation without ever providing a satisfactory explanation of why they justify employing the Intel-compatible personal computer concept. This defect was inadequately addressed in post-trial assertions that, in the Microsoft case, the narrow framework was appropriate (Fisher and Rubinfeld 2000a, 88-90).

The case allegedly neatly managed not to involve any of the complexities than undermine a structural approach. In oral testimony, he effectively shifts the burden of proof to Schmalensee. This succeeded despite the usual presumption that the prosecution must prove. In fact, Fisher's analytic argument implies that, unless overwhelming contrary evidence exists, Schmalensee's approach is preferable.

Even Fisher's treatment of network effects is almost consistent with the arguments in Chapter 5. As argued in Chapter 8, Fisher's conceptual discussion of tactics is unsatisfactory.

The theory section of his direct testimony starts with the standard textbook principle that competitive firms cannot affect price but monopolists can. He concludes "A monopolist can charge supra-competitive prices because the constraints imposed by rivals are loose and ineffective" (par. 25, 10). From what follows, this is meant to indicate that "supra-competitive" prices are precluded by a threat of entry.

He goes on to distinguish between market power, any failure to correspond with the textbook description of pure competition, and monopoly where the departure is substantial (paras. 26-8, 10). He notes "When present only to a small degree, market power should not be of antitrust concern" (par. 27, 10). His effort to explain suggested that the magnitude and duration of the excess over competitive prices determined whether the difference was significant (par. 28, 10). He concludes with comments on monopoly from "innovation, superior marketing, or historical accident," indicating that the importance and innovative character of the software industry necessitate preventing use of anticompetitive practices (par. 29, 10-11).

Anticompetitive is too legal a term. The standard economic term is inefficient and is usually used here. What is more important is that the problem of translating the criteria into useful measures was evaded. Fisher and Warren-Boulton simply stated their opinions.

Fisher distinguishes four issues in appraisal. They are identifying monopoly power, considering network effects, treating anticompetitive acts, and inefficient use of monopoly power to extend control to other markets (par. 30, 11). The last two are treated in Chapter 8.

His criteria for judging start by noting that the conventional approach is to define a relevant market and assess whether the market share gives control over price (par. 32, 12). He warns that the market definition should encompass all sources of competition. He specifies three–substitution by consumers to other products (demand substitutability), substitution by producers to other products (supply substitutability), and entry of new productive capacity (paras. 32-6, 12-13).

These arguments reflect the broad view of competition that he presented in prior writings and rejected in the case. His supply-substitutability criterion, moreover, constitutes a critical unmet challenge to asserting the existence of an effective applications barrier to entry. Schmalensee's analysis stresses how strong the supply substitutability effects are. The government never responds. The gfof (par. 18, 18-19) quotes these propositions but predictably also never uses them.

After noting the similarity of his views to DOJ merger guidelines (par. 37, 14), Fisher concludes by recognizing the need to consider entry prospects (paras. 38-9, 14-15). Ignoring these prospects until his oral testimony is another key flaw of his applications to the case. All his concepts are valid but too vague to implement, as his applications to the case demonstrate.

Warren-Boulton's effort to define monopoly, in contrast, is essentially an extended statement of the textbook definition of control over price (paras. 26-32, 12-15).

The treatment of network effects follows similar lines. Neither side ever indicates the existence of the extensive literature. This permits the government to ignore the drawbacks. In treating network effects, Fisher starts with initial general remarks in his theory section (paras. 40-45, 15-16). Further conceptual points are made during the appraisal of Microsoft's operating-system monopoly (paras. 66-70, 25-7). Warren-Boulton again is terser and comes close to a definition loose enough to imply no software upgrade can succeed. Schmalensee counters with an overly brief dismissal of the theory and concentrates on showing that the history of software shows that entry is possible.

Fisher's initial review starts with a sentence indicating that economies of scale and network effects are barriers to entry arising in the case (par. 40, 15). Definitions follow. For economies of scale, he uses the standard definition, strictly speaking valid only for single-product firms, of falling average costs (par. 41, 15). That of network effects is "the attractiveness of a product to customers increases with the use of that product by others" (par. 42, 15). He adds that with network effects, a firm with a large market share may gain monopoly power "by innovation, marketing skill, historical accident, or any other means" (par. 43, 15-16).

He recognizes that this may occur without anticompetitive acts and adds the truism that this does not justify subsequent resort to anticompetitive acts (par. 44, 16). As noted, he subdivides such acts into ones extending the monopoly to other markets or ones protecting the current monopoly (see Chapter 8). His last general point was "In the absence of anti-competitive conduct, market forces and developments can erode monopoly power based solely on network effects ..." (par. 45, 16).

A subsequent clarification makes explicit "there is nothing inherently anti-competitive about network effects" (par. 68, 26). He then asserts without elaboration, "The existence of network effects also implies that the effect of anti-competitive contracts or conduct will not be dissipated merely by terminating the anti-competitive contracts or stopping the anti-competitive conduct" (par. 69, 27). Thus, a durable effect is postulated without proof.

As with his analysis of monopoly, Fisher presented evaluation criteria for network effects that seem more stringent than those actually used in the case. His theoretic argument again admits more vulnerability than the government claims.

Warren-Boulton again is both less detailed and more problematic. He stresses the costs of conversion in terms of software purchase, retraining, new hardware, and file updating (paras. 49-50, 21-2). Thus, big payoffs must accrue to shifting operating systems. The barriers arise with any software changes. The Warren-Boulton argument, thus, at least comes dangerously close to asserting that software updating is unattractive. The case record makes clear what every experienced computer user knows. Upgrades are frequent.

Under cross-examination, Warren-Boulton inadvertently provided another illustration of the problems of using insider comments. Warren-Boulton notes that Nathan Myhrvold, a Microsoft executive and brother of witness Cameron, was cognizant of Brian Arthur (November 19, 1998, a.m., 85). The cited document is a memorandum with a draft of a proposed public response to criticism (GX 994). Myhrvold somehow inferred a viewpoint closer to Liebowitz and Margolis and Schmalensee than to Arthur and Warren-Boulton. Myhrvold, by creativity or obtuseness, sweeps aside wrong choice and lock-in problems and talks of how displacement is the norm in software. He also describes a prevailing low-price strategy for Microsoft (3-5).

The government economists' reading of the documents is the sole support for the conclusion that such lock-in effects apply to Windows. Neither proof of the existence of a network-effect shield for Windows nor an explanation of how it arose is provided. Both sides recognize that none of the conventional barriers to entry exist. Programmers and the funds to pay them are widely available. Thus, some unusual problem must exist to preclude entry. The network-externality contention is the only available rationale.

Whether network effects are truly the right explanation in theory or practice is doubtful. The tacit assumption is that inefficient acts are more likely to succeed because of network effects; this is another leap. More critically, the assertion ignores all the challenges, including Fisher's, to belief in the efficacy of anticompetitive acts and the importance of network effects. (See Chapters 4 and 5 for the theory and Chapter 8 for the applications to the case.)

Schmalensee's statement deals tersely but correctly with the general defects of network-effects arguments and to emphasize the evidence suggesting their absence in the Microsoft case. He too simply asserts the defects of the claims. Most notably, he only cites the software history components of the draft manuscript of Liebowitz and Margolis (1999).[1]

Schmalensee's summary was:

> Some economists have suggested that extensive network externalities in the microcomputer software industry make this industry prone to "tipping" and "lock-in." But they have relied on certain highly abstract economic theories that imply no more than that "tipping" and "lock-in" are *possible*—and even then only under a set of specific assumptions seldom if ever encountered in real-world industries (par. 74, 37, emphasis in original).

In a footnote omitted here, he chooses to reference only an article arguing that adverse impacts on competition in software arise from network effects. The paragraph ends with assertion that the concept is not applicable to software. After further skeptical comments about tipping, he adds:

---

[1] The first reference to Liebowitz and Margolis was par. 36, 19. Others are par. 59, 29; par. 80, 40; and par. 612, 314.

Some economists have also argued that the software category leader gets "locked-in" and that its dominance will persist. "Lock-in" results from very high switching costs. In theory, this might come from network effects that make it costly for individual users to switch unless many others also switch. But history provides no support for this "trapping-state" view of the world (par. 76, 38 footnote omitted).

The review of the theory in Chapter 5 suggests that Schmalensee understated the drawbacks. Katz and Shapiro's discussion of sponsorship suggests that network effects are simply barriers to entry. When the prospects are good, a promising new system is simply another example of the good investments that, as Schmalensee points out, get funded. In short, network effects are far less unique and important than the government claimed.

Fisher's Direct Testimony on the Monopoly

The portion of Fisher's direct testimony supporting the existence of a Microsoft operating-systems monopoly (paras. 62-78, 22-31) relies entirely on insider opinions. Fisher starts by reviewing OEM assertions that no alternatives existed (par. 63, 22-5, none of those cited was a trial witness). This is followed by the assertion that Microsoft's market share is "very high and stable" (twice in par. 64, 25). He next states without explanation that high market shares and barriers to entry prove the existence of monopoly power (par. 65, 25).

He then asserts that network effects are important (paras. 66-71, 25-9). Again the reliance is on statements by industry sources only one of whom, Microsoft's Brad Chase, was a trial witness. The quotations state the obvious, but not conclusive, point that applications are important. Then Fisher interprets (paras. 72-3, 29) the memorandum by Joachim Kempin of Microsoft (GX 365) as admission that the company does not fear competition.

This last involves not just relying on, but misinterpreting insider views. Kempin's memorandum clearly recognizes that too high prices could inspire efforts to create a rival operating system. Fisher quotes a dismissive statement about the ability of an OEM such as Compaq singlehandedly or collectively to mount such a challenge. Fisher, among other things, thus ignores fears Kempin stated, two paragraphs later, that an Intel-led consortium is another, more dangerous threat. The thrust of the memorandum in any case is that the prevailing Microsoft low-price strategy is sound.

This selective quotation was repeated in gfof (par. 49.2, 94-5). The gfof's treatment of monopoly (par. 15, 9-15; paras. 17-28, 16-48) largely parallels Fisher's. More quotes are added, including many from Fisher and Warren-Boulton, as is the allegation that the dependence creates fear (par. 15.2, 14-15). A section (par. 19, 20-7) explicitly dismissing alternatives is a more significant elaboration. Quotations are again the proof throughout.

Fisher turns (paras. 74-7, 29-30) to Schmalensee's statement that Microsoft faces competition from the stock of previously sold Windows programs. Fisher's dismissal involved tacitly narrowing further the definition of the relevant market by contending that new computers are more important and thus critical (par. 77, 30). He adds the suggestion that improvements in hardware increase the attractiveness of new computers. However, he and the government also criticize Microsoft practices towards the supposedly unimportant upgrade market.

He further contends that the restrictions on licensing to computer makers limits competition from the installed base (par. 77, 30). The OEMs can neither resell these licenses nor continue to sell an old version once a new one appears. He talks of the barriers to a secondary market in old operating systems resulting from these restrictions on the resale of licenses to use Windows.

The Fisher argument seems to confuse flows with stocks. New computers may be the main outlet for new flows of Windows. This does not eliminate the large stock of existing computers with old versions of Windows. That stock was what Schmalensee was discussing. Again, questions arise about whether these conditions would prevail without Microsoft's strategy of a low-cost, often-improved Windows. If Windows became unattractive, OEMs could begin offering computers without operating systems. Independent software suppliers could then stockpile older versions of Windows, and piracy could increase. More critically, people would not buy new computers so often. Moreover, Microsoft continues to supply earlier versions of its operating system (mfof par. 358, 161-2).

Fisher's arguments involve conflicting views about the implications of frequent updates. His oral testimony (January 1, 1999, p.m., 19-20; June 3, 1999, a.m., 11-14) notes that monopolists also innovate; this presumably recognizes that upgrades have desirable attributes. However, his direct testimony points out that updates necessitate changes in applications software (par. 165, 80). During cross-examination in June 1999, he more bluntly notes this removes the stability of the interfaces (June 3, 1999, a.m., 21-2, quoted gfof par. 164.4.1, 309). Suddenly, upgrades are undesirable.

The central problem with these last comments is that they are another venture into areas outside his expertise. He was responding to technological claims by Microsoft that it placed restrictions on how OEMs presented Windows to ensure system stability. His arguments are an effort to suggest that, in fact, the goal was to restrict competition. A direct statement and proof that significant competitive impacts arose is the preferable approach in an economic analysis. Fisher starts from the uncontroversial point that upgradings by definition upset the prevailing stability. Since he is not a computer scientist, he cannot judge either what role, if any, Microsoft should play in smoothing the effects of upgrades or whether or not that role justifies the criticized controls on OEMs. This offhand venture into computer science, nevertheless, was employed by the government to disparage Microsoft claims of preserving the integrity of Windows (see Chapter 9).

His plunge into technology, moreover, seems to ignore that upgrades are so common that regular users of computers as well as computer professionals expect such changes.

Schmalensee's Approach

Schmalensee's analysis is a vigorous assertion that ease of entry is so great that Microsoft must act as if it were a pure competitor. His presentation differs from that used here. He starts with a section (II) on software competition that delineates basic propositions that he supports by reciting evidence from industry experience. Evidence on one proposition, that leaders get displaced, receives particularly close attention. He concludes that the facts suggest a vigorously competitive industry.

A longer section (III) argues that the differences between an operating system and an application do not permit monopoly. The discussion is a treatment of the competitive pressures on Microsoft. His development includes arguing that network effects impede, but do not preclude, entry into software including operating systems. In short, as the government tries to deny, Schmalensee starts with a general argument that entry into software is easy and adds explicit discussion about why the peculiarities of operating systems do not preclude entry. A key associated point is that no special characteristics impede entry into browsers.

His Section II develops a conceptual framework illustrated by industry experience. This includes an extended review of successful displacement of leading programs. Section III starts with evidence indicating that the arguments of Section II are applicable to operating systems. He begins with a survey of the evidence about the ability to create an operating system and attract programs. He reviews the history of operating-system competition and concludes with examination of existing threats from other operating systems and alternatives to the personal computers.

Then he develops and employs a framework for arguing that these pressures force Microsoft to behave competitively. He contends that a combination of low and falling (on a quality-adjusted basis) prices, innovation, and heavy investments in inducing programmers to write Windows programs show that Microsoft does not act like a monopolist. The pricing concept proposed by Schmalensee is known as limit pricing, but it is a question to Fisher in oral testimony (January 11, 1999, p.m., 49) that explicitly introduced the term into the case.

To support his conclusions, Schmalensee seeks to justify the conclusion suggested by observation of software pricing that Windows seems cheap for a monopolized product. He testified, "I think it's very common-sensical that a monopolist of the kind described here could charge many hundreds of dollars for Windows. And it strikes me as absolutely at odds with common sense that such a monopolist would settle for a $50 computer system" (January 21, 1999, a.m., 20-22). In his direct testimony, Schmalensee reported Gates's claim that low prices and innovation are needed to withstand competition (par. 124, 58-9). The assertion came in an interview given to Schmalensee.

His calculations suggest that a monopolist would charge $1,980. A major consequence of this conclusion is that the perceived impotence of existing rivals arises because Microsoft has preempted them in pricing, promotion, and innovation. His oral testimony (January 20, 1999, p.m., 44) indicates that Schmalensee developed the conceptual framework in 1992 for prior work for Microsoft.

Actually, the numbers are redacted from his direct testimony. The price was treated as a trade secret, but in open court, $50 or $65 was used. For example, Fisher employs a $65 price (June 1, 1999, p.m., 13). On January 21, 1999, a.m., 49, Lacovara notes use of a $65 price in an exhibit and asks Schmalensee whether this is the actual price. Schmalensee describes it as that used by "convention" in open court and above the actual price to computer manufacturers. This produces several pages of bickering about the secrecy (50-53). Fortunately, Schmalensee based his numbers on a supporting document that is available without redaction (see below).

He argues, in conclusion, that Fisher and Warren-Boulton have incorrectly analyzed the situation (see below). The successive criticisms are for reliance on a structural approach, illogically too narrowly defining the market, and, therefore, incorrectly appraising Microsoft. He suggested that examination of behavior was more appropriate.

The Problem of Structural Analysis

Schmalensee presented the vision of a marketplace with so many competitive pressures that structural analyses are inappropriate. He argues that behavioral measures be stressed because the nature of the threats implies that the usual weaknesses of structural measures are acute. His basic case for preferring a behavioral approach is that it can handle all the influences on competition without having to decide the exact extent of the market (paras. 176-7, 88-9). To remain consistent with prior work, he makes the obvious addition that a behavioral approach is appropriate when the boundaries are unclear and thus controversial (par. 178, 89). He adds scholarly support from Fisher (1979).[1]

He then notes reasons why this is true of software. His first example is the tendency of all types of software to incorporate previously separate features. Therefore, absorption by other programs, entry, the installed base, and piracy are restraints (par. 179, 89-90). Then the relevance to Microsoft is noted (paras. 180-81, 90). He indicates Microsoft is constrained by an installed base of its older operating systems, the existence of rivals, and the threat of piracy. In particular, the installed base means that software developers and users must be persuaded to accept a newer system (par. 181, 90, repeated January 14, 1999, a.m., 25).

In attacking the government's relevant-market definition, he starts with the basic problem that the Netscape/Java platform and every other threat are outside the market (par. 182, 90-91). This point is reiterated orally (June 22, 1999, p.m., 18-32). He then explicitly mentions Apple and observes that the government's logic would imply that if Apple integrated a browser, it too should be sued (par. 183, 91).

He adds that the government improperly uses short-run arguments to treat long-run issues (paras. 184-6, 92-3). As this section does not explicitly state, the attack on Microsoft's predation stresses long-run effects, but only the short-run impacts of competitive threats are considered relevant. As discussed below, the importance of long-run ramifications is closely related to their current influence on Microsoft. Schmalensee asserts and the government denies a profound current effect.

He concludes that only a behavioral approach can treat these influences. He adds that, given the potential entry of any software producer, software, in which Microsoft has about 10 percent of the market, is another possible relevant market. He notes these measures are not meaningful share figures but indicate how much potential competition exists (par. 187, 93-4).

Reynolds (2001, 30-32) adds that statistical problems arise in sensibly implementing the government's definition. He notes that Windows NT for servers was included but the Unix-based operating systems for Sun and others not using Intel processors were excluded. He undertakes adjustments that reduce the Microsoft share from the 96 percent share claimed by the government to about 80-83 percent. This is the net effect of differences

[1] While the attribution is correct, the wrong journal is cited.

between his sources and the government's, the exclusion of Windows NT, and the inclusion of Apple. The government argument that adjustments do not make a great difference is probably valid as long as the structural approach is accepted. However, concerns about a structural approach remain.

Starting with Schmalensee's rebuttal testimony (June 22, 1999, p.m., 19-20), he has proposed the alternative view that the government logic implied that platform competition was the relevant concern. Post-trial writings expanded on the suggestion (Evans 2000, Evans and Schmalensee 2000a and 2000b, and Evans, Nichols and Schmalensee 2001). This puts the Netscape/Java platform and Windows with Internet Explorer in the same market.

Evans and Schmalensee (2000a) aver problems for the government's charge of uncompetitive behavior when stress is on platforms. They start by asserting a lack of economic justification for rejection of concentration on platform competition. Then they present reasons why such recognition would undermine the government's case on both the monopoly and the predatory response sides. The main point in the monopoly arena is that the Netscape/Java platform faced the same "applications" barrier challenges as any other alternatives. Evans and Schmalensee then state in several ways that the government evaded the defects of the argument that Netscape/Java was able uniquely among all possibilities to comprise a threat. Only admission that the entry-barrier claim was defective justifies taking the middleware threat seriously (2000a, 62-3).

On the predation side, Evans and Schmalensee note that adoption of the platform-competition model hurts the charges of illegal tying and predatory pricing. If Windows and Netscape Navigator are platforms, integrating Internet Explorer into Windows is simply another natural expansion of Windows. The switch to a platform approach also forces better analysis of whether the effort to respond to competition to Windows was predatory. All this leads them to assert "Thus, sophistry by misleading market definition is at the heart of the government's case."

From a purely analytic viewpoint, this approach is less satisfactory than the original position that no structural approach captures all the complexities. Evans and Schmalensee probably present the platform-competition viewpoint as that most consistent with the government case. In most respects, however, it is preferable to retain the behavioral approach and the sharper criticism it allows.

Fisher and Rubinfeld's attempt at rebuttal is further evidence of the superiority of explicit rejection of relevant-market concepts. They claim their conclusions are "essentially independent of market definition" but those of Evans and Schmalensee rely on "a tortured market definition"

(2000a, 89). The Fisher and Rubinfeld exposition of the point provides a variant on Fisher's effort to suggest the middleware threat is outside the relevant market (see below). They end by asserting that in any case, however the market is defined, Microsoft took predatory actions against Navigator and Java (90). While wrong, the latter assertion at least recognizes that market definition is inappropriate in this case.

The basic difficulty in any situation is that pressures differ in intensity and kind, but a structural analysis requires deciding which forces are relevant. The cut-off point for recognizing important competition is too subjective and too easily, as in this case, left badly explained. The platform-competition viewpoint ignores challenges from alternatives to personal computers and that other reasons might better explain the creation of Internet Explorer (see Chapter 8). Any structural approach leads to arguing about whether operating systems, platforms, or browsers are "separate products." This obscures the critical issues of whether the threat was credible and the response efficient.

However, several commentators (e.g., Hall and Hall 1999, 14, 16 and Economides 2001a, 14) suggest departure from standard relevant-market arguments was asking too much of a judge. Reynolds (2000, 128) quotes Boies's assertion in Heilemann's book that no judge understands an expert and thus only evaluates whether the expert knows what he is talking about. This may be unfair. Jackson made comments in court suggesting an ability to comprehend economic arguments. The defects of his findings may lie in his well-publicized desire to establish an unchallengeable case against Microsoft (see Chapter 10). The implicit rationale for a shift to platform competition is that, if a relevant-market approach must be used, the platform-market view is the least-worst alternative.

Schmalensee on Competition

As noted, the core of Schmalensee's treatment of competition is first to show why competition in software generally is intense and second indicate that the reasoning applies to operating systems. The first analysis begins with discussion of the special economic characteristics of software, turns to ease of entry, notes the changes that prevailed, and then states the consequences.

He starts by noting that the industry cannot be purely competitive because marginal costs are virtually zero and zero prices mean ruin (paras. 29-31, 16-17). Schmalensee accuses the government economists of sticking too closely to textbook standards. As the discussion of Fisher argued, his fault arose in inadequate execution of principles akin to Schmalensee's.

Schmalensee's next point is that software competition is "to lead or create a category" (par. 32, 17-18). Network effects imply that the entrant must provide a significant improvement over existing software. Such advances and thus displacement are feasible. Such turnover often has occurred. Therefore, software prices are restrained by an ever-present fear of displacement (paras. 32-35, 17-18, par. 37, 19-20).

He then develops at length the evidence that barriers to entry are not significant. In this discussion, he understandably often uses Netscape as an example. The Netscape case is indeed a paragon that anyone might note. More critically, the arguments have major direct implications for the case. His discussion tacitly undermines the government's vision of Netscape as a weak innocent, readily defeated by Microsoft.

He starts by noting the existence of at least 12,000 firms, 200 entrants since 1991, and 190 initial public offerings since 1997 (par. 38, 19). He proceeds to indicate the large number of programmers (2 million in the United States and 5 million worldwide) (par. 40, 20-21), the availability of capital (par. 41, 21), and the mobility of these resources (paras. 43-4, 22). He uses Netscape as an example of a company able to attract funds and programmers (par. 41, 21-2). He notes that technical advances in hardware create opportunities to innovate in software (paras. 45-6, 23-4). A network of specialized publications and Internet sites ensure wide knowledge of developments (paras. 47-9, 24-5). Many distribution channels exist including low-cost ones such as the Internet (paras. 50-51, 25-6). The last is an unsubtle criticism of the government's effort to denigrate downloading (see Chapter 9).

He then turns to the implications. He notes the lack of precise definitions but suggests the concern is preventing efficient new competition because entry costs are high relative to benefits (paras. 52-3, 26). He suggests that three factors–sunk costs, switching costs, and network effects–might, but do not, impede entry.

He notes that the pressures to innovate mean that incumbents as well as entrants are regularly incurring sunk costs in new programs but the costs are not prohibitive. He contrasts the $10 million Netscape spent to get its first browser to market with the outlays of $500 million on Viagra, $1 billion on a new Gillette razor, and $1.5 billion for a new Motorola chip factory (paras. 55-7, 27-8). His initial treatment of switching is to refer to studies such as Liebowitz and Margolis that show its occurrence (par. 58, 28-9). The next part of the section is a history of displacements in applications (paras. 61-73, 30-37). Similarly, the treatment at this point of network effects simply indicates they can be overcome (paras. 59-60, 29-30). The review of displacements is followed by further observations, the first of which was that on tipping cited above.

He proceeds to argue that the result is product improvement and falling prices; he uses office suites as his example of falling prices (paras. 78-81, 39-41). Then he expands on his initial discussion about why prices are above marginal costs and adds that the rate of return on successful products must reflect the risk of failure (paras. 82-88, 41-3).

The next section is the defense against the monopoly charge. While his section II tended to use industry experience to demonstrate concepts, section III focuses on the empirical issue of competition in operating systems. Three themes are developed–barriers of entry are not high, Microsoft, therefore, acts competitively, and the government treated competition defectively. As elsewhere, the argument is grounded in a conceptual model. Ease of entry is treated with examples. Analytic points are made on competition and its treatment by the government.

He begins with the critical problem of inducing independent software vendors (ISVs) to write programs for a given system. He necessarily recognizes that persuasion is required, but argues that a pre-existing position can be and often is overcome. Thus, he affirms that the attractiveness of an operating system depends upon the availability of supporting applications. Thus, success requires following creation with attracting ISVs. He suggests that dominance indeed may not be enough. Microsoft sees it necessary also to provide direct stimulus, investing $630 million per year in support of ISVs (paras. 98-105, 47-50).

He argues that the ability of Apple and other operating systems to attract applications suggests that the difficulties can be surmounted. He concludes with a section that argues the applications barrier is not high. He notes that switching costs do exist and thus the entrant must overcome the impact (paras. 114-15, 54-5). This seems to relate to his earlier points that the entrant must provide a major improvement and such improvements are possible.

Schmalensee then reviews the history of operating systems to show that many displacements occurred including several Microsoft successes at replacing its earlier operating systems (paras. 117-36, 55-64). He then describes threats from middleware, other operating systems, and alternatives to the personal computer (paras. 135-60, 63-79). A similar discussion is in mfof (paras. 199-239, 89-107).

The discussion includes a section on key implications. The first is that the experience is inconsistent with the vision of instant tipping and a lock-in (paras. 125-7, 59-60). Transitions are more gradual than tipping theories suggest but occur, so lock-in does not. He then argues, similarly to his views on applications software, that technical progress in hardware facilitates creation and introduction of new software (paras. 128-9, 60-61). He notes that the development and switching costs are higher for an operating system but so are the rewards of success (par. 130, 61-2). Then the middleware threat is used as an example that competition can start from software other than an operating system (par. 131, 62).

The review indicates that Microsoft is cognizant of these challenges and acts accordingly. This suggests a critical aspect of the case. Stripped down, the Microsoft defense starts with awareness of and response to challenges and adds that the reaction is to provide a better, cheaper product than the competitors did. The case centers on whether or not antitrust enforcers can distinguish efficient from inefficient response.

Necessarily all Schmalensee can establish is that many rivals are anxious to displace Windows and that Microsoft is concerned. The credibility of the threats can be and was challenged. Unfortunately, the government economists, the government attorneys, Judge Jackson, and the Circuit Court all evaded the question of what comprises a sensible basis for judging credibility. The only basis is that Fisher and Warren-Boulton believed that Schmalensee was wrong. As noted, Fisher and Warren-Boulton, in turn, relied on documents. That is not economic analysis.

Schmalensee also observes that Warren-Boulton ignored the portions of Joachim Kempin's December 1997 e-mail that recognize competitive threats and proposes not raising the price (par. 164, 81) (see above).

Schmalensee next describes the innovations with Windows (paras. 165-9, 82-4) and how as a result the quality-adjusted price has fallen. Schmalensee shows that Microsoft added features, several of which, when purchased separately, each sold for more than Windows (par. 172, 85-6). He calculates that the combined price of the 1994 operating system and just two of the previously separate programs was $261. The price of Windows is redacted, but testimony, as noted, suggests a price around $50-65. Mfof (par. 38, 161) proposes a broader vision of improvements in the functionality and features of Windows. This could be taken to mean improving existing components and new ones that were previously nonexistent as well as those once separate.

Such inclusion of extra features reinforces Schmalensee's view that Windows sells for much less than the monopoly price. The mfof, of course, indicates this evidence and the failure to refute it (paras. 356-9, 160-62). McKenzie (2000b, 39-44) precedes a similar discussion of added features with data suggesting a falling constant dollar price of Windows.

Schmalensee ends his discussion with criticism of the government's economists' assertions about monopoly. He concentrates on Warren-Boulton, ostensibly because his was the fuller treatment. The stress allows recalling his unique slips. Schmalensee emphasizes the defects in Warren-Boulton's treatments of profitability. Schmalensee prefaces this criticism with a flat observation that high profits are inevitable with success in software (par. 195, 96-7). He next notes that Warren-Boulton disregarded warnings, including one coauthored by Fisher, about why accounting data are defective for economic analysis (par. 196, 97 citing Warren-Boulton par. 62, 28). Schmalensee adds that Warren-Boulton's consideration of price/earnings ratios ignores that they are influenced by growth expectations; high expectations, such as would prevail with Microsoft, would produce high price-earning ratios (par. 197, 98, citing November 19, 1998, a.m., 26-7).

Warren-Boulton also erred by asserting without proper discussion that, in effect, the demand for Windows was inelastic (paras. 199-200, 98-9, citing Warren-Boulton par. 37, 17). For reasons discussed below, the latter is equivalent to accepting Schmalensee's views of Microsoft's behavior; Schmalensee notes this (par. 201, 99-100).

Schmalensee (par. 195, 96) mercifully restates Warren-Boulton's assertion (par. 61, 27) that operating system costs are a rising percent of computer prices as an assertion that operating system costs have not fallen as rapidly as computer prices. Schmalensee then makes the obvious point that, since the underlying economics are affected by different forces, the trends also can differ. He ends with recollection that his quality-adjusted numbers refute the charge. Nevertheless, gfof (par. 38.1.2, 64) repeats the contention.

He also reiterates earlier points. Schmalensee thus notes that a high share is likely in software because network effects produce leadership but leaders are readily displaced (par. 190, 94-5). Thus, the share-based Department of Justice merger guidelines to which Warren-Boulton (and Fisher) refer are not applicable (par. 198, 98). This understates the uselessness for the case of the guidelines. Moreover, the leadership is derived from superior performance (par. 191, 95). Warren-Boulton's dismissal of competitive threats relies on an inappropriate short-run viewpoint (par. 193, 96). This last is closely related to the debate on a proper interpretation of Microsoft behavior, but not Schmalensee's clearest presentation of the point (see below).

He also repeats his criticism of Warren-Boulton's claim that Microsoft charges a noncompetitive price; this ignores that the purely competitive price would be zero (par. 30, 16-17; par. 192, 95-6). This is too kind. Warren-Boulton's treatment seems to be yet another example of unsubstantiated speculation whose basis is unknown. Schmalensee ends this section with an undeveloped declaration that price differences are common; a footnote associates this with price discrimination.

This review of Schmalensee may be contrasted to Economides's post-trial critique. Economides (2001a, 14) contends without elaboration "a full and coherent view of a *dynamic* market definition was never presented."

(Emphasis in original.) Given that he does not even list Schmalensee in the bibliography, it is difficult to know what shortcomings produced this conclusion. Certainly, as recognized above, Schmalensee's argument lacked the completeness of a scholarly treatise and perhaps went too far in the other direction.

Earlier in his paper, Economides presented a conceptual treatment of why competition in a network industry, while unconventional, is still efficient. He starts with (1) recognition that in a market with network effects the winner will dominate in Microsoft fashion, (2) this will arise without "anti-competitive" acts, (3) forced changes are "futile and counterproductive," and, in particular, (4) adding firms will not help. However, (5) vigorous competition to become a winner will prevail. (6) Divestiture may create inefficiencies. (7) The benefits of success as well as the cost of entry are high and thus competition may be greater compared to non-network industries. (8) The advantages of incumbency are formidable but not insuperable. This is little different from Schmalensee's analysis.

At best, the discussion can be viewed as a debate over which model of competition is more valid economically. At worst, it involves conjectures about industry development that no one can confirm. At a minimum, this indicates the failure of Fisher and Warren-Boulton seriously to address these arguments.

The Government Response 1: Defending Structure

A basic defect of the government case is relentless, never justified advocacy of the concept of share of the relevant market. It elicited comments from Fisher to deal with the issue. In his rebuttal phase testimony, Fisher was asked to comment on Schmalensee's views on structural analysis. Fisher's response began:

> Well, Dean Schmalensee basically refused to define any market at all because he found that either difficult or impossible. And stemming from that, I think there are a whole series of problems leading to–how shall I put it–leading to a lack of systematic thinking and to some muddled results (June 1, 1999, a.m., 6-7).

However, every Fisher point is simply one of disagreement that largely has nothing to do with the choice of framework. For example, Boies asks Fisher a misleading question about whether freedom of entry into software is a meaningful question. Fisher's answer ultimately concludes that such a statement ignored the network barriers to entry (10-11). This ignores that Schmalensee argued for valid reasons that such barriers were surmountable.

Eventually, Fisher gives two examples of facilitation of entry that he asserts prove the superiority of a structural approach. The first is the invention of an automobile that uses methanol and thus facilitates breaking down a hypothetical gasoline monopoly. (Fisher and Rubinfeld (2000a, 90) talk of root beer becoming a substitute for gasoline.) The second is the creation of a railroad to California that undermines a California monopoly of "some fairly bulky product" (15-18).

The primary defect is that the examples illustrate, rather than solve, the problem of a purely structural analysis. In addition, the Netscape/Java threat was to assume part of the function of Windows. Fisher's examples, moreover, are fanciful. Had he considered the broader phenomenon of market-widening by improved transportation and communications, the problems of a structural approach would have been even clearer. The gfof (par. 40.2.1, 72-3), nevertheless, repeats the argument. (The government transforms the bulky commodity into crude oil, in which railroads long ago ceased to be a major transportation mode.)

Upon cross-examination, Lacovara introduces a quotation from Fisher noting "market share is at best a very rough indicator of market power"(June 2, 1999, a.m., 58). Fisher's extended response is that, nevertheless, his approach is better than Schmalensee's (59-63).

The attack on Schmalensee in the gfof starts with criticism of Schmalensee's behavioral approach. The summary point is "Refusing to define a relevant market, Dean Schmalensee opined that Microsoft cannot be a monopolist because it does not behave like a monopolist" (par. 39, 70). The first part of the charge is Fisher's. The rest is assertion that Schmalensee's conclusions are invalid. Later, the government tries a fuller, but behavioral, refutation (see below).

The conceptual attack on a behavioral approach at its best is only further assertions that Schmalensee is wrong about disputed questions. The criticism started with the allegations, examined in Chapter 6, of inconsistencies with prior work. A summary of the Fisher points just noted follows. More briefly, the gfof adds that the absence of a current threat from Netscape/Java further supports the government's market definition (par. 40.2.3, 74).

Earlier in the gfof, an effort is made to defend the structural approach by noting, "Other 'platform' products, such as Internet browsers and Java, are not good substitutes for operating systems because they cannot function without an operating system" (par. 19.1, 20). The threat central to the case is thus twice dismissed to make a point. The broader criticism is that dismissing by quotation each alternative is not sufficient to disprove that collectively they restrain Microsoft (par. 19, 20-27).

Again, the government shifts time horizons. The support provided is that Schmalensee "conceded" that no present competitor constrains Microsoft. Schmalensee's argument is that the potential threats suffice to limit Microsoft's current behavior.

The last criticism is mendacity. Schmalensee's point that market share is misleading due to special industry conditions is attacked for supposedly ignoring two other things, the constraints by other competitors and the height of barriers to entry (par. 40.3, 75). The government knew that these issues were central to Schmalensee's arguments.

This government's effort to save the structural approach (par. 42, 75-85) seems actually to illustrate the drawbacks. Schmalensee is correct that the government's vision that the threat to Microsoft comes from entities outside the market is problematic. This debate over the structural approach, moreover, is less important than the government tries to assert. In developing its response, the government must follow the by now standard principle that conduct and performance measures support the market definition. The real issue is whether the monopoly charge can withstand Schmalensee's criticism. The rest of the government effort deals with this.

The Existence and Interpretation of Price Discrimination and Other Problems

The government, in passing, also charges Microsoft with price discrimination (par. 38.3, 66-9). This starts with another use of Fisher's point that market power can become monopoly power. The most important assertion is that Fisher used the existence of price discrimination to infer monopoly power (par. 38.3.1.ii, 66). The citations are to redirect (January 11, 1999, p.m., 41) and recross (January 13, 1999, a.m., 26) testimony. The first is described as indicating that price discrimination suggests an ability to earn supranormal profits; it actually only says that price discrimination implies market power. The second is correctly said to argue high and sustained market power suggests monopoly power. This does not contend that the discrimination is a clear indicator of monopoly power.

Moreover, the remainder of the quoted answer only indicates an explanation is needed for his comment. The examination (27-36) shifts instead to a series of questions suggesting that, in theory and software practice, discrimination is common among firms with nonmonopolistic market power. In any case, Fisher never clearly argues that the discrimination indicates monopoly power for Microsoft.

Gfof supports the quotations by redacted examples of alleged price discrimination. The mfof (paras. 348-55, 156-60) objects to the form and substance of the claim; this response presents the points raised in the recross of Fisher. The reply (par. 349, 157) starts by criticizing the government effort to hide that price discrimination often occurs without monopoly power. It is added that Fisher's purported use of discrimination to infer monopoly power is inconsistent with his writings (par. 350, 157). Then Carlton and Perloff are cited as supporting the Microsoft interpretation (par. 351, 157-8).

The government (gfof par. 38.3.1.iii, 66) counters with a further, irrelevant quote from Carlton and Perloff indicating that many firms cannot discriminate. Microsoft (mfof par. 353, 159) contrasts Fisher's evasion of questions about the prevalence of discrimination in software to evidence in the case about discrimination by Netscape (par. 354, 159). Then a redacted response is made to the redacted evidence on operating-system pricing (par. 355, 160).

All this ignores the more fundamental problem that the charge of discrimination is wildly inconsistent with the government's model of competition. Discrimination is undertaken to favor more price-sensitive customers. Given the postulated absence of competition for Windows and the weakness of the OEMs, no such more sensitive consumers should have existed. By the government's assumption, no rival existed to undersell. Nothing differentiated OEMs from each other in price sensitivity. In short, whatever differences prevailed must have reflected economic differences among OEMs.

Judge Jackson (cfof par. 64, 33), nevertheless, accepted and embellished this charge. He asserts the discounts were granted "depending on the degree to which the individual OEMs comply with Microsoft's wishes." This is unsubstantiated, misleading, and unnecessarily pejorative. By definition, a discount is provided to reflect some benefit received. An act willingly undertaken to secure recompense is not obeisance.

The government throws in fanciful charges worth mentioning only because Judge Jackson also adopted them. The first is the government's complaint that the price of Windows 95 was raised to equal that of Windows 98 when the latter was issued (par. 35, 57-60). Jackson parrots this (par. 62, 32). However, he earlier (par. 57, 29) also incorporates Fisher's complaint about the lack of a secondary market. Jackson, as did Fisher, fails to notice that the continued availability from Microsoft of earlier versions is why no secondary market exists.

Microsoft disputed the price-increase charge (mfof paras. 359-62, 162-4). However, that response and the original government charge (par. 36, 57-60) are redacted into incomprehensibility. The original government statement starts with a Fisher assertion that the price should not have risen and moves to the evidence. However, none is public. The mfof starts arguing that the government failed to consider both royalties and discounts (par. 359, 162). It adds that no evidence of intent was introduced (par. 360, 162-3). Then the response to the data analysis is redacted.

Again, what is important is ignored. Customarily, old products disappear when new ones appear. Thus, even still to offer Windows 95 is an unusual boost to competition. Economic logic suggests that Microsoft would want to price Windows 95 at levels that encourage a shift to Windows 98 and, thus, would perhaps raise the Windows 95 price. After all, the standard response of discontinuing the product makes the price infinite. This would occur whatever Microsoft's monopoly power.

The second charge is even more bizarre. The government (par. 38.2, 65) unearthed a memorandum debating whether to charge $49 or $89 for the upgrade to Windows 98 from Windows 95 and asserted this shows that Microsoft had discretion over price. At least three problems arise with the assertion.

First is the misuse of language. The only discretion proved is the trivial one that any firm, whatever the market structure, can quote any price it desires. Monopolistic discretion has two further elements. The desired price must be attainable and at a level that allows monopoly profits. All the government has shown is that Microsoft has enough market power to set and maintain a price. It is not illegal to set the profit-maximizing price, again whatever the market structure.

The government does not help by adding the gratuitous conjecture "there is no reason to believe that price would have been unprofitable." Choosing a higher over a lower price has no relationship to whether either yields monopoly profits. The claim about profitability suggests an ability to judge the appropriate price of Windows belied by the discussions of that price. The price-choice argument is just another example of piling on material without regard to the merits.

This leads to the second concern that the assertion is inconsistent with the contentions in its evaluation of Microsoft's actions to promote Internet Explorer. The upgrade-price critique implies a duty of Microsoft to sacrifice profits for no reason. The Internet-Explorer arguments attack sacrificing profits to meet a competitive threat.

A third objection is that again an expedient change of focus was made. The government's case otherwise heavily stresses that computer improvements means such frequent replacement that OEM distribution is what matters. Suddenly the upgrade market is critical because it allows using another memorandum. Nevertheless, Jackson (cfof par. 63, 32-3) parrots the statement.

Barriers to Entry in Theory and Practice

The government's treatment of barriers to entry mixes together various general points and statements noting the drawbacks of the threats that Schmalensee indicated. These are better separated.

Fisher's testimony provided the basis for the essence of the government's argument. Fisher argues that the threats are not immediate or real enough to matter. Fisher contends current conditions differ from those when Windows became dominant. He notes (June 1, 1999, a.m., 55) that the industry was smaller and thus the benefits to ISVs of writing programs was smaller. Eventually (57-9), he is asked about Schmalensee's point that a large share of a small market may be preferable and attract ISVs. The response is that this is not happening.

The basic error is that, as the question implies, the larger market size, while increasing the benefits of writing a Windows program, also raises the payoff to becoming the leader in an application for a promising rival operating system. The assertion of greater difficulty to compete ignores Stigler's 1951 observation that a larger market makes entry more profitable. Profitability, in turn, is what determines entry (recall Chapter 3). Despite these drawbacks, the gfof (par. 42.4.2.i, 83) extensively quotes Fisher's first answer. An alternative argument, which is not developed, would be that the growth of the number of available programs has drastically increased the cost of entry.

As noted above, Fisher is prompted into saying that ease of entry into software is not the critical question. It was also indicated that the question oversimplified Schmalensee's position on competition in operating systems. Schmalensee argued that freedom of entry was all that matters in browsers (see Chapter 8) but, as noted, addressed the special problems of operating systems. His summary presentation of this point, moreover, termed the government's contrary assertions about browsers a "red herring" (par. 3, 1). The government twice uses the Fisher quote on the irrelevance to operating systems (e.g. par. 40.1.3.iii, 72; par. 43.i, 86); the second citation justifies a heading calling Schmalensee's argument on operating systems a red herring.

The government (par. 48, 93) selectively cites several pages of Fisher testimony (June 1, 1999, a.m., 18-23) to suggest that Schmalensee considers too long a time horizon. As gfof does not note, Fisher agrees that a long-term perspective is appropriate (19). He proceeds to argue that the relevant time frame for estimating competitive threats is different (and by implication shorter) from that relevant for predation analysis. Schmalensee's core contention (par. 184, 92) is that the payoff to predation depends on the persistent absence of competition. This implies that Fisher's assertion is wrong since the prospects for competition throughout the recoupment period matter. At best, Fisher can claim that it is unreasonable to insist on certainty about later years. Moreover, if the time frame for monopoly analysis should be shorter, it still may be longer than Fisher believes.

An earlier discussion (par. 45.i, 88) cites other parts (14-15, 25-6) of the same Fisher session that argue the variant that potential threats do not disprove current monopoly power. This could be paraphrased as stating that Schmalensee's long-term time horizon allows too much consideration of hypothetical developments. Either way, this is another distortion since Schmalensee used the valid inclusion criterion of impacts real enough to influence price. Fisher (14) uses the invalid metaphor of the grandfather's warning about the danger of a wolf in "Peter and the Wolf," ignoring that Peter really captured a wolf. Moreover, this attack on concern with conjectural developments could apply to the government's emphasis on a possible middleware threat.

Another complaint following immediately (par. 45.ii, 88) is

Dean Schmalensee's position, as Professor Fisher testified, proves too much. It implies that "any monopolist who took action to preserve its monopoly and saw a threat worth taking action would be able to argue successfully that the fact it took the actions means that it can't have monopoly power." Fisher, 6/1/99am, 13:12-20.

This misstates. Schmalensee makes a fuller, sound defense. This involves efficient response to multiple threats. Part of that defense is what Fisher recognizes, but regularly ignores in practice, the difficulty of distinguishing between efficient and inefficient responses to rivalry.

The gfof (par. 47, 91) makes matters worse by further undermining the government's case. It states, "Dean Schmalensee's speculation that operating-system neutral, web-based applications developed on the Internet could some day erode the applications barrier to entry (Schmalensee, 6/23/99am, 36:15-41:22) also does not mean that Microsoft lacks monopoly power." The raison d'etre of the case is denigrated into Schmalensee's idea to make a point. Similarly, the claim that Microsoft could vitiate the threat by securing a large browser share is another restatement of the case.

The government supports the charge with a quote from an unavailable Gates transcript that AOL "doesn't have it in their genes to attack us in the platform space" and observing the inability of Schmalensee or Fisher to find examples (par. 47.1, 92). The Gates quotation is another example of reliance on inappropriate material. A middleware threat real enough to justify the case should persist whoever owns Netscape Navigator. This is but one example of the government's effort (see Chapter 9) to deny that the

Netscape/AOL merger that took place during the trial provided potent potential competition for Microsoft. The reliance on Schmalensee and Fisher is another illustration of use of the economists for appraisal of issues on which they are not experts.

In its zeal to show Gates feared middleware, the government twice cites views about the danger attributed to Gates by Steven McGeady (par. 56.1.ii, 115-16; par. 359.2.1, 631). The critical part of the quote says "If you begin to get a few leading-edge application developers that are developing for the Netscape environment, then that makes that environment that much more attractive both for end users and for other applications developers." The mfof (par. 260, 116) notes this inconsistency but omits a second sentence indicating that this start would stimulate wider entry.

Moreover, the fuss discussed in Chapter 8 over dealings with Apple suggests the updating of Office for the Macintosh was central to Apple's survival. (See Fisher, par. 153, 76-7.)

The gfof (par. 42.1, 75-7) goes beyond attacking concepts; the substance of Schmalensee's arguments are stated misleadingly. It starts "Dean Schmalensee conceded virtually all of the critical facts that underlie the applications barrier to entry." The major examples are discussions that recognize problems of entry exist. This ignores his conclusion that these barriers have been and still can be overcome. The government includes a Schmalensee statement that raising Windows prices would be profitable. This disregards that such statements are the basis for his argument that Microsoft's prices are too low to be monopolistic.

The second and more extensive part of the response is another demonstration that each threat considered by Schmalensee is not presently strong enough by itself to undermine Windows. As usual, the approach is to find quotations from people including Fisher (e.g., June 1, 1999, a.m., 13-15, cited gfof par. 45, 88) who dismiss the threats.

Another illustration suggests the resort to assertion. Fisher (January 11, 1999, p.m., 41) states:

> And the notion that operating systems such as Linux or Bee-OS (phonetic) [actually Be OS] or OS/2 or even Apple are really going to succeed in taking away much, if any, of the business from Microsoft Windows, is a joke. Of course it's not true.

In any case, the attack on separate threats is another evasion. Schmalensee's argument, in effect, is that collectively these forces constitute a mass of rivals, one or more of which might develop into a significant competitive threat. Recognition of this ever-present danger drives the low price, rapid innovation strategy.

The Body-Count Problem

As suggested, the government argues that the larger number of existing applications increases the difficulty of entry. (See gfof par. 42.4.2, 82-3, relying on assertions of Fisher, June 1, 1999, a.m., 53-4 and 56-8, and Warren-Boulton, November 24, 1998, a.m., 48-9.) The argument might imply that expanding the number of applications automatically increases the difficulties of entry and Windows has reached the point at which no one can compete. Microsoft's statements are a reminder that the larger size of the market increases the payoff to securing a given market share and makes competition more feasible. The latter view is more consistent with economic theory than the government's view.

The government denies that "applications in a few key categories" would produce entry into operating systems. Entry required "both (1) a large, diverse, and frequently updated set of applications and (2) assurances to users that such applications will be available in the future" (gfof, par. 27.1, 43). The basis is quotations (paras. 27-31, 43-52). The evidence provided is that the government economists, Microsoft, and those who deal with it do not see an extant competitor to restrain Microsoft. The argument again is overdone. The description of Apple (par. 31, 51-2) comes close to suggesting impending ruination.

In work completed after the publication of his book, McKenzie (2000a) investigated the claim that 70,000 applications existed and could not find supporting evidence. He did determine the number was an estimate covering programs for every operating system Microsoft had produced (5). Examination of what was available on Amazon.com suggested an offer of far fewer, 8,301, for all operating systems. After suggesting why even this number is inflated, he moves on to a summary critique of the case.

McKenzie traced the number to the testimony of John Rose of Compaq. Rose took care to stress the number related to every program that Windows could run and was so large because Microsoft ensured that its new operating systems would run programs designed for earlier operating systems (February 17, 1999, p.m., 20). Upon redirect examination, he was asked whether the typical customer used all 70,000. He replied "Boy, I hope no. No. Typically what we see is some users use about three to five applications. Some users may use ten" (February 19, 1999, a.m., 48).

Schmalensee and the Microsoft attorneys make three main counterarguments. First is that existing software including operating systems is displaced (Schmalensee paras. 116-31, 55-62). Second is that Microsoft spends about $630 million per year to assist applications developers (Schmalensee par. 102, 49). Third was an effort to undermine during the trial the implicit theory that as the number of applications increase it becomes more difficult for an alternative operating system to succeed.

The Microsoft attorneys tried several approaches to the last. One is to suggest that a small core of programs account for most use and thus simply attracting the development of such programs would suffice to start a new operating system. Schmalensee consistently criticizes the stress on the numbers of applications available rather than the existence of enough important applications to attract customers. Schmalensee (paras. 112-13, 53-4) notes that a few types are critical. He later denies the importance of numbers and reiterates the role of key applications on the basis of "common sense" (January 14, 1999, a.m., 9-10 and 16-20). (See January 19, 1999, a.m., 48-51 and January 21, 1999, a.m., 35-8 for further comments.)

Another effort was to ask the government economists about their computer use; see Warren-Boulton, (November 24, 1998, a.m., 19-21) and Fisher (January 6, 1999, a.m., 55-6). Fisher states (January 7, 1999, a.m., 30-31) that concern exists with "both the writing of very popular applications and with the breadth of applications." Discussion with Fisher moves on to suggest that it might be more attractive to be first mover with a newcomer such as Linux than to attempt competing against a successful Windows application (January 6, 1999, a.m., 55-66). Given the number of potential customers, sales sufficient to justify development costs might be more easily secured by selling to a large proportion of those adopting a new operating system. While that system might have many fewer users than Windows, it still could have large numbers. See mfof (paras. 279-82, 124-6) for a summary.

In short, the government failed to prove the importance of the applications barrier to entry.

The Other Elements of Competition

The final section is labeled a refutation of the claim "that Microsoft's other behavior is inconsistent with monopoly power" (par. 50, 103-7). The government just cites Fisher and Warren-Boulton on the incentives of even a monopolist to innovate and cultivate applications developers. The treatment adds in the claim that piracy and an installed base do not restrain Microsoft. This is another effort to misuse observational equivalence.

A Tale of Two Theories of Competition

As suggested, by the time the trial was completed, the government had developed and advocated both of the mutually-inconsistent possible responses to Schmalensee. The first was to produce a vision of price restraint that preserved monopoly. The second was to deny price restraint. Fisher, the government, and possibly even Warren-Boulton supported both theories. The government's strong case (par. 49.1, 93-4; par. 49.2, 94-5) that full exercise of monopoly power was the correct model is immediately followed by justification of the monopolistic-restraint alternative (par. 49.3, 95-9). However, that in turn is followed (par. 49.4, 99-103) with a summary of Fisher's attempt to show that the prices are profit maximizing.

Each model was developed through eliciting appropriate responses in oral testimony and weaving them together in the findings. Fisher managed fully to articulate both, but after the trial expressed preference for the first. Warren-Boulton makes statements consistent with both.

In his direct testimony, Fisher just stated the obvious point that Schmalensee "only" proved short-run profits were not maximized (par. 78, 31). In oral testimony, Fisher noted (January 11, 1999, p.m., 49) that a limit price may still leave "supernormal profits" (January 13, 1999, a.m., 23). He later gave explanations of how these profits were used. The introductory statement is:

> It takes some of its profits in the price of complementary products, both current complementary products and later prices–I'm sorry–later products in time. It takes some of its profits in the form of protection for its monopoly, and it does that in the form of the restrictions that it imposes on OEM's. And–well, in summary form, I think that's it. It's a rather longer story (January 12 1999, a.m., 19).

Two follow-up questions elicited the longer story (19-22). The first response indicates that sales of Office and Windows upgrades are the main complementary revenues. He notes Office has a higher price than Windows. It is implausible, however, that it is preferable to reap the monopoly profits from a product, Office, facing competition rather than from the operating system Fisher tells us faces no competition. Economides (2001c, 22-3) adds that the advantages of a low operating-system price would accrue to all the applications suppliers and that, as is not the case, the Apple version of Office would have been cheaper since the Macintosh operating-system monopoly belongs to Apple, not Microsoft.

The answer to the second question starts with another assertion of the desire to preserve the applications barrier to entry. Fisher then turns to recognition that, if Microsoft wants to require computer manufacturers and others to abide with onerous terms, compensation in such forms as a lower price for Windows must be provided.

Judge Jackson suggested another example, greater future sales of Windows, and Fisher agreed. Gfof (par. 49.3.1, 95-8; par. 49.3.2, 98-9) presents the argument and citations leading to the Judge's suggestion and

Fisher's response (January 12, 1999, a.m., 24-5). A stronger affirmation and a discussion of the incentives for competitive firms to keep prices low emerged later (January 12, 1999, p.m., 66-7). Jackson was pleased enough with the argument that he incorporated it into his fof (par. 65, 33). However, this is Schmalensee's argument in favor of presuming a competitive limit-pricing strategy.

Worse, if a low price promotes growth of Windows sales, a superior browser might also do so. The government stresses one type of promotion and denies the other. If pressed, the government undoubtedly could fabricate an explanation of why the situations are different. Its arguments simply assume away the advantage of a Microsoft browser; using Netscape suffices. As endemic in the case, the government's world is one in which every circumstance neatly is consistent with its charges against Microsoft.

Cross-examination of Fisher (January 13, 1999, a.m., 23) tried to secure admission of the similarity of views. The mfof (par. 342, 154) notes this but cites Fisher's discussion on redirect of the concept rather than his statement under cross-examination. Fisher, having admitted some relevance, tries to minimize by asserting that the entry of new operating systems is not "at the forefront of Microsoft's corporate mind." This inspires Lacovara to remind Fisher that talking about the corporate mind is inappropriate. This is another reminder of the stress on interpreting Microsoft memorandums and the objections raised by the Microsoft attorneys.

Fisher's effort simply to give an alternative explanation for limit pricing undermines the government's case. Once it is admitted that Microsoft failed to maximize short-run profits, its exact goals become unclear. The essence of limit pricing is that if enough threats exist, Schmalensee is right. The government must prove that the restraint still leaves monopoly profits. Such proof would be difficult because of the profit-measurement problem about which Fisher warned in the IBM case. Fisher again simply asserts. The mfof (par. 344, 150-51) correctly notes that Fisher provided "no basis to distinguish" among the explanations.

Among the other defects with these charges is the problem of reconciling them with his analysis of Internet Explorer. In particular, Fisher's explanation of limit pricing invokes a complementary-revenue argument that he asserts is invalid for Internet Explorer. Inconsistencies also arise between his limit-pricing model and his predation analysis (see Chapter 8).

In post-trial work with Rubinfeld, Fisher reverts to the restraint from maximization explanation and dismisses his assertion the price was profit maximizing as correction of errors by Schmalensee. Fisher and Rubinfeld state "We believe that Microsoft's pricing of its operating system–in particular, its contractual prices to original equipment manufacturers–is consistent with profit maximization by a firm with monopoly power" (2000b, 13-14). This is another use of the fallacy.

This is preceded by what is essentially repetition of Schmalensee's point. Fisher and Rubinfeld recall that with zero marginal costs profit maximization is revenue maximization, which occurs when the elasticity of demand is one. They give an argument similar to Warren-Boulton's that the elasticity at prevailing Windows prices is less than one. Rubinfeld and Fisher make the right conclusion that prices are not profit-maximizing.

The Fisher-Rubinfeld (2000b, 14) explanations are maintaining a large customer base, encouraging the sale of other software, discouraging piracy, and compensating computer manufactures for accepting "onerous restrictions." Aside from piracy (a Schmalensee explanation), these are those stated in Fisher's oral testimony. It is questionable whether these explanations are better than or even greatly different from Schmalensee's.

With this theory, the difference in views is about whether the reduction in monopoly profits that Schmalensee postulates and Fisher-Rubinfeld accepts retains or eliminates monopoly profits. The Fisher-Rubinfeld argument for conclusion that monopoly profits exist is assertion that none of the threats suggested by Schmalensee is credible. As noted, even the potential of the Netscape/Java platform is dismissed because it has not materialized. However, if the threat was unreal, the case has no basis.

However, the fatal flaw is that the argument is entirely conceptual. No evidence is provided that reality is closer to the Fisher model than to the Schmalensee view.

Oral testimony was elicited from both Fisher (June 1, 1999 a.m., 6-7; gfof par. 49.1.i., 88 says June 2) and Warren-Boulton (December 1, 1998, a.m., 43-5) rejecting a limit-pricing explanation and arguing that the price did maximize short-run profits. Fisher (par. 63, 22-5) and Warren-Boulton (paras. 38-40, 18-19) argued, on the basis of statements by Microsoft and other computer industry firm executives, that Windows faced no current competition. Fisher argues that the threats are long run and thus too distant to affect prices; this reflects his rejection of Schmalensee's contentions that the threats are real enough to affect Microsoft's behavior. Lacovara cross-examining Fisher (June 3, 1999, a.m., 6-9) tries to suggest that the threats may have been more immediate. Both economists assert that waiting for entry before cutting prices is the optimum strategy. As discussed below, Fisher also tried to show that sufficient changes in Schmalensee's assumptions made the current price profit maximizing.

The government (gfof par. 49.1, 93-4) notes "First, limit pricing–lowering price and thus sacrificing revenues today in order to deter entry tomorrow–is irrational if potential rivals know that the firm can lower price later, if and when competition emerges." The paragraph concludes by stating the obvious implication of the premise–Microsoft does not need to employ limit prices. Fisher (June 2, 1999, a.m., 6-7) makes the same argument.

However, as also already noted, the section immediately following argues that the limit-price charged still leaves monopoly profits. The government's straddling is a stunning concession that the government's certainty about Microsoft's monopoly power is not great enough to determine what constraints exist. Monopoly then is not obvious and possibly as constrained as Schmalensee argues. The government characteristically fails to make any citation of the relevant literature or go beyond assertions in stating its conclusions.

Microsoft contends that the government's case implies a monopoly so impregnable to competition that it can maximize short-run profits. In his oral testimony, Schmalensee argues that the government's assertions about Microsoft imply an ability to maximize short-run profits (June 23, 1999, a.m., 9). In earlier testimony, he noted that this impregnability assumption ignored that future effects, such as the growth-of-use idea Fisher took from Jackson, did affect current pricing decisions (June 22, p.m., 36-9).

This is more critical than Microsoft recognized. Schmalensee's influence-on-current-price criterion is economically valid and coherent. The rational-expectations approach that has revolutionized macroeconomics suggests that Schmalensee understated the importance of prospects. Fisher and the government excessively shift time horizons. The only legitimate defense of differential treatment is that different horizons are applicable for different purposes. This was not made. It is indefensible in this case. In particular, the Netscape/Java platform cannot be trivial as an influence on Windows pricing and the crux of predation with Internet Explorer. The predation charge starts with inclusion in Windows and thus an effect on the price of Windows.

Evans and Schmalensee (2000a, 71) note "If a durable, impenetrable barrier to entry protected Windows, Microsoft would have no reason to charge anything lower than the short-run profit-maximizing price." They then note that "the government's economists" adopted this view during the trial.

The Microsoft attorneys also adopted this view. In his summation (September 22, 1999, p.m., 40), John L. Warden argues in the course of casting scorn on a monopoly-price argument based on assertions by Fisher and Warren-Boulton:

> But if Microsoft were a monopolist with the power to control price, you don't need a Ph D. in economics to figure out that Microsoft would always charge the

short-run profit maximizing price because it would have no fears of competitors coming in with lower prices and bidding away the business.

To the extent that he recognizes a Microsoft defense, Judge Jackson (cfof par. 65, 33-4) adopts a limit-price interpretation (see Chapter 10). Since it defends Jackson's decisions, the brief for the appeal to the Circuit Court (2001, 61) also reverts to Fisher's original theory.

The Economics of Profit Maximization in the Case

As Chapter 3 showed, long-established economic theory shows that, at the profit-maximizing price for a monopolist, the elasticity of demand is one or greater (in absolute terms).

This result occupied a key role in the case. Schmalensee's calculations on whether Microsoft maximized short-run profits and of Fisher's effort at refutation both explicitly rely on this result. In contrast, Warren-Boulton (par. 37, 17) presented a numerical example that implied that the demand for Windows is inelastic (less than one) to prove Microsoft is a monopolist. Schmalensee (par. 200, 99) noted this misstep and the inconsistency with oral testimony that profits were maximized. McKenzie (2000b, 30-31) also caught the slip. The gfof (par. 49.3.2.11, 99) presents a quotation of Fisher that omits his explanations. Without checking the original (January 1, 1999, p.m., 16-17), a reader would incorrectly presume that Fisher had repeated Warren-Boulton's error.

Despite the criticism, the gfof (par. 19.3.2, 90) reiterates the argument citing first Fisher (June 1, 1999 a.m., 27) and then Warren-Boulton (par. 37, 17). Judge Jackson (cfof par. 19, 7) describes the impact of an operating-system price increase as "trivial."

Schmalensee and Fisher on Pricing Windows

Fisher argues that Windows prices rose over time, a point endorsed by the government. He stated:

> I have looked at what's happened to Microsoft's operating system price over time, and it isn't falling, and I don't believe it's falling even on a quality corrected basis. And for that matter, it isn't even constant. It's rising. And Microsoft appears to have set its price without regard, not for competition. Now, I don't mean–perhaps I should say that Microsoft has no constraints on it. That's not true (January 11, 1999, p.m., 42, cited gfof, par. 38.1.1(i), 63). (The remainder of the answer seems awkwardly to indicate that an optimal price exists for any monopolist and that Microsoft has monopoly power.)

Even on cross-examination in the rebuttal phase after viewing Schmalensee's direct testimony, Fisher reaffirms his belief but indicates that he cannot quantify the revenue impacts (June 3, 1999, a.m., 14-17). The question then arises about whether, if the rise occurred, it provided for recovery of the cost of developing Explorer. A more basic concern is that economics indicates that it is changes in demand-cost relationships, not market structures, that produce price changes.

Schmalensee, in contrast, presents (Appendix B, summarized paras. 162-4, 80-81) an effort to estimate the profit-maximizing price for Windows. A separate paper by three economists from National Economic Research Associates (NERA) developed the work for the case (Reddy, Evans, and Nichols 1999). (On January 20, 1999, p.m., 35-45, Schmalensee restates the argument under cross-examination. His redirect testimony, January 21, 1999, a.m., 9-25 returns to the argument. June 23, 1999, a.m., 5-23 presents reactions to Fisher's criticisms.)

The start of the estimate is the classic rule of economics that, in equilibrium, Abba Lerner's monopoly ratio (of the gap between price and marginal cost to price) equals the reciprocal of (the absolute value of) the elasticity of demand (see Chapter 4). By accounting for the inclusion of Windows in a computer, rearranging and plugging in assumptions about the components of the formula, the optimum price can be calculated.

Reddy, Evans and Nichols examine how with a zero marginal cost for operating systems the relation changes and can be solved for the optimum price for computer operating systems. The following shows the derivation with tacit steps added and the price of computers net of operating systems shown as a variable instead of the estimated actual number fitted into the equation. The differences from the prior notations relate to the distinction between the price of the computer and of the operating system. The subscript o is used to denote variables relating to operating systems; a c subscript applies to computers; n, to computers net of operating systems. The results are:

$$E_o \equiv P_o/Q * dQ/dP_o; E_c \equiv P_c/Q * dQ/dP_o$$

$$\frac{P_o}{P_o} = \frac{1}{E_o} \equiv \frac{1}{P_o/Q * dQ/dP_o}$$

$$= \frac{1}{P_c/P_c * P_o/Q * dQ/dP_o} = \frac{1}{P_o/P_c * [P_c/Q * dQ/dP_o]}$$

$$= \frac{1}{P_o/P_c * E_c} = \frac{P_c}{P_o E_c} = \frac{(P_o + P_n)}{P_o E_c};$$

$$\frac{P_o}{P_o} = 1 = \frac{(P_o + P_n)}{P_o E_c}$$

$$P_o E_c = (P_o + P_n); P_o E_c - P_o = P_n; P_o (E_c - 1) = P_n$$

$$P_o = P_n/(E_c - 1)$$

As a concession to possible objections such as Fisher made, Reddy, Evans, and Nichols modify the analysis for additional revenue R from other products. They consider in theory and practice how the profit-maximizing price would decline if Windows sales were presumed also to generate sales of other products (presumably mostly Microsoft Office and upgrades of Windows).

The additional-income argument comes dangerously close to accepting theories that monopoly power in one realm can be leveraged to create a monopoly in another. It concentrates on the wrong benefits of increased Windows sales. The model has Microsoft earning monopoly profits from realms in which it has greater existing competition than in operating systems. At least two Windows office suites other than Microsoft Office exist. In any case, whatever the problems with the modification, it was sufficiently conciliatory to defuse substantial criticism.

The impact of complementary revenues on the optimal price was much smaller than that of either elasticity or computer price. The lower importance lies in the low level of auxiliary revenues compared to computer prices. The derivation involves adding ancillary income R to the formula.

The impact of complementary revenues on the optimal price was much smaller than that of either elasticity or computer price. The lower importance lies in the low level of auxiliary revenues compared to computer prices. The derivation involves adding ancillary income R to the formula.

$$\frac{P_o + R}{P_o} = 1/E_o = \frac{1}{P_o/P_c * E_c} = \frac{P_c}{P_o E_c} = \frac{(P_o + P_n)}{P_o E_c};$$

$$\frac{P_o + R}{P_o} = \frac{(P_o + P_n)}{P_o E_c}; P_o E_c \left(\frac{P_o + R}{P_o}\right) = P_o + P_n;$$

$$E_c (P_o + R) = P_o + P_n; P_o E_c + R E_c = (P_o + P_n);$$

$$P_o E_c - P_o = P_n - RE_c; P_o(E_c - 1) = P_n - RE_c;$$

$$P_o = \frac{P_n - RE_c}{(E_c - 1)}$$

The actual price and other important derived numbers, as noted, were redacted to incomprehensibility in the public version of Schmalensee's direct testimony. The NERA study, however, starts with a $50 price, and nothing is hidden.

The base case used was a zero marginal cost of Windows, an elasticity of two, and a $1,950 computer price. The price assumptions come from data in the case. Since studies of computer demand price elasticity are unavailable, NERA and Schmalensee base the choice on values typically arising in studies of other industries. The elasticity assumption implies that Windows should sell for the same price as the computer. As noted, that was set at $1,950. This contrasts to a price of about $50-$65 actually charged.

What is key is that higher computer prices raise, and higher elasticities and additional sales lower the profit-maximizing price of Windows. An optimal price closer to that actually charged depends on prevalence of higher elasticities and auxiliaries and lower computer prices.

Fisher explores this (June 1, 1999, p.m., 6-18 with amplifications on redirect June 4, 1999, a.m., 6-15). He observes that computer prices are falling sharply and that a $1,000 price is now more appropriate. This change does not deal with pricing in past years and, by itself, still leaves the profit-maximizing price well above the actual.

Fisher thus goes on to challenge Schmalensee's elasticity assumptions. Fisher proposes looking at a demand elasticity at the upper limit Schmalensee thought might possibly be considered. An elasticity at the limit of 5 produces a profit-maximizing price of $187.50

Thus, Fisher must also raise the auxiliary revenues from NERA's $125. $160 in supplemental revenue yields a $50 price. The result is arithmetic. The validity remains unproven.

The one problem ignored is that elasticities are constant only with logarithmic demand curves. For example, the linear demand curves drawn in textbooks have a constant slope so the elasticity level varies with the p/q ratio. Since q falls as p rises, the ratio and elasticity rises as price rises. Too many assumptions must be made to deduce the linear demand curves consistent with the different models of operating system competition.

In any case, Fisher's work is both inconsistent with the limit-price with monopoly profits explanation and a treacherous argument. It may be (and seems) wrong. If it is right, it undermines the case. The Windows on which profits are maximized presumably includes Explorer. However, a predatory price is not short-term profit maximizing.

In many of its statements (e.g., mfof par. 83, 34), Microsoft seized upon a Fisher statement about coming within a few hundred dollars of the actual price as admission of failure. The higher figure, of course, results from rejecting one of the assumption changes made by Fisher.

Fisher both in earlier oral testimony (January 12, 1999, p.m., 13-18) and in his piece with Rubinfeld (2000b, 13) uses the implausibility of high elasticity at the actual Windows price as support for his restrained profit-maximization argument. Critics such as Hall and Hall (1999) have noted the limitations of this, namely the concession to Schmalensee implied.

The Remedy Phase: Another Theory of Monopoly

As noted, in the remedy phase, the government shifted from emphasis on the quantity of applications to the importance of critical applications as Schmalensee and Microsoft had argued. (Recall from the above that similar arguments slipped into the gfof.) In the relief phase, the government enlisted new experts and reused Felten. These blindly accepted the charges against Microsoft while jettisoning the applications barrier to entry that was the core of the violation case. The proposed remedy was to split Microsoft into an applications company and an operating system company. The remedy proposals are predicated on accepting the view that a few core programs are what matter.

In the statements supporting breaking up Microsoft, a major claimed advantage is the allegedly greater incentive of an independent applications company to develop versions of Microsoft Office for other operating systems, especially Linux (Shapiro 2000 and Henderson 2000). The government's arguments supporting its break up proposal endorse this conclusion (Plaintiffs' Memorandum in Support of Proposed Final Judgment, April 28, 2000, 28). The availability of Office will stimulate the use of the operating systems.

This clearly denies the assertions in the case that providing the most critical applications is not a sufficient stimulus. In line with the opportunism that was endemic in the government case, no attention was given to the tacit renunciation of the applications-barrier-to-entry argument. In his Findings of Fact and Conclusions of Law, Judge Jackson swallowed completely the government's claim that what mattered was that a large number of applications existed.

Logic and the history of Microsoft suggest, moreover, that a breakup of Microsoft is not needed to ensure that, if the economics are favorable, a Linux Office would emerge. Word and Excel, the main components of

Office, were originally designed for the Macintosh operating system and, despite some maneuvering discussed in the case, are still maintained for the Mac. As Chapter 10 notes, many observers including some sympathetic to the government's case feel that divestiture is an excessive reaction of dubious value.

This alternative theory is only part of the remedy. Proposals also were made and accepted to micromanage Microsoft's behavior. Their review is inessential here.

Conclusions

Traversal through the arguments leaves unsatisfied Fisher's requirement that monopoly power must be distinguished from market power. The government, as stated, successfully won by asserting the charge of monopoly was not refuted. However, the need was proof, and that provided was clearly suspect and probably fatally flawed.

Another neglect in all the discussions is the Baumol, Panzer, and Willig (1982) concept of contestable markets, an effort more precisely to delineate whether firms must behave competitively given the prospects of entry. Particularly given the mass of strong participants whose existence Schmalensee underplayed, his vision of constrained competition constitutes a formidable challenge to which the government never responded. The best that the government could do was to assert that every element in his refutation was overstated. These claims were often unsatisfactory and do not coalesce into a coherent complete reply.

Schmalensee set a standard that highlights the basic dilemma of antitrust, distinguishing inefficient behavior from vigorous competition. Schmalensee's stress is upon the dangers of damning simple vigorous competition. Fisher, in effect, responds that Schmalensee's approach is too lenient towards monopoly. These are the implications of their respective views of the case.

The relevant issue is which argument is sounder public-policy advice. The need is to establish theoretic and practical guidelines to identify the alleged inefficiencies. The government did not even pretend to provide coherent criteria of appraisal. Instead, the government often asserts that actions are consistent with the existence of monopoly. That these practices are also consistent with competition is ignored. Unfortunately, this fallacy was perpetuated in the court decisions. Much of the government's response is clearly misleading.

As many have argued, Schmalensee's model is far more plausible than the government's. Schmalensee's argument has compelling elements. First is that it is hard to believe $50-$65 is a monopoly price.

Second, the vision in the Kempin memorandum of a consortium of the OEMs, Intel, AOL Time Warner, and perhaps others creating a rival to Windows if prices rose significantly seems realistic. One of the existing approaches could serve as a basis. Yet another variant of Unix might emerge. The material in the case indicates that already many Unix-based systems exist. Linux is one. Subsequently, Apple adopted Unix for OS X, a radical revision of the Macintosh operating system.

Third, Gates has good reason generally to fear rivals. The pioneers in many critical software realms have vanished. The Intel-compatible personal computer first overtook Apple and eliminated many lesser existing firms. The evolution allowed other OEMs to surpass IBM, the originator, as a supplier. In time, the vaunted mainframe and intermediate sized computers suffered. The same might occur for the personal computer.

Finally, a network is essentially just another type of status quo. The underlying theory ignored in the case indicates that willingness to enter can produce the investments needed to promote the rise of a promising innovation. Schmalensee's view of Netscape as an example of such stimulation makes more sense than the government's assertion that the threat was unique. The government fails to treat these drawbacks.

Chapter 8 Microsoft's Tactics: Predation, Tying, and Threats in Theory

The government's attack against Microsoft's tactics unnecessarily complicates the issues, probably again to obscure. The numerous charges all translate into assertions that Microsoft sought vigorously but inefficiently to buy customers for Internet Explorer. The vigor is undisputed. Inefficiency was unsubstantiated.

The government fails at the basic task of defining measurable criteria of guilt. This naturally precludes development of a coherent empirical argument. Instead, the government relies on a complex but unsatisfactory and unsubstantiated chain of conceptual points to condemn Microsoft. In short, the analytic base is invalid, and the supporting evidence, nonexistent.

To create an impression of anticompetitive acts, the government bloats the description of Microsoft's actions. The government argues that everything was done only to preserve Microsoft's operating-system monopoly by eliminating the Netscape/Java platform hazard and that solely by predatory acts Microsoft overwhelmed Netscape. Every action to promote Internet Explorer is described as harm to rival browsers. Such "harm" is the necessary consequence of competing successfully. A problem arises only when the displacement is inefficient. Such inefficiency was never proved.

The government contends at every possible opportunity that the threat was obvious and the response was clearly illegal. Mention of the protection or use of the operating-system monopoly occurs about 190 times (including 40 in the table of contents). The material presented proves not to support the charges against Microsoft.

Lacking evidence, the government relies only on claims by Fisher and Warren-Boulton that predation is the only plausible explanation of the behavior. The economists, in turn, base their conclusions solely on allegedly incriminating sentences from documents from Microsoft and others.

Unlike the material generated in the case, the exposition here separates treatment of concepts from review of implementation. This chapter treats theory; practice is in Chapter 9. The division was undertaken to handle a basic dilemma about the case. Full review involves extended discussion of the details. This obscures the absence of a supporting framework. To lessen the problem, the arrangement here first highlights the analytic problems and isolates the examination of details.

The government, Microsoft, and many external commentators accepted the customer-purchase interpretation. The problem was that this was muted and stress was on minutely examining the details of implementation. Customer buying is a standard business practice. Therefore, attack on Microsoft must prove that its practices went beyond a permissible response to competition.

The government's case is largely presentation of undisputed facts about what Microsoft did (see Chapter 9). The government shows that Microsoft employed many tactics to improve its competitive position *vis-à-vis* Netscape. This effort naturally was accompanied by recognition of the objective to compete and win. Extensively presenting such details of customer buying creates a bad impression. In particular, a major element of the government's case is frequent, often repetitive, citation of Microsoft memorandums exhorting better performance.

While this sufficed for the case, it is not proof. The memorandums support nothing more than the existence of competitive challenges that are clearly broader than a middleware threat and the determination to win by making a better product and vigorously marketing it.

Including a browser as a component of Windows without a price increase and vigorously seeking to improve and promote that browser are not conventional predatory acts. As the government tries to ignore despite the reminders from Microsoft, such actions are usually viewed as beneficial. More critically, creating Internet Explorer is an act that is radically different from predation by selling below cost. Apparently, some alternative theory was employed; proof was limited to mention of raising rivals' cost. This mention lacked even definition of the concept, let alone an effort to demonstrate its applicability.

One possible view is the undesirability of any Microsoft advantage. The government seems to argue any reaction is illegitimate and dismisses the possibility of increased profits by providing Internet Explorer. Given its alleged monopoly in operating systems, Microsoft should not be allowed to be that aggressive. This seems the implicit basis of the government's case.

Microsoft counters these were the strivings of a vigorously competitive firm to compete fairly. It was responding to a broader challenge that antedated Netscape, competing fairly, and leaving Netscape a viable competitor. Its victory was won by making Internet Explorer superior to Netscape Navigator. The government counters that the improvements were merely facilitators of the predatory actions.

Netscape's strong initial position implies the desirability of extensive efforts to buy into the market. The Microsoft defense is that, as an entrant into browsers Microsoft needed extra steps to overcome an incumbent. Thus, mfof defends Microsoft's practices as promoting Internet Explorer "when Netscape held a commanding position" (par. 1508, 674). (See also par. 384, 173; paras. 766-7, 352-3.) This is an issue not readily unraveled.

The arguments are complex, and their identification and evaluation, therefore, is difficult. Each issue has several parts. The central role of existence of an operating-system monopoly, the confirmation of this importance by Fisher, and the deficiencies of the proof are treated in Chapter 7. Monopoly does not ensure that inefficient tactics would succeed. Attention here turns to the tactics case. Throughout, the allegation of an operating-system monopoly is ignored but only to avoid repetition.

Discussion begins with note of the contribution of the expert economists. Two overriding issues are examined–the competitive pressures faced by Microsoft and its reaction to them. The questions are not neatly separable, but here the pressures are surveyed before giving an overview of the reaction. Then the prospects for browser monopoly are examined with stress on Fisher's analysis.

Given the government's shift towards a customer-buying interpretation, the importance of that concept to the case is discussed next. In particular, the case record indicates that inefficient buying is impossible to appraise. The ensuing section shows that the government also adopted an invalid market-share measure of eliminating the middleware-platform threat.

Examination is made of the conceptual aspects of the charge that the creation, integration, and pricing of Internet Explorer were inherently predatory. The next sections examine the conceptual aspects of the predation charge against Microsoft. Fisher's approach to predation and its success, its use by the government, and their criticism by Schmalensee and Evans and by the Microsoft attorneys are explored.

The final area considered is the addition of other charges–Intel, Apple, IBM, Sun, and RealNetworks. In each case, some aspect of the Netscape/Java issue arose; only the Sun portion does not involve direct concern over Netscape. In every case, separate issues also arose. These include charges of suppressing software rivalry from Apple, Intel, RealNetworks, and IBM and sabotaging the multiplatform characteristics of Java.

Exposition ends with a summary and conclusions.

The Expert Economists Problem (Again)

Again, the contributions of Fisher and Schmalensee are critical. They made comments on the basic economic issues associated with the case. They make very different points. Once again, Fisher is particularly problematic. As noted in Chapter 6, his basic framework of introduction, theory, and application to the case fragment his discussions. He sometimes separates and sometimes mixes together treatments of the issues. Even when pulled together, the treatments are unsatisfactory. Fisher states the advantages of extending a monopoly, claims that an existing monopoly can promote such an extension, and argues for an opportunity-cost measure of predation. The sacrifice of browser income rather than the cost of producing Explorer would be the measure.

The only further point about his organization that is needed here is that his treatment of browsers in his evaluation of the case starts and ends with points about the underlying issues. In between, he reviews dealings with different types of firms. The last do not differ sufficiently from gfof to merit consideration here.

Fisher (see below), moreover, introduces an undesirable extension of the fixation on documents. He bases arguments on the absence of documents. This is a determination no one can make. Beyond the basic problems with reliance on documents, it is impossible to prove nonexistence. Something might have been overlooked. It presumes that either the plaintiff or the defense attained perfection in locating relevant documents and that the plaintiffs' attorneys faultlessly selected material for Fisher to view. The argument, moreover, seems to shift the burden of proof to the defendant. It is the plaintiffs' charges that need the substantiation. This is only one element of a willingness to extend his opinions far beyond the realm of economic expertise (see Chapter 9).

More critically, Schmalensee again sticks closer to the substance than does the government. He provides extensive evidence to support clear theoretic arguments. In this case, he indicates the problems of creating a monopoly in browsers and disputes the opportunity-cost approach. The main problem is that the evidence tends to overwhelm the arguments. His theoretic points actually are better documented than in his treatment of the operating-system monopoly and largely cover the essential points.

Why Internet Explorer: Microsoft's Objectives and Their Attainment

A critical issue is the distinction between concern with all the competitive threats resulting from Netscape Navigator's strong position and concentration only on the middleware-platform threat. As often indicated, the government case centers on the contention that Internet Explorer was created only to end the Netscape/Java platform threat to Windows. The treatment of the issue is unsatisfactory. The narrowing of the challenge is a leap unjustified by the underlying economics of the case.

Accord exists only that Microsoft was concerned about the rise of this challenge but that implementation did not materialize. Microsoft chose to accept the contention that it was worried about middleware competition. The primacy of the threat is disputed.

The limitation of hazards has the convenient feature of closing a major hole in the case. The usual vision of harm is ruining a rival. That clearly did not occur. Stress on platforms implies destruction of Netscape is unnecessary. Microsoft wins simply by reducing Netscape's role sufficiently to eliminate the platform peril. Unlike eradication, the end of the danger is not readily measurable. The constriction allows the government to claim it was irrelevant that Netscape was thriving. Mere assertion suffices. It recalls the gangster in "Guys and Dolls" who forced people at gunpoint to use his dice without indentations. Others threw, and he told the outcome.

The failure to eliminate Netscape also weakens any charge of browser monopoly. Inefficiently protecting an operating-system monopoly creates another form of potential Sherman-Act violation. Monopolizing of operating systems was the only charge that was upheld through trial, appeal, and post-appeal negotiations.

Memorandums indicating the browser war was ended were introduced as proof. This is opinion, and, more critically, its use presumes that those quoted used the same concept of victory as the government employed. To make matters worse, the government at times denies that the threat was realistic. If this is so, Microsoft was victorious without any effort and is being prosecuted for wasting money fighting a phantom.

Barksdale's cross-examination produced another favorite quote. Asked about whether Marc Andreessen really had bragged he would reduce Windows "to a set of poorly debugged device drivers," Barksdale replied that the statement is and was a joke. He added that Andreessen was young and often made statements "that has gotten us in trouble." He ends by saying that Netscape only hoped partially to assume Windows' platform characteristics (Barksdale, October 20, 1988, p.m., 72-3).

The treatment again is government assertion, Schmalensee response, and government counterargument. Chapter 7 indicated the contention in Schmalensee's direct testimony of multiple competitive threats to Windows and his subsequent arguments that the government's justifications for taking the platform threat seriously implied entry barriers were not high. Microsoft's attorneys agreed (mfof 147-55, paras. 199-235).

The government theory about why Internet Explorer was introduced can be attacked in at least two ways. The argument may be wrong. Microsoft might have had other reasons for pushing Explorer. Many are possible and are suggested in the case material and comments. Microsoft saw a competitive threat from the Internet. Microsoft saw creation of Internet Explorer as the best way to meet the challenge. Microsoft worked strenuously and simultaneously to improve Explorer and to promote its use. Alternatively, the threat might be real, but Microsoft responded properly.

Admittedly, Andreessen's claim proved an irresistible target. Exhortations to defeat the threat abound in Microsoft documents. However, the evidence suggests the statements were largely empty posturing.

Reynolds (2001, 4, 47-51, 67-8) considers the Netscape platform threat totally implausible. He bases this on judgment that accomplishment is difficult and, in any case, would create applications that run on any browser. Conversely, a good operating system must still be available (28). He treats the Netscape "choke hold" as a barrier to Microsoft's ambitions in Internet content, services, and server-software (4).

A broader chokehold argument is possible. As several commentators suggest, Netscape Navigator potentially was a textbook downstream monopolist whose elimination, contrary to Fisher (see below), was efficient. The classic reason of eliminating monopolistic pricing would apply. Reynolds, in fact, also raises this point in his arguments that Microsoft's free-browser policy was efficient.

Other possible concerns are the prospects for wide moves to Internet access using devices other than personal computers employing operating systems other than Windows. In short, a broader version emerges from Reynolds, the Internet itself, not Netscape, is the threat; Economides (2001c, 25) makes this point. Once again, a supporting exhibit exists. Ron Whittier of Intel quotes Maritz "Internet is a platform ... " (GX 279).

Schmalensee's arguments about entry threats in both browsers and operating systems are applicable to discussions of a Netscape monopoly. The crux is that the Netscape monopoly was one ripe for elimination by entry. The other key presumption is that Microsoft seems an appropriate entrant. However, the government's view that browsers can be monopolized implies concern over irresistible monopoly. The government ignores that preferring a Netscape downstream monopoly is inefficient. In short, entry may have everything to do with the competitive threat to Windows of the Internet and nothing to do with Andreessen's platform reveries.

McKenzie (2000b, 224) argues that Sun was the true threat. He adds that Netscape was "a stalking horse" for server manufacturers in their battle with Microsoft. As he notes elsewhere (132), this involved provision of Windows NT for servers. (Also see Muglia's 1999 testimony.) Heilemann

(2000) stresses the lead role Sun played in forging an antiMicrosoft coalition.

Finally, another explanation, apparently too simple for experts to consider, is that entry into interesting areas is standard Microsoft practice. Microsoft typically enters many activities, possibly because of just a general belief it can serve the market better. Evidence of this is strewn through the case and in Liebowitz and Margolis (1999, 135-229). Their review of Microsoft's history shows that the company has tried with variable success to provide its version of almost all the major types of software.

Starting with spreadsheets and word processing programs for the Apple Macintosh, Microsoft attained leadership in both realms on the Macintosh and with Windows. Then their combination into the Office suite of programs cemented this dominance. This is only the most successful example. Microsoft has entered into other widely used program types as databases and financial management. It offers reference books on disks and an online service to rival AOL. Hall and Hall only hint at this tendency towards entry with comments about a tendency of Microsoft to seek dominance only of certain types of software (1999, 40). This record shows that browser provision is less radical than the government tried to suggest.

Finally, the government's argument presumes implausible deftness by Microsoft. An effort as resolute as the government postulated should have produced substantial damage to and even ruin of Netscape.

Thus, three alternatives exist to the Netscape/Java platform explanation–Schmalensee's multiple-threat argument, the expanded Reynolds Internet as threat, and the Microsoft as inveterate entrant model. All deserve more consideration than the government gave them. Indeed, each seems more plausible than the Netscape/Java platform hypothesis. As noted above, it seems merely the fiction needed to convert the government's conjectures into an antitrust violation.

The Bases of Suspicion: An Overview

The government, as noted, contends that Microsoft's sole concern was the Netscape/Java platform threat. The government adds that Microsoft was aware of Netscape's financial weakness. Thus, only to undermine the Netscape/Java platform challenge, Microsoft adopted tactics to exploiting that financial weaknesses. By implicit reference to the earlier treatments of Microsoft's importance in operating systems, the response to the threat is transformed from responding to competition to preserving a monopoly. These broad charges break down into components mostly treated in Chapter 9.

This section focuses on the Microsoft documents used to support the charges of concern and awareness of Netscape's financial status. The memorandums do not confirm the government and Fisher claims of illegal behavior. Often a single provocative statement introduces pedestrian treatments of prevailing conditions and how best to respond. The suggested responses invariably are providing better products and promoting them more effectively. Most arose after the introduction of Internet Explorer.

In particular, the evidence presented does not support the claim of exclusive concern over the middleware threat. Other challenges were often mentioned in Microsoft documents. Again the only support is opinions from Fisher or Warren-Boulton based solely on examining memorandums.

The components include the cut off Netscape's air supply remark McGeady attributed to Maritz, writings by and interviews with Gates, and pronouncements by other Microsoft executives.

Gates's May 1995 piece "The Internet Tidal Wave" (GX 20) is a statement of the challenge. Gates starts by stressing the profound effects that he expects from the Internet. He turns to the competition. These are, in order of discussion, Novell, Lotus, Sun, Adobe, Apple, Netscape, and the emergence of an Internet access device cheaper than a computer. His description of Netscape notes a 75 percent usage share and that its platform ambitions would "commoditize the underlying operating system" (cited gfof par. 54, 113). He concludes outlining a response strategy centered on producing "the best Internet server as an integrated package." This recognition of broader threats also appears in other cited Microsoft documents.

To suggest that fear of the platform competition, nevertheless, was the only inspiration of the free-browser decision, the government quotes interviews with Gates (only one of which was posted) after the introduction of Internet Explorer noting the resulting unfavorable impact on Netscape's revenue (paras. 298.4-298.5, 521-3). The available material from October 1995 (accurately quoted gfof par. 298.4, 521) only observes that Netscape's stock-market value reflects difficult-to-meet expectations. Those not posted mentioned the alleged harm to Netscape's business plan from free browsers. Gates insists that he was doing no more than factually answering a question. Below it is argued that not harming Netscape, but market pressure, is the most plausible explanation of free browsers.

To reinforce, Fisher and the government cite a memorandum from November 1996 (more than a year after the introduction of a free Internet Explorer) in which Netscape's business situation is discussed (GX 100); it proves description. Other memorandums are mentioned to show that the desire to compete inspired aggressive efforts to secure acceptance (par. 299.3, 524-5). Many do or die messages, particularly Chase's April 1996

"Winning the Internet platform battle," are cited (GX 39, GX 465, GX 510, GX 512).[1]

Chase advocates wide adoption of Internet Explorer and various ways to attain it. Chase's description of Internet Explorer as "a no revenue product" is seized upon as the epitome of predatory intent. The two clarifying sentences talk of otherwise "we will loose (sic) the Internet platform battle" and "leadership on the desktop." Therefore, the statements only show that Microsoft considered the challenges justified providing a free browser. The rest of the statement discusses actions to meet the goals. Much attention is devoted to securing support from many channels. These include vigorous efforts to make deals with ISPs.

Fisher uses the Gates interview material and a 1997 statement by Microsoft president Steve Ballmer (par. 125, 57, cited omitting quotations gfof 298.2, 518) as proof of predatory intent. The paragraph starts by describing GX 100 as something undertaken at Gates's personal direction to see Netscape's vulnerability, an unsubstantiated charge. Fisher dismisses the "colorful language" defense because the "language accurately describes the purpose and effect of Microsoft's conduct..." (par. 126, 57-8). Apparently, he is asserting the meaning since the quotations do not support his interpretation. (See Fisher January 7, 1999, a.m. 75-6, cited gfof par. 298, 516; Warren-Boulton direct par. 190, 83 cited in toto gfof par. 297.2, 515.)

Considerable evidence suggests that the vulnerability-to-predation interpretation of Gates is wrong. Netscape's survival did not depend on browser revenues, it had financial backing, and Gates was clearly aware of these realities (Rosen 1999, par. 30). Moreover, the material was produced too long after the introduction of Internet Explorer in August 1995 to be important efforts to influence the strategy.

Browser Monopoly: Feasibility, Windows as a Support for Internet Explorer, Internet Explorer as a Support for Windows

The vision about only thwarting a middleware platform coexists with contentions, mainly by Fisher, that Microsoft sought monopoly in the conventional sense. This section examines Fisher's approach, Schmalensee's response, and the government's reaction.

Fisher argues that Microsoft mounted a campaign to monopolize browsers, that the Windows monopoly assists the creation of this monopoly,

---

[1] GX 465 is GX 39 plus appendixes. GX 510 is an April 4, 1997 update of GX 39; GX 512 is GX 510 plus a cover indicating numerous recipients of whom Cameron Myhrvold is the only one prominent in the case.

and that the browser monopoly would protect the operating-system monopoly. The ability of a browser monopoly to protect the operating-system monopoly, its effects on Netscape, its effect on Microsoft, and the ultimate impacts on consumers are dubious. See Mfof (paras. 376-83, 170-73, esp. par. 382, 172).

A browser-monopoly charge, moreover, raises the troublesome point that the browser war is, therefore, a fight between Microsoft and Netscape for monopoly position. Fisher's direct testimony (see below) hints at a possible rationale. That rationale is not stated, let alone justified. Conversely, the existence of monopoly in operating systems or browsers is not conclusive proof of antitrust violation since a monopolist still can defend its position by efficient actions.

Three issues arise with a browser monopoly. The first is the feasibility of a browser monopoly. Second and most interesting is whether the operating-system monopoly facilitates creation of a browser monopoly. The third issue of benefit to Microsoft is trivial; success can only help.

The problematic reinforcement issue was obfuscated by Fisher and ultimately given only token support by the government. The economics and their treatment are sufficiently interesting to justify examination. Fisher's efforts to provide an analytic basis prove only to show how a new monopoly aids an old (see below).

As also discussed below, the argument is not seriously pursued. The government perfunctorily repeats the assistance charge (par. 405.6, 762-3). However, it moves towards treating access to the Windows desktop as simply a form of payment (par. 238, 433-5). Ignoring the absence of evidence, Judge Jackson held Microsoft guilty of seeking to monopolize browsers, a finding upturned on appeal (see Chapter 10).

Fisher and Schmalensee present conflicting but incomplete views. The debate is between Fisher's assertion that a browser monopoly is possible and facilitated by the Windows monopoly and Schmalensee's denial. Fisher's general principles and the applications to the case are unsatisfactory mainly because again they rely on assertion. Here the simpler argument that a browser monopoly is possible is treated first. Then the invalid assertion that the Windows monopoly promotes a browser monopoly is reviewed.

Fisher's chronic failure to cite the relevant literature again caused serious faults. As Chapter 4 shows, better arguments than Fisher presented exist in principle for asserting a monopoly in one realm can be employed under some circumstances to create a new monopolist. However, the requisite conditions are unlikely to arise. Even the creators of these theories expressed doubts about their applicability to the Microsoft case. Therefore, substantiation of the claim that the operating-system monopoly facilitates a browser monopoly requires assurance that the special conditions prevail. Schmalensee showed more familiarity with the literature than Fisher and recognized problems that Fisher tried to obscure.

Feasibility analysis for browser monopoly involves no additional and perhaps one fewer conceptual issues than operating-system monopoly. Since browsers are a new development, an applications barrier to entry is likely to be smaller. Appraisal requires applying the proper analytic principles to the economic peculiarities of browsers.

The assertion that a browser monopoly is possible introduces the browser portion of Fisher's applications section. The argument is completed in his conclusions. In between is material on Microsoft's actions to promote Internet Explorer and then brief review of data on a rising market share. This is his indirect evidence of success.

His treatment starts by asserting without elaboration, "It is probable that in the absence of intervention, Microsoft will obtain monopoly power in the market for Internet browsers" (par. 79, 31). He next reiterates that browsers are a separate product in the sense of being separately priced (par. 80, 31). He presents three questionable justifications (par. 80, 31-4). His first is that substantial separate demand exists. His proof is a long quotation of Cameron Myhrvold about the role of ISPs as distributors (par. 80a, 31-2). This ignores the case-undermining points that ISPs do not charge and heavily utilize distribution channels such as mailings that the government contends are ineffective.

Fisher follows with quotations about the desire for choice (par. 80b, 33) and even browserless systems (par. 80c, 34). This methodology fails to show whether providing Internet Explorer really restricts choice or whether the demand for browserless operating systems is large enough to justify deleting browsers.

His third point is "Barriers to entry (including network effects and the results of Microsoft's conduct)" preclude competition. In particular, the bundled browser "effectively prevents companies from successfully entering the browser market unless they successfully enter the operating system market at the same time" (par. 81, 34, a similar statement appears par. 22, 8).

These claims involve several suspect tacit assumptions. First is whether inclusion inefficiently removed the ability to sell browsers. Fisher's arguments depend on his assertions that the optimum provision of browsers is as separate products that are sold. If the correct model is of free browsers and remuneration from server software and Web sites, Fisher's presumptions are invalid (see below). Consequently, loss of browser revenue does not require, as he suggests, replacement by operating-system income.

A second issue is whether the mere presence of Internet Explorer is a substantial disincentive to adopting another browser. This is based on a vision of stupid, ignorant, lazy consumers that permeates the government's case. A third is whether the provision, integration, and perhaps other Microsoft actions also impede use of other browsers. The continued usability of Netscape Navigator in Windows belies this (see Chapter 9).

Fisher's treatments of the tie between the operating-system monopoly and a browser monopoly are invalid. His summary contains tautological assertions that an existing monopoly can create a new one. His first truism is that if enough of the new product is tied, a dominant role is attained (par. 9, 3-4). After recognizing the objections to leveraging arguments, he adds another tautology that the critiques are incorrect when the tying "maintains an existing monopoly or secures a new monopoly" (par. 11, 4).

He states that if Microsoft's monopoly power in operating systems is used to create a monopoly, serious consumer harm will result through monopoly pricing of Internet services (par. 15, 6). This indicates the consequences of his assertions. However, it is inconsistent with his frequent claims that Microsoft did not expect significant income from the Internet. Plausibility and evidence are dubious. The government, nevertheless, dutifully includes the argument (gfof par. 405.6, 762-3, see below).

Fisher gives a first list of inappropriate actions, namely those emphasized in the case, taken to promote the browser monopoly (par. 19, 7). He asserts without elaboration that the operating-system monopoly system is being used (par. 21, 8). This is followed by another discussion of Microsoft's tactics (par. 22, 8-9). Some involve Windows such as the tying and the requirement of icon display so that this is tacitly supporting material.

In his theory section, he further discusses leveraging. He begins by again asserting that monopoly can be leveraged and promising to show why this is undesirable (par. 55, 19). He changed the subject from the controversial question of possibility of leverage to the less disputed one of resulting harm. He supports by illustrations.

The first is what he correctly describes as a classic example in leverage analysis. It is a monopolist securing a monopoly in a product that uses the monopolist's product as an input in a fixed proportion. This increases the profits by allowing price discrimination (par. 56, 20). He ignores the problems of determining whether or not discrimination lowers welfare.

The second is another classic case of the profit gain from entry into the consuming industry when the input product is used in variable proportions (par. 57, 20). He ignores the equally classic point that an efficiency gain is involved. The third relates to profits in markets in which the acquired product is an input (par. 58, 21). Since he does not expand, it is unclear whether he is merely describing one form of benefit or suggesting entry into further areas.

The fourth is entry into another product that prevents competition in the monopolist's market (par. 59, 21). The threat feared by the monopolist is that independent availability of the other product facilitates entry into the monopolized business. Fisher suggests (par. 60, 21) that this example is directly applicable to the case. He ends again stating that extending monopoly is bad (par. 61, 21-2). All his cases treat the advantage of independently establishing new monopolies that assist the old.

In his concluding comments, he indicates why he believes leveraging will be effective. A statement about the operating-system monopoly promoting a browser monopoly (par. 238, 108) is followed by a few sentences on the status of Microsoft's effort. He then lists forces that raise barriers to entry if the monopoly arises (par. 239, 108). The alleged limits on distribution by OEMs and ISPs derive from the ownership of the desktop. That ownership, if it exists, exists now. However, he adds the claim that dominance is self-perpetuating. This is inconsistent with the displacement of Netscape Navigator.

He then notes the browser will preserve the network-effect grounded operating-system monopoly because the entrant must secure a browser (par. 240, 109). He ignores that at worst the entrant could adopt Netscape Navigator. Implicit in these arguments is a response to those who argue the government is choosing (badly) between monopolists. He is tacitly asserting that a Windows with an Internet-Explorer monopoly is more formidable than a Netscape browser monopoly. Since he has not proved the feasibility of any browser monopoly, which would be worse is fruitless conjecture.

The government adds "the browser market was not mature, and penetration of the market was low, when Microsoft entered" (par. 389.4, 732). (The basis is unclear; the supporting quotation is an unrelated statement by Fisher.)

The government's overall approach, however, suggests belief that the preferable argument was that browser monopoly was possible. The government emphasizes the desire to preserve the operating-system monopoly to hide its inability to prove that the operating-system monopoly facilitates a browser monopoly. However, this had little effect on the case. Leveraging was never seriously examined despite Judge Jackson's finding that illegal tying occurred.

Schmalensee presents Internet Explorer as an efficient means to increase the attractiveness of Windows. While most of this is best treated in the section on the creation of Internet Explorer, the observations on leverage need mention here. They appear in his section (VI) asserting defects in the arguments of Fisher and Warren-Boulton. This deals with several areas. The relevant element here is the criticism in the closing section of arguments central to the browser-monopoly debate. Schmalensee again concentrates on the issue in the case of the implausibility of a browser monopoly and ignores the broad theoretic drawbacks in the government's appraisal.

Schmalensee (paras. 332-4, 166-7) criticizes Fisher and Warren-Boulton for failing to provide evidence of consumer harm, the success of exclusion, and how recoupment would occur. He then claims three faults in the Fisher and Warren-Boulton analysis. The first is that they did not demonstrate that the challenged actions prevented distribution of Netscape Navigator (paras. 336-7, 168-9). He adds that the government economists have a tacit, unsubstantiated theory that a Windows monopoly automatically produces a monopoly over software (implicitly including browser) distribution (par. 337, 168-9). This reiterates his introductory statement that, in the analysis of Microsoft tactics, the claim of an operating-system monopoly was a "red herring" because, not only do other options exist, but access to the desktop could be and was bought from the OEMs (par. 2, 1-2).

The second defect that Schmalensee considers is the treatment of Netscape as a threat outside the market. He notes the inconsistency between taking the Netscape/Java threat seriously and asserting an applications barrier to entry and a market limited to Intel-compatible personal computers (paras. 338-9, 169). Third, he reiterates that the government lauded adding features to Netscape Navigator, but not to Windows. Therefore, the attack on including and integrating Internet Explorer into Windows damns Microsoft for behavior for which the government praised Netscape (par. 340, 170).

He has a footnote (par. 522, 269) citing Bork (1978) that claims of harm from tying are "controversial among economists." Schmalensee's clearest treatment of tie-in sale theory, however, was during his first cross-examination (January 19, 1999, a.m., 29-32). After reminding Boies that tie-in is a legal term, Schmalensee points out that the theory discusses aiding both entry and price discrimination. He clearly states twice (30-31) that discrimination may not be undesirable. His statement on entry says that tying can work under some circumstances if economies of scale prevail.

In his discussion of why access to the Windows desktop is not a barrier to entry, he noted that the foreclosure assertion is akin to the essential-facilities concept in traditional antitrust. He asserts that the Windows desktop does not meet the legal definition of an essential facility–being vital to the potential user and unavailable in any other way (paras. 367-71, 186-8). (The definition comes from a standard textbook on antitrust.)

The government responded to Schmalensee by obfuscation of the distinction between preservation and extension. Chapter 7 reviewed both the government effort to distort Schmalensee's views on entry into operating systems and Evans and Schmalensee's suggestion that shifting emphasis from operating systems to platforms weakened the government claims. Consideration of platforms better explained the addition of Internet Explorer to Windows and made clear that the proper analysis was of the profitability of Windows (2000, 63-4). While they are right about the proper way to view Internet Explorer and profitability, concentration on platforms is not clearly the best way to proceed.

As discussed in Chapter 7, the government initially tries to dismiss the argument by asserting "Dean Schmalensee's contention that entry into the microcomputer software industry is easy is a red herring" (heading for gfof par. 43, 85). However, the government's assertion was designed to argue that ease of entry into software did not apply to operating systems. As also reviewed in Chapter 7, Schmalensee dealt with the peculiarities of operating systems. What is of interest here is that in treating the application to browsers, the government effectively capitulated.

The critical comment in the section asserting the irrelevance of Schmalensee comments about a monopoly of software distributions is

> Whether Microsoft had monopoly power over software distribution has nothing to do with whether the exclusionary restrictions in the ISP and OLS agreements were anticompetitive. They were anticompetitive because they served no legitimate purpose and erected barriers to successful distribution of browsers by Microsoft's rivals [because Fisher (June 1, 1999, a.m., 60-2) and Warren-Boulton (paras. 182-3, 80-1) said they did] (par. 238.1, 433).

Later it is stated "Microsoft needed, not monopoly power over OLSs and ISPs, but only the ability to pay valuable consideration" (par. 238.2, 434). This is the stunning concession of a customer-buying interpretation.

Competition as a Bidding War

As suggested, the government's treatment is one of many that recognizes that the charges reduce to claims of inefficient customer buying. Schmalensee's red-herring comment (par. 3, 1-2) includes, as noted, observation that access to the desktop can be purchased. He later (par. 396, 203) describes Microsoft's deals with OLSs, ISPs, ICPs, and independent software vendors (ISVs) as providing compensation more valuable than Netscape was willing to provide. He adds that Netscape had the assets to make such an offer.

Fisher makes tacit acknowledgements. In treating deals with ICPs, he refers to valuable concessions (par. 182, 87). Fisher's model of monopoly-protecting limit pricing similarly includes compensating OEMs for accepting inconvenient terms. As not noted, bargaining to alter the arrangements could be undertaken. Fisher also explicitly noted that Netscape could outbid Microsoft (June 1, 1999, p.m., 57, cited gfof par. 380.1, 699). This also undermines his effort to suggest one monopoly can be used to leverage the creation of another.

In contrast, Schmalensee's distinction between monopoly of the operating system and control of software distribution implies the need even for Microsoft to pay for rights on the desktop.

Several commentators on the case have made similar arguments. Liebowitz and Margolis (1999, 260-2) properly evoke the Coase theorem (1960, 1988) or more precisely the part of Coase's analysis dealing with efficient bargaining to argue that the OEM aspect of the case is simply a battle over the property rights to the desktop. Coase's enormously influential article indicates that where such bargaining is possible, efficiency will result regardless of the initial assignment of rights. The rights go to the party to which control is more valuable. Fisher's analysis has the further implication of suggesting that Liebowitz and Margolis are correct in presuming that efficient bargaining is possible. Klein (2001, 58) makes the property-rights argument without reference to Coase. McKenzie (2000b, 106) calls the Microsoft deal with AOL customer buying.

This interpretation deprives the case of the hint, however badly developed, that the operating-system monopoly creates differences with other predatory-pricing cases. The uses of resources consisted of integration of Explorer, requiring display of the Internet-Explorer icon at installation, and including in Windows easier access to specific service and content providers. These uses have a value, and with enough of a payment Netscape could have overcome them if it had the superior product.

If the standard economic assumption of rational behavior by Netscape is added, the government's case vanishes. A rational Netscape would have incentive to outbid Microsoft if the prospects for a Netscape/Java platform were as great as undertaking the case implies.

The usual objections to a presumption of rationality have less than their usual (nearly nonexistent) validity. Netscape already had substantial financial backing, and, as its eventual purchase by AOL illustrates, large firms with concerns about computer software were willing and able to finance promising new technologies. Similarly, naiveté fails as an explanation. Founder Jim Clark and Jim Barksdale who took over had long business experience; a leading venture capitalist backed and advised Netscape. Moreover, the companies that might have financed Netscape could communicate with Netscape on its prospects. Indeed, the evidence in the case suggests that such communication arose.

These influences and the financial backing they provide also make a deep-pockets explanation implausible. The main defect of a deep-pockets argument is the underlying assumption of difficulties in securing outside financing to allow survival. Netscape got as far as it did because it could attract capital. In particular, its purchase by AOL illustrates how promising ideas are financed. Resolution of the predation charges still depends on whether the acts are inefficient.

The government's review of offers of special treatment in Windows ignores this essential point. The government never gets past reporting the actions. Their efficiency is never measured. These favors are a form of price cut. The government indeed stresses that access was valuable and could have been sold instead of bartered.

Thus, the opportunity-cost concept advocated by Fisher (see below) is applicable; the worth to Microsoft of access is its market price. Opportunity costs are relevant and known to firms. Therefore, Microsoft would base its offers on its estimates of willingness to pay for access. The problem with Fisher's approach is that he goes too far by contending that an outsider observer also can determine these expectations.

Fisher tried to minimize the importance of the customer-buying approach by dismissing the behavior as "raising rivals' costs". Chapter 4 noted the work by Salop and Scheffman (1983, 1987) on raising rivals' costs, its expansion, and criticism. Their 1987 article is one of Fisher's two literature citations (par. 133, 63-4). The work, however, was a prime example of the new industrial organization of which Fisher was critical. In the case Fisher and the government often used, but never explained, the raising-rivals'-costs phrase.

In his rebuttal testimony, when questioned about raising rivals' costs, he stated it is a "well-studied and documented" economic doctrine (June 1, 1999, p.m., 62). The terminology can be taken as mere acknowledgement of existence but that interpretation is inconsistent with his use of the material. Similarly, the gfof often uses the phrase or ones similar to it.[2]

In the trial, the phrase is used to suggest without substantiation illegitimacy of Microsoft's actions. The described acts do raise rivals' costs because the Microsoft efforts raised costs by introducing competition for Netscape.

As Schmalensee responded to Boies (January 19, 1999, a.m., 52-5), this demonstrated the defects of the raising-rivals'-cost concept. One aspect of Schmalensee's defense of Microsoft is the implausibility of the conclusion that these actions ended the Netscape/Java threat to the applications barrier

---

[2] overview 6, par. 89.4, 196; 89.6, 197; par. 168, 319 (2); par. 176, 334; par. 179, 344; par. 185.2, 350; par. 241, 438; par. 241.3, 440; par. 242, 441; par. 291.1, 503; par. 361, 638; par. 364, 645 (5); par. 364.3.iii, 646; par. 366.1, 651; par. 370.1, 667 (2); par. 380, 699 (4); par. 380.3.1.2.i, 702; par. 380.3.2.iii, 704; par. 380.3.3, 704; par. 380.3.3.1, 705; par. 381.2, 711.

to entry. More critically, he pointed out the problem of distinguishing between inefficient acts and legitimate competition. This is central because the case is more a raising-rivals'-cost than a traditional predation case.

The Proper Criterion of Success

The government clearly used the wrong measure to determine Microsoft's success whatever its goal. The government asserts that a large market share for Internet Explorer sufficed to end the middleware threat. The apparent rationale is Microsoft memorandums that stress the importance of browser share (gfof par. 359.3, 631-3) and make getting a larger share than Netscape the basis of victory. This is another example of relying on shares when the level of sales is the relevant criterion.

As discussed in Chapter 4, shares are a widely-used but defective indicator of monopoly power since that involves position relative to rivals. It is the absolute size of sales that determine whether investment in a platform is justified. However, the high-browser-market *share* argument is explicitly used to deny the need for monopoly (par. 359, 630). As suggested but never quite said in mfof (par. 380, 171; par. 384, 173), preoccupation with share is more consistent with a desire to overcome the Netscape browser monopoly than with fighting the middleware challenge.

The basis is set in the direct testimonies of both government expert economists. The clearer statement comes from Warren-Boulton. He asserts that anticompetitive results can arise if the rivals had a low enough market share to discourage writing to another platform (par. 153, 68).

Developing a Netscape/Java platform and merely seeking to stay viable are among the investment opportunities open to Netscape. Payoff depends upon the relation of the amount expended compared to the amount gained. The latter depends on the absolute size of use. Netscape's payoff depends upon securing enough users to justify the expense of creating a universal platform. This is recognized in the mfof (par. 387, 174-5); this points to an inconsistency with statements (gfof par. 26.2.3.2, 38-40; par. 27, 42-8) making installed base the criterion of operating-system viability.

If the market is large enough, even a small market share may suffice to produce enough profits to justify the action. Similarly, if market growth is high enough, the amount of use can increase despite a falling share. A share by definition is the ratio of the firm's activity to that of the total universe. If the rise in industry activity is great enough, a firm with a falling share could still have increased activities. If industry activity doubled from one billion to two billion and the share went from 75 percent to 45 percent, the firm goes from 750 million to 900 million.

Schmalensee's rebuttal testimony presented the essence of this argument. In the first germane response, he cited growth of Netscape use to 50 million with 100 million expected by 2001. He notes "that's an extraordinary base from which to become a platform" (June 21, 1999, a.m. 25). Schmalensee was then asked a series of questions that imply defects in the government's presumptions. The first is whether anything in economics justifies making a "50.01" percent share the criterion of victory. He says no. He is then asked whether the government provided empirical support, and again he says no. Reinforcing questions were added. One allowed Schmalensee to deny that Fisher had provided any citations (June 21, 1999, a.m., 26-8).

It is not disputed that the growth of the Internet increased the amount of use of Navigator. Thus, the data exercise about market share discussed in Chapter 9 involved paying enormous attention to an irrelevant number.

The only theoretic way to rescue the share argument is to argue, contrary to the facts, that only one browser could be viable and, therefore, a large share for Microsoft spelled the ultimate doom of Netscape. In addition, the presumption of a one-browser monopoly is justification for Microsoft acting to avoid a downstream monopoly. Market share, therefore, is relevant to proving attractiveness compared to Navigator, but it does not guarantee that the rival Netscape/Java platform cannot emerge.

Fisher, as discussed above, emphasizes the prospect for a browser monopoly. One section, however, contains mention of preventing threats by limiting rivals' market shares (par. 92, 42-3); this is supported by quoting Maritz, Chase, and a third Microsoft executive on the desirability of a large share.

However, the rest of his section discusses alleged benefits to Microsoft of succeeding. These are independent of how success is produced and also fanciful. The first is the alleged removal of the need to provide Internet Explorer for other operating systems or "support standards and technologies that are not tied to the Windows operating system" (par. 93, 43).

This statement is incomprehensible, and the supporting quotations make matters worse. The cited Microsoft executives indicate that success of a browser requires providing support for browsers on other platforms. That need does not disappear with a monopoly, so it is inconceivable that the monopoly could be maintained if browsers were not provided for other operating systems. What he meant about other support is left unexplained. Perhaps, he is arguing that Macintosh applications such as Office would cease.

This was followed by a quotation of an Allchin objection (GX 354) to encouraging crossplatform activities rather than promoting Windows (par. 94, 43-4). A Gates reply (GX 475) not reported by Fisher indicates the need is to show the superiority of Windows to Java (see below).

Fisher then states the obvious implication of success, developers would not work on rival platforms (par. 95, 44); he unnecessarily conditions this result on Microsoft restraint from supporting other technologies.

The government effort continues with a book quotation (gfof par. 359.3.i, 632) asserting that Gates felt a share of at least 30 percent would make Web masters too uncertain to commit irreversibly to a single browser. This is at best suggestive of a better but also dubious argument that a significant Microsoft presence might delay the emergence of programs written to the Netscape platform.

The gfof misleadingly evoked Fisher to support the argument (par. 359.3.iii, 632). In cross-examination, Lacovara pressed Fisher on his criteria for the elimination of the platform menace. Fisher indicated that he could not tell exactly what Internet-Explorer market share ended the platform threat. Lacovara reminded Fisher that his deposition indicated it was the number of users that was critical. Fisher agreed (January 6, 1999, p.m., 32-3). After pressing about the market-growth implications for Netscape's viability, Lacovara shifted to the share necessary to attain monopoly and gets an answer that a 50 percent share produces market power (35).

A further exchange (January 7, 1999, p.m., 34-6) involved Fisher not knowing whether or not the number of users of Netscape Navigator had fallen but apparently expecting that the usage had declined. The government (par. 359.3.iii, 632) cites testimony it elicited (January 11, 1999, p.m., 57). In it, Fisher restates the criterion as becoming big enough to eliminate the incentives to write for a Netscape platform. In short, Fisher realizes that share is the wrong criterion if the threat is a middleware platform.

As the government notes in a repetition of the citation (par. 371.iii, 672), Fisher mentions (58) of a Microsoft memorandum claiming victory with a 50 percent share. This last aside is the only hint of acceptance of a share criterion. The source is GX 515, a chain of e-mails from February 1998 dealing with the status of Internet Explorer. The most substantial shows a chart indicating a December 1997 Internet-Explorer share of 40 percent with a forecast of a 59 to 68 percent share in 2001. Another included memo comments that "the browser battle is close to over." However, Brad Chase commented "no one should count netscape (sic) out ...."

A third citation (par. 390.1.i, 733) of Fisher is followed by noting that Warren-Boulton thought 70 percent was required (par. 390.1.ii, 733). Examining the citation (December 1, 1998, a.m., 15) shows that this too was response to Lacovara. Mfof (par. 385, 173-4), noting these assertions and the conflict between them, termed the effort "simply pulling numbers out of the air ...."

A critical implicit government premise is that Microsoft believed that high share was critical to defeat the Netscape/Java platform. The better possible explanation is that, in fact, Microsoft believed that high share was needed simply to compete in browsers. Again, the point is that share is more relevant to competitive position than to the economics of a middleware platform. Once again, the government misused Microsoft material.

Asserting that Microsoft shared the government's premise is unacceptable. Adopting that view implies that the expert economists prefer lay opinions to what economic theory indicates. The dependence on documents distorted professional judgment.

Whinston (2001, 76) contrasts Microsoft's recognition that the number of users determines the attractiveness of Netscape Navigator with the court's decision that share is critical. Whinston charitably attributes the court's view to belief that only the more popular browser would be served. Judge Jackson actually clearly repeats the error that developing a middleware platform requires a large market share (cfof paras. 376-86, 187-92). Whinston make the proper response that both browsers might be supported.

This discussion implies the need for a more stringent criterion than the government used. In measuring success, several considerations arise. If the concern is the viability of maintaining and extending Netscape, it must be demonstrated that the number of customers is too small to justify survival. If the issue for whatever reason is a monopoly in browsers, then the demonstrations must accord with previously discussed economic principles. The government's case about browser monopoly is at least as defective as the treatment of operating-system monopoly. The market-share indicators of success are dubious. The claims that the AOL $4.6 or $10 billion purchase of Netscape does not prove viability are unconvincing to a degree to justify using such government pejorative terms as unreliable.

The Creation of Internet Explorer as a Predatory Act: The Basic Principles

As noted, the creation, zero pricing or use subsidy, and integration of Internet Explorer were deemed intrinsically predatory. Again, two radically different positions were adopted. The government claims Internet Explorer was created only to fight the middleware-platform danger. Microsoft retorts that the objective was to meet the Internet challenge. Microsoft further argues that it did so by the procompetitive actions of providing a better browser and making it free. Another claim is that the decisions antedate the creation of Netscape. Attention turns to arguing that the government overstated Microsoft's ability to coerce.

Warren-Boulton's criterion of separateness is the best (par. 71, 28). He specified sufficient demand to make separate supply efficient. Fisher properly defined separate as being offered and priced separately (par. 80,

31-4). In particular, the computer owner should pay the distributor for that browser. Warren-Boulton and Fisher added that bundling limited choice. Thus, the government economists stated the problem correctly. It is their conclusions that are debatable. As Chapter 9 shows, the government attorneys overreached by also considering irrelevant definitions of separate.

With this argument, Microsoft is guilty of the predatory acts of forcing a zero price, pushing Netscape aside, and making Netscape competition difficult by integration and the requirements imposed on OEMs. These restrictions are requiring inclusion of Internet Explorer and displaying an Internet-Explorer icon after Windows is initially installed. However, the OEMs are free to precede Windows installation with their own program that may make another browser the default choice.

An alternative view is that the natural economic outcome is for bundling browsers as part of an operating system. With this granted, the government case changes to asserting that the optimum approach for Microsoft was to buy a browser. In this case too, the government still contends that neither integration nor any restriction of how OEMs treat the browser is justified.

Clearly, the biggest blow to Netscape is displacement by Internet Explorer. This is simply creating competition. What needs proof that never emerged is that this competition was somehow inefficient. The move to a free browser is another harm to Netscape, but it may be unavoidable and is beneficial to consumers. Under both theories, integration is a tertiary issue. Integration makes a difference only in precluding deletion. This matters only if the user is constrained for capacity. While extensive claims of such problems were made (gfof paras. 166-73, 315-31) and accepted, this ignores the expanded ability of computers to store programs.

The economics of inclusion is another realm in which Schmalensee introduces the germane economics into the case. Indeed, he provided the only economic appraisal. Fisher and Warren-Boulton only make scattered, dubious remarks. The gfof is characteristically ramshackle. However, since Schmalensee's analysis includes a response to Fisher's comments, the latter are discussed first.

After discussing Microsoft's concerns about browsers, the meeting with Netscape, and supposedly parallel efforts with Apple and Intel, Fisher presents an interpretation that creation of Internet Explorer was an investment without expectation of return and thus predation (paras. 124-39, 53-66). Chase's "no revenue product" remark is recalled (par. 124, 55-6). This is followed by the presentation, criticized above, of Gates's views (par. 125, 56-7) and claims that this material proves the case (paras. 126-8, 57-8).

Fisher next attacks the contention that Internet Explorer would be profitable because it increased sales of Windows (par. 129, 58-9; quoted gfof par. 163.1.1, 305; par. 163.2, 306; par. 311.3.1, 546, and 311.3.2, 546-

7; see also January 7, 1999, a.m., 46-7). Fisher's case has five components. His first reason is lack of supporting documents. Under cross-examination, he replies to questions about other revenues "I do know there is not a hint in contemporaneous Microsoft documents that that's what they were thinking about in terms of those revenues. That appears to have been invented in the middle of this trial" (January 7, 1999, a.m., 17). Similar statements are made elsewhere (January 12, 1999, a.m., 34; June 1, 1999, a.m., 40, 63).

The second, best, but still-invalid point was that all that was needed to promote Windows use was a good browser. The key flaw is the neglect of the economics of procurement. What Microsoft wants is the economically most attractive browser. This involves price and quality. It is argued above that faith in the ability to produce superior products characterizes Microsoft's business strategy. Dependence on Netscape had disadvantages, particularly difficulties of agreeing on a satisfactory price and those of reliance on a downstream monopolist. Thus, promoting a new browser could have been preferable.

Fisher next asserted that the alleged effort to discourage Netscape development of a Windows browser disproved interest in promoting browser use. His fourth point is that provision of an Apple version promoted a competitor. The final contention is that the stress on share is indifference to levels. Curiously, the justification is a further charge about Netscape. Microsoft is accused, without even a supporting document, of seeking to disable Netscape and thus reduce browser use. (The reprise in Fisher and Rubinfeld 2000b, 20-21 omits reference to Netscape.)

These last three arguments are specious. The interpretation of the alleged deal with Netscape goes far beyond the government's claims of market sharing. Microsoft was accused of wanting displacement, not elimination. The Apple point ignores that part of the cost of entry into browsers is to serve the major operating systems. Fisher is conjecturing about whether the direct effects on Windows offset the gains in attractiveness of Explorer. Given Netscape Navigator for the Macintosh, Microsoft would not have greatly reduced Macintosh sales by not providing its own Macintosh browser. This, moreover, is another example of inconsistent treatment of rival operating systems.

Finally, the comment about share ignores that with the expansion of the Internet, a rising share means more sales. The mfof (par. 777, 357-8) tries to show this by citing Fisher (June 3, 1999, p.m., 53-4) on recognition that Netscape had probably increased distribution of browsing software. The charge about Netscape again goes far beyond the evidence.

Schmalensee counters that Internet Explorer is an indispensable (June 21, 1999, p.m., 68), sensible, and profitable improvement to Windows. His discussion starts with background information (paras. 205-34, 102-17). Key points are that addition of features to operating systems is common and all operating systems include browsers (paras. 216-23, 107-10). More examples of adding previously separate products appear in a later section (par. 508, 261-3). Allchin's direct testimony (1999, paras. 261-76, 99-107) provides a fuller survey. Mfof (paras. 656-69, 301-8) gives similar detailed information on the other operating systems. Gfof indicates that, while others do not link browsers, they all provide them (paras. 114-16, 228-41).

Schmalensee indicates that bundling lowers distribution costs and, therefore, addition of features is common with computer programs and many other products (paras. 236-7, 118-19). Moreover, to attract more customers, some of these additions will appeal only to some consumers (paras. 238-47, 119-22). More critically, he warns of the difficulty of identifying which additions are appropriate (paras. 514-19, 265-7). Schmalensee adds that inclusion of a browser sells Windows (par. 556, 285) and asserts that benefits arise to Internet users and programmers (paras. 224-34, 111-17; par. 205, 102).

Schmalensee indicates that the existence of opportunities for ancillary income makes the marginal cost of browsers negative and precludes charging for them (paras. 242-8, 121-4). This argument was never refuted. Hall and Hall (1999, 41-2) note that free browsers are so ubiquitous and attractive to service and content providers that the natural price is zero. Thus, competitive pressures are another influence. Therefore, the justifications for an included free browser seem compelling.

Apparently in response, the government notes and rejects an uncited Microsoft claim that wider use of Explorer would increase Windows sales because of features in Explorer attractive to applications developers (gfof par. 312, 548-50). This is rejected because the features were added after the free-price strategy was adopted and do not apply to versions of Explorer for other operating systems. The objections focus on a narrow part of the claim and arbitrarily rule out benefits that were not foreseen.

Schmalensee sees no evidence of significant demand for the browserless operating system demanded by the government (paras. 501-6, 258-60). He argues that Weadock's claims that some corporations want such operating systems is based on an exaggeration of the difficulties of disabling a browser (par. 503, 258-9). He later suggests such a version be labeled "**Now with integrated Web-browsing** *disabled* **at no extra charge!!!**" (par. 598, 308, emphasis in the original).

His discussion treats implicitly the browser-buying alternative favored by the government. The superior-quality argument presented below implies that Microsoft should prefer to distribute Internet Explorer rather than Netscape Navigator. Further arguments can be made.

Securing Netscape Navigator and giving it away eliminates the downstream monopoly, but possibly at a cost. Given such a cost, the often-noted existence of extensive Microsoft outlays on creating Internet Explorer must be related to the possible costs of buying Netscape Navigator. The record of the discussions with Netscape make the latter's insistence on royalties a barrier to procurement (Rosen 1999, paras. 22-5). Similar problems might have arisen with other browser suppliers.

The issue of optimum provision of a browser involves another classic economic problem of optimizing how firms secure the resources that they employ (see e.g., Coase 1937; Stigler 1951, 1968; and Williamson 1975, 1985). In particular, the economics literature tries to grapple with defining the conditions that determine whether something is purchased or produced within the firm. This theory generally calls for a market test to sort out the conflicting claims about what is best. The tacit government theory is that the applications barrier to entry precludes a fair test. However, as standard in the case, that argument needs to be made explicit and tested. Stigler's vision that self-production is more likely when the number of suppliers is limited seems germane to the Microsoft case.

When operating systems include browsers, operating-system suppliers no longer are indifferent about browser provenance; a downstream monopoly concern arises. Curiously Hall and Hall (1999, 43-4) follow their argument that the natural browser price is zero with acceptance of Fisher's view that Microsoft could have met the demand without creating Internet Explorer.

Schmalensee also recognizes that the introduction of Internet Explorer is a consumer benefit. Browsers become free (paras. 269-82, 134-41) and a quality-improvement race is initiated (paras. 255-82, 127-33; June 21, 1999, a.m., 7-9, 11-19). This created competition for Netscape and ultimately produced a browser better than Netscape's. Whatever its motivation, Microsoft won the browser war by producing a better browser.

He adds that Netscape's decision to stop charging for Navigator was based more on the superiority than the zero price of Explorer. Extensive quotations from software reviews are used to support the point. He asserts that parity of quality was reached with Internet Explorer version 3.0 (paras. 256-8, 127-9). This is summarized in Mfof (paras. 425-34, 192-6). Given that Netscape was charging whenever possible for Netscape Navigator, Internet-Explorer use began to rise (paras. 277-8, 138).

The government separates its response. The first treatment stressing AOL starts arguing the claim is false and irrelevant (par. 239, 435). The first supporting point is that Internet Explorer was not superior when "Microsoft extracted its exclusionary agreements and is not clearly superior today" (par. 239.1, 335). Elaboration (par. 239.1.1, 435-6) indicates that only quality comparable to Netscape Navigator was offered AOL. Assorted AOL complaints about quality are purported to prove lack of subsequent "material" superiority (par. 239.1.2, 436-7). This is the closest the gfof comes to supporting the allegation that clear superiority did not exist "today." Two quotations from Colburn's testimony specifying complaints at unstated times are the only possible support. The restrictions on distributing other browsers are deemed another indication that quality was not superior (par. 239.2, 437). The AOL choice is asserted to result from promotional benefits rather than superior quality (par. 239.3, 437-8).

The later treatment starts by claiming that "implementation of new predatory practices" rather than the introduction of a superior version of Internet Explorer better explains the rise in share (par. 381.1, 711). The first quotation, from Fisher (June 4, 1999, p.m., 5-7), shows that this means that the AOL deal rather than the introduction of Internet Explorer 4 better explains the share rise. In prior uncited testimony, Fisher (June 4, 1999, a.m., 9) set the rise in share as "roughly at the same time as the introduction of IE 3." Thus, Fisher concludes superior quality is not the explanation.

The government next points out that neither raising rivals' costs (par. 381.2.1, 711-12) nor predation can succeed unless sufficient product quality is attained (par. 381.2.2, 712). While true, this is another stunning concession since it implies the impossibility of determining the dominant influence. In commenting, the mfof (par. 429, 194) takes the opportunity to use Schmalensee's recognition (January 19, 1999 a.m., 53-4) that the raising-rivals'-cost concept can condemn efficient competitive behavior.

To suggest Internet Explorer is not really superior, the government sought reviews outside Schmalensee's computer-focused magazine universe less favorable to the superior-quality conclusion (paras. 381.2-381.4, 711-16). As usual, no effort is made to prove the alternative selection is better than those undertaken by Schmalensee and by Liebowitz and Margolis. Judge Jackson concludes that the assertion of superiority has "only equivocal support" (cfof par. 195, 95).

The last is difficult to reconcile with the "sufficient" quality requirement and unnecessary. The government apparently argues Internet Explorer manages to be good enough to compete without being superior to Netscape Navigator. This is another implausible coincidence. The balancing presumably is undertaken because victory by an inferior product seems more predatory.

The prior arguments are what matter. Schmalensee stresses the impact of Internet-Explorer quality; the government, the zero price. Observational equivalence alone precludes proof of the government's claim. If zero is the natural price, the allegation remains invalid.

This suggests that Schmalensee's emphasis (par. 556, 285) on promoting Windows sales, while part of the explanation, understates the case. The issue is not estimate of incremental changes, but concern over survival. These fears, moreover, arise only from the pressure to provide a browser. The much-mentioned middleware-platform menace becomes at most an additional incentive and more probably just the government's fantasy. The government case becomes implausible for another reason.

As noted, the gfof discusses the zero-price aspect of Internet Explorer (paras. 295-317, 514-63) after review of the efforts to promote Internet-Explorer use. Detailed discussion is in Chapter 9 because the contention lacks substance. The argument starts by noting that Fisher and Warren-Boulton disagree with Schmalensee about the ability to charge for browsers. Similar confrontations among the expert economists comprise response to other defenses such as the stimulus to Windows and the prospects for ancillary incomes.

The *Journal of Economic Perspectives* Spring 2001 symposium on the case focuses heavily on the relationship of inclusion to economic theories of tying and exclusive dealing. All draw upon the prior work on tying by Whinston (1990) and Carlton and Waldman (1998, 2000). Klein (2001, 55-60) takes the position closest to mine. He concentrates on exclusive dealing with ISPs and tying. His ISP comments are treated in Chapter 9.

He observes (56-7) that two elements of models of successful tying, exclusivity and cost to consumer, are inapplicable to adding Internet Explorer to Windows. His treatment of the requirement to display an Internet-Explorer icon starts with a long discussion (57-8), illustrated by the Compaq dispute, why this should be considered a dispute over property rights to the desktop. In this comment, he notes that Microsoft did not demand removal of a Netscape Navigator icon. A comment discussed below about Microsoft's explanations follows (58-9).

He turns (59-60) to the third issue of payments to OEMs to favor Internet Explorer; he argues Netscape could have competed at reasonable cost. This involves customer buying, rather than tying. Klein apparently recognizes this; he places quotation marks around tie.

Whinston (2001) only considers exclusive dealing and tying. He uses arguments close to Klein's but is more equivocal about the interpretation. Whinston precedes his appraisal with a sketch of the relevant issues from the case and with review of the relevant theory. Turning to application, he argues that the situation is one in which models of successful exclusive dealing seem applicable (73-4). He stresses economies of scale due to zero marginal costs and fixed costs to recover, network effects, and the high value of preserving the profitability of Windows.

As with Klein, the fit to tying models seems "less well." Whinston stresses less "precommitment" because Internet Explorer can be removed and the zero marginal cost to Netscape of getting added (74). He adds that a dispute in the case was whether other forces offset these considerations. He then notes that little "satisfactory" can be said about exclusionary contracts (his term for all the accords to promote Internet-Explorer use). He points out that the economics justify a negative price and that payments are to serious users (74). As he does not note, this justifies Microsoft's behavior.

Whinston's next paragraph (74) presents a highly qualified endorsement of the efficiency of integration. The argument that the integration is not different from prior additions to Windows "seems plausible." He adds that the validity depends upon lowering distribution cost. He notes "tension" between a distribution-cost saving and the claim Netscape could still distribute freely.

He pauses to note that Microsoft did "remarkably little" to defend its exclusionary contracts. He sees problems in forming the response because a less restrictive agreement could have produced the desired results (74). He then argues that the e-mails should be taken seriously. However, he admits that they are consistent with both a desire to hobble Netscape and to create a superior product (75). As the rest of the article recognizes, this still does not prove that the response was inefficient.

His distribution cost-advantage point is recognition of the advantage of bundling a browser with an operating system. Further questions arise about whether a superior browser could overcome the disadvantage or whether Netscape could have provided incentives to Microsoft to adopt Netscape Navigator. A superior browser will necessarily displace and thus harm Netscape Navigator. A desire to hobble is not inefficient if it occurs by superior performance.

His evaluation begins with the impacts on Netscape (75-7). Nonexclusivity and the existence of other outlets such as large users who reconfigure and downloading should make the effects small. However, Microsoft's employment of bundling and, if the government is correct, foreclosure of the most attractive outlets, could produce larger repercussions (75). Evaluation is mingled within discussion of evidence about the declining share of Netscape Navigator (76-7).

He notes that the result is lesser use of Netscape Navigator than "otherwise would have been" (76-7). By noting this might be due to the superior quality of Internet Explorer, he elliptically recognizes that a share decline occurs with any successful form of competition (77). He adds that, nevertheless, the evidence is "most consistent with" considering tying and deals for access as influences.

In turning to welfare impacts (78-9), he tacitly recognizes that tying and deals need not be inefficient. In his short-run analysis, he only treats the welfare loss due to lesser availability of Netscape Navigator. This seems too close to the classic problem of confusing harm to competitors with harm to competition. To make matters worse, he confines concern to the limited number of contracts with OEMs to promote Internet Explorer. He restricts comment to the observation that more onerous restrictions are conceivable. He turns to the uncertainty of the economics of also providing a browserless Windows. He then recognizes the uncertainty about long-run impacts.

He concludes with recognition that the theory still has significant limitations. It can provide guidance, nevertheless. He notes the court's "decision stands in marked contrast to the conclusions that emerge from the discussions above" (79). This apparently means Jackson was clueless about the germane economics.

While the lead article in the symposium, by Gilbert and Katz (2001), mentions the theories stressed in the other two pieces and notes the charges, the relationship is not pursued. Emphasis is on broader issues (see below).

Predation in Theory: Fisher's Model: Nature and Drawbacks: 1 Opportunity Cost

Predation was treated inadequately. First, the dubious status of predation in economic theory was largely ignored. That occurred despite evidence that such skepticism should be applied to the case. Fisher's treatment of predation again consists of general conceptual arguments in his review of relevant economic principles and applications in his discussion of the case. Again, the two are unrelated.

Instead of selling below production costs to reap higher future revenues on sales of the predatorily priced product, Microsoft is accused of selling Internet Explorer for less than it otherwise could have to protect the profitability of Windows. The less-than-possible-charge part of the argument collapsed from recognition that browsers were included with all operating systems and the question was the profitability of that addition.

However, a profitability-preservation charge remained central to treating the peculiarity of the case. The government claims predation by a free tie-in to Windows and inducing others to adopt Internet Explorer. This involved a cost, no revenues (at least according to the government), and, therefore, a reduction in Windows profits. This is a tacit raising-rivals'-cost approach to predation. As Schmalensee noted (January 19, 1999, a.m., 52-4), this ignores the criticisms, made here in Chapter 4, of post-Chicago theories of predatory behavior. The government definition encompasses efficient as well as inefficient competitive responses and provides no way to determine whether inefficiency actually occurs. The idea of reducing profits to preserve profits is a strange type of predation.

In the theoretic treatment, Fisher introduces a difficult-to-implement generalization of the concept of predation. He first presents three definitions of predation (paras. 46-8, 16-17), but his last is the fullest. It is "A predatory anti-competitive act is one that is expected to be profitable in the long run only when taking into account the supra-normal profits to be earned because of the adverse effects on competition" (par. 48, 17). While he does not say so, this is akin to Ordover and Willig's "would not be profitable without the additional monopoly power resulting from the exit" (1981a, 9). Both suffer from Fisher's prior warnings about the problems of measuring profits and the further difficulties of determining that a profit change is due to increased monopoly power.

In amplification, he notes that his definition involves opportunity cost, all lost profits (paras. 49-53, 17-19). He then correctly argues that standard criteria such as the Areeda-Turner test are special cases of his (par. 54, 19). This terse discussion ignores the enormous literature Areeda and Turner inspired (see Chapter 4). The debates involved the problems of establishing a test that could be implemented. Fisher's generalization appears to be another complication that cannot be implemented in practice.

Concern over Fisher's opportunity-cost concept led to a further discussion (June 1, 1999, a.m., 7-8). He again tries to argue that while problems arise in principle with applying the opportunity-cost concept, they do not occur in the Microsoft case:

> They took actions that were simply not profitable at all on any standard.... Well, one version is it's just a deliberate money-loser. A second version says, well, you don't charge the price you could have charged. You don't earn all the profits you could have charged....
>
> Actually, a seriously deep understanding of–well, I can't help it–of economics leads to the view that these are, in fact, the same thing properly considered. Counting that as a cost, revenues will, in fact, be below cost. That is not to say that this is necessarily easy to do. In this case, I think it's extremely easy to do, but it isn't always (the omissions are repetitions and clarifications).

Whether viewing the case or broader implications, Fisher's clarification overstates. The "deep understanding" point is only a restatement of theoretic argument for using opportunity cost. The last-quoted sentences understate the implementation problems.

The opportunity-cost criterion works with deals to provide Explorer separately from Windows but only because it is consistent with Areeda-Turner. However, whether below-cost selling prevailed (or is even a meaningful concept) in the bundling of Explorer in Windows remains dubious. More critically, this is incidental to whether or not he was right to dismiss contentions that complementary revenues, rather than predation, explained the marketing of Explorer. The government's economists ignore the criticisms, including Fisher's, of the predation concept.

As several commentators (e.g., Klein 2001, 6) have noted, Fisher's effect-on-competitor criterion comes from Ordover and Willig (1981a, 1981b). Klein adds that the criterion automatically prevents a monopolist from competing with a rival. He might have better said "alleged monopolist." This reiterates what Schmalensee said in the trial.

A parallel discussion (Gilbert and Katz, 2001, 33) also notes the relevance of Ordover and Willig but leaves its use in the case implicit. Gilbert and Katz want to extend Ordover and Willig to cover weakened as well as ruined competitors, presumably better to encompass the case.

Schmalensee and Evans indicated the deficiencies. They also correctly added that similar problems arise in implementing Fisher's reduced-Windows-profits criterion. Schmalensee's effort in the trial to remedy this made all the critical points and provided limited, but appropriate, references to the literature (paras. 531-5, 275-6). Schmalensee recalls the two-pronged test that the U.S. Supreme Court established in the Brooke-group case. The test requires proof of selling below appropriately measured costs to be supplemented by evidence of a dangerous probability that the losses could be recouped (par. 569, 292). Fisher is faulted for an unworkable measure of cost and failure to present evidence about recoupment.

Mfof (par. 695, 319) presents a fuller statement of the criteria. It recalls an explicit objective to remove a competitor, unprofitable except for the benefits of monopoly.

Schmalensee (June 21, 1999, p.m., 40-49, 77-81; June 24, 1999, p.m., 24-5) and Evans (2000) properly warn that acceptance of Fisher's concept would dangerously expand the concept of predation. Schmalensee notes that Fisher's criterion might ban any price cut in response to unexpected competition (June 21, 1999, p.m., 44-7). He later warns about the difficulties of estimating lost revenue (June 21, 1999, p.m., 77-80). The mfof (paras. 698-700, 320-2) reiterates these points. It adds "Fisher performed no analysis to support his sweeping, albeit irrelevant, assertion ... [about revenue prospects]" (par. 699, 321). Schmalensee's comments imply the Fisher concept automatically makes any response of a firm to a competitive threat predatory.

Schmalensee's approach has the problem of suggesting that Microsoft has profits to reduce. This would support Fisher's vision of restrained but still monopolistic profits. This would explain Schmalensee's stress on income from increased sales of Windows and ancillary activities.

Fisher's addition of the further requirement that the firm possesses monopoly power lessens, but does not eliminate, the problem. Even a monopoly is allowed to compete. Thus, the undesirability still depends on establishing anticompetitive effects. As the case illustrates, determining when a firm crosses the line from acceptable market power to unacceptable monopoly is difficult. Evaluation, indeed, may exceed the powers of the legal system. An even greater problem is the implications for the behavior of a monopolist. The Fisher rule seems to ban any competitive response. In short, Fisher's criterion involves the problems discussed in Chapter 4 of improving on Areeda and Turner.

Predation in Theory: Fisher's Model: Nature and Drawbacks: 2 The Predatory Price that Recoups

As his applied discussion indicates, Fisher is faced with the difficulties of adapting standard analysis to the case. His treatment of predation starts by arguing several usual questions do not arise. The predatory act is not lowering prices to create a monopoly and then raising them, but creating a new "product," not charging for it, and promising never to charge for it (par. 130a, 60). He adds that, in fact, a negative price (i.e., subsidies to use), not a price above costs or specifically average total costs prevails (par. 130b, 60; par. 130d, 61). The payoff comes from preserving the profitability of Windows (par. 130e, 61).

To confuse matters further, he refers to the additional profits from a browser monopoly (par. 130e, 61) but immediately denies Microsoft expected income from any ancillary products (par. 130f, 61). The last again follows from lack of supporting documents. He included one further statement that the true motive was damaging Netscape (par. 130c, 60). He uses McGeady on air supply as his evidence.

He presents a list of supporting points, two of which, a negative price and the desire only to injure rivals, are repetitive. He adds the operating-system monopoly, creation or preservation of barriers to entry in operating systems by the free browser, and high investments in creating and distributing Internet Explorer (par. 131, 61-2).

The claim that difficult issues are avoided is reiterated and followed by an unsubstantiated assertion that the situation allows use of his profit-sacrifice test rather than the usual cost test (par. 132, 61-2). He adds that Microsoft lost money to raise rivals' costs although this "didn't make sense" and made agreements to restrict distribution of Netscape Navigator (par. 133, 63).

Examples follow. He mentions the restrictive nature of accords with ICPs (par. 134, 63). The restrictions on Intuit are noted (par. 35, 63-4). He then more fully discusses dealings with Apple (paras. 136-9, 64-6). He next turns to a survey of Microsoft actions (paras. 140-209, 67-97) that does not differ enough from the gfof to merit separate treatment. He ultimately reviews the success against Netscape (paras. 210-33, 97-107) and concludes with competitive consequences (paras. 234-42, 107-10). The success is deemed evidence that his recoupment criterion is met.

Fisher's oral testimony tried to clarify these arguments. He claimed:

> Yes, I can. In the first place, you have to understand what the question means. In an ordinary predatory pricing case–maybe no predatory pricing case is truly ordinary–there is a predatory price on some product. It's supposed the competition will then be driven out and that there will then be a recoupment phase, typically when the price of that product goes up. That's not what's going on here. What's going on here is there is a predatory price on a product, but the purpose of the predation is to protect Microsoft's operating-system monopoly, and in some sense Microsoft has already begun to recoup that, because it recoups it in the knowledge that it is protecting the monopoly. (January 7, 1999, a.m., 14-15; he adds that what would have happened had Microsoft not acted cannot be determined.)

The second elaboration only slightly better states the key point, "Microsoft is recouping in the form of freedom from–its freedom or increasing freedom from the threat of losing its monopoly power" (January 12, 1999, a.m., 31-2). Both of these statements are inferior to the direct testimony.

By making his points in a broader discussion including what he deems clear evidence of guilt, he conceals his actual argument. To make matters worse, the wording seems designed to suggest that each difference from the usual conditions helps, rather than complicates, the case. Profit preservation is normal behavior. That the profits may come from a monopoly does not prove that their defense is inefficient. He should have taken the missing further step of explaining raising rivals' costs because that is what he is alleging. His tacit view is that Microsoft is preserving its operating-system monopoly by inefficiently raising rivals' costs.

Schmalensee provided the only useful discussion in the case. When asked by Boies, Schmalensee (January 19, 1999, a.m., 52) termed raising rivals' costs as "slippery." When Boies asked why, he was told "because competition on the merits can raise rivals costs, as well as [can] anticompetitive actions." Boies then asked whether use of the concept generally meant conduct was not anticompetitive (January 19, 1999, a.m., 53). Schmalensee described the term as "a convenient umbrella" for "certain anticompetitive practices." He reiterates that the concept has the "analytic problem" that "perfectly legitimate pro-competitive practices that also have the effect of raising rivals' costs" (January 19, 1999, a.m., 53-4).

To see the problems, the economics must be treated more explicitly. Contrary to Fisher's claims, the differences between this case and conventional predation cases make his arguments suspect. The process is marketing a browser. Whether it is a separate product or a feature is immaterial. What matters is the total costs and benefits of introduction at an efficient charge. The analysis must recognize that many different quality situations could prevail. The polar cases are that everyone agrees that

Internet Explorer is superior to Netscape Navigator or conversely everyone considers Netscape Navigator better than Internet Explorer. With mixed visions, some might select one browser, some the other, and some both.

At the efficient charge, whatever it might be, an unambiguously superior browser would capture all the market. If Internet Explorer were that dominant browser, Netscape Navigator would disappear. Similarly, if Internet Explorer attained recognition for superiority among a significant number of users, Netscape Navigator would be greatly displaced. In either case, the sales and profits of Netscape fall. Thus, the-save-for-impact-on-rivals rule fails because even fair competition produces such a profit decline. By construction, this loss is more than offset by the benefits to consumers of a superior browser and Microsoft's profits.

Inefficiently low pricing of Internet Explorer lowers Netscape's profits more. This also reduces Microsoft's profits, but, as always, the lower price is a consumer benefit. However, the definition of inefficient is that the costs exceed the benefits so welfare is less than at the optimum price.

The government is caught in a trap Fisher constructed. To prove the case, it must show that profits were reduced excessively. However, Fisher cannot repudiate his demonstration that accounting data give invalid measures of economic profits. Thus, Netscape's profits are ignored. Fisher and the government must resort to the fall-back position that the charges for Internet Explorer were too low.

However, the case generated no data on what would be optimal. The government relies on the mass of information discussed here in Chapter 9 to suggest underpricing. This requires denying that a negative price is optimal and exaggerating the importance of Microsoft's aggressive promotional activities. What is critical is that the only element of Microsoft's activities in which a special advantage is possible is with OEMs. The competition for favoritism with every other type of company is clearly one of competitive bidding. The firm with the superior browser will win.

However, in the arguments devised by the government, Microsoft has rigged the OEM situation to preclude fair competition by integrating Internet Explorer into Windows. This contention is built on the invalid premise that maintaining two browsers strains the capacity of both the computer and the mind of its user. Once this is rejected, the ability of Netscape to secure OEM access becomes no different from attracting other potential distributors.

The gfof asserts that preserving the monopoly was the recoupment. Again, the support is from quotations. None of these is Fisher or anyone else on recoupment. Only Microsoft's motivations are treated. Another sample of memorandums including Chase's GX 39 is used to recall Microsoft's interest in market share. Fisher is quoted at length asserting that the only motivation is preservation (paras. 301-5, 534-40). These quotes treat both the desire to preserve and the alleged lack of evidence on other motives.

Later a paragraph is devoted to the January 12 Fisher quotation (par. 309, 544). Still later, the gfof further discusses other possible Microsoft motives. The claim that Windows sales would be increased is dismissed mainly by reporting Fisher's appraisal (par. 311, 544-8). This is followed by criticism of the claim that one way that Windows demand would rise is because of the attractiveness of interfacing features in Internet Explorer. The objections are that these features came after the pricing decisions, do not explain provision of Internet Explorer for other operating systems, and could have been separately placed in Windows (par. 312, 548-50). The claim that provision of Internet Explorer stabilizes interfaces is then criticized. This involves Fisher's observation that updates destabilize (par. 312.4, 550, quoting June 3, 1999, a.m. 22; see also direct par. 165, 80).

Then the ancillary revenue claim is discussed. The first criticism is the lack of documents (par. 313.1, 550-1, citing Fisher June 1, 1999, a.m., 40; direct par. 130, 60). The second is that, through allowing changes in home pages and shell browsers, revenues were sacrificed and probably were not significant to begin with (par. 313.2, 551-5). Then, the other examples of free software are considered as irrelevant, mostly because the other software does generate significant revenue for ancillaries (par. 313.4, 556-7). The irrelevance depends upon the validity of the prior claim that ancillary income from Internet Explorer would not be comparable to those for the other programs.

Then the government answers a defense that no one would seriously make, that the matching by Netscape proves profitability to Microsoft (par. 313.4.2, 557-8). The discussion ends with slaps at Schmalensee. He is faulted for not trying to guess what revenues Microsoft could have expected (par. 314.1, 558), understating costs, overstating benefits (by rejecting the lost-revenue hypothesis), not accepting the government's explanation of motivation, not accepting the claim that Netscape did not have to be eliminated, overstating the importance of AOL, and asserting that other threats existed. In short, he criticized the government's case.

The Microsoft attorneys employ a two-pronged response. First, they indicate that the evidence clearly refutes the argument that a conventional predation model applies. Netscape was not driven from the market; Internet Explorer is not unchallenged; victory has not produced price increases. However, the prior shows that Fisher is using a raising-rivals'-cost model. The Microsoft attorneys recognize and criticize this in their second line of attack. The mfof contains early in the discussion of the browser war a clear statement that the alternative visions of true monopoly and sufficient share exist (par. 381, 172). This is followed (paras. 382-7, 172-5) by an attack on the inadequacy of the proofs offered about either concept.

Early in the treatment of the predation charge, Fisher's claim of loss of revenue from selling Internet Explorer is noted (par. 696, 319). The failure to recognize that Windows is the product, the absurdity of arguing that Windows was sold at a below-cost price, and the invalidity of an income-sacrifice criterion are indicated. The invalidity of the last stems from incompatibility with the standard vision of losses to be recouped (par. 698, 320). The danger that any response to competition would fail Fisher's test is stated (par. 700, 321-2). This is followed by summary assertion that the inclusion was profitable, Netscape is not in danger of elimination, and no prospects of recoupment exist (par. 701, 322). It is asserted that Chase's "no revenue product" remark only reflects that Internet Explorer is a component of Windows (par. 702, 322-3). Moreover, the government gave no proof that the addition was unprofitable (par. 703, 323).

A response to government charges follows (paras. 705-23, 323-32); much of that is cited above. Then the government's failure to quantify the costs and benefits of Internet Explorer is criticized. Then it is argued that Netscape was never threatened with extinction and its acquisition guarantees survival (paras. 753-9, 347-50).

The final subsection (par. 760, 350) starts by noting failure to show expectation of recoupment by higher Windows prices; instead, the government attacked the forever-free policy. The discrepancy between Fisher's claim that the browser war was won and the absence of higher Windows prices was noted (paras. 761-2, 351). This constitutes conclusive, if perhaps superfluous, refutation of a conventional predation charge.

Then attention turns to the Fisher monopoly-profit-preservation concept embraced by the government. Three defects are claimed. First is reiteration of the argument that the decision to create Internet Explorer antedated the creation of Netscape (par. 764, 352). Second is that none of the documents used by the government support the monopoly-preservation argument (par. 765, 352). Third, what is proven is platform competition against an entrenched rival (par. 766, 352-3). This appears an awkward effort to say that only a desire to compete was shown. The use of the material by the government is attacked as an inability to distinguish predation from vigorous competition and ignoring that Microsoft faced an entrenched rival (par. 767, 353-4). The elaboration notes that gaining against rivals does not necessarily reduce competition.

Then, Fisher's worst statements of his case are mocked. The mfof notes "At one point, Fisher suggested that Microsoft might have been 'recouping' at the same time it was engaging in the allegedly predatory actions themselves" (par. 768, 354). Fisher's "knowledge of protection" comment is noted. A resposte followed "Such a theory of, in essence, 'psychic recoupment' is wholly foreign to predation analysis" (par. 769, 354). Then, they note the fundamental problem that recoupment simultaneously with the price cut is not predation (par. 769, 354).

This relies on testimony elicited from Schmalensee. The first indicates prices that are simultaneously predatory and monopolistic are not considered in economic theory (June 22, 1999, p.m., 41-2). The second indicates that he has seen no government discussion of recoupment (June 21, 1999, p.m., 86).

The criticism concludes by contending that the record belies Fisher's assertion that the development of other browsers was retarded. The examples aside from efforts by Sun are only shells over Internet Explorer (par. 770, 354-5).

The literature dealing with or inspired by the case tends not to discuss the use of raising rivals' costs. The clearest exception encountered is Lopatka and Page (1999, 210-14). They reject the raising-rivals'-costs claim because the actions mentioned by the government have, as argued here, effects too minor to matter. Lopatka and Page (1999, 211) add that Microsoft refrained from truly damaging actions such as making Netscape Navigator inoperable in Windows. Economides (2001c, 26-31) made a similar criticism.

Coate and Fischer produced (2001) a more thorough critique; their stress is on the failure to quantify. Their attack on Fisher starts with the implausibility of the middleware threat. They argue that no facts such as that other applications have spawned an operating system were provided, the probability of success was ignored, and generally the unique status of Netscape was unproven (847-8). As noted, actually Fisher at times seems to see a low probability of success.

Coate and Fischer (848-9) next criticize Fisher's analysis of predation for denying the increased-Windows-sales and web-portal-income benefits. They use (850) Fisher's assertion that browsers are a natural monopoly as criticism of Fisher's attack on concern with market share. Coate and Fischer see this as the natural focus of a firm worried about who would be the monopolist. My critique is that, in this case, rising share is no different from rising absolute sales.

Their next concerns are two aspects of the failure to quantify, treatments of the implications of differences in the quality of the two browsers and of the actual economics of alternative distribution methods. They argue that, if only one browser is distributed by OEMs, Netscape Navigator will be selected only if significantly better. If it is significantly better, Netscape should be able to compete with Microsoft with ISPs (850). Lifting their one-browser assumption, all Netscape had to do to secure OEM acceptance was to provide at zero cost a browser that at least a significant minority of users considered preferable, or even worth having as a backup.

Coate and Fischer (850-51) note that, given AOL's distribution methods, Fisher should have quantified his assertions about the attractiveness of alternative distribution modes. Their final complaint is that since adding features to software is the only way to generate new sales, Fisher needed, but failed to present and implement, criteria for judging the efficiency of adding Internet Explorer.

While some details of the Microsoft response can be challenged, the fundamental problem remains. Fisher's opportunity-cost and recoupment-by-profit-preservation rules damn any defensive actions by an established firm facing new competition. A critical corollary is that the approaches cannot distinguish between inefficient victimization and defeat by a superior competitor.

It is indicative of the problems that so many of the commentators (e.g., Salop and Romaine 1999) including those hostile to Microsoft postulate an eventual price rise. The overly intricate case developed by the government forced resort to an indefensible concept of recoupment.

Attainment of the criterion would be another case of an implausibly neat outcome. The government did not try proof. The government assertions so often criticized here are an effort to disguise that the case is untenable. All this simultaneously explains why Fisher explicitly proposed an opportunity-cost rule and tacitly advocated a raising-rivals'-costs model and why the suggestions should be rejected.

Judge Jackson's Conclusions of Law opts to ignore the problem and talks of a charge for Explorer as part of the price of Windows (32). However, he terms Microsoft's behavior "predacious." In context, this means predation other than by below-cost sales.

The Limits to Microsoft's Power

In viewing the charges about marketing Internet Explorer and other disputes, the government stresses the importance of Microsoft to other firms and ignores the importance of other firms to Microsoft. In every situation, this greatly weakens the government's case. In at least two, the disputes with Intel and the battle with Sun over Java implementation, the interdependencies destroy the government's argument. The Sun case has interesting aspects that merit attention here. The Intel case is so farfetched that only cursory examination is needed.

A central government theme is, because no viable alternative exists, wide subservience to Microsoft prevails. The vassals include the original equipment manufacturers, Intel and other microprocessor makers, applications developers, Apple Computer, online services, Internet service providers, and Internet site operators. Their ability collectively to mount a counterattack also is ignored. Schmalensee's analysis, in contrast, is built on rejecting the vision of impotence.

At least three categories of participants exist. Intel is sui generis. It needs a good operating system, but Microsoft needs a good microprocessor. Thus, the prevailing situation is properly termed as the Wintel system. Nevertheless, again with its bent for overkill, the government portrays even Intel as a serf and takes seriously alleged Microsoft threats not to support a new generation of microprocessors from Intel (gfof par. 333.1, 594). The charge is wildly implausible because the economic realities made the threat idle. However, Judge Jackson accepts the assertion (cfof par. 102, 51).

Again, Microsoft made sure that the obvious argument was not missed. Maritz devoted a section of his testimony (1999, paras. 307-39, 117-32) to relations with Intel. He concludes (par. 339, 132), "Neither Intel nor Microsoft can intimidate the other. They are large, sophisticated, enterprises, each fully capable of looking out for its own interests." Mfof (par. 1363, 613) paraphrases. The statement Carl Shapiro (2000, 11-13) filed for the government to support the breakup of Microsoft relates how both companies regularly finance competition for the other.

This does not go far enough. The same conclusion holds for most of the main actors in the case. More critically, the point has nothing to do with the central case. This is particularly true of Intel, which was only remotely involved in the middleware threat.

A second category consists of firms that similarly need a good operating system but do not play as critical a role as Intel. These consist of the computer makers and software developers. The third category is those in online services, Internet service, Internet sites, and Apple Computer. What they need is the best available browser.

The needs of the computer manufacturers and software companies for an operating system does not reduce them to impotence. Microsoft, in turn, needs the support of these other participants. As noted, collectively, they are strong enough to finance a rival operating system. In any case, software manufacturers were targets mainly in their role as Internet users.

Allegedly, the computer desktop was a critical battleground. In yet another government straddle, the manufacturers are portrayed as both the consumers' representative and impotent to ensure that the best option is made available. The government presents quotations from Fisher and Warren-Boulton noting the role of computer manufacturers. Two sentences from Warren-Boulton suffice here. "As Microsoft has acknowledged, OEMs are in the business of satisfying their customers. They are exceedingly unlikely to market a product that does not meet consumer demand" (par. 160, 71; quoted gfof par. 176.1, 334).

Evidence appeared that the manufacturers sought more flexibility in how browser options were presented. Manufacturers had options to promote other browsers and would have widened them if Navigator were sufficiently better. If strong reasons to resist the Microsoft demands existed, the restrictions would have been overcome. Computer manufacturers could at a price overcome the Microsoft restrictions. The only thing left of the government case is the bidding-war concept previously expressed.

Allegedly unfavorable treatment by Microsoft, for example, particularly disadvantaged IBM. The government ignores that IBM, because of its diversity and resources, is the computer manufacturer best able to withstand Microsoft pressures. The government shows little or no recognition of the differences among these dependencies or of Microsoft's dependency on these organizations.

Even the relationship between Microsoft and the program developers who generated the (supposedly 70,000) applications involves interdependence. The success of Microsoft makes these programmers want to provide Window applications, but not necessarily exclusively. Microsoft wants these programs enough to invest in assisting their development. Given the package, computer manufacturers consider Windows the best operating system to offer, again not necessarily exclusively.

Again, the Schmalensee framework produces recognition missing in the government's efforts. He notes the importance in Microsoft's business strategy of assistance to software developers (paras. 101-5, 48-50). He reflects a viewpoint stressed by Microsoft executives (see Maritz 1999, paras. 136-51, 51-5; Allchin 1999, par. 283, 108-9). What is more critical is that whatever the relationship, it is irrelevant to browser marketing. Few, if any, programs need directly to incorporate browsers. If provision is desirable, the same consideration apply as to others seeking browsers.

The Other Disputes

The disputes with Intel, IBM, Apple, Sun, and RealNetworks are problematic for both the case and external observers. All involve conflicting testimony and technological issues. Each battle was presented only by partisans and unclearly treated. Resolution requires more evidence and expertise rarely possessed by attorneys and economists. Moreover, veracity, rather than economics, is central.

Nevertheless, some appraisals are possible. Each case was more complex than the government alleged. Economics does suggest why the charges are overblown. One case, the dispute with Sun over Java implementation, has characteristics that merit greater attention than the other matters. Most fundamentally, the dispute proves to hinge critically on the economic concept of rational decision making. In addition, insight is provided into Sun's interests in the case. Another incentive is that the Microsoft executive testifying on the case made the technical issues clear.

The Intel issues involved compatibility of Intel software with the planned update of Windows and Intel's desire to include previously separate capabilities into the new version of the Pentium processor. (The Microsoft side is mfof paras. 1352-401, 608-32.) The IBM affair is a mixture of disputes over IBM's strategy in promoting systems and applications software and other ancillaries and over royalty payments. One issue seems to be the withholding of marketing allowances, a decision understandable when IBM was running advertisements disparaging Windows. Settlement was reached. As argued above, Intel and IBM are too strong to bully successfully, so the charges are implausible.

The conflicts with Apple involved a patent dispute between Apple and Microsoft and missteps by Apple management that had placed the company on the verge of ruin. Apple wanted to promote a program called QuickTime, get technical support for QuickTime, and secure an updated Office for the Macintosh. Microsoft wanted to promote its software over rivals. This at a minimum applied to its alternatives to QuickTime and Internet Explorer, issues treated separately by the government.

On the broader issues, both sides clearly desired to resolve the patent disputes. (Apple is mfof paras. 1402-81, 633-65; Maritz 1999 paras. 340-88, 133-52 also summarizes on Apple.) At worst, the threat not to provide a new version of Office is still only another way to buy customers. The government's stress on the importance of Office is another conflict with the applications-barrier-to-entry claim. Again, proof of excess is needed. Another interpretation of the dealing is that for modest compensation through better treatment of Internet Explorer, Gates preserved Apple. This maintained a market for software, avoided a giant public-relations disaster, and aided Internet Explorer.

The question of Apple's QuickTime does not warrant much attention. The issues are similar to, but the stakes are much smaller than, those with Netscape (as discussed in Chapter 9). The material provided is not sufficient to resolve the conflicting explanations. Some Microsoft memorandums suggest that is another case of proposals to incorporate Microsoft technology. This would make the dispute economically identical to that with Netscape. The failure is all that is clear. That outcome has the same implication as the inability to reach a deal with Netscape. Resolution without renunciation of QuickTime suggests that any threats that were made were not credible. Finally, any charge about Apple is another example of threats outside the government's cozy Intel-compatible personal computer relevant market.

The RealNetworks case is too sketchy to understand (mfof paras. 1482-97; 665-71) but seems another dispute over competing technologies.

The dispute with Sun over implementation of Java proves the most interesting. The issues are more straightforward. Their essence was well outlined by Microsoft's Muglia and is instructive for understanding the prospects for a middleware platform. The conflict is the only place in the case in which even a hint is given of the broader rivalry between Microsoft and Sun. Finally, the dispute seems to boil down to an issue critical in economic analysis, the sophistication of economic entities. Thus, further discussion is warranted.

First, the defects of the other charges need recapitulation. While reinforcing the appearance of Microsoft as an aggressive competitor, the expansions also undermine the claim of a unique Netscape/Java platform challenge. Intel, IBM, and Sun surely were too strong to threaten.

Finally, the proposals to limit activity were rejected, and most of the disputes over relationships with Microsoft were settled. Dispute settlement is something else that could occur whatever the monopoly power of Microsoft. What matters is that the resolution did not involve capitulation. Only the company best able to resist, Intel, undertook possibly significant concessions. The economic realities imply greater plausibility to the view that Microsoft had legitimate concerns to which Intel responded.

Polluted Java

Microsoft's modification of Java is one of the few incidents stressed by the government that has economic implications, and they favor Microsoft. The polluted Java charge involves the basic problem that it violates the standard economic assumption of an informed consumer. The practical validity of this assumption is often challenged. The challenge is inappropriate here. The users are programming professionals.

The government refers 14 times to the effort as pollution, a term used in a document secured (paras. 318-27, 564-85). The full charge was "Kill cross-platform Java by grow (sic) the polluted Java market." This turns out to be the "strategic objective" at the start of a proposal of unstated provenance on Java. In particular, the discussion explicitly states an objective to demonstrate the advantages of Windows-based Java over a cross-platform form (GX 259). The government turns to other exhibits for confirmation. In each, another single overstated sentence is used (GX 351, 518, and 1334). Two of the three also support the concept of promoting a Windows-specific Java.

Microsoft's Muglia was cross-examined on these exhibits. He asserts that GX 259 was a junior employee's 1997 draft that went no further than her supervisor (February 26, 1999, p.m., 13-16).

The action was the design of a version of Java that ran on Windows (mfof par. 1199, 535) and did not support some features of Java (gfof paras. 320-23, 565-74). The government tries to suggest that applications developers could be tricked (gfof par. 331, 590-91) or forced into using the Windows specific version (par. 329, 588, consisting only of a sentence asserting such forced use). The government argument stresses, among other things, that Microsoft supposedly concealed that its version was designed to work only with Windows (par. 331, 590-1).

Muglia's testimony better lays out the issues than Sun's attack. The mfof (paras. 1197-276, 535-68) is a terse version of Muglia's direct testimony on the subject.

Java was developed to protect Sun's servers from personal-computer competition (Muglia paras. 40-3, 20-1; mfof paras. 1213-19, 542-5). Several problems arise with using Sun's version of Java. The first is a cross-platform language is limited to capabilities shared by all operating systems. Muglia indicates that universality imposes the limitation of forcing exclusion of features unique to specific platforms. As the systems advance, the universal language can and should expand. Muglia adds that Sun failed to upgrade as rapidly as possible and often disregarded backwards compatibility.

Muglia argues that Java is well supported by Microsoft. The Microsoft implementation added Window-specific features, supplied new universal features, and better implemented Java. Mfof adds that Microsoft provided a choice that the developers could correctly evaluate (paras. 1199-206, 535-40). Later, the mfof suggests that the alternative was needed because of deficiencies in the Sun version of Java (paras. 1252-64, 558-64).

Hall and Hall (1999, 34-6), a collaboration of an economist and his software developer son, presents similar comments about the limits of a universal language and notes the problems in developing Java applications. Gifford (1999) similarly presents the dispute as a competition between languages and also examines weaknesses similar to those noted here in the attack on Microsoft's entry into browsers. Economides (2001c, 25) describes the search for a universal language as a "pipe dream."

Schmalensee similarly views this as providing an alternative to programmers that, if preferable, will be adopted (as have other modifications of languages that he cites) (par. 149, 71-2). He presents an economic justification for Microsoft's actions. He notes "Developing platform-specific *options* for Java developers may make Sun (and Plaintiffs) unhappy, but it is certainly not anti-competitive. It offers developers (and ultimately consumers) greater choice." He adds that modification of computer languages and their transformation into new languages was common.

The criticisms of the government's vision of Microsoft dealing with dolts apply here to imply that Schmalensee is right. It strains credulity that programmers do not know the characteristics of the software that they adopt.

Summary and Conclusions

The above implies the government had no case. The issue is whether Microsoft's practices were clearly inefficient. The key aspects of this are (1) whether there was a monopoly to protect, (2) what was the threat, and then (3) was Microsoft's response inefficient? Everything else is embellishment. The details hide the failure to prove either monopoly or predation. Schmalensee and the Microsoft attorneys made this point. However, the need to respond to the mass of specific charges buried these basics. The theoretic weaknesses were too gently noted.

The government used invalid concepts and totally neglected quantification. The government's case depends critically upon its unproved assertion of an operating-system monopoly. A far-fetched concept of threat and a similarly preposterous vision of response were concocted. Their sole justification is that they might be consistent with the facts. The government often asserts, but never tries even feebly to prove, that its interpretation of the record is conclusively superior to all others.

Even the most prointervention suggestions about how to judge predation (e.g., Bolton, Brodley, and Riordan 2000; Salop and Romaine 1999) require explicit specification and probably quantification of the benefits and costs of challenged actions. The five-stage Bolton, Brodley, and Riordan (2000, 2264) process is not fulfilled, even badly. The requirement starts with a market-structure study, which the government attempted. A review of the predation scheme should follow.

Bolton, Brodley, and Riordan, in developing this obligation, require evidence of exclusionary effects on rivals and of injury to competition and competitors. Such evidence was absent. Only the middleware conjecture was provided. A recoupment analysis, something that is totally absent, should have ensued. Proof of selling below cost also is needed. The closest the government came was its unconvincing effort to suggest browsers could profitably have been sold separately.

The final test is to prove the absence of a business justification or efficiency defense. The government relies only on Fisher and Warren-Boulton assertions of the sole motive. These are pretextual. Both Bolton,

Brodley, and Riordan and Salop and Romaine expect the more traditional outcomes of a ruined rival and price increases by the predator. Ending the middleware threat and limiting the profit decline do not satisfy the criteria.

The government never presents a meaningful qualitative statement of the issues. It bull-headedly denies what even Judge Jackson had to recognize (cfof par. 408, 204). Microsoft increased competition in browsers. By ruling out obvious benefits, the government's argument necessarily leads to the conclusion that the results are inefficient. Judge Jackson and the Circuit Court of Appeal erred. They rejected the claim that no benefits arose but still accepted the undocumented charge that the net effect was bad.

As Chapter 7 argued, there was no monopoly to defend. The contention on which the case also depends, that the only concern of Microsoft was the Netscape/Java platform, is patently false. Gates's overview of threats considered (GX 20) far more than Netscape and was not clearly directed only at the middleware question with Netscape.

The concern with browser share is not, as the government contends, evidence of fear of Netscape Navigator as middleware. The size, not the share, of Netscape Navigator determines whether it is profitable to design a platform. Since share is an indicator, albeit very imperfect, of importance, concern over share is evidence of fear of Netscape as a monopolist of the Internet. The assertion of concern only over middleware is a lawyer's trick, the only model of behavior that cannot be refuted (or confirmed) by the evidence. Whether the AOL purchase is valued at $4 billion or $10 billion, it is not ruin. With Netscape Navigator still in business, the supposedly predatory campaign did not eliminate a rival.

Fisher's profit-preservation model only indicates that in the worst-case scenario a Netscape monopoly and other threats could undermine the viability of Windows. With or without this worst-case hypothesis, conventional predation does not exist. Microsoft's decision to make Internet Explorer a component of Windows means that only a raising-rivals'-cost form of predation might be applicable.

Use by Fisher and the government of the raising-rivals'-costs concept as a mantra is more obfuscation. It ignores that, even within the Salop and Scheffman model, both whether such strategies are feasible and what the welfare effects occur depends upon the circumstances. Critics identified other problems. The government, by sloganeering, avoids noting these difficulties. For Microsoft's actions to be inefficient, the losses to Netscape must exceed the gains to consumers and Microsoft. Proof would be difficult and is not attempted. Again, it seem that the government took the most convenient available theory that could not clearly be refuted or confirmed.

More likely, predation is meaningless in this case. Microsoft is trying to compete with an entrenched rival. The objective is not eventually to raise prices to recoup its costs. The goal is only to make Internet Explorer an effective competitor for Netscape Navigator in the browser realm.

With the fall of the middleware-platform threat motive and a plausible predation model, everything else becomes fluff. That froth is defective as evidence of anything. The easy target is the government's reliance on the vision of underpowered computers used by idiotic, ignorant, indolent, impatient consumers. Indeed, this could be said to be the whole case. The only reason inclusion and integration of Internet Explorer in Windows, the requirements on OEMs, and all the deals with others would be anticompetitive is that consumers are incapable of choosing for themselves.

Aside from violating the basic principles of economic theory, the incompetence model is implausible. The incorporation of a browser and displaying an icon are neither burdens on computer capacity nor overwhelming advantages in the browser-selection process. The lack of strain is clear. The absence of advantage starts with the reality that a shift is not that hard. If Netscape Navigator were an attractive option, installation of it and the requisite icon by OEMs would have been greater. The government's fuss about OLSs and ISPs is stunning concession of yet another way to thwart Microsoft's design and licensing decisions. The efforts to downgrade downloading and carpet bombing as alternatives are another misuse of the limited capacity and limited intelligence presumptions. The ICP charges are empty.

Of the various auxiliary charges, those on Intel, polluted Java, and IBM are totally implausible. Intel and IBM could not be plausibly threatened; the Java argument rests on another assertion of stupidity, now by experienced programmers. While Apple and RealNetworks were weaker than the others, they resisted the pressures on their software. Even if adoption of Internet Explorer was the price of a new Macintosh version of Office, this is not necessarily inefficient.

Moreover, the review in Chapter 9 of how the fluff was presented suggests further problems. Too much "evidence" consists of phrases that superficially seem damning. The government never validates the conspiratorial interpretation that it provides. Inefficiency is never measured. Instead, the government and its expert economists assert often and vigorously that they are right.

All this ignores the undercurrent in the case that Netscape was a sore loser. A section in mfof (paras. 435-8, 196-7) cites evidence of inattention to marketing. The discussion of the competition to serve AOL suggests inadequate Netscape efforts to respond. Klein (2001) notes that Netscape used the wrong price strategy towards ISPs (55) and the possibility of a general Netscape inattention to the imperatives of marketing (59).

Chapter 9 Microsoft's Tactics: Predation, Tying, and Threats in Practice

In this chapter, the details of the discussion of Microsoft's tactics are examined. To document the problems with the case, the government's case is evaluated extensively. This seeks to overcome the misleading impressions in government statements and journalistic accounts. The review begins by explaining how the material was presented in the case.

Following the government, actual discussion starts with review of a June 21, 1995 meeting between Netscape and Microsoft. The government version is that Microsoft proposed "naked market sharing" and was rebuffed. Surprisingly, the evidence is sufficient to narrow the dispute between Netscape and Microsoft.

The next area presented is the charge that the creation, integration, and pricing of Internet Explorer were inherently predatory. The analytic aspects are treated in Chapter 8; here the details are appraised.

The zeal of promotion is the other government concern. The government showed in great detail how Microsoft bought customers in each of three realms: (1) original equipment manufacturers (OEMs); (2) Internet service providers (ISPs) and online services (OLSs); and (3) Internet content providers (ICPs). The rules governing the treatment of Internet Explorer by computer manufacturers are considered unduly restrictive and designed only to hinder the distribution of Netscape Navigator. Similar challenges are made of the terms of agreements with ISPs, OLSs, and ICPs contracting to favor Internet Explorer. Therefore, the arguments in each of the three realms are reviewed next here.

Separate treatment of these issues is followed by examination of the government's assertions about the combined effect of these restrictions. The government presents a vision of optimum browser distribution in which the channels in which Microsoft was particularly successful are deemed the most effective and those in which Netscape was unchallenged are ineffective. The government appraisal is much too neatly designed to overcome the inapplicability to the case of more conventional concepts.

Attention turns to the consequences of Microsoft's actions. First, the debate on how to measure browser-usage change is sketched. Then, the government's conclusions about the change in share and their effect are noted. Then the treatments of damages by the government and Microsoft's (valid) claims of benefits from its actions are explored. The impacts on Netscape including the implications of its purchase by AOL are covered next.

The next and most problematic issue is long-term consequences. A critical defect with the government's case is the absence of a clear opportunity to harm by raising prices. As mfof notes, the government never claims that the price of Windows would rise if the Netscape/Java platform threat dies. Such an argument among other things would undermine the assertions made that the Windows price was the optimal monopoly price. As a result, the government must resort to reliance on speculation by Fisher about the innovation lost in a world ruled by Microsoft.

Comparisons to the Source Documents

Treating the complexities of the substance again is made more difficult by the forms the participants used to present the case. The gfof and the other key reports differ from each other and me in deciding where an issue belongs. The treatment proves convoluted. The discussions in the case again start with the documents, are epitomized in the direct testimonies, further developed in the oral testimony, and recapitulated in the proposed findings of fact for each side (gfof and mfof, respectively). A difficulty prevalent throughout the case is that of explaining the roles in developing the case of the different participants. The economists, the other witnesses, and the attorneys all contributed. As noted, the economists acted as synthesizers on whom the attorney relied heavily and indeed excessively. To see the problem, it is necessary to review how the attorneys and expert economists treated the topics identified here.

The findings naturally serve legal ends. This produces many excesses such as overstatement, repetition, and choice of the most derogatory possible way to characterize what is being attacked. The government's stress, of course, is on highlighting the desire to harm Netscape. At any excuse, the government cited material purporting to support its theory of Microsoft's motivation. The government handled creation of the Internet Explorer by frequent unsubstantiated assertions that the only motivation was the middleware challenge. This ignores many quotations in the government exhibits that suggest otherwise.

The presentations particularly by the government are scattered, fragmented, duplicative, inconsistent, and uncoordinated. The government breaks the issues into many points, looks at each part, and provides no overview. Many Microsoft actions are noted and invariably condemned without regard to plausibility or internal consistency. Padding and frivolity abound. Indeed, several charges are wildly implausible. Citation is made of numerous variants of the same arguments and even multiple submissions of the same document. Every presentation starts with flat assertions. While some are unelaborated, most are followed by supporting material. These in most cases are quotations or descriptions of someone else's views.

Examination of key issues is spread among separated sections of the gfof. In developing the argument, the treatments of each issue prove both incomplete and anticipatory of later sections. In critical cases, conflicting treatments of the same issue are isolated from each other. These include the evidence on Microsoft's motivations, the attractiveness of different browser distribution methods, and particularly the extent of Netscape Navigator distribution by OEMs. Typically, each component then is treated in multiple, separated discussions.

The government's discussion of tactics starts with a section giving what proves the first of several treatments of the platform threat and Microsoft's reactions (III, paras. 51-62, 108-32; paras. 53-6, 109-18 browsers; paras. 57-9, 118-28 Java; paras. 60-2, 128-32 the combined threat). The negotiations with Netscape (IV, paras. 63-72, 133-71), the dealings with Apple on QuickTime (IV, paras. 72-83, 132-90), and discussions with RealNetworks (IV, par. 84, 190-3) are examined in the next section. A large section follows successively reviewing different elements of Microsoft's strategy (V, paras. 85-317, 194-563). These start with another review of Microsoft strategy (A, paras. 86-90, 194-8). The first topics are pressures on Intel (A, paras. 91-2, 198-203) and creation of Internet Explorer (B, paras. 93-174, 204-333).

This last subsection is particularly problematic. It covers only the effects of the presence of Internet Explorer. It devotes much attention to trivia, fails adequately to explain the creation, largely leaves the decision not to charge separately to the later subsection on predation, and anticipates the next subsection on OEMs. It mentions the restrictions on OEMs and the (two) disputes (with Compaq and IBM) arising from these and other restrictions (par. 128, 249-50). The IBM case, however, has almost nothing to do with Netscape. The critical failing is stress on technical feasibility, when the germane issue is economic preferability.

The next portion treats actions towards OEMs (C, paras. 175-211, 334-406) including the disputes with Compaq (paras. 197-202, 363-84) and IBM (paras. 205-7, 387-90; paras. 207-10, 390-404).[1] The OEM subsection

---

[1] The in-between paragraphs deal with other issues.

focuses on conditions for licensing Windows that the government alleges were designed only to hamper Netscape. The treatment of the impacts of these actions on shipments of Netscape Navigator with new computers does not appear until the final section and there is separated into two unsatisfactory parts.

Coverage moves to ISPs and OLSs (D, paras. 212-57, 407-66) and ICPs (E, paras. 258-82, 467-92). Illogically, this incorporates the first of two efforts to refute Microsoft's claim that it won by introducing a superior browser; this concentrates on the AOL choice of Internet Explorer (par. 239.1, 435-7). Dealings with Apple (paras. 283-92, 493-510) and RealNetworks (par. 293, 510-12) related to browsers are examined. A concluding portion argues that the prior comprises predation (paras. 295-317, 514-63). A major element of the last is the argument that Microsoft preempted the most desirable distribution channels and left the unattractive ones to Netscape. This reiterates and tries to synthesize material in prior sections; the concluding section (VII) further repeats twice.

A section (VI, paras. 318-56, 564-627) is devoted to polluting Java (paras. 318-41, 564-609) and the Intel software issue (paras. 342-56, 610-27).

The final section (VII, paras. 357-410, 628-774) deals with consequences. This is divided into five main parts. The first and longest asserts Microsoft success (A, paras. 357-82, 628-724). This comprises a rambling, disorganized effort to show the attainment of an Internet-Explorer market share large enough to end the middleware danger. The first aspect sets up the case for looking at browser share (paras. 358-60, 630-38). The case that Microsoft preempted the most attractive distribution channels is restated (paras. 361-8, 638-63). Data on the rising market share of Internet Explorer are introduced (paras. 369-70, 663-71). The supposed implications are noted (par. 371, 671-3).

Another attack on Schmalensee concludes the subsection and is itself subdivided. The discussion mostly responds to his criticism of the government's data (paras. 374-9, 674-99; par. 382, 716-24). However, a few conceptual disagreements appear. The subsection starts asserting the superiority of the government's market-share criterion over the correct market-size measure used by Schmalensee (par. 373, 673-4). A longer discussion (paras. 380-81, 699-716) deals with a succession of further issues. The unexplained phrase raising rivals' costs is evoked to challenge Schmalensee about options open to Netscape (par. 380.1, 699). Then the government tries to defend Fisher's gross underestimate of Netscape Navigator shipments by OEMs (paras. 380.2-380.3, 699-706). Downloading is denigrated again (paras. 380.5-380.6, 706-10). Finally, the government again tries to refute Schmalensee's superior-product defense (par. 381, 710-16).

The remaining main subparts indicate the danger of a browser monopoly (paras. 383-92, 725-34), try to deny that the AOL merger undermines the case (paras. 393-6, 735-48), make statements about harm to competition (paras. 397-403, 749-58), and finally assert damage to consumers (paras. 404-10, 759-74). The harm-to-competition subsection is a reiteration of the assertion that the middleware-platform opportunity and the innovations it would produce have been thwarted (paras. 397-403, 749-58).

This suggests flaws critical to the case. It is only proved that Internet Explorer has outcompeted Netscape Navigator, but the fundamental claim that the victory is inefficient remains unproven. Speculation replaces proof.

Allegations about Microsoft's motives appear in six places in gfof. The first two are those mentioned of the section on the subject and the introductory material at the start of the section (V) on tactics. In addition, the concluding subsection on predatory pricing (paras. 295-317, 514-63, esp. paras. 295-8, 514-23) makes comments. The remaining three discussions are scattered in the final section (VII) on impacts. They appear as a preliminary to the treatment of Internet Explorer's rising market share (paras. 358-9, 630-3), as an introduction to the subsection on the establishment of a browser monopoly (paras. 384-7, 725-30), and as a prelude to the subsection on harm to competition (paras. 398-400, 749-52).

The mfof moves more linearly. The first germane section (VI, paras. 369-460, 167-208) is a denial of the browser-monopoly charge. The next (VII, paras. 461-523, 208-36) responds to the charge of blocked distribution channels. The benefits of an integrated browser are then asserted (VIII, paras. 524-692, 236-318). Then, a response on predation is made (IX, paras. 693-770, 318-55). Consumer benefits are claimed (X, paras. 771-800, 355-68). The OEM agreements are defended (XI, paras. 801-965, 368-440) with extensive attention to Compaq and IBM. The other promotional efforts are justified next (XII, paras. 966-1196, 440-535) with extensive attention to the AOL deal. The other issues are examined (XIII, paras. 1197-497, 535-671). These are the Java dispute with Sun, the meeting with Netscape, and the discussions with Intel, Apple, and RealNetworks.

Schmalensee's discussion is even more integrated than mfof. He stresses that the introduction of Internet Explorer is an efficient means to increase the attractiveness of Windows. This is stated in his initial conclusions (paras. 4-5, 2). The bulk of his report is supporting evidence. His examination of operating-system competition reviews similar past additions of features to Windows (III, paras. 167-72, 82-6). His treatment of browsers starts with the benefits of integration (IV, paras. 205-52, 102-25). He moves to the benefits to consumers of the browser war (V, paras. 253-320, 126-60).

He responds to Fisher and Warren-Boulton (VI, paras. 321-42, 161-70). He next treats the absence of serious impediments to distribution of Netscape Navigator (VII, paras. 343-94, 171-202 and VIII, paras. 395-486, 203-50). He asserts the absence of a tie because browsers are natural additions to operating systems (IX, paras. 487-528, 251-72), and the absence of predation (X, paras. 529-92, 273-303). Schmalensee's assertions are directed at prior government claims and, as shown, received response. As with Fisher, the material is treated, if at all, here under the appropriate topics.

I attempt unified treatment of each issue. One section covers creation, integration, and charging. Similar amalgamation is employed on OEM restrictions and their effects and the comparative attractiveness of distribution channels. Some cross-references are provided.

Marc Andreessen's Midsummer Night's Nightmare: Naked Market Sharing

A much-discussed issue was what happened at the June 21, 1995 meeting between Netscape and Microsoft. (June 21 is roughly the date of Midsummer's Night Eve.) A memorandum by Marc Andreessen of Netscape, written during or right after the meeting, suggested that Microsoft tried to persuade Netscape not to produce a browser for Windows 95. This charge was often used as a critical example of Microsoft's violation of antitrust laws.

The opening arguments (October 19, 1998, a.m., 34-41) featured excerpts of a videotaped deposition of Gates about knowledge and appraisal of the charge. Then material suggesting concern over competition from Netscape is used to suggest the denials of knowledge of company culpability are false (42-50). Gfof (paras. 63-72, 133-71) presents the fullest discussion of the charge; mfof (paras. 1277-351, 569-608) gives the response.

Reynolds (2001, 57) cites a newspaper article in which Boies called this contention "the heart of the case." (See Reynolds 55-60 for a treatment of the discussion reaching conclusions similar to mine without specific reference to the available material.)

Fisher uniquely among the expert economists stresses these negotiations (paras. 97-108, 44-9). Drawing upon Barksdale's deposition, Fisher talks of drawing a line between Windows 95 and other operating systems (par. 98, 45). Examination of Barksdale's direct and oral testimony indicates that is one of several after the fact descriptions he adopted. Fisher then evaluates.

He contrasts Gates's denials (par. 101, 45) with what he considers overwhelming evidence to the contrary (paras. 102-13, 46-51).

Fisher accepts the assertions of Barksdale and Andreessen. The reporting of Andreessen's charges by an AOL executive (GX 34) is treated as confirmation (par. 108, 48-9). Fisher adds quotations from Microsoft. All but one relate to the undisputed desire to persuade Netscape to abandon its platform ambitions. However, one Microsoft official twice lists the goal "Move Netscape out of the Win32 Internet client area" (GX 24, cited par. 107, 47-8). Gfof (par. 65.3.ii, 135-6) quotes an earlier memorandum (GX 952) by the same executive stating cooperation "would really be a veiled effort on our part to move them off of the Windows client."

The government, in contrast, accurately but antagonistically, conveys that the issue centered on how much Microsoft technology would be incorporated into Netscape's Windows 95 product. While the details are unclear, the essence is undisputed. Microsoft was suggesting adopting enough technology that Netscape Navigator for Windows 95 would not have independent platform capability (par. 66.2, 137; par. 67.2, 139-40).

Moreover, the government even describes the suggestions as so subtle that Barksdale only realized their implications during the June 21, 1995 meeting (paras. 66.1-66.2, 137-8). The naked-market-sharing charge then blooms from that recognition. Much of the substantiation consists of Microsoft memorandums about the desire to wrest leadership from Netscape (by producing a better browser).

Much material on the subject is available within the case record, and it suggests that the debate is less over what was proposed than on divergent views about the implications. In particular, the nature of Microsoft's proposal for cooperation is undisputed. Both sides, properly interpreted, agree that Microsoft proposed a partnership in which Netscape would market a full line of browsers but rely on Microsoft platform technology as the basis for Netscape's Windows 95 browser.

Moreover, this discussion took place around the question of cooperation between Microsoft and Netscape. Once again, the technological requirement of some interaction explains the meeting. Microsoft and the designers of Windows programs need to cooperate to ensure the applications work. Microsoft suggested using more technology than Netscape wanted.

The discord on the software-adoption proposal seems mostly interpretive. Microsoft, at least after the fact, believed that this accord was in the best interest of both firms. Netscape, again at least after the fact, considered this an outrageous proposal to restrict Netscape's potential. Well after the fact, charges of further pressure were added.

Given this record, it becomes possible to reach conclusions independent of disputed facts about the details. These include how much authority Dan

Rosen, the Microsoft executive heading the presentation team, had to make offers, and the nature, vigor, and timing of the offers.

According to Barksdale and Andreessen, Microsoft offered close cooperation and even an investment if Netscape refrained from competing with Microsoft in supplying browsers for Windows. Andreessen's statement is one paragraph in his notes on the June 21 meeting. That paragraph talks of being asked to stay away from a Windows 95 version of Navigator (GX 33).

Barksdale's initial discussion repeats this point and adds the claim that otherwise "Microsoft would crush Netscape, using its operating-system monopoly, by freely incorporating all the functionality of Netscape's products into Windows" (par. 25, 16). This seems only a melodramatic appraisal of the decision to create Internet Explorer. His expanded discussion (paras. 105-14, 59-65) talks of drawing a line between Windows. "Microsoft proposed that we build products that would run on top of the Windows operating system and browser" (par. 110, 61).

In his oral testimony, Barksdale gave several clarifications. In two (October 21, 1998, a.m., 51-4; October 22, 1998, p.m., 36-9), he indicates that it is drawing the line in a fashion that moved Netscape away from serving Windows 95. In the second exchange, Barksdale adds that Microsoft stepped across the line by competing in browsers. The Microsoft attorney (John Warden) suggests that the real objection is to adding Internet Explorer to Windows (October 22, 1998, p.m., 39).

Mfof (par. 1345, 604) asserts a Barksdale court retreat (October 27, 1997, p.m., 71); this relates to describing the idea as a gradual withdrawal (October 27, 1997, p.m., 69-71). Such a modification is essential to plausibility since development of both Windows 95 and an appropriate update of Netscape Navigator must have been in advanced states for the August 1995 launch of Windows 95. The proximity of the launch and the primitive state of Internet Explorer at the time would seem to limit severely Netscape adoption of Microsoft technology.

To suggest pressure to accept Microsoft's proposal, Barksdale quotes Rosen on the relationship to needed technical assistance, "It certainly isn't independent" (par. 25, 16; par. 111, 62).

Rosen agrees with Barksdale about the types of coordination that were considered. Rosen *was* seeking to secure the maximum utilization of Microsoft technology by Netscape (par. 39). However, fuzzy terminology in his testimony, Barksdale's, and the two fofs make the exact nature of the proposal unclear. It may indeed have involved the possibility of building on top of Internet Explorer, but Rosen only talks of using Windows (paras. 88-99, paras. 118-21). Rosen also indicated that he talked about Microsoft's willingness not to produce browsers for other operating systems (paras. 97-

9). The discord on substance involved whether Microsoft's restraint from providing non-Windows browsers was contingent on Netscape's building on top of Microsoft technology and accompanied by a threat. Rosen denies both (par. 114).

The statement of Christopher Jones of Microsoft adds details. A single remark in this deposition was used by Fisher (par. 105, 46-7) and the government (par. 67.2.11, 140) as evidence that a conspiracy was involved. In interrogation about the June 21 meeting, Jones was asked whether Microsoft wanted to persuade Netscape not to compete. He replies (GX 1469, 582) "absolutely" but adds the idea was to convince Netscape of the value of such action.[2] (Rosen (par. 86) notes Jones was 25 at the time.)

The full text indicates the Jones testimony reinforced Rosen's. The discussions with Jones preceding and following make clear that the goal was to persuade Netscape to adopt Microsoft programs to provide platform capability (574-606). In the process (575), he cites Andreessen's claims about making Navigator a platform and remarks "I am not in the business of shipping partially debugged devices" (575). Later when asked about the "consequences" of Netscape seeking to develop platform capability, he responds that Microsoft stressed its commitment to remaining a platform (583-4; further statements are made, 602). His summation was "There was no consequence. We were in the platform business" (544).

This is followed by denial of the charge of withholding support technology (584-5); he added that the suggestion was "a joke" (600) because he wanted Netscape to use Windows. Mfof (par. 1322, 590-91) gives different quotes in a similar vein.

Whatever the offer, it gave Microsoft the benefits of a promotion of its technology whose adoption ended the Netscape platform challenge. Rosen's testimony and Jones's deposition both suggest belief that, as Gates argued, such an arrangement would have been mutually beneficial.

Rosen argues that the arrangement harmonizes with a vision of market prospects that he believed was shared by Microsoft and Netscape. That argument held that "client" browsers, ones used by Internet viewers, would not be profitable. However, "server" software used by content providers and attractive Web sites would be the source of profits (par. 44). Exploring adoption of Microsoft technology, moreover, tested Barksdale's claim that he wanted better relations with Microsoft (paras. 35-8). Gates (GX 22, May 31, 1995) indicates that he too believes that clients do not make money but servers do, and that a deal with Netscape based on this premise would be mutually beneficial.

---

[2] His deposition is one in a series that is paginated as one document, but each person's statement is made a separate exhibit.

However, this involves the implicit assumption that the eventually-admitted excesses of Andreessen's platform claims inspired rethinking by Netscape. Acceptance would occur only if Netscape believed that such abandonment of platform ambitions had proven the optimal strategy. Barksdale views the proposal as disastrous to Netscape's prospects, presumably because he did not wish to abandon its platform ambitions.

Andreessen and Barksdale had strong motivation to develop interpretations that characterized Microsoft as a predatory firm. Rosen similarly was trying to defend the company. If all were honest, what remains about the basic suggestion is a discord corresponding to the interests.

Given that Netscape initiated the suggestion of a financial stake, its discussion is innocuous. The investment proposal is a means of transforming Netscape from a competitor into a partner. This is similar to the strategy of buyouts at attractive prices McGee indicated was employed by Standard Oil. To be sure, an investment is not a full merger. However, the offer can be interpreted as conditional upon Netscape acting as if it were a subsidiary. This interpretation makes the proposal more a Clayton Act merger issue than a Sherman Act restraint of trade or monopolization issue.

The government argued that the deal cannot be a "legitimate" joint venture because Netscape would cease to produce genuine Windows browsers (par. 70, 156-61). The adjective legitimate is what is critical. By definition, a joint venture is an arrangement in which two or more firms undertake what they might each have undertaken separately. It is this elimination of separate activities to which the government was objecting.

The treatment adds the valid point, evident from the refusal, that Netscape did not consider this a mutually beneficial deal. It was noted that, because of the need for a high-quality browser, eliminating Netscape Navigator for Windows 95 was harmful to Microsoft (par. 70.3, 158-60). However, elimination was not proposed.

The remaining issues are whether the deal Rosen outlined demanded excessive compensation for the investment and the implications of any threats that were made. The inherent economics resolve the issues independently of the truth about disputed facts.

The relevant economic principles imply first that Rosen's offer is an indication of the minimum economic value to Microsoft of the deal. Bargaining might elicit a better offer. The relevant indicator of adequacy to Netscape is acceptance. Netscape's rejection then means the deal was too unsatisfactory to negotiate.

The portion of gfof attacking Microsoft's defense (paras. 68-70, 147-61, paras. 71-2, 168-71) basically asserts that Netscape's interpretation is correct. The effort to impeach Rosen is too convoluted and secondary to treat fully. As usual, the contribution is atmosphere rather than substance.

The government adds Barksdale's complaint that a specific need for assistance from Microsoft was denied (par. 70.4, 161-7); Microsoft replied that the technology had not been created. Barksdale's collection of staff memorandums is then cited as evidence of pressures on OEMs, ISPs, and ISVs not to deal with Netscape (par. 70.4.3, 167-8).

Evans and Schmalensee stress that the offer was rejected with impunity (2000b, 98). The rejection has clear implications for the economic relevance of threats, if they had been made. Netscape's refusal indicates that it did not think the threats credible. Netscape's decision to reject the suggestion and the resulting survival cast doubt on the case against Microsoft.

However, the government's case is that the threats were implemented and succeeded. Thus, an inconsistency prevails between Netscape's expectations and the alleged outcome. Netscape believed that it could profitably develop a platform. The government argues that Netscape failed because Microsoft was irresistible. The government only considers the outcome and, thus, stresses outcomes regardless of expectations. This shift of focus is typical of the case. Elsewhere, false expectations or even the absence of expectations are the basis of charges against Microsoft.

A further point is that the government's extensive concern over a Microsoft failure that seems to involve sinister behavior is more evidence of the overall defects of the case. Given the lack of clear evidence of illegal acts by Microsoft, the government piled on evidence suggesting illegal motives. The abortive dealings with Netscape become another example.

Mfof (paras. 1341-4, 601-4) postulates a Netscape effort to fabricate antitrust action. A critical consideration is that Andreessen's memorandum was turned over to an outside counsel who immediately contacted the Antitrust Division (GX 1259, cited mfof par. 1342, 602-3). The mfof adds that market division was not among the complaints. Examination indicates that the closest the letter came was charging that if Netscape tried to compete with Microsoft, Microsoft "will competitively harm Netscape." During Barksdale's testimony, Warden for Microsoft asked questions to indicate the lack of specifics (October 26, a.m., 27-8) and Boies countered with one bringing out more supportive quotations (October 27, 1998, a.m., 30-4). The profusion of complaints about predation in Netscape e-mails and the heavy resort to internal and external legal support suggests at a minimum a preoccupation with antitrust. McKenzie (2000b, 199-201) reaches a similar conclusion.

The Creation of Internet Explorer as a Predatory Act: The Criticisms

The key task here is to convey the deficiencies of the government's treatment of browser-creation issues. As suggested in Chapter 6, the effort started with overweighing the witness list with specialists on technical issues. Three (Farber, Felten, and Weadock) wrote only about browser provision and integration; one (Felten) was selected as a rebuttal witness. Half of a third witness's direct testimony (Soyring) treated inclusion.

Microsoft responded extensively. Allchin's testimony systematically deals at length among other things with the nature (paras. 75-150, 30-57; paras. 184-203, 68-75; Appendix A, 127-35) and history of Internet Explorer (paras. 204-60, 75-99). Schmalensee provides another view (paras. 205-52, 102-25). Mfof (paras. 524-609, 236-81) synthesizes and responds to gfof on the technical issues; then the business decisions are reviewed (paras. 610-92, 281-318).

These government witnesses and gfof failed to provide substantive information. They could prove the obvious points that browsers can be made separate and concealed but could not and did not treat the germane issues of optimal procurement and pricing of browsers. This is part of extensive efforts to assert that the presence of Internet Explorer is an encumbrance. The argument relies on the presumption of limited computer capacity rejected above.

A large subsection of the gfof (VB, paras. 93-174, 204-333) is devoted to arguing that the creation and integration into Windows were intrinsically anticompetitive. Much of that subsection belabors undisputed questions of technical feasibility. It shows that Microsoft could have designed Internet Explorer differently, not that options other than those chosen by Microsoft were more efficient. The result is a document too tedious fully to criticize. The treatment of the fundamental economic issues is strewn through the section, each part is inadequate, and a whole never emerges.

Lengthy assertions are made that, in some sense, browsers are not "included" in an operating system. Since the government's charge is that provision with and integration into Windows are the undesirable acts, the relevant types of separation are independent provision or including as a removable component. The government presents extensive data (par. 96.1, 206-7; paras. 115-16, 228-41) on the universality of browser provision. This, as noted, parallels similar presentations by Schmalensee (paras. 216-23, 107-10) and the Microsoft attorneys (mfof paras. 656-69, 301-8) and thus is another stunning concession. The government tries to save this by stressing that the other browsers were separable and could be removed before computer shipment. In short, all this mainly reiterates the claim that Microsoft should have bought a browser.

This recognition transforms the same operating systems that were considered unimportant in monopoly analysis into major concerns. To be sure, the references do not assert importance. However, the alleged unimportance of these operating systems suggests the irrelevance of everything they do.

The portion arguing that browsers are separate mainly deals with differences unrelated to the central issue of universal provision with an operating system. These include pure definition (par. 96.2, 207-8; par. 96.4, 208-10; paras. 98-100, 212-15), physical separability (par. 96.1, 206; paras. 113-17, 226-41), separate appraisals in magazines (par. 96.3, 208-9), separate distribution to those not receiving it with an operating system (par. 97.1, 210), the existence of rivalry between Netscape Navigator and Internet Explorer (par. 97.3, 211), and decisions to chose a different browser (par. 112, 225-6). The Microsoft response (paras. 670-85, 308-14) indicates that the definition of an operating system differs among observers and evolves with technology.

The third problem area of the gfof is a part contending (presumably large) costs associated with accepting Internet Explorer (paras. 167-73, 315-31). First, higher technical support and testing costs are imposed on OEMs (par. 167, 315-18). Secondly, the cost of adding Netscape Navigator was raised and thus installation was discouraged (par. 168, 319). However, the bulk of the concern is that the presence of Internet Explorer adds complexity, causing difficulty for users (paras. 170-71, 320-30). This discourages use of another browser.

While OEMs clearly incur costs, their consequences are unproven. However, the consumer-damage charges are frivolous. As many newspaper and trade-magazine articles attest, the history of the personal computer involves substantial increase of operating and storage capacity. The ability to handle browsers is readily determined by any computer user. Using Macintoshes of various vintages and different Intel-compatible personal computers, I find all have both Internet Explorer and Netscape Navigator installed and working well with both operating systems.

With these issues considered, the treatment of the underlying predation charges can be examined. The basic argument is presented with the usual reliance on a string of quotations that falls far short of adequate proof. Therefore, the essence must be painfully inferred.

The primary argument is that Internet Explorer was created, combined, and integrated only to undermine the competitive threat from Netscape by discouraging the use of other browsers (par. 93, 204-5).

The government (par. 102.i, 216) cites Fisher's assertions (par. 80, 31) that browsers are best provided separately with a charge to users. Later, the government turns to the claim that the decision thwarted demands for operating systems without browsers (par. 111, 222-5). This last is supported by quotations from executives from some OEMs and by Weadock indicating that demands for browserless operating systems exist among corporations wishing to block access. In anticipation of the obvious rejoinder that not providing a modem and a means of access would also block access, it is claimed these alternatives are "often less efficient." Vigorous claims again substitute for proof. The more basic question is whether this implicit challenge to Schmalensee is correct. While the claim allows subsequent complaints that this need is not met, the gfof and the courts do not develop the initial assertions or analyze the economics of providing two versions of Windows.

Again using quotations from Weadock and various industry sources, it is asserted that separation of the browser facilitates standardization of installations within a corporation (par. 104, 217-21) and breaks upgrading into separate tasks (paras. 109-10, 221-2).

Only one section directly deals with the creation of Internet Explorer. The treatment first contends that the timing of the decision making indicates Internet Explorer was only a response to the emergence of Netscape Navigator (paras. 118-26, 241-7). The argument is based primarily on ambiguities in Allchin's testimony. His discussion of the history (paras. 204-60, 75-99) suffers from imprecision. However, the critical portion (paras. 228-34, 84-7) indicates a team in place in August 1994 based on proposals made in April. Gfof (par. 119, 242-4) presents documents that indicate the absence of such plans in 1994. However, two Microsoft memorandums that the government posted but did not cite suggest that the allegation is incorrect. The first from October, 1994 (GX 128) talks about efforts to buy browser rights. The second (GX 134) from December indicates that the Spyglass browser had been leased. Memorandums from 1995 about promoting Internet Explorer are used to suggest a decision after the appearance of Netscape Navigator (par. 124, 246).

The contention (par. 125, 246-7) that inclusion was only to thwart the middleware problem is backed by three quotes from Microsoft (GX 623 and 521 and Allchin oral testimony) and assertions from Warren-Boulton (November 24, 1998, p.m., 37-8; November 24, 1998, a.m., 59) and Fisher (par. 143, 67; January 1, 1999 p.m., 10-11) that the objective was to foreclose competition. Fisher's direct testimony based its conclusions on quotations from 1997 (GX 48, 56, 202, 204) about the effectiveness of linkage as a competitive strategy to infer, contrary to arguments presented in Chapter 8, that only the desire to end the Netscape/Java platform threat explains the action.

This has several defects. First, response is not an antitrust violation. Proving the desire to compete does not prove predation. Second, timing is suggestive but not conclusive. The decision might have reflected other influences recognized only after Netscape Navigator appeared. Third, again the evidence is unsatisfactory.

The mfof expands at length on timing (par. 697, 320) and its implications (paras. 704-21, 323-31). Related material appeared earlier in mfof (paras. 612-15, 282-4) followed (paras. 616-55, 284-301) by more detail largely from Allchin's direct testimony. The primary supporting evidence is that Netscape founder Jim Clark's deposition indicates that Gates informed Clark before the release of the beta version of Netscape Navigator that a browser would be given away with Windows (par. 697, 320; paras. 706-8, 324-5). An article in *USA Today* on April 20, 1994 reporting the inclusion of Internet access is also noted (par. 627, 290). (While introduced as exhibits, the Clark deposition and the article were not posted.) Further supporting material is cited without discussion (par. 708, 425).

Mfof (paras. 713-21, 327-31) adds that, with a decision made in 1994 before Netscape shipped its first browser, the juiciest documents in the case become irrelevant. Gates is correct in his deposition that the decision was to make Windows a better product and had nothing to do with Netscape. Strictly speaking, the denial was overdone since anything that improves Windows in browsing, even if previously planned, hurts Netscape.

Maritz's alleged 1995 air-supply remark becomes even more pointless. The 1996 studies of Netscape's finances become routine business research. In addition to being misread, Gates's October 1995 *New York Times* interview similarly is unrelated to why Internet Explorer was created. Whatever the history, all the statements were made after the release of Internet Explorer. The government's reliance on such material is inconsistent with rejection of after-the-fact material favorable to Microsoft.

In the gfof, the assertion that monopoly power was used to force licensing appears in a heading (to par. 126, 247). The exposition starts by stating what Microsoft did (paras. 126-7, 248). Then the claim is made that for lack of a viable alternative, acceptance was forced despite "clear demand" for Windows without Internet Explorer (par. 128, 249-50). (Par. 143, 270 reiterates this with a heading attributing the action to use of the operating-system monopoly). The evidence is that Compaq wanted to remove the Internet-Explorer icon.

The next charge is that the decision to integrate also was done only to end the middleware threat (paras. 129-30, 250-1). The proof is quotations from Microsoft that integration makes a better product. The favorite quotation is again an isolated sentence "We will bind the shell to the Internet Explorer, so that running any other browser is a jolting experience." (See GX 334, 485, and 684–the same exhibit "How to Get to 30% Share in

12 Months.")[3] Nothing before or after indicates what this means. The memorandum outlines an aggressive campaign to promote Internet Explorer using every tool at Microsoft's command including "leveraging Windows." Making the browser superior and marketing vigorously are also important strategies. The desirability of a larger share is taken for granted, but with only a 30 percent goal credibility as a rival, rather than the middleware threat, is the likely concern.

Judge Jackson (par. 172, 86) helpfully interpreted jolting as "having unpleasant consequences for users." Without any obvious basis, he further associated this with a peculiarity that Internet Explorer can unexpectedly become employed in some circumstances even when another browser was selected as the preferred option (par. 171, 83). The importance of inadvertent use of Internet Explorer is unclear but far short of important sabotage. Evidence in the case indicates the ability of Netscape Navigator to run efficiently in Windows.

As noted above, several efforts were made by Microsoft to show the advantages of integration (Allchin (paras. 76-104, 31-40); Schmalensee (paras. 224-34,111-17); mfof (paras. 526-64, 237-60)). All relate to technical matters whose implications are not made clear to lay readers. Page and Lopatka (1999) provide an independent critique.

The technologically based attack on Windows design follows in gfof (paras. 130-42, 251-70). After reiterating the criticism of inclusion, integration is assailed as only a means to defeat Netscape (paras. 145-6, 271-6). Numerous memorandums are cited asserting that closer integration is an effective competitive strategy (GX 47, 48, 49, 50, 51, 53, 113, 202, 205, 334, 354, 355, 480, 655). This proves neither that this is an illegitimate form of competition nor that it is the only reason for integration.

After returning to technology (par. 147, 276-9), the government claims Microsoft thwarted the demand for browserless operating systems (par. 149, 279-80); a long discussion of the feasibility and desirability of excluding Internet Explorer follows (paras. 151-62, 280-305). Then Fisher's (par. 129, 58-9) claim that Internet Explorer did not promote the demand for Windows is reiterated (par. 163, 305-7). Substantial quotes of the original Fisher statements, related oral testimony, and a superfluous Warren-Boulton

---

[3] Par. 129, 251 cites GX 684 and attributes it to Chase despite the lack of any author indication; par. 146, 274 and par. 230.iii, 424 cite GX 334 and assign it to Chris Jones because this version includes his cover memorandum. An entirely different line is quoted without attribution from GX 485 (par. 60.2, 130); it does have a hand-written cover sheet reading "Brad Chase online doc's." Jackson credits jolting experience to Chase (par. 172, 85). However, Jackson later refers by name to the document and attributes authorship to "a group of Microsoft executives" (par. 276, 136-7).

statement (par. 187, 82), that excluding Netscape would lower the value of Windows, are used.

The next claim is that the rules were not needed to preserve the integrity of Windows (par. 164, 307-11). The most relevant of the many quotes provided are typical Felten assertions that other methods existed. The section has several technological pronouncements by Fisher and Warren-Boulton. Indeed, it builds on a point about updates presented by Fisher (June, 3, 1999, a.m., 22 clarifying direct par. 165, 80).

Fisher starts with the truism that updates force changes. He argues that this undermines Microsoft claims that its actions are needed to prevent instability; the government uses the point several times. Whatever the use, the problem is a familiar one that Fisher's point is not conclusive. Change can be excessive, and a need may exist for Microsoft to prevent such excesses. A further point is that this concern about excessive change is another reminder that the lock-in concept central to the monopoly case fails adequately to incorporate updates.

Finally, gfof asserts that the quality-related justifications are invalid (par. 165, 312-14). The justification (par. 165.2, 312-13) is that Fisher (January 1, 1999, p.m., 6-7) and Warren-Boulton (November 24, 1998, p.m., 22-3) believe it would be better to have a choice between browsers.

Buried in all this verbiage are hints at a characteristic of computer use that the government handles with its characteristic opportunism. Generally, the computer user is treated as a helpless, ignorant individual. That many of these individuals have gained experience never emerges in the trial. However, many treatments appear of the existence of a large portion of users affiliated with corporations and other organizations. Large organizations can and do customize. Schmalensee (par. 353, 177-8) cites data that 41 percent of new computers go to organizations large enough to customize installations.

Nevertheless, the primary government emphasis is dumb customers. When convenient, Microsoft is attacked for strategies that manage to gull the stupid and raise costs to the sophisticated. This is another example of the government's incessant claims that conditions perfectly fit the charges.

Fisher (paras. 157-8, 78) presents, but fails to resolve, a key related problem. He notes that software can be designed in many ways and a efficiency gain can be claimed. However, blanket acceptance would exempt anticompetitive actions from scrutiny. Rather than present principles, he presents another ukase, "In the present case, the anti-competitive effects are large; the technological benefits appear to be small or non-existent." The first half reiterates conclusions disputed here; the second is another assertion outside his expertise. This reflects the impossibility of appraising the desirability of innovation. He is implicitly evoking Ordover and Willig and ignoring the criticism they received. This is based on accepting the view that Netscape was foreclosed from effective distribution.

Mfof counters that the tied product cannot be identified, i.e., the government cannot specify what software is extraneous (paras. 565-6, 260-61). Much space is devoted to asserting that Felten regularly failed to remove Internet Explorer (paras. 566-96, 262-73). Then the technical advantages of integration are presented (paras. 597-609, 274-81).

Relying heavily but not exclusively on Allchin, mfof (paras. 610-55, 281-301) reviews the history of Internet Explorer. While often too vague, the discussion makes essential points. The review, for example, starts (par. 610, 281) noting the desire to match IBM and Apple operating-system characteristics. Among the confusing information, clear evidence is provided of plans made before the creation of Netscape for inclusion of a browser in Windows (paras. 612-13, 282-3). The review of browsers in other operating systems follows (paras. 656-99, 301-8). It is then recalled that, as the needs expand, so does the content of an operating system (paras. 670-77, 308-10).

The next point is that "A Web Browser Is Not, by Definition, an Application" (heading for section VIII G, before par. 678, 311). The development (paras. 678-85, 311-14) basically argues that the integration of Internet Explorer makes it an intimate part of Windows. This begs the issue of whether such integration is optimal. The final subsection (paras. 686-92, 315-18) tersely covers other issues. Several treat why the design of Internet Explorer precludes the proposed removal or separation. The alleged demand for separate browsers and the desirability of providing a browserless Windows are challenged as unproven (par. 689, 316). Similarly, it is noted that the design does not preclude organizations from selecting Netscape Navigator (par. 690, 316-17).

As noted, the gfof discusses the zero-price aspect of Internet Explorer (paras. 295-317, 514-63) after review of the efforts to promote Internet-Explorer use. This allows incorporation of material from these sections. These uses are so minimal and readily comprehensible that they can be incorporated here. The argument starts with the fact of a free browser and the presumption that the goal was to ruin Netscape (paras. 296-8, 514-23).

The first step is an effort to show Microsoft thought that Internet Explorer could profitably be sold separately. This cites 1995 Microsoft memorandums debating whether to charge for Internet Explorer or at least some extra features (par. 296, 514-15). The supporting memorandums only indicate conjectures that charging would be profitable. Mfof (par. 710, 325) indicates that the evidence relates to rejected suggestions by marketing personnel that extra features for Internet Explorer be included in a package of Windows extras. This seems a correct reading of the documents.

Then with excessive quotations, gfof reports the decision to bundle without charge (par. 297.1, 515). Warren-Boulton's argument (par. 190, 83) that a charge could have been made is included. Then the predatory impact is stated, bolstered by a combination of assertions by Fisher and Warren-Boulton, McGeady's claim about cutting air supply, indications such as statements by Gates to journalists that a free browser was injurious to Netscape, and numerous 1996 memorandums about the vulnerability of Netscape. The barrage is divided into a basic statement (par. 298, 516-18) and later presentation of the Gates interview stuff and additional supposedly reinforcing material (paras. 298.4-298.5, 521-3). Again, most of this material was generated after the introduction of Internet Explorer, some in late 1997.

It is noted that Netscape was charging for Netscape Navigator and shifted to free provision only in response to "Microsoft's predatory strategy" (par. 298.3, 519-20). Barksdale with concurrence by Warren-Boulton is the support (par. 192, 84).

Then the government takes Netscape's side on the question of whether it was seriously trying to charge (par. 298.33, 520). Schmalensee had indicated (paras. 269-73, 134-5) that Netscape allowed many customers to secure Netscape Navigator without charge. Barksdale was pressed on this in oral testimony and argued that the company had imperfectly attained objectives to charge (October 20, 1998, p.m., 97-8). The government ignores these admissions. It states that Microsoft is claiming its practice "simply mirrored" Netscape. This seems a straw man. Schmalensee's discussion only indicates the problems of charging. As discussed above, he elsewhere argues that other forces would inevitably force the price to zero.

The government, in any case, moves on to recalling the large development and marketing expenses incurred by Microsoft (par. 299, 523-33); this includes noting the incentives discussed in prior sections. The handling of Microsoft's outlays has the curious feature that the accessible material starts with Fisher's citation (par. 122, 54) of a Microsoft reply to an interrogatory indicating an expenditure of at least $100 million per year. Despite the fact that this is much more than the reported spending on Netscape Navigator, the number remains unchallenged. Mfof (par. 727, 334) indicates that it does not contest the number although much (relating to marketing expenses) is based on hearsay.

Gfof (par. 300.1, 533) uses an assertion by Warren-Boulton (par. 189, 82-3) to contend the price to OEMs had to be reduced because of the burden of taking Internet Explorer. This is a more ambiguous statement than Fisher's pronouncements. It is added that the deal with AOL harmed Microsoft's own online service, MSN (par. 300.2, 534). The harm would arise because AOL would also have desktop placement. Chase has argued that Microsoft gave this access because Gates realized it was little different from that AOL already received from the OEMs. The government's discussion employs a quotation from testimony Schmalensee gave at another trial stating the truism that evaluation requires consideration of everything that affects price. The statement supports the undisputed relevance of consideration of the effect on MSN. The use of Schmalensee seems another effort to suggest defects in his arguments in the case.

Another attempt is made to argue that the goal was only to protect the operating-system monopoly (paras. 301-11, 534-48). This again includes many memos about the desire for browser-use share and many quotations of Fisher with repetition within the section and with prior sections.

Gfof attacks as "pretextual" the claim that "negative pricing was part of a profitable plan to distribute widely the platform-aspects of its browser, including APIs, in order to increase demand for Windows" (par. 312, 548-50). The Microsoft assertion in plainer English is that Windows benefits from making Explorer available and an attractive platform for software developers. The criticisms are that the ability to interface with applications was added after the adoption of free pricing (par. 312.1, 548), does not apply to Explorer for other operating systems (par. 312.2, 548-9), could have been incorporated into a browser that was sold (par. 312.3, 549-50), and does not stabilize the access because of the changes through updates (par. 312.4, 550).

Only quotations support the first three points. Those on the timing talk about componentization, which promotes adoption of Internet Explorer rather than making it more attractive to programmers. Apple is treated with a Microsoft expression of interest in attracting Apple and Fisher's comments (par. 129, 59). Oral testimony (June 1, 1999, a.m., 42, 44) of Fisher is the sole justification for advocating separate provision. Similarly, Fisher's oral-testimony version (June, 3, 1999, a.m., 22) of his comment on updates is the basis of the government's assertion on stability.

Only the first criticism has even limited validity. Even here, it is unclear that gains from later developments should be ignored; again, the insistence on anticipation seems unreasonable. That the gains only occur in Windows does not eliminate them. That the capability could be incorporated into a browser with a price greater than zero assumes that that price was viable, precisely what is at issue. The existence of changes might lessen but does not necessarily eliminate the greater generation of programs.

The treatment turns to other revenues (par. 313, 550-8). Again, Fisher's lack-of-documents argument is cited (par. 313.1, 550-1). Indeed, frequent use of the assertion is shown (direct par. 130, 61; January 7, 1999, a.m., 17; June 1, 1999, a.m., 40, 64, 68).

Then in another expedient repudiation of the claim of relentless search for advantage, Microsoft is accused of relinquishing ancillary income (par. 313.2, 551-4). The first example is that OEMs are given freedom to promote other browsers. This contradicts the earlier claims of tight restrictions hindering such promotion. It is supported by oral testimony (January 12, 1999, a.m., 35-6) by Fisher, correctly summarized as arguing that allowing changes in the default start page, as Kempin's oral testimony indicated he permitted, showed indifference to auxiliary income.

Microsoft also permits provision of browser "shells" that disguise that Explorer is employed and direct users to a home page controlled by the creator of the shell (par. 313.2, 551-4). The shell browser presumably shared at least some of the purported disadvantages of adding a second browser. Similarly, ISPs, OLSs, and ICPs can change start pages (par. 313.2.2.2, 553). A quotation from Warren-Boulton's oral testimony (December 1, 1998, a.m., 13-14) supporting the argument follows (par. 313.2.3.i, 554). This seems another stunning concession that competitive pressures exist.

The next step (par. 313.3, 554-5) is to argue that these other revenues are small. One rationale is assertions by Fisher (January 7, 1999, a.m., 50-2; June 3, 1999, a.m., 25-6). The other is that Barksdale says Netscape's revenues from auxiliary sources are not sufficient to recover his costs. This ignores his direct testimony that the combination of these revenues and server software sales kept Netscape viable and conflicts with the government's claim that the AOL acquired Netscape because it generated substantial auxiliary income.

It is then alleged that the analogies Microsoft made to other free software are not applicable to Internet Explorer (par. 313.4, 556-8). Elaboration starts with a claim by Fisher (January 7, 1999, a.m., 44-5), that these benefits are dubious. Two examples of free software cited by Microsoft are challenged because the suppliers (Apple and Intel) do not make everything free. Two others (Adobe and AOL) are alleged to have better auxiliary-income prospects. Moreover, provision by AOL puts pressures on others, such as operating-system suppliers, also to include free browsers.

It is next noted that Netscape's defensive move to a zero price does not prove that price is profitable to Microsoft (par. 313.4.2, 557). This is true because the reaction reflects Netscape's position, not Microsoft's.

Severe problems arise with the government's treatment of Schmalensee's analysis. The government's criticism of Schmalensee's application to the case of the implausibility-of-predation argument starts by claiming that Schmalensee's benefit analysis relates to "benefits that occurred after the fact" (gfof par. 314.1, 558, probably echoing Fisher's dismissal because of the absence of supporting documents).

Then Schmalensee is criticized on various grounds (paras. 314-17, 558-63). The first is another attack on the claim that the benefit is increased sales of Windows (par. 314, 558-9). This too is deemed an unexpected benefit. Schmalensee is faulted for not analyzing expected revenues (June 24, 1999, 15); however, he correctly argued that such forecasts were unlikely to be helpful. Warren-Boulton (par. 193, 84) is the source of a lack-of-documents charge.

A further claimed problem is that Schmalensee understated the costs incurred by Microsoft by ignoring marketing costs (par. 314.2, 559). Apparently pushing Fisher's argument that Internet Explorer could have been sold, the government adds that Schmalensee ignored that many of the (supposedly nonexistent) benefits could have been produced with a nonzero price for Explorer (par. 314.3, 559-60).

Fourth, Schmalensee is criticized for failing to analyze Microsoft's motivations (par. 314.4, 560). This is deemed inconsistent with prior writings endorsing Scherer's call for such inquiries. However, Schmalensee's accurately conveyed reply (June 24, 1999, p.m., 43) was that he is now less confident about the workability of the test without overwhelming evidence. His fault is only that he does not share the government's belief that it secured conclusive proof from Microsoft documents.

The government next contends that Schmalensee's claim that no predation occurred because Netscape survived ignored that eliminating Navigator's dominance (par. 315, 561) ended the middleware threat. The government's argument is that already criticized of asserting Microsoft only wanted to end platform competition.

Again relying on Fisher (June 3, 1999, a.m., 20), the possibility AOL will switch back to Netscape Navigator is denied (par. 316, 561). The final criticism is denial that other threats exist (par. 317, 562-3). One justification is that the Netscape threat was unusual. Another starts using Fisher's contention (see Chapter 8) that the payoff is preservation of the profitability of Windows. This is supported by a Fisher statement (January 1, 1999, p.m., 31) making the point and a Fisher complaint (January 1, 1999, p.m., 32) that the success might have stifled emergence of the Netscape/Java platform. Then Schmalensee is quoted as recognizing that a $9 increase in the price of Windows sufficed to recoup the $600 million investment. These comments are unconnected to each other and Schmalensee's argument about the implausibility of a conventional predation charge.

Again much evidence appears of vigorous competition by Microsoft and the consequences of success, but only assertions by Fisher and Warren-Boulton support the presumption that the competition was inefficient.

The concluding section has a portion on the consequences of entry that start (paras. 384-6, 725-30) reprising attacks on creation. Memorandums on wanting high shares are used to suggest a desire to monopolize (paras. 385-6, 727-8). A quotation from Warren-Boulton (par. 387.1, 729, citing direct par. 89, 39-40) that network effects preserve a browser monopoly is used. Warren-Boulton's statement is surrounded by related quotations about reinforcement and feedback. The data indicating a high share are recalled (par. 388, 730). Then it is argued that barriers to entry will preserve that monopoly (par. 389, 730-32). This is based primarily on Fisher material cited above.

Dealing with the OEMs

The government's treatment of restrictions on OEMs displays most of the defects criticized above. It is a confusing, bloated, dubious effort to assert that restrictions were imposed on OEMs solely to win the platform war. As indicated above, the OEM issues overlap with the creation issues. The result is another subsection impossible satisfactorily to describe. To convey the problems, the government's arguments are treated here in the order presented.

The main proposition is clear. The OEMs must live with the consequences of Microsoft's design decisions. Moreover, requirements on OEMs went beyond that of mandatory inclusion of Internet Explorer in Windows. The government asserts that the rules governing the installation of Windows were designed only to win the platform war and gave such an advantage to Internet Explorer that the use of a rival was materially discouraged.

More concretely, the assertion is that requirements about how Windows initially loaded when a computer was started for the first time and requiring display of an Internet-Explorer icon at initial start up were both imposed to defeat the middleware threat. The wording suggests that other, less direct, influences are more important than the icon display. It is doubtful, however, that the broader charge has anything but cosmetic value. A far more extensive description of restrictions is facilitated. Characteristically, a more arcane, less comprehensible procedure is made the more critical.

That argument, however, is only a small part (paras. 175-7, 334-9) of the subsection. Assertions are made about OEM efforts to create start-up tutorial programs that the government considers desirable (par. 176, 334-6). Microsoft restrictions allegedly harmed such endeavors (paras. 178-85, 340-53). After pausing to claim that "recent" relaxation of the restrictions is inadequate (par. 186, 353-4), the government attacks Microsoft's defense of the requirements (paras. 188-94, 355-62). The remaining and larger portion of the discussion (paras. 195-211, 363-406) is predominantly review of disputes with Compaq and IBM. Mfof (XI, paras. 801-965, 368-440) responds to the charges including those about Compaq (paras. 871-901, 398-413) and IBM (paras. 902-65, 414-40).

The problems start with the title of the subsection "Microsoft imposed a variety of other anticompetitive restraints on the OEM channel in order to impede rivals such as Netscape" (before par. 175, 334). The usual charge that the restrictions are intended only to stem the browser platform threat follows (par. 175, 334). Not content with a single expression, the subsection frequently injects (see below) further restatements.

Discussion of the use of startup programs by OEMs uses documents to show the purpose was to introduce users to a computer (par. 176.1, 334-5). Examples of such programs ensue (par. 176.2, 335-6). A redacted summary of the terms imposed by Microsoft follows (par. 176.3, 336).

Then appears the charge "By contrast, when OEMs customized their PCs in ways that threatened Microsoft's objective of gaining browser usage share, Microsoft moved quickly both to enforce and to augment its restrictions" (par. 177, 336). At this point, it is noted that Microsoft made display of an Internet-Explorer icon mandatory at the initial startup (gfof par. 177.1, 336-7). Klein observes that, while the display of the icon was not clearly desirable (1999, 15), it was not sufficient to displace Netscape Navigator; it was not displaced until Internet Explorer became better (14).

Gfof then claims that further restrictions were imposed to limit browser competition. Despite the defects of both fofs, it is clear that the government distorted the history in stating the charge. The treatment (par. 177.2, 337-9) begins with a Gates memorandum to Kempin expressing concern about favoritism, unrelated to the startup sequence, by OEMs to other browsers and OLSs other than MSN (GX 295). A memorandum from Maritz dealing with the value to AOL of access to the Windows desktop is termed a response to Gates (GX 297). This is because Microsoft discovered that the startup programs gave options to select browsers and other programs. An unelaborated point from a Kempin slide presentation "Control over start-up screens, MSN and IE placement" (GX 401) is used as evidence of a desire to react.

In treating these charges, Mfof joins in claiming a red herring (par. 837, 384). Mfof notes that these requirements had nothing to do with browser choice. This is shown by a variety of arguments including an overblown defense of the rules as ensuring proper use of Windows (par. 839, 384; paras. 842-50, 386-9). Nevertheless, the key points about limited effects on browsers are made. That the Maritz memorandum is not a reply to Gates, but not the other problems with the government's assertions on the history, is indicated (paras. 840-41, 384-6). Nevertheless, Judge Jackson accepted the government's tale (cfof par. 212, 103).

Gfof used a list of newly stated restrictions, none of which is prohibition of programs with signup options, as evidence of response (par. 177.3.1, 338-9). The first requirement is continuing to demand display of the various icons, folders, and menus including the Internet-Explorer icon. The Windows startup sequence cannot be modified. Special OEM programs may not run after the Windows startup. This is treated as a major restriction. Fisher (par. 148, 71-4) makes a similar argument. Another is adding icons larger than Microsoft-supplied icons. The government pauses again to charge acquiescence due to lack of choice (par. 177.3.2, 339). Quotations previously used to indicate an operating-system monopoly are reiterated.

Then a claim is made that restrictions were imposed on a feature called "Active Desktop" to prevent its use to feature "third-party brands on the desktop" (par. 177.4, 339). Redaction, however, appears where an explanation of the restriction would be expected. Since the charge is a stretch, the loss of detail is inessential.

The section on damages to OEMs and users begins (par. 178, 340) with reiteration of broad assertions about Microsoft's motives that have little to do with what follows. The first charge, supported by lengthy quotations from OEMs, is that the ability to provide startup programs was made too expensive (par. 178.1, 340-2). The cited complaints from IBM and Hewlett-Packard relate to startup programs, but those from Compaq, Dell, and Gateway involve other effects of the requirements. A comment follows that the value of Windows was lowered and excluding browser rivals is the only possible explanation of incurring this loss (par. 178.2, 342). The support is listing but not quoting part of Warren-Boulton's direct testimony. Examination (paras. 189-94, 82-3) discloses conjectures about damages including a failure to charge separately for Internet Explorer.

Selective enforcement is portrayed (par. 178.3, 342-2) as evidence of capriciousness. Again, flexibility is as bad as rigidity. Flexibility, moreover, seems more consistent with concern over the integrity of Windows than with fighting Netscape. Rules designed only to battle would never be altered. Nevertheless, the government later (paras. 189-90, 355-7) returns to this argument.

This is followed by the assertion that Microsoft saw these alternative startup sequences as an effective device to promote the Netscape/Java platform (par. 178.4, 343-4). The supporting quotations, however, describe the browser threat without mentioning how OEM startup programs would assist.

At this point, the dubious arguments used to oppose the inclusion of Internet Explorer are modified to attack the restrictions on OEMs. Adding additional icons such as for Netscape Navigator is alleged to increase clutter, confusion, and, therefore, support cost (par. 179.1, 344-5). This was a powerful incentive not to add Netscape Navigator (par. 179.2, 345-6); it also increased cost to corporate users wishing to standardize (par. 180, 347). In between these assertions comes the first effort to refute statements by John Rose of Compaq (a Microsoft witness) that his company's removal of Netscape Navigator was not due to foreclosure by Internet Explorer (par. 179.3, 345-7). The apparent crux seems how to interpret Compaq's agreements with AOL. The government contends they are less restrictive than Rose and Microsoft believe.

Treatment turns to the harm to Netscape from loss of the superior promotion in a startup sequence (par. 181, 347-9). Opinions that icon display is less effective are the relevant support. As usual, excess arises. Soyring is quoted as claiming that selecting an alternative browser requires "sufficient technical skills." He claims that he found it difficult. Making what I find a trivial task seem so difficult is a defect far worse than those the government stresses. Moreover, after sticking to material from industry insiders, the government quotes Warren-Boulton's assertion of computer expertise.

This is followed (par. 182, 349) with claims that Fisher and Warren-Boulton showed other effects. As quoted or in context, the Warren-Boulton statement (par. 177-8, 78-9) is mostly another criticism of restrictions on startup programs. In a sentence not quoted, he adds that the prohibitions apply to running programs including browsers after end-user boot. However, automatic running of browsers is not an option likely to be adopted. Fisher's contribution is conjecture (par. 148, 72) that a ban on larger icons is important.

Undocumented assertion of raising OEM and end-user costs to protect the operating-system monopoly follows (par. 183, 349). Then comes also unsubstantiated recapitulation of the charge of harm to startup programs and higher support costs.

Response to Microsoft's arguments follows. Schmalensee's observation that icons are readily added is criticized using earlier arguments about the costs of such additions (par. 185.1, 350). A statement by Kempin that browsers are added is attacked (1) because one example is only a shell over Internet Explorer and thus less difficult to add and (2) because offering of Netscape Navigator has declined (par. 185.2, 350-1). Similarly, Kempin's statement about the ability to run a program before installing Windows is claimed inconsistent with complaints about the difficulty and a Microsoft memorandum predicting the OEMs would not use the option (par. 185.3, 351-2).

After all this, gfof (par. 185.4, 352) notes statements by Microsoft witnesses that alternatives exist but retorts that they are less effective than the foreclosed options. One support is a complaint by a Hewlett-Packard executive that the restrictions prevented use of its preferred startup option. A cross-reference is the supposed support for the claim of superiority of foreclosed options. That cross-reference (par. 366, 650-60), however, is a discussion of the alleged drawbacks of downloading and mail distribution.

Mfof stresses the mitigating effects of these options. It indicates that OEMs could install any software including other browsers and add any icons (mfof paras. 807-8, 370-71; repeated par. 825, 378) and make another browser the default choice (par. 816, 374). Users can delete icons (par. 824, 378). The restrictions still allow an OEM program to initiate startup (paras. 853-4, 390-91) and to appear at other points during loading (paras. 855-8, 391-3). What proves to be a letter to Compaq allowing it to run a program including "non-MS advertisements" (GX 292) is cited as evidence. (To be sure, the Microsoft attorneys go overboard and say this is government agreement.) These restrictions do not eliminate the ability to offer choices of software (par. 866, 397-8). This suggests that the government charge is not elimination of the option, but making it less attractive.

These government claims are dubious. The superiority of the programs over the other options is questionable. Moreover, if that superiority existed, Microsoft could pay to have Internet Explorer made an option. The Microsoft restrictions are not as severe as claimed.

Gfof then argues the lessening of requirements (paras. 186-7, 353-4) is inadequate. The problems (par. 187, 353) are that past damages cannot be undone and the basic challenged rules remain. This discussion (par. 187.2, 353-4) identifies the further restriction of not allowing promotion of anything but the OEM and ISPs during a ISP signup routine. This clearly is not a major impediment.

The remaining sections of the criticisms of practice argue that Microsoft's justifications are unsatisfactory. Microsoft wants consistency of experience, preservation of product quality and good will, and prevention of fragmentation. That Microsoft allowed exceptions is the sole objection to the consistency-of-experience rationale (paras. 189-90, 355-7). Examples of such exceptions are given first. Fisher (par. 166, 81) and Warren-Boulton (par. 161, 71-2; paras. 171-8, 76-9) then are the chosen source of justification for the claim that these exceptions undermine consistency. Thus, again we have a questionable assertion involving computer science evaluated by economists.

The government's discussions of exceptions provide more inconclusive anecdotes. Citation of Fisher and Warren-Boulton on issues of computer science is frequent. The government's case is that the rules are only to end the Netscape/Java platform threat. The evidence does not indicate that the exceptions are part of meeting the challenge or that the exceptions are granted on an arbitrary and capricious basis.

The criticism of the preservation of quality and goodwill defense (par. 191.2, 357-8) is more intricate, largely because it is used to make broader points. The first complaint is that the restrictions are unnecessary because the OEMs will maintain quality. This (par. 191.1, 357) uses Warren-Boulton's argument (paras. 83-8, 36-9; par. 161, 71-2; paras. 181, 80) that, in effect, market forces on OEMs suffice to preserve quality and goodwill. This is a curiously Austrian argument to come from Warren-Boulton. Moreover, the controls allegedly do not preclude adding features that the government claims could harm quality (par. 91.2, 357); this is a variant on prior claims of inconsistent enforcement by Microsoft. Another objection (par. 191.3, 358) is that other operating-system suppliers do not impose restrictions.

It is indicative of the problems with the government's case that both Klein (2001, 58) and Gilbert and Katz (2001, 32) associate the argument with the Internet-Explorer icon requirement. Emphasizing icon requirements reflects their more obvious impacts.

The final attacks relate to alleged faults in Kempin's testimony (paras. 191.4-193, 358-61). All seem frivolous. The concern that some shells are defective is refuted first by noting some are not (par. 191.4, 358-9). The same Gates statement (GX 295) presented as the basis of new restrictions is reused as evidence that harming Netscape was the true motive. Another statement about allowing variations concludes the support.

An effort to impeach Kempin's testimony follows (paras. 191.5-192, 359-61). The first complaint is that his definition of preventing tampering means requiring Microsoft approval. This is a switch from condemning laxity to attacking rigidity. The second is lack of first-hand knowledge of the effects of removing Internet Explorer; this is another use of the demand for irrelevant knowledge.

The third point is that he was wrong that the restrictions had long existed. This combines one point in his testimony in which he notes the practice was never allowed and recognition elsewhere that the demand was later made explicit.

Kempin's comment that the Gates memorandum (GX 295) was not necessarily related to Netscape is deemed incredible. However Kempin only indicated (February 25, 1999, a.m., 19) that Gates did not mention Netscape. Kempin added that he knew what was meant. Once again, wariness is treated as unreliability.

The penultimate point refers to an earlier discussion (par. 187.2, 354) of Kempin's treatment of restrictions on Netscape. The defect seems to be making a statement about the absence of restrictions on promoting Netscape Navigator that did not explicitly mention the ISP provision that he twice discussed. The final point was the conflict between Kempin's statement that the restrictions were routine and the government's failure to find examples.

The next issue involves statements by Kempin about degrading Windows (par. 39) and allowing consumer choice (par. 13). Degradation concerns are refuted by claims that the restrictions prevented IBM from using a startup program Microsoft considered effective. What Kempin said about choice was that removing the Internet-Explorer icon "If anything" limits choice. The government counters with its claim that the presence of the icon discourages adding a Netscape Navigator icon.

The fragmentation argument is criticized because some of the restrictions have nothing to do with preventing fragmentation (par. 194, 361-2). Felten is quoted on the ease of removing the Internet-Explorer icon. Warren-Boulton on OEMs' concern for the consumers and Fisher's assertion that updating undermines stability are tossed in as supposed further support. These comments are unrelated to the Microsoft practices being criticized.

In a later subsection arguing that Microsoft's acts were predatory, a portion (par. 299.4.3, 429-32) alleges expensive efforts to secure OEM promotion of Internet Explorer. However, most of this was redacted. A Netscape memo on an offer to Dell of unstated incentives (GX 182, GX 236) and Barksdale's reports of promises of price cuts (par. 299.4.3.2, 531) appear.

The treatment of the effect of these restrictions on OEM decisions is meretricious. In one portion of the concluding section dealing with the effects of Microsoft's action, the claim is made that by the beginning of January 1999, "Netscape was present on the desktop on only 1% of PCs OEMs shipped" (par. 364.4.3, 648). The proof is that Fisher said so and that is "consistent" with Barksdale's testimony. Barksdale's figure (October 27, 1998, p.m., 12) was quoted in the prior paragraph (364.4.1.iii, 647) as setting the share at 10 percent.

Later a more substantial effort is made in the guise of refuting Schmalensee's contrary arguments (par. 380.3, 700-706). Much verbiage is expended on minimizing Goldman Sachs's due diligence findings on the Netscape/AOL merger that 22 percent of computers were shipped with Netscape Navigator. An introductory claim (par. 380.3.1, 700) is made that Schmalensee did not refute Fisher's 1 percent figure. The treatment of the 22 percent figure starts with Fisher's statement "I don't actually know where the 22 percent number comes from (par. 380.3.1.3, 703 quoting June 4, 1999, a.m., 28)." Thus, the government presents what seems a confession of ignorance to refute what is obviously the most impartial available estimate. Fisher actual concern was over the lack of elaboration.

The government's appeal brief (2001, 75) calls the AOL material "one ambiguous statement." That statement is then presented: "Estimate client [i.e., the Navigator browser] on 22% of OEM shipments with minimal promotion."

A higher 31 percent figure from Schmalensee (January 21, 1999, a.m. 43-5) is attacked (par. 380.3.1.2, 701-3) because part of this was access to Compaq for which Netscape paid and because of an alleged error in treating Packard Bell. The payment point (reiterated par. 380.3.2, 704) comes from Fisher's oral testimony (June 11, 1999 p.m., 55-6) terming this raising rivals' costs.

Another quote (par. 380.3.2, 704) from Fisher's testimony (June 11, 1999 p.m., 58-9) argues that, nevertheless, Netscape is not receiving enough OEM shipment to become a threat to Microsoft. The mfof (paras. 490-93, 220-2; paras. 813-15, 373-4) reviews the disparity between the claims and reality. The government discussion thus distorts the facts and fails again to analyze their cause and consequence.

As noted, the OEM subsection of gfof concludes with examples of the alleged consequences. The government unearthed two disputes between Microsoft and OEMs, namely Compaq (paras. 197-202, 363-83, heavily redacted) and IBM (paras. 203-10, 386-404, this is a summary of Norris's testimony). These disputes comprise almost all the concluding portion and collectively receive more attention than the Internet-Explorer rules for OEMs. The Compaq dispute involved Internet-Explorer requirements. Internet Explorer was a secondary issue with IBM.

The theme in this portion is that Microsoft too aggressively enforced its requirements. The actual charge was "Microsoft used its monopoly power to force OEMs into taking actions to hinder products or industry developments that threatened its operating-system monopoly" (heading before par. 196, 363).

The Compaq section is an extended discussion of a dispute over a desire to remove the Internet-Explorer icon. However, the start is a discussion redacted to incomprehensibility that Compaq got special treatment (paras. 197-9, 363-6). The essence of the dispute is then given (paras. 200.1-200.6, 366-71). A further effort to discredit Rose occupies more space than the actual issues (paras. 200.7-201, 372-81). The treatment of Compaq closes with more debilitatingly redacted material on favors granted (paras. 202-3, 381-4). What emerges is simply a fight over property rights that got resolved.

On the way to the IBM discussion, the gfof pauses to assert that discounts were given for making Internet Explorer the default browser (par. 203.2, 384), for preserving the Microsoft-dictated Windows interface (par. 203.2, 385), and for following hardware guidelines with validation by

Microsoft (par. 203.3, 385-7). Again almost everything is redacted. Eventually, IBM becomes the focus (paras. 203.3.2-205, 386-90). This portion treats dealings with IBM on Internet Explorer. This related to marketing allowances contingent on supporting Internet Explorer.

The gfof then digresses to quotes (par. 206, 390) from a Gateway employee. One citation indicates that Microsoft was distressed at Gateway's internal use of Navigator and that cooperating in marketing with Microsoft was contingent on a proMicrosoft attitude. The other noted that Dell benefited from cooperating with Microsoft rather than Netscape. The remaining material (paras. 207-210, 390-404) views all the issues with IBM ending with recollection of the marketing-allowance point (par. 210.3, 404).

Several points of substance emerge. First, the material supports the Liebowitz and Margolis view that this was a fight over control of the desktop. Moreover, the battle was over more than browser choice. Conversely, a bargaining interpretation explains why Microsoft tried to maximize its rights and why it relented. In any event, again the treatment fails adequately to prove barriers to access. This presumably is why so much stretching and inconsistency arose.

Microsoft's assertion of copyright privilege to ensure more favorable treatment of Internet Explorer on the desktop is only a predictable effort to tilt the assignment in its favor. Similarly, having clauses limiting the distribution of rival browsers by those agreeing to favor Explorer is a predictable try at maximum gain.

More broadly, the charges against Internet Explorer collapse to inclusion and initial icon display that give an advantage. The attack on a free browser is feeble. The long gfof section on browser provision without integration by operating system providers is certainly one of the stunning concessions claimed in mfof.

Some general points emerge from this review and are applicable to the discussions of other Microsoft tactics. The aggressive Microsoft efforts to secure advantages in its dealing with the OEMs and others indisputably constitute vigorous competition. The question is whether the response was inefficient. The problems of claiming predation are discussed in Chapter 8.

The restrictions on OEMs were "purchased" by providing access to Windows. Access to Windows was an aspect of the deals with others. In these cases, what was provided was inclusion in special folders on the Windows desktop. Those negotiating with Microsoft believed, apparently incorrectly, that this placement was valuable. However, placement of Internet Explorer itself and links to others on the desktops are commodities with implicit values. Netscape could have trumped them by paying enough to the OEMs and others.

Dealings with OLSs and ISPs and ICPs

In dealing with OLSs and ISPs and in the next section treating ICPs, the gfof is straightforward about the transactions. The undisputed point in all cases is that Microsoft vigorously pursued favored treatment from OLSs, ISPs, and ICPs. Adoption of Internet Explorer and limits on promoting Netscape Navigator were secured. That this was buying access was clearly recognized (e.g., gfof par. 212.3.2, 407; par. 224, 418-19). Illegitimacy arises again because the effort was only to defend the operating-system monopoly (par. 212.4, 407). Thus, the payment was "a very large bribe" (par. 224, 418). This is justified only by Fisher and Warren-Boulton statements about inducements being given. Describing the action as bribery is another example of substituting deprecation for analysis.

Remarks on the importance of ISP/OLS as distribution channels and Microsoft's resulting interest in favorable treatment appear as introductory material (paras. 212.1-212.3, 407; par. 213, 408-10). Then the restrictions on ISP and OLS in the agreements are described (paras. 214-20, 411-15). Assertion follows, on the basis of one quotation, that Microsoft feared that, without these agreements, Netscape Navigator would be preferred (par. 221, 415-16). Review is made of Microsoft's success at securing agreements (paras. 222-3, 416-18). Description ensues of what Microsoft gave signers (paras. 224-32, 418-27). A claim then is made that the desired results arose (par. 233, 427-8).

The remainder of the subsection is appraisal (paras. 237-57, 431-66). Again, shifts of focus arise. The first portions criticize the conceptual basis of the Microsoft defense (paras. 237-9, 431-8). Purported damages then are treated (paras. 240-48, 438-48). Then attack is mounted on Microsoft's justification of its tactics with ISPs and OLSs (paras. 249-57, 448-66).

Here the descriptions of the arrangements are cursory, and stress is on the government's complaints. In particular, the degree of restriction is not examined. The critique developed applies to total bans on shipping Netscape Navigator, rather than the limits on shipments actually imposed. Therefore, debates over the enforcement of the requirements are irrelevant to my arguments. Nothing is added about already noted portions of the subsection dealing with subsidiary issues.

The restrictions imposed differed somewhat among and even within the three categories of dealings. The more restrictive OLS and ISP agreements required adopting Internet Explorer as the default browser and limiting promotion and actual distribution of other browsers (paras. 215-17, 411-14). In return, OLSs and ISPs received Internet Explorer, technical assistance, access to source code, software allowing customization including the ability to select that default home page, and at times cash payment (par. 225, 419-22). Less restrictive accords also were made (par. 219, 414).

With ISPs, two levels of treatment were devised. Platinum-level ISPs agreed to restrict promotion of other browsers, implement Internet-Explorer-specific technology that could degrade access by other browsers, not pay other browsers to promote their content, and exclusively use Internet Explorer. This produced inclusion in a special folder; again, the listing facilitated access. The gold level gave promotion off the desktop in exchange for not making another browser the default.

The customization point (par. 225.4, 420-22) is used to show a willingness to sacrifice income for MSN. Again, flexibility is as good a charge as rigidity. More critically, changing the home page is such a clear essential for OLSs and ISPs that competition would have forced that concession. In addition, changing home pages is simple outside the world inhabited by the government attorneys.

To reinforce, the government argues placement on the Windows desktop is a valuable resource whose use was a major element in Microsoft's competitive strategy (paras. 227-36, 422-31). In particular, placement on the desktop was so important to OLSs, ISPs, and ICPs that they accepted onerous terms for that access (par. 233, 427-8). Moreover. such access harmed MSN.

In developing this case, the government first presents the views of Fisher and Warren-Boulton that Windows was used as a promotional tool and, according to Fisher (January 12, 1999, a.m., 27), Microsoft sacrificed income. The government then argues with typical supporting quotations that access is important (par. 228, 422-4) and describes the creation of desktop folders in which links to participating ISPs and OLSs would appear (paras. 229-32, 424-7). The last paragraph (par. 232, 426-7) presents a series of quotations building the case that Gates decided that securing the AOL deal justified harming MSN. Quotes on perceptions of the attractiveness of inclusion follow (par. 233, 427-8).

The AOL deal is the government's prime example of sacrificing MSN (paras. 234-36, 429-31). Microsoft's defense (Chase par. 31, 12) is that it discovered that AOL had deals with OEMs giving desktop placement and could not understand why AOL wanted the same status from Microsoft. Microsoft devised a compromise in which AOL and other OLSs and IAPs would appear in a desktop folder. Users then could open the folder and connect with a preferred listed company. The MSN icon would still appear on the desktop. Chase is useful in presenting information about aspects of the deal that the government ignored.

In attacking Microsoft's defense, the first point is that Gates's denial in his deposition of the importance of Windows as a promotional outlet conflicts with memorandums about his prior concerns (par. 237.1, 431). Then Schmalensee's argument that the value to AOL of placement is low is attacked (par. 237.2, 431-2). The first criticism is that the deal was expected to be beneficial. The second is that the deal lowered the cost of dealing with OEMs. This point is valid qualitatively; quantification is needed to prove importance. A similar argument by Chase is less aptly answered by claiming failure to recognize, as Colburn of AOL did, the power of Microsoft over OEMs (par. 237.2.3, 433).

Then points already discussed are raised. First is the customer buying answer to Schmalensee (par. 238, 433-5). Next is the partial treatment of browser quality (par. 239, 435-8).

The government turns to harm in the form of a lower share for Netscape (paras. 240-48, 438-47). The deals are seen to have caused significant harm by raising rivals' cost by restricting the ability to use OLSs and ISPs as distributors (par. 241, 438-41). This is another incarnation of the vision of dumb, lazy consumers who will stick with the default browser (par. 241, 438-41). A further problem is that this is the stunning concession that the supposedly irrevocable choice made at initial booting can be reversed by another irrevocable decision in selecting an ISP or OLS.

Next data on impacts are examined (paras. 242-8, 441-8). Consideration is given to information secured by both Microsoft (par. 243, 441-2) and the government (paras. 244-8, 442-7). Presentation of the latter starts with the overall change in usage shares (par. 246, 443). Then attention turns to an effort to compare usage by consumers whose service has an accord with Microsoft to those who do not (par. 247, 444-7). The data indicate that Internet-Explorer use is much greater for customers of ISPs with accords with Microsoft. This subsection ignores extensive efforts by Schmalensee to refute these data (Appendix D, paras. 100-116, D-55-66; paras. 474-87, 213-19); a later attack on Schmalensee (see below) provides the response.

This is followed by examples of the areas–retail, business, and downloading in which Netscape does better than Internet Explorer (par. 248, 447-8). The mention of downloading ignores the many efforts to denigrate the downloading option.

The attacks on tactics begin the first of two statements that Microsoft overstated its flexibility in enforcing the contracts (par. 250.1, 448-9; par. 250.2.1.3, 452; par. 254, 458-9). It is noted that testimony from Myhrvold and Chase about the flexibility remaining in practice to ISPs and OLSs in providing browser choice was inconsistent with the contract (par. 250.1, 448-50; par. 250.2.1.3, 452).

One discussion (par. 250.2, 450-52) of the limits of downloading precedes the last example of restrictions; a short further statement follows the example (par. 250.2.2, 452-3).

Only later does the government respond to the defense that the contracts were deliberately not enforced. The government contends that often the requirements were enforced and, when they were not, they could have been and this inspired compliance (par. 254, 458-61).

Moreover, the wavers granted in April 1998 were not sufficient to eliminate the damage to competition (par. 255, 459-61). The changes did not cover AOL and other key contracts (par. 255.1, 460). Other wavers were incomplete (par. 255.2, 460). The damage had been done, again mostly because Fisher and Warren-Boulton said it was (par. 255.3, 460-61). Cross-references supplement the last charge. One refers to the summary of usage data (paras. 369-70, 633-71). Another relates to assertions about the preferability of OEM and ISP/OLS as distribution channels (par. 363, 640-45). The last refers to a later summary of the usage data (par. 388, 730).[3]

The gfof returns to the subject in the subsection on predation. To a summary of its prior arguments is added examples of payments for gaining users (actually termed "gaining browser usage share") (par. 299.4, 525-9).

The attack adds, "Microsoft's agreements frustrated access providers' desire to offer customers a choice of browsers" (heading for par. 251, 453). This restates pejoratively the truism that choice is altered by the commitment to Explorer. The support is quotations claiming a desire for choices. For example, it is added "AOL wanted–but was not allowed–the flexibility to offer its users a choice of browsers" (par. 251.2, 454). (Also see par. 273, 478-80 on ICPs.)

These signer reactions are examples of the chronic tendency to ignore the voluntary nature of contracts. The essence of the contracts was agreeing to prefer Explorer. The complaints by firms making the agreement reflect denial of the consequences. Here as in every other example with OEM, ISP, OLS, and ICP, the correct description is that those accepting a Microsoft offer naturally wanted more but concluded that on balance the benefits were worth the sacrifice. In short, the point is a convoluted way to reiterate that Microsoft bought customers.

Then gfof employs the usage data to attack contrary claims by Microsoft (par. 252, 456-7). First, material in Myhrvold's testimony is criticized; then note is taken of the later discussion of Schmalensee's data analysis.

A paragraph follows stating, in effect, that the disappointing results from the referral folders do not disprove exclusionary effects of the other restrictions (par. 256, 461). This is true by definition; the two are unconnected. The only support provided is citation of the location of the Schmalensee and Myhrvold discussions of the poor results from the referral

---

[3] The reference is "II.B.3.c; ¶ 388.2." Par. 388 is in VII.B.3.c. II.B.3.c is par. 32 on barriers to entry.

folder. More critically, this is a stunning concession of the irrelevance of the deals.

Turning to Microsoft's defense that the restrictions were needed to ensure adequate compensation for Microsoft's assistance, the government notes that the option of cash payments was available (par. 257.1.1, 462-3). This is true but leaves open which route is most profitable. The next charge is that the restrictions are greater than needed to ensure that customers secured through Windows use Explorer (par. 257.1.2, 463).

This is followed by noting that having features in Windows that facilitate Internet access does not justify the exclusionary requirements (par. 257.2, 463). This seems true but irrelevant. The features vindicate inclusion and integration, but not making deals.

Finally, the claim only a cross-marketing agreement was involved is attacked. The restrictions are considered not to be "routine" cross marketing because they are more restrictive. In particular, Netscape imposes looser rules (par. 257.3.2, 464-5; par. 281.1, 488-9).

Then it is argued:

> Microsoft's agreements are not typical cross marketing agreements for a more fundamental reason. In typical cross marketing arrangements, the product being marketed is a profitable product. But Microsoft's effort to purchase browser market share can be explained only as a strategy designed to weaken Netscape and protect Microsoft's operating-system monopoly (par. 257.3.2.4, 466).

The validity depends critically upon the government's assertion that Explorer is the product. The Microsoft assertion that Windows is the product implies that a profitable product is being cross-marketed. More critically, the government is only repeating that it thinks the restrictions are inefficient. The subsection should have proved that Microsoft made predatory payments for access; it does not.

The treatment of ICPs (paras. 258-82, 467-92) is similar to, but much less interesting, than the ISP/OLS section. The start (par. 258, 467) is another undocumented assertion of valuable concessions only to preserve the operating-system monopoly. Allegations of importance of and interest in ICP agreements follow (paras. 259-63, 467-70). Discussion ensues of enticements including a feature called Channel Bar on the Windows desktop (paras. 264-5, 470-71) to secure favored treatment (paras. 266-73, 471-7). Channel Bar apparently was a window containing icons linking to ICPs that was open on the desktop in the default configuration of Windows (Poole 1999, par. 48, 15-16).

Note is taken (par. 269, 473-4) that Microsoft preferred "strategic barter" of access over a charge. Poole used "strategic barter" in his oral testimony (February 8, 1999, a.m., 34). The interpretation is "In order to obtain access to the Channel Bar and placement within the Windows desktop, ICPs had to agree to Microsoft's restrictions, despite the ICPs desire to enter into promotional and distributional deals with competing browser companies, like Netscape" (par. 273, 478-9). Again, the voluntary nature of the deals is ignored. More supporting quotations follow (paras. 274-5, 479-80).

Then the unremarkable conclusion is reached that the deals captured customers from Netscape (paras. 276-9, 480-85). The development consists of more assertions about illegitimate defense of monopoly by gaining browser share. Two quotes from Poole's oral testimony "conceding" uncontested parts of the case are the most direct evidence presented. First (February 8, 1999, a.m., 67), he agrees that the ICP agreements were to increase browser share (quoted par. 277.2, 482). Second, he agrees that one reason to gain share was to fight the browser threat (February 8, 1999, a.m., 18, quoted par. 277.3, 483). Microsoft admits both threats and the desire to compete to overcome them. Such an admission is not proof that middleware was the only threat.

Inserted (par. 278, 484) into the discussion is an attack on another oral statement by Poole (February 8, 1999, a.m., 29-30) that the unproven nature of Channel Bar, rather than "to gain browser share to thwart Netscape" was the basis for the incentives. The government counters with evidence of willing buyers of access and documents indicating the promotional goals.

At most, these and other uses of Poole are efforts indirectly to criticize the way he evaded the issue of promoting Internet Explorer. He goes no further explicitly than noting that a goal was to encourage Internet connection (par. 67, 23). Otherwise, he stresses promoting technology incorporated in Internet Explorer (paras. 55-6, 18-19). He preferred to concentrate on how little the effort, whatever the goals, accomplished.

Again, the government closes the review with denunciations. First, it is asserted Microsoft was wrong that the effects were small (par. 280, 485-8). However, the discussion only shows Microsoft expected some effect. The criticism starts by arguing, correctly, that the failure of Channel Bar does not mean benefits were not expected (par. 280.1, 485-6). The support is Warren-Boulton (November 30, 1998, p.m., 32). A Fisher claim (par. 197, 93) that the damage "has already occurred" is tossed in.

Another specious attack on Schmalensee follows (par. 280.2, 486-7). He is correctly cited as asserting (par. 470, 241) that the Channel Bar option was too short-lived to have a major impact. The government counters that the share of Internet Explorer rose dramatically in that period. This is the classic fallacy of asserting correlation implies causality. This is followed by the assertion that Schmalensee's analysis of ICP agreements ignores:

the contemporaneous evidence that Microsoft entered into these agreements in the context of its other anticompetitive actions and with the expectation that they would impede its rivals and for the purpose of protecting its dominant position in operating systems (par. 280.2.2, 487).

This presumably seeks to suggest that it is Schmalensee's appraisal, not the government's, that fails to synthesize. It is yet another stunning concession that ICP accords are at most a small element in Microsoft's competitive efforts.

A confusing treatment of Intuit follows (par. 280.3, 487-8). The apparent point is that the deal transformed planned nonexclusive use of Internet Explorer to exclusive employment.

Again, the treatment ends by arguing that the agreements lack justification (other than increasing use of Explorer) (par. 281, 488-92). Also again the ordinary-cross-marketing defense is criticized as ignoring the restrictive nature of these agreements (par. 281.1, 488-9). The claim that Microsoft benefits from association with ICPs is criticized because Microsoft's restrictions do not include a ban on association with other browser providers (par. 281.2, 490). Again, Microsoft is being criticized for not being restrictive. Moreover, lack of exclusivity may lower but does not eliminate the benefits.

The remaining points state the obvious:

1.   Promoting use of other Microsoft technologies cannot be the sole rationale (par. 281.3, 490-91). The cited quotes of Poole's direct testimony (par. 62, 20 paras. 90-100, 32-6) only assert that a benefit to technology arises. As noted, the testimony is overly coy about directly promoting Internet-Explorer use. While the government's usual arguments about seeking to increase browser share would have sufficed, the response consists primarily of describing actions that, as is not noted, are more consistent with promoting Internet-Explorer usage.
2.   The deals are not necessarily the best way to promote Internet use (par. 281.4, 491). This is an excuse to repeat Fisher's claim that the treatment of Netscape showed that Microsoft did not care about usage and comparable statements by Warren-Boulton.
3.   Giving a better deal is again "offering a very large bribe" (par. 281.5, 491-2).

The subsection ends with reiteration of the claim that all this was only to defend the monopoly with Fisher and Warren-Boulton quotes as the evidence (par. 282, 492).

After discussing dealings with Apple (paras. 285-92, 493-510) over the push to adopt Internet Explorer and alleged pressures on RealNetworks not to support Netscape (paras. 293-4, 510-12), the gfof notes (par. 294, 512-13) that independent software vendors also received better technical support for favoring Internet Explorer.

Klein (2001, 50-55) is similarly skeptical of the attacks on these efforts. He views the AOL deal as simply Microsoft competing on merit no different from price or quality difference (50-52). He observes that, because the strategy was unlikely to eliminate Netscape Navigator, it could not be a case of victory by eliminating a superior rival (53).

He notes an alternative explanation that, because of the value of preserving its operating-system monopoly, Microsoft could outbid Netscape (53-4). He suggests that, because of the benefits of defeating an incumbent, the argument is not always applicable (54). He notes that the government used the simpler point that Microsoft paid too much because it incurred expenses for which it gained no income (54). Klein describes this as ruling out as anticompetitive the benefits of future Windows income (54). This concentrates on the key issue of appraising the basic raising-rivals'-cost element in the case. The government went further than Klein indicated and rejected the increased-sale defense.

The Net Effects: The Restricted Distribution Claims

A key government claim is that Microsoft has cut off all the attractive options and left the unattractive options to Netscape. The result was a precipitous decline in Netscape's market share.

The contention involves unsubstantiated arguments about both the effectiveness of alternative distribution channels and Netscape's access to each. The best distribution outlets allegedly were the OEMs, OLSs, ISPs, and ICPs. The government asserts that browser distribution through this assortment of companies is far more effective than direct distribution by mail or computer.

The support, as noted, is scattered repetitively in several sections. The subsections on each category of supposedly superior distribution source are keyed to the central theme. The attractiveness is stated, and an effort is made to show that Microsoft has preempted all of them. Again, the substantiation consists of quotations. Prior sections treated the claimed outcome. Here, review is made first of the scattered attacks on the supposedly inferior options. These are mail distribution (carpet-bombing), downloading, and retail sales. Then a sketch is provided of the more integrated approach to distribution taken by Schmalensee.

The first government effort to show that downloading is "not an efficient channel of distribution" appears in the subsection on OLS/ISP (par. 250.2, 450). The bases are that a Chase demonstration omitted steps in the download and took place on a higher speed Internet connection than available to many customers, Chase says access is difficult, and the AOL deal prevents telling that access to Navigator exists (par. 250.2.1, 450-52). This establishes greater difficulty. not insurmountability.

Thus, the government provides the standard collection of quotations asserting that the options that cannot be preempted are inferior to those that can be (par. 366, 650-60; paras. 380.5-380.6, 706-10). The usual problems arise. The most basic is whether the evidence proves the difficulties truly create a substantial disadvantage. Two obvious problems arise with the choices of sources. Barksdale (10 citations) is the main source. This comes from his effort to show that Netscape is damaged but not fatally. That balancing act involved claiming that Netscape proved the feasibility of downloading but the technique was not good enough to maintain its competitive position. Fisher is quoted nine times as an expert on the software industry.

Again, Fisher and Warren-Boulton are heavily relied upon as support for the conclusions about which channels are most effective (paras. 362-3, 638-45), that Microsoft's efforts harmed Netscape by "raising rivals' costs" because the remaining distribution alternatives are inferior (paras. 364-6, 645-60); much other concurring opinion is presented, however. AOL's reliance on carpet bombing, is justified by subscriber revenues that Netscape does not get (paras. 366.1-366.2, 651-4). However, if it is correct that the profitability lies in server software and web sites, then the distribution might be justified by promoting those incomes. The need of Netscape to respond to this competition is characterized as raising rivals' costs (par. 364, 645-6); this is a stunning concession to Schmalensee's point that the concept is too broad.

The loss of revenues from browser sales is treated as an impediment to response (par. 367, 660-61). The discussion moves to summarize the losses of outlets (paras. 367.1.2-367.2.3, 661).

Microsoft provides several efforts to refute that the supposedly preferable channels were foreclosed. This is the subject of two sections (VII and VIII) of Schmalensee's testimony. VII is evidence for his assertion that the government uses a mistaken theory of monopoly in software distribution. The first point is that the Windows desktop is one of many distribution channels (paras. 346-7, 172-4), and, moreover, not the most important (paras. 348-9, 174-5); the latter is particularly true for business customers (paras. 353-4, 177-8). The experience with MSN and early versions of Internet Explorer shows placement on the desktop does not guarantee success (paras. 350-52, 175-7). OEMs have great freedom to add icons and folders to the desktop (paras. 355-2, 178-83). Therefore, access can be purchased from OEMs as well as Microsoft, and while it is cheaper to negotiate with Microsoft than numerous OEMs, the cost difference may not be great (par. 363, 183-4). Thus, Netscape could purchase access (par. 364, 184). Others have done so extensively (paras. 365-6, 185).

This leads Schmalensee to suggest that the contrary arguments are an invalid effort to term the desktop an essential facility (paras. 367-71, 186-7). He turns to arguing Netscape has successfully distributed through many sources (paras. 373-9, 188-93); he concludes by noting the implausibility of Fisher's claim that installing software is inordinately difficult. Then data supporting Schmalensee's argument are presented (paras. 379-92, 193-201).

Schmalensee's subsequent treatment of the other accords is largely factual. While based mostly on public reports, the material is duplicative of direct testimony of Microsoft executives–Chase on AOL, Myhrvold on other OLSs/ISPs, and Poole on ICPs. What is new is further data analysis, challenging the government claims that the accords greatly contributed to use of Internet Explorer (paras. 445-76, 227-44; based on Appendix D, paras. 100-116, D-55-66).

Mfof (paras. 470-523, 211-36) similarly reviews the different distribution channels. The efficacy of downloading is noted (paras. 474-87, 213-19) with heavy citation of Netscape's success. Further discussion (paras. 517-21, 233) attacks claims of difficulties in downloading.

The government's theory is intrinsically too glib. As already noted, by extolling so many options in which many participants exist, the government implicitly undermines its contention that Microsoft monopolized all the superior outlets. Indeed, it engages in deception to overstate the decline of Netscape's distribution by OEMs and wordplay to overstate the importance of ICPs. Conversely, it gives AOL an importance from which it retreats in discussion on the impact of AOL's acquisition of Netscape.

A Digression on Browser Use Data

As noted, the expert economists became ensnared in a sideshow over which of two rival methods of measuring browser use was better. An economic analysis should avoid trying to verify the storm of conflicting claims and limit coverage to consideration of the economic significance, if any, involved.

Schmalensee relied on telephone surveys of users that showed little change in Netscape Navigator's share of use. The government employed data recorded by servers about visits to various sites. These data showed a sharp decrease in the Netscape share. Much time was devoted to arguing the merits of the two sources. All three experts engage in their direct and oral testimonies in a debate over which side's chosen data on browser usage are better. This is accompanied by lawyer-like overstatements. Schmalensee calls the government data "grossly flawed" (heading for par. 229, 165). The findings of fact are similarly concerned (gfof paras. 377-9, 679-98; par. 382, 716-24; mfof paras. 389-424, 175-91). Just why the share decline justified so much attention never was made clear (see above).

The evaluations seem outside the expertise of an economist. Therefore, ideally the three experts and I should have refrained from involvement. Substituting a survey-data specialist for one of the several weak witnesses on both sides seems preferable (at least after reading the record).

The radical differences in presentation, moreover, preclude comparison. Schmalensee presents the only coherent treatment with discussion of methodology. It includes extensive treatment in the main text (paras. 288-317, 143-59; paras. 379-92, 193-201; paras. 445-76. 227-44) and an 84-page appendix stating the case for preferring the data that he used to those used by the government. Mfof (paras. 389-424, 175-91) summarizes Schmalensee and later comments. The gfof has scattered comments (cited elsewhere in this chapter). Fisher (paras. 225-34. 102-7) and Warren-Boulton (paras. 136-50, 61-7) are sketchy and only present results.

The essence is clear. Each side stresses the clear limitations of the other's data. The time period covered by the Microsoft surveys is longer than that of the government data, and the survey can secure more information than available from visitor data. However, the visitor data should be error free; the surveys depend on often-faulty memories. Moreover, a summary provided by Schmalensee about the differences between the data indicates that they differ little in the most recent periods covered, but in earlier years, Netscape had a larger share in the advertising-visit data than in the surveys.

However, an economist can evaluate the usefulness of these data. At least two concerns arise. First, the existence of two diverging data sets suggests difficulties in accurately assessing conditions, particularly in the earlier years of the Internet. The characteristics of the two data sets as discussed by both sides suggest intrinsic problems. Both sides display unwarranted confidence that they can measure the change. Barksdale testified about the unreliability of available data (October 21, 1998, p.m., 12).

Second and most importantly, the debate inspires attention to what the two sides should have tried to measure. For reasons discussed above, this is a case of Koopmans's measurement without theory. Usually, the government presents theory without measurement. Both faults undermine the case. Questions arise about whether the government has correctly specified Microsoft's goals. It is certain that by ignoring the absolute size of Navigator usage, the government is using the wrong measure of strength. It is the amount of use that affects the income potential and the justification of creating the Netscape/Java platform. Finally, it is unclear why so much fuss was placed on the exact magnitudes involved.

The Government's Case: An Overview on the Harm to Netscape and to Competition

The last section of gfof treats harm (paras. 357-410, 628-774). The government contends that the favored position of Internet Explorer in Windows together with Microsoft's deals with other companies fatally and illegally harmed Netscape. This effort to prove Microsoft did more than outcompete Netscape is divided into four parts. The first covers the probability of what is called a browser monopoly. The actual claim is that Netscape was prevented from becoming a competitive platform and this precluded the benefits of such a success. This is followed by an effort to explain how a multibillion-dollar sale is consistent with ruin. The last two parts deal with broader implications. As is typical, some arguments are anticipated in earlier sections, and the concluding section repeats much from prior sections.

The propositions presented are that a high share, rather than monopoly, was needed to end the Netscape/Java threat, the channels in which Microsoft imposed restrictions are by a convenient coincidence the most attractive browser distribution channels, Netscape's share has fallen, the acquisition by AOL does not matter, and thus Microsoft is attaining a monopoly in browsers.

At least three issues arise. First is whether the foreclosures, in fact, greatly increased the difficulties for Netscape. Conclusive data are not available on the efficacy of different distribution outlets. The second is, as noted, whether the advantage is due more to illegal practices, legitimate marketing efforts, or to the superiority of Internet Explorer. The third is whether Netscape was severely harmed. The evidence on these points is nonexistent.

The discussion again presents the invalid share criterion (paras. 359-60, 630-38); the basis is Microsoft documents and statements by Fisher and Warren-Boulton. The government's case starts with the premise that a browser share sufficient to end the threat was Microsoft's goal (par. 359, 630-33). This is followed by arguments about why the usage figures the government employed are preferable to the shares of installations used by Schmalensee and other justification for the government's methodology (par. 360, 633-8).

Then it is noted that Microsoft's "other exclusionary and predatory conduct" harmed Netscape (paras. 367-8, 660-63). The conduct is the zero price and the accords. The undesirable effects are loss of customers, use, and revenues. Again a loss of Netscape Navigator use is precisely what Microsoft was seeking; the loss of revenue point is a reiteration of the claim that Netscape lacked financial resources. Once again, the government uses unsubstantiated characterizations to damn the consequences of successful competition.

Eventually (paras. 369-70, 663-71) the data on browser-share changes are presented. Treatment starts with review of the government's data analysis. Then data from Microsoft that confirm the case are noted. It is mentioned that the result is the expected impact of raising rivals' cost, backed by Fisher's testimony that the concept is well recognized in the economic literature. Then an effort to measure the effects of ISP contracts with Microsoft is discussed. It then is asserted that victory statements from Microsoft and conclusions by Fisher and Warren-Boulton prove the middleware threat was killed (par. 371, 671-3).

Schmalensee's dissent is criticized (paras. 373-82, 673-724), initially with the same arguments as used against his treatment of predation. These are that the threat has been eliminated, other challenges are not realistic, and predation discourages the rivalry (par. 373, 673-4). Yet another data battle follows with criticism of the data he uses (paras. 374-9, 674-698). This continues later with response to his criticism of the government data (par. 382, 716-24).

Then comes an effort to refute his assertions about the damages to Netscape. This starts with obfuscation. Schmalensee's assertion that Netscape can still outbid Microsoft is criticized for ignoring raising rivals' costs (par. 380.1, 698-9). Schmalensee actually criticized the raising-rivals'-cost concept for its inability to distinguish predation from efficient response to competition. A more proper interpretation was that the cost barriers were surmountable.

His rejection of the outlet-foreclosure assertion inspires more material on the drawbacks of downloading and carpet-bombing. The supporting quotation is an unsubstantiated claim by Fisher (June 1, 1999, p.m., 56) that such response is "raising rivals' costs."

Then comes a battle over different data, those discussed above on OEMs installation of Navigator (paras. 380.2-380.3, 699-704). Quotation of supporting testimony by Fisher (January 1, 1999, a.m., 55; June 6, 1999, p.m., 55-6, 58-9) throws in his claim that the threat was thwarted (par. 380.3.2, 704). Denunciation of the data Schmalensee presented then resumes (par. 380.3.3, 704-6). Then comes criticism for considering mail distribution and downloading as viable (par. 380.5, 706-10). Less frivolously but no more satisfactorily, a response discussed above is made to the claim that Internet Explorer won because of its superior quality.

Finally, Schmalensee's criticism of the data used by the government is reproved (par. 382, 716-24).

The government then returns to the presumably abandoned argument that browser monopoly was possible and vital to Microsoft (paras. 383-91, 725-34). The government again argues browsers are a market (par. 384, 725-6), that Microsoft sought to monopolize (paras. 385-8, 725-30), and succeeded (par. 386.1, 727-8; par. 388, 730). The government asserts barriers to entry in browsers ensure monopoly power can be exercised (par. 389, 730-32). Fisher's assertions (par. 239, 108) about the prospects for monopoly are noted. Then claims of a high probability of success and harm are justified only by quotations from Fisher and Warren-Boulton (paras. 390-91, 732-34). More Fisher and Warren-Boulton quotes follow reiterating that elimination of rivals was not required (par. 390, 732-4).

Again, a long, tenuous chain of reasoning is implicit. Once more, the monopoly assertion must be accepted. It must be demonstrated that use of the Windows monopoly was essential to the success of Explorer. Then it must be proved that such success produced a monopoly that killed the middleware threat.

A further problem is how to benefit from a browser monopoly given Fisher's zero-price and zero-ancillary-revenue arguments. Fisher never indicates how monopoly profits can be reconciled with a free browser. Neither possible explanation is consistent with the government case. The gains can only come from charging more for Explorer or by auxiliary income. The government's case stresses the commitment never to charge and contends that auxiliary income is unlikely.

The essence of all this is that given the inherent weakness of a predation charge, the absence of a satisfactory proof of monopoly power, inconsistencies in the government's argument, and the plausibility of the alternative revenue claim, the government's case seems inadequate justification for any action, let alone that of dismembering a major, successful corporation.

Other commentators have similar criticisms. For example, Klein (1999) argues that, granting most of the government presumptions (except perhaps that Explorer generates ancillary revenues), it still is impossible to determine whether Microsoft engaged in predation or just lowered price in response to competition. The existence of competition would force the provision of a browser, but, if free browsers were available elsewhere, provision of Explorer would require supplemental revenues to justify the investment.

Did Microsoft Succeed? Damage to Netscape after the $10 Billion Sale

During the trial, Netscape was sold to America Online (AOL) for stock initially valued at $4.3 billion and rising in value to $10 billion by the time of completion. Therefore, the government must explain what harm resulted.

Much was made of this. Mfof (par. 47, 20) gives the initial value and notes (par. 254, 113) the rise to $10 billion at the time the deal closed. Then the higher figure is repeated (par. 449, 202; par. 754, 348). McKenzie (2000b, 117) reiterates this information. Lacovara (June 3, 1999, a.m., 58) talks about "this $4 billion or $10 billion acquisition." Judge Jackson (cfof par. 299, 148) uses $4.3 billion. Schmalensee, writing before the deal closed, includes a $4.2 billion value almost every time he refers to the merger (par. 434, 222; par. 435, 223; par. 537, 277; par. 540, 279; par. 541, 279; par. 544, 280; and par. 577, 298).

Considerable effort was devoted to asserting that Microsoft had harmed Netscape. Some aspects of the government's effort to stress damages and minimize the deal are in earlier sections. In particular, the predation subsection (paras. 296-308, 514-44) intermingles assertions of a desire to harm Netscape and indications of success (esp. paras. 296-8, 514-23).

Overkill occurs again. Gfof (par. 307.1, 541-2) claims, based on assertions by Barksdale, Andreessen, and Warren-Boulton, that Netscape's ability to innovate was decreased. Netscape had to cut back on activities. This ignores the external financial backing available. Then the effect of Microsoft's distribution efforts on Netscape's distribution and the resulting need to offer inducements are sketched (par. 307, 542-3). This ignores that this is the normal effect of getting competition. It is further claimed that the development of other browsers was discouraged (par. 308, 543-4). This contrasts with Schmalensee's observations (June 21, 1999, a.m., 7-12) that the competition from Microsoft put pressure on Netscape to improve Navigator.

Judge Jackson embraces both views. He first (par. 379, 189-90) accepted the government charge that Netscape was forced to reduce efforts and thus innovated less than it otherwise would have. He later (par. 408, 204) notes the improvements in browsers produced by the competition.

The government also denies that AOL's ownership of Netscape is a threat to Microsoft (par. 316, 561-2). The payments by Microsoft and Microsoft's power to predate supposedly make continued use of Explorer likely. This argument is more fully developed in a discussion devoted to whether AOL would change browsers or revive the browser threat (paras. 394-6, 738-48). Fisher (January 6, 1999, a.m., 21-4) presents the case against shifting to Navigator; he contends the deal with Microsoft is too attractive to renounce. The final point is to dismiss again the threat of entry and thus Schmalensee's conclusion that this threat makes predation futile (par. 317, 562).

In the conclusion, the government tries further to explain away the AOL acquisition of Netscape (paras. 392-6, 735-48). The government presented three nonsense reasons why the AOL purchase is irrelevant. First, after two pages of statements that the purchase was not for the browser because the browser was declining, the government notes "AOL instead purchased Netscape because of Netscape's portal, server and e-commerce product" (par. 393, 735-8).

Users were attracted by default when using Netscape Navigator. AOL material with, as usual, a few Fisher quotes are the support. To deal with this, the claims are modified "To the extent AOL valued the browser, it was only as a means of feeding traffic to Netscape's portal site, not for its potential to develop into an alternative platform" (par. 393.3, 737). In short, by another convenient coincidence, Netscape is big enough to be worth $10 billion as a portal but too small to implement the Netscape/Java platform alternative. This statement downplays the necessity of keeping Navigator viable to preserve the benefits of the purchase. Schmalensee (June 21, 1999, p.m., 35-6) noted this. Such preservation maintains the potential to create a Netscape/Java platform.

Again, analytic and empirical problems arise. Netscape's complaints during the case are inconsistent with the material generated in evaluating the merger. The latter indicate that Navigator was valuable. The material is strewn about the transcripts but epitomized in the mfof. The cross-examination of Fisher (January 6, 1999, a.m., 23-30) introduces material from the press conference announcing the merger; the value of Navigator and the intention to promote it were stated. Rebuttal-phase cross-examination (June 3, 1999, p.m., 40-80) introduces the Goldman Sachs and other merger-related material. An assertion about interest in the browser appears (45). Schmalensee (June 21, 1999, p.m., 31-41) presents a discussion, based on these documents, that Netscape and Netscape Navigator are viable. He reinforces later (June 21, 1999, p.m., 87-99).

Schmalensee also presents a slightly different view (June 21, 1999, a.m., 24-5). He contends (based on the denial by Barksdale) Netscape "never seriously intended" to become a competing platform. Schmalensee then notes that Goldman Sachs indicated Netscape serves 50 million users and will serve 100 million by 2002. He believes this provides a sufficient base to justify developing a middleware alternative.

Mfof (paras. 448-60, 201-8) summarizes. It cites sealed AOL documents indicating interest in Netscape Navigator as valuable "on its own terms" as well as the basis of a popular web site and determination to strengthen market position (par. 449, 202). Another document shows AOL recognized its importance as a customer (par. 451, 203). Then the obvious point is made that a shift might occur (paras. 452-5, 203-5). The remaining discussion (paras. 456-60, 205-8) argues that the government misled. The main point is that the government cited AOL documents that for public-relations reasons deliberately understated the value of Netscape Navigator.

Mfof (par. 756, 348-9) indicates that the due-diligence studies Goldman Sachs conducted on the merger indicate that a large base of installed Navigators exists and Navigator was considered a valuable asset.

Nevertheless, Judge Jackson (cfof paras. 299-304, 148-52) minimizes the importance of Navigator to AOL. Moreover, if the government were right, it aids Microsoft by suggesting that browsers are only means to the profitable end of providing content.

The second government claim is that AOL will not revive the threat (par. 394, 738-45). Three reasons are given. First is that Microsoft's campaign against Netscape will scare AOL and AOL is too dependent on Microsoft (par. 394.1, 739-40). The first point is implausible economics. What was then AOL and is now AOL Time Warner surely has the resources and independence to mount a challenge if it seems profitable. Dependence really means Microsoft provided a superior product, contrary to charges elsewhere.

Second, again misusing the browser-share criterion, the absence of a prospect for a large share is said to discourage mounting a platform challenge (par. 394.4, 740-44). It is admitted that AOL adoption of Netscape Navigator would greatly increase share. This is deemed unlikely because AOL then would not appear in Microsoft's Windows Online Services folder and Microsoft might provide sufficient inducements to prevent a shift. The third part of the second argument is that, at best, this would be a new threat; the original challenge failed (par. 394.3, 743-5).

Third, other AOL challenges to Microsoft are unlikely (par. 396, 745-6). This point too is finely subdivided. The first is that AOL has denied interest in entering operating systems (with Schmalensee used as a confirming witness). Second, Gates suddenly becomes credible when stating "AOL doesn't have it in their genes to attack us in the platform space." Third, AOL abandoned plans to develop a low-cost alternative to the PC.

Then the government contends that AOL will not try to compete more vigorously in browsers. This is based on AOL assertions that it does not plan to compete and Fisher's conclusion in oral testimony (June 4, 1999, a.m., 52-3) that the acquisition did not affect Microsoft's monopoly power. (The cited remarks were redacted because they comment on a redacted exhibit.)

It is next again alleged that the deal with Microsoft is so good that it will continue (par. 394.4, 740-44). Since Fisher says so (June 2, 1999, a.m., 17-

18; June 1, 1999, p.m., 66), it is too late for Netscape to succeed (par. 395, 744-5). Finally, Netscape will not compete in other ways because it has no present plans to do so (par. 396, 745-8); quotations appear about operating systems and devices simpler than computers.

Mfof (paras. 753-9, 347-50) adds to evidence of the viability of Netscape and the boost given by the AOL deal a reminder of the animosity of AOL toward Microsoft (par. 758, 349-50).

The idea that a company mighty enough eventually to take over Time-Warner would remain quiescent whatever Microsoft does is at least dubious and probably absurd. As argued in Chapter 7, the existence of AOL Time-Warner and similar well-financed actors in the arena makes Schmalensee's model of behavior heavily restrained by the threat of entry the most attractive.

Fisher and Rubinfeld, as part of their effort to discredit the Evans-Schmalensee argument, include the gratuitous comment that the $4 billion value at announcement is more germane than the $10 billion at closing (2000a, 91). The substance of their attack, however, is reiteration of (1) the inferior channel charge, (2) the observation, oblivious to its irrelevance, that Navigator's share fell radically, and (3) stress on the value of the portal without recognition that such value depended on the continued viability of Netscape Navigator (2000a, 92-4). Fisher and Rubinfeld, nevertheless, assert "We can most charitably call both points [of Evans and Schmalensee] misleading." The two points were that distribution of Navigator still was wide and that selling out to AOL hardly comprises failure. Thus, the resort to invective to hide defective arguments persisted after the trial.

Thus, clearly this is predation without a victim. A simple predation model was clearly invalid. The claims about AOL are specious. Were a platform profitable, this giant and its partner in browser development, Sun, could develop it. This alone makes the government's charges frivolous.

Beyond Netscape: Probable Dangers from Monopoly

To this point, the government has failed to show why economic efficiency is reduced by the provision of a free browser and competition to improve browser quality. Harm to Netscape is not relevant. The government must demonstrate further damages. In the absence of evidence, the government becomes even more speculative in assessing broader consequences. Its peroration (paras 398-410, 749-74) lists all the losses that the government and its experts can imagine. The essence is that innovation will cease unless Microsoft is curbed. The usual collection of quotations, mostly repeats, appears.

First, it is noted that the lack of a competitor means continued use of Microsoft standards, another truism (paras. 398-403, 749-54). Claims of thwarted competition follow (par. 403, 754-8). Fisher and Barksdale are sources of affirmation. An assortment of Microsoft material indicating a desire to succeed is added. These start with another use of the Gates's interviews about Netscape's vulnerability.

The government postulates various specific losses:

1.   Preventing the emergence from the Netscape/Java platform of competition in operating systems producing more systems and more innovation at a lower price (par. 405, 759-62). The support comes from industry statements that innovations are desirable and the usual assertions from Fisher and Warren-Boulton. This merely restates the case.

2.   Discouraging alternatives to the PC (par. 405.4, 761-2). The sole justifications given are quotations from Microsoft executives stating that such devices are a threat. This is another stunning concession. It admits another, previously denigrated reason for Microsoft's Internet-Explorer strategy.

3.   "Deterring new developments" (par. 405.6. 762). This generic charge is an excuse to insert more quotes of Fisher and Barksdale. Fisher, Warren-Boulton, Barksdale, and Andreessen are quoted on general chilling effects on competition and innovation.

4.   Additional injury (par. 405.6, 762-4). This too is an excuse to quote. A remark by Scott Vesey of Boeing about the benefits of competition appears. More substantially, Fisher's charge (par. 15, 6) that Microsoft will extract a toll on the Internet is introduced. Again, the government is oblivious to the stunning concession involved. Both possible interpretations conflict with the basic arguments in the case. The toll can only be collected by higher prices of Windows or auxiliary income. Fisher ruled out the prospects for the latter and the government made that conclusion a cornerstone of the case. A higher Windows price may indeed be the outcome of successful browser monopolization. However, accepting Gates's forever-free assertion caused the government to refrain from explicitly claiming prices would rise. Fisher's explanation of recoupment reflects this recognition of the drawbacks of a price-rise claim.

5.   Reduction in the ability to choose browsers (par. 406.1, 763-4); this again restates the case.

6.   Preventing innovations by Netscape (par. 406.2, 764); this blindly accepts a Barksdale claim.

7.   The harmful effects of integrating Internet Explorer into Windows (par. 406.3.1, 765-6); this is another restatement of the case.

8.   The costs imposed on OEMs by limiting start-up display options and requiring display of the Internet-Explorer icon (par. 406.3.2, 766-7).

9.   The earlier complaints about undesirable effects on Java and Intel's Native Signal Processing (paras. 406.3.2-406.3.3, 767) are reiterated.

In short, this section only sums up the prior arguments. The essence remains a claim of severe damage to Netscape by actions that made Windows less attractive to consumers. The reduced-attractiveness conclusion is based on ignoring the benefits of a better, cheaper browser and stressing dubious charges of harm. The damages to Netscape and thus to innovation are speculative.

This is followed (paras. 403-10, 767-74) by shifting to specifying how lessened innovation would arise. This is effectively yet another presentation of the applications-barrier and predation-to-preserve-it hypotheses. The core is quotations from Fisher about the virtues of competition and his speculation that without antitrust intervention Microsoft will dictate innovation in computing (par. 408.1, 768). As should be clear by now, Fisher passionately believes that Microsoft can throttle competition and innovation. Again, others are expected to accept this vision solely because he says so. This far exceeds what any expert can confidently state.

The first specific complaint is that innovation depends on Microsoft support (par. 408.2.1, 769). Three memorandums from the same exhibit (GX 921) are cited. All indicate that Microsoft sometimes misses deadlines. One also notes that Microsoft must be persuaded to cooperate. A memorandum from Andreessen asserting that McGeady remarked that Netscape was necessary competition for Microsoft was also noted. None of this is either controversial or indicative of anything but normal business practice. For the power to be harmful, operating-system monopoly must prevail. Ill effect is then inferred from complaints from McGeady (par. 408.2.2, 769-70). He only states the predictable frustration with delay. As yet another irrelevant citation, quotation is made of some Microsoft failures mentioned in Engstrom's oral testimony.

Next is the charge that Microsoft rather than the market controls innovation. The first set of instances is again that deadlines are missed (par. 409.1.1, 770-71). This consists entirely of memoranda indicating that the release of Windows 98 was delayed until the completion of Internet Explorer 4. The remaining examples are reiteration of prior charges. The first is inconvenience to large companies seeking to customize (par. 409. 1.2, 771-2). Then the challenged activities such as the disputes on Java and Intel's Native Signal Processing and accords to promote Internet Explorer are recalled (409.2, 772-3). The treatment closes with Fisher statements postulating unspecified harms to innovation from failure to thwart Microsoft (par. 410, 773-4).

Thus, the critical issue of harm is treated only by repetition of prior speculation and new, even less substantial ruminations.

Summary and Conclusions

The chapter started by showing the different ways in which the issues were treated in key case documents. A review of the June 21, 1995 meeting between Netscape and Microsoft indicates that the event did not deserve the attention it received. At worst, Microsoft sought to buy out a competitor that refused and suffered only from new competition.

The government's treatment of the creation and integration of Internet Explorer rarely raises economic issues. The economic assertions are suspect. They involve in particular heavy use of Fisher's conjectures on the issues and invalid assertions that adding Internet Explorer overloads computers and the minds of incompetent consumers. The predatory-pricing charge is made entirely from assertions by Fisher and Warren-Boulton on the economic prospects of Internet Explorer. These include Fisher's belief that a separate charge for Internet Explorer was feasible and categorical, but unsubstantiated, rejection of the defense that Microsoft would increase income from Windows and other products.

The treatment of OEMs exaggerates the importance to browser competition of restrictions on OEMs. The treatment of deals with ISPs OLSs, ICPs, and ISVs only shows an eagerness to compete. The associated vision of foreclosing the most attractive distribution outlets seems too pat.

Finally, the assessment of damages is nonexistent. The government cannot even prove substantial harm of any sort to Netscape. What happened to the vaunted Netscape/Java platform is a mystery. The government tries to pretend the merger with AOL is irrelevant. Consumer damage consists of the possible losses of a wonderful new operating system and other innovations. Fisher's ruminations are the evidence.

In short, the government has presented a substantial amount of material, but none of it proves inefficient behavior.

Chapter 10 After the Facts: Decisions and Commentary

Much followed the Findings of Fact. New challenges and responses occurred within the legal system. First came decisions by Jackson, and then statements from the attorneys about the next phase. This all culminated in the Circuit Court of Appeals decision on the case.

As Chapters 1 and 6 indicated, a parallel universe of commentary arose even before the start of the trial and continues. Journalists, lawyers, and economists, among others, have had their say. Melding all this seems unfeasible and is clearly unrewarding. Thus, focus is on the court decisions and commentary that clarifies the debate.

Thus, the Judge's three decisions and the Court of Appeals decision are viewed. Given how closely these follow the gfof, the review is limited.

The Judge Responds: Findings of Fact, Conclusions of Law, and Final Judgment

As noted in the preface, the implausibility of Judge Jackson's Findings of Fact inspired my effort to learn the basis of his arguments. When originally read as an isolated document, Jackson's Findings of Fact seemed a collection of dubious arguments. When reread immediately after intensive reading of the critical documents in the case, Jackson's efforts appear a slavish restatement of the government's case. This extends to accepting the indefensible assertions. Thus, almost nothing is gained by closely examining Judge Jackson's Findings. The government's remedy proposals and their acceptance also do not raise analytic questions beyond those about the effects of a break up discussed in Chapter 7. How the government would micromanage Microsoft is not critical here.

The comparison is aggravated by the by now well-examined deficiencies of Judge Jackson's presentation of his decisions. As one circuit court judge complained, Jackson simply stated his facts. Neither his Findings of Fact nor his Conclusions of Law contains any formal use of the case material.

The Findings of Fact cite nothing; the Conclusions of Law only cites the Findings of Fact.

Even when he quotes from exhibits in the case including the juicy quotes, he fails to provide citations. All the possible routes to treatment are problematic. Reynolds (2001, 8-9) simply noted (by citation of several journalistic appraisals) the acceptance of government arguments and proceeded to criticize the Findings without concern over origin. One of his sources, Heilemann (2000, 305), says "only one or two [Findings of Fact] were remotely favorable to Microsoft, while the remainder of the document could have been written by the DOJ."

The alternative of tracing origins and noting radical changes seems inordinately tedious. The minimum need is familiarity with the government's case. However, the bases are not always immediately apparent. Indeed, in a few cases, searching gfof for a key word in the Judge's Findings failed to unearth a basis.

However, Jackson produced a more coherent presentation than the government did. Most critically, the discussion is more logically ordered. A narrative, rather than assertions invariably followed by quotations, is employed. At times, he does better than the government in stating the case; often he makes the argument worse.

To understand his Findings of Fact and Conclusions of Law and the Circuit Court decision, the formal legal issues in the case need note. The primary charge is illegal defense of a monopoly. This encompasses all the government's points. First, the existence of monopoly must be shown and then it must be demonstrated that Microsoft took illegal acts to protect that monopoly. The second charge is that Microsoft sought to create a browser monopoly. Third, that effort involved illegal tying of Internet Explorer with Windows. Fourth, this comprised exclusive dealing.

These charges are unrelated to how the case was organized. It was essentially a trial on the first charge. The other three charges seem only specific forms of illegal methods.

Jackson in his Findings thus follows the government in starting with the allegation of an operating-system monopoly and proceeding to discuss promoting Internet Explorer. Parts II (paras. 18-32, 6-15) and III (paras. 33-67, 16-35) of the cfof handle monopoly. The discussion is divided between the relevant market (in II) and Microsoft's position (in III). He presents the government's case whole. He is fixated about the applications barrier to entry (68 mentions in the cfof). Therefore, because the applications barrier renders competition impotent, he ignores Schmalensee's arguments about ease of entry (par. 30, 14).

The only sign that Microsoft presented a case is recognition that the evidence is inadequate to determine whether Microsoft charged a monopoly price for Windows (par. 65, 33-4). However, he avers that this does not matter because the low price may reflect goals other than underselling competition. He uses his promotion-of-future-Windows-sales example. As he fails to note, he is effectively saying that the government failed to prove its claim Microsoft charged the short-run monopoly profit-maximizing price for Windows. However, Fisher's explanation of the restrained maximization conclusion is implicitly preferred over Schmalensee's.

The remainder of the cfof moves through the rest of the arguments. He starts with a largely descriptive view of the Netscape/Java platform threat (paras. 68-78, 35-40). He then discusses alleged Microsoft efforts to fight the threat. He starts with the June 21, 1999 meeting between Microsoft and Netscape (paras. 79-92, 40-47). He goes on to Intel (paras. 94-103, 48-52), Apple QuickTime (paras. 104-10, 52-5), RealNetworks (paras. 111-14, 55-7), and IBM (paras. 115-32, 57-67). These treatments also echo the government. Thus, my criticism of implausibility, that most of the attempts failed, and the irrelevance of the IBM dispute to middleware are all ignored.

At this point, Judge Jackson undertakes his version of the case against Internet Explorer and its promotion (paras. 133-356, 66-177). He adds nothing to the government's case, fails to ignore any of the questionable points, and continues to shun the defense.

Discussion can be confined to key examples of adopting bad government arguments. He accepts the government's suggestion that technical feasibility rather than economic attractiveness should govern software design (paras. 175-85, 87-91). The dispute with Compaq is taken to illustrate a desire to promote Internet Explorer over Netscape Navigator (paras. 230-36, 114-17). This ignores that the dispute was only with one company and only involved removing the Internet-Explorer and MSN icons. The Apple deal also is his last example of excessive promotion of Internet Explorer (paras. 341-56, 169-77).

He turns to impacts (paras. 357-85, 178-92). This includes yet another battle of share data (paras. 360-74, 179-86). He adds confusion by introducing a third set—"estimates that Microsoft executives cited to support their testimony" (par. 360, 179-80). These otherwise unexplained data are deemed sufficiently different from those used by Schmalensee that the government's data are preferred to those Schmalensee used (par. 371, 185). The clearest problem with this is that he fails to substantiate.

The next portion moves to causes. This includes recognition that quality (par. 375, 186-7) and a zero price (par. 376, 187-8) were factors. He adds the undisputed point that because of the Netscape-Navigator lead, promotional activities were needed for Internet Explorer (par. 376, 187-8). He ignores that the government never tries to prove the efforts were inefficient.

An inept effort follows asserting that the browser threat was ended. First, the February 1998 battle-is-over memorandum is quoted (par. 377, 188). Then recognition is taken of the large increase in the number of users of Netscape Navigator. He concludes that, nevertheless, the larger share of Internet Explorer precludes developing the platform (par. 378, 188-9). Thus, he too uses a share criterion where a size criterion should have been employed. He goes on to deny the Netscape/AOL merger affects the situation (paras. 380-83, 190-1).

He then accepts all the charges of "polluted" Java (paras. 386-407, 192-204).

He concludes with a three-page discussion of impacts. He starts admitting that competition in browsers was increased (par. 408, 204). This is his sole concession to Microsoft in the whole document. This is supposedly offset by the numerous defects of Internet Explorer. These are not meeting the demand for a browserless operating system, the alleged disincentives (confusion, degradation, and lack of memory) to installing Netscape Navigator from the mere presence of Internet Explorer, and the ability of Internet Explorer unexpectedly to launch. He throws in the failure of Intel to develop Native Signal Processing (par. 410, 206).

He then claims unjustified distortion of competition by hobbling the rise of the Netscape/Java platform. He admits that that the evidence does not prove that the platform would have had the claimed effects but losing the potential is bad enough (par. 411, 207). Then, he echoes Fisher in suggesting that the actions intimidated rivals (par. 412, 206-7).

While the Findings of Fact were a total triumph for the government, the Conclusions of Law made one modest concession. Every charge but exclusive dealing was upheld. Again, the misuse of monopoly charge involved the existence of a monopoly and an effort to preserve it by illegal means. He handles the existence of monopoly (3-7) by a summary statement of the key conclusions of the Findings of Fact.

The treatment of the illegal defense starts with review of the law (7-9). He summarizes the middleware-platform threat (9) and moves to evidence. He starts indicating that the efforts to influence Intel, Apple, RealNetworks, and IBM and the dealing with Netscape are evidence of improper actions (9-10). Again, he is unconcerned about relevance, plausibility, or success. Moreover, the only aspect of this explicitly treated is the alleged effort to persuade Netscape not to provide a Navigator for the newest versions of Windows. A reference to the relevant Findings of Facts is all that is ever said in the Conclusions of Law about the pressures on Intel, Apple, and RealNetworks not to undertake software developments.

He then shifts to subsequent strategies. The familiar issues arise–OEM restrictions including bundling (10-14), the efforts with what he calls IAPs (14-17), ICPs, ISVs, and Apple (17-18), and polluting Java (18-19).

In concluding, he adopts a vision of predation close to Fisher's. He notes the costs and the forever-free policy. He sees no return to Internet Explorer and claims that neither greater sales of Windows nor auxiliary incomes can explain the decision. Therefore, it must be to preserve the applications barrier to entry (20-21). He does not bother to mention the resulting preservation of profits Fisher tossed in to satisfy the standard criteria of proof. Instead Judge Jackson uses evasive terminology. He describes the behavior as "predacious" (20). Later he talks of the "predatory nature of the firm's conduct" (21).

The Circuit Court decision (2001, 42) concludes that here Judge Jackson is using a definition of predation different from traditional economic models. The Circuit Court indicates the absence of liability for predatory pricing. Thus, apparently for Jackson, predation is an umbrella for anything deemed inefficient. This is an expansion more dangerous than Fisher's.

His next decision is particularly unsatisfactory. Ignoring the government's move to a reduction-of-Netscape-share argument, he asserts a desire to monopolize browsers. He uses as his prime example the alleged failed effort to move Netscape outside the Windows browser realm (22-4). He concludes that while the effort suffices to justify the finding, the rising Internet Explorer share reinforces the decision (24).

The stress on the alleged offer to Netscape conflicts with the "dangerous probability" of success criterion that Judge Jackson cites (21). Failure to secure acquiescence means a zero probability of success, the farthest possible distance from a dangerous level.

He turns to tying (25-34). The focus is in rebutting the earlier Circuit Court of Appeals decision on tying Internet Explorer into Windows. He uses the separate product argument (29) to defend a decision of tying. He adds the claim that since a price was paid for Windows, the browser was not really free (32). Again, he makes an argument that undermines his conclusions. Suddenly, he is accepting the Microsoft view of Internet Explorer and denying the consequences.

The refusal to uphold the exclusive dealing charge completes the weirdness (34-9). After swallowing the foreclosure of the best outlets, Judge Jackson now contends that too few outlets were foreclosed to constitute exclusive dealing (38).

The Appeal as Judge Jackson's Revenge

The appeal covered three areas–the Conclusions of Law, the failure to conduct hearings on a remedy, and the bias against Microsoft demonstrated in interviews given to journalists during the trial and published afterwards. The appeal largely upheld the illegal use of monopoly charge, rejected the browser monopoly charge, and required reconsideration of the tying charge. The government agreed to drop the tying charge. The Circuit Court also concluded that the remedy phase was too short. The bias charge was deemed serious enough to justify some reversals of the conclusions of law, requiring a fuller remedy hearing, and transfer of the case to a new judge. However, the request for dismissal was denied.

A large part at the end of the decision (106-25) was devoted to criticizing Judge Jackson's remarks during the trial to reporters. The Circuit Court sees a dilemma. The evidence is hearsay, but this is because Judge Jackson used the embargo to preclude investigation (108).

The discussion ultimately included citation of the quotation indicating Jackson deliberately crafted his findings of fact to limit the Circuit Court ability once again to overturn him (125). This was one of several quotes. The first indicated belief that building light meters into camera illustrated inappropriate product integration (109). Such integration emerged from market decisions reflecting the greater convenience to users. No monopolists were involved. Thus, the example further undermines Jackson's credibility. Other Jackson statements displayed animus towards Gates and other Microsoft executives (110-12) even likening them to drug dealers and other criminals (111-12).

Several statements indicated that trust in the government (112), uncertainty about his competence (112), and a desire to shock Microsoft (113) motivated his decision on a remedy. The last is another example of Jackson's peculiar outlook. As reported, he presents the familiar joke about mule training starting by hitting the mule to get attention as if it were novel.

This last is another invitation to similar remarks. In particular, W. S. Gilbert had his Lord Chancellor in *Iolanthe* use "hoodwink a judge who is not over-wise" as an example of what a lawyer should avoid to demonstrate probity. This seems precisely what the government did not shun, and Jackson clearly did not notice.

The Court concluded that the taint, nevertheless, was not sufficient to justify overturning the Findings of Fact or Conclusions of Law. Only the remedy was subject to readjudication. The justifications were that a full reversal would "unduly penalize plaintiffs, who were innocent and unaware of the misconduct" and that Microsoft's objection were limited (122). Given the extensive government effort to produce an emotional response, innocence seems dubious. That Microsoft's complaints were limited is even more questionable. Its broad objections incorporated many of the hundreds of Judge Jackson's Findings.

Judge Jackson's remark that he crafted his reports to constrain the appeals is saved for last with rationalizations of why even this does not disqualify. The judges purport to believe that this is a mere statement of the desire to provide an extensive record. The judges feel that Jackson succeeded. Clearly, this conclusion conflicts with mine. I see Judge Jackson as blindly accepting an economically unsound government case.

This restraint clearly severely and adversely affected the earlier sections of the appeal decision. Having allowed themselves to be constrained, the judges then adopted most of the findings, again including ludicrous ones.

Their treatment added analytic support and literature citations that Jackson, Fisher, Warren-Boulton, and the government attorneys had failed to provide. Explicit review of Microsoft's arguments also appeared. The rationales remained tortured. From an analytic view, the rejections were insufficient. This is another illustration of the limitations of courtroom appraisal of the vigor of competition,

The literature review (11-14) that prefaces the detailed review of the charges deserves note for what it chose. Of all the many articles on network externalities, the court picks Katz and Shapiro (1985). It is unclear why one of the earliest formal treatments was preferred to the more relevant Katz and Shapiro (1986), Arthur's broader statement of the concerns, or the *Journal of Economic Perspectives* symposium stressed in Chapter 5. Shelanski and Sidak's (2001) review of divestiture is noted next. Nodding to Schmalensee, Schumpeter is cited.

The court ends with its most extensive literature comments. These contrast Salop and Romaine (1999) to Cass and Hylton (1999). Salop and Romaine are correctly characterized as concerned with the competitive impacts of behavior in high-tech network industries. No more is said so that neither the failure of the government to meet the Salop-Romaine criteria of proof nor the deficiencies of the Salop-Romaine analysis is addressed.

Similarly, Cass and Hylton are correctly portrayed as skeptical, but the depth of their skepticism is not conveyed. Again curious diction arises. Cass and Hylton are describes as "equivocating on the antitrust implications of network effects." This suggests lack of concern. However, further comments correctly indicate that Cass and Hylton argue that the impacts of network effects is equivocal. Therefore, it is difficult to appraise such effects, which is their central point. The court returns to Shelanski and Sidak for further arguments about the problems of appraisal.

Then comes the first of many efforts to evade the problems with the case. Microsoft is characterized as not claiming "anticompetitive conduct should be assessed differently in technologically dynamic markets. It claims only that the measure of monopoly be different" (13). These unelaborated statements have no clear meaning. They are a poor summary of Schmalensee's view that structural tests are always questionable and are particularly dubious in this case. The court is only introducing its decision to prefer Fisher and Warren-Boulton over Schmalensee.

The acceptance of the monopoly charge starts with adoption of the government's structural arguments (15-19). First, Apple can be ignored because the Macintosh operating system is an imperfect substitute (16). Thus, again Apple is made simultaneously unimportant and, in assessing promotion of Internet Explorer, important. Alternatives to the PC are dismissed next (16-17).

At this point, the court turns to the problem of middleware as a threat from outside the market. (17-19). Again it is decided that because the threat is potential, it can be ignored. It is argued the law allows consideration of such possible threats. Again, the fundamental contradictions are ignored. In a structural approach, the threat should be in the market. Whatever the model, an influence cannot be potential (i.e., unimportant) and important. We are back to my conclusions in Chapter 7 that a structural approach is undesirable and the supporting arguments are inconsistent.

The court then agrees that, in the market as defined by the government, Microsoft has a high share that reflects limits to competition. Indeed, the court argues that the strength lies in the applications barrier to entry. Again, the not-inconsistent fallacy arises. Creating some applications for other operating systems is not inconsistent with disincentives for others to devise more programs (20). The court then displays another failure sensibly to resolve the debate. Microsoft's point that far less than 70,000 applications are needed to attract customers is noted (21). A long quotation of Judge Jackson is presented suggesting that, nevertheless, the idea that more is available is a powerful marketing tool (21, quoting cfof par. 37, 17-18).

The idea that the quality of Windows attracts applications is dismissed by a series of irrelevant assertions. It is admitted that the position of Windows may have been attained by superior foresight or quality but the case is about maintaining the position by illegal means. The barrier to entry gives a power to preserve a position regardless of quality. The "barrier is thus a characteristic of the operating system, not of Microsoft's popularity, or as asserted by a Microsoft witness, the company's efficiency" (22). Thus, superiority is irrelevant because it is irrelevant.

Finally, the court dismisses the argument that because of the importance of getting updated applications, Microsoft incurs the same costs as any developer of operating systems in attracting software developer. The Court then note that some such as Bain (1956) consider such difficulties a burden while Stigler (1968, 67) does not. The court concludes that this does not matter because the argument does not apply to still usable applications for older Microsoft operating systems (22-3).

The court twice uses the not-inconsistent-with-monopoly fallacy to reject Microsoft's contrary-behavior arguments (24, 25). As with the government and Jackson, the Circuit Court of Appeals, therefore, conveniently ignores the broader argument that Schmalensee, Maritz, and the mfof (par. 176, 80; par. 250, 112) presented of easy entry and many known and unknown threats preventing exercise of monopoly power.

Following another pattern in the case, the court sets good rules for judging anticompetitive conduct (25-8) and ignores them. Both the icon requirements and the controls over how Windows load are deemed anticompetitive for the same reasons stated by the government and Jackson (29-35).

The argument starts with a particularly bad statement of the high-share fallacy. A high share is needed to attain a critical mass (28). Microsoft is deemed guilty of preventing attainment of that critical mass (29). The availability of conflicting testimony is used as an excuse to accept the consumer-confusion attack on the requirements to display the Internet-Explorer icon (lumped into an unnecessary attack on all the display requirements) (30-31).

Acceptance follows of the charge that even the more arcane requirements on start-up protocols are anticompetitive. The rationalizations here are problematic. The Gates memorandum about unfavorable treatment of Internet Explorer by OEMs (but not the allegedly supporting documents) is used again (31-2). A letter from Hewlett-Packard expressing irritation is used as evidence that the restrictions are harmful. The court then recognizes that these complaints do not prove inefficiency. Its assertion of such harm starts with the overstatement that the restrictions prevent OEM promotion of rival browsers (32). All that was proven is that promotion might be more problematic. Eventually, the court reaches its conclusion that the efforts improperly harmed Netscape (33).

This is followed by a long attack on Microsoft's argument that its copyright privileges justified its actions. This "argument borders on the frivolous" (33). Since these are not central or economic issues, no comment is appropriate here. Eventually, the court turns to the Microsoft defense that Netscape was not significantly excluded. The response is parroting the exclusion-from-most-effective-outlets claim (35). This discussion is curious in treating the secondary copyright defense more prominently than the primary limited-economic-impact response.

In treating integration, the court identifies from cfof three problems: the exclusion from the Add/Remove utility, inadvertent overriding of preferences, and commingling of code. All are deemed anticompetitive (37-8), but the evidence on the inadvertent override is deemed insufficient to justify liability (40). The Add/Remove-utility point is a particular oddity. It had been mentioned in passing in gfof. Jackson's Findings of Facts (par. 170, 84-5) discusses the issue, and in his treatment of tying in the Conclusions of Law, he presents the deletion as an example of how Internet Explorer was tied (32). However, it is hard to see why such an inclusion would have been made after making Internet Explorer unremovable. More broadly, this part of the decision seems an unwise repudiation of the caution stated in its earlier decision about inclusion.

In treating IAPs, the Circuit Court identifies four charges (1) free browsers, (2) payments for securing customers, (3) creating a program useful to IAPs in customizing their offerings, and (4) making that program free. It is noted that an attractive price is desirable and that preserving profits is not the usual form of recoupment (42-3). Given this, the failure of Judge Jackson to find predatory pricing, and the failure of the government to object, the free browser and the free customizing software are deemed not to violate the Sherman Act (42). The creation of the special software is also not a violation (42). However, the requirements imposed are deemed too restrictive because of their exclusionary effect on Netscape (42-7).

The ICP deals were not illegal because Jackson's Findings of Fact did not support his Conclusions of Law (47). However, Jackson's elevating the casually mentioned deals with ISVs to a major problem was upheld (48). The court went on also to swallow whole the Apple (49-51), polluted Java (52-6), and harm to Intel (56-8) charges.

The only interesting thing about accepting the charge of bartering Office for better treatment of Internet Explorer is that Apple is suddenly described as having "a not insignificant share of worldwide sales of operating systems" (51). The Java charge is narrowed to attack on the promotion of alternative Microsoft technology (53-5). The allegedly deceptive alternative method for designing a Java program is denounced (55-6). That Microsoft designed its own Java Virtual Machine (JVM), a program that allows Java to work in other environments, was deemed innocent (52-3). The Intel aspect is more curious. Native Signal Processing is ignored. The sole concern is discouraging an Intel JVM. This inflates a single paragraph in cfof and the single sentence (18) in the Conclusions of Law, both in sections dealing broadly with Java.

The Circuit Court (58-9) then adds rejection for lack of supporting evidence of what it calls the course-of-conduct section of the Conclusions of Law. The basis is that the section supposedly postulates a general Sherman Act liability beyond that associated with the specific condemned actions. This seems a clear misreading.

Unlike the Circuit Court, Jackson did not state a violation of the Sherman Act when describing separate Microsoft actions. The "course of conduct" section, which Jackson labeled "Microsoft's Conduct Taken As a Whole" (19), seems a blanket statement that everything previously discussed was illegal (19-21). The Circuit Court characterization as "broad, summarizing conclusions" (59) suggests some recognition of this proposition. What prompted the conclusion of a general charge on top of the specific allegations, affirmation of most specifics, and the rejection of them as a package is unclear.

The last element in treatment of illegal preservation of monopoly is denying that questions about the reality of the middleware-platform threat undermine the case. The murkily presented basis is that such a reality-check requirement is a dangerously permissive standard (59-62).

On the basis of freedom of entry (66) and the inadequacy of the proof, the Circuit Court rejects the charge of attempting to monopolize browsers (62-8). Thus, while Jackson chose to be vague about the government's victory without monopoly claim, the Circuit Court endorses the assertion. Both approaches ignore that the contention is invalid.

At greater length, the Circuit Court indicates the need to rehear the tying charge (68-90). Most of the discussion is an extended argument that, as Schmalensee indicated, adding previously separate programs into other programs is common. Four existing criteria exist for an illegal tie: (1) the products are separate, (2) the firm has market power, (3) the products cannot be bought separately, and (4) a substantial volume of commerce is affected (70). The tendency to add components to software necessitates reconsidering the separate-product criterion (77, 82-3). These points justify overturning Judge Jackson's decision that the tying was per se illegal and requiring reexamination on a rule-of-reason basis (85). A warning is added that, in other software cases, a per-se rule may apply (86).

Requirements of proof are set. First, it must be shown that Microsoft unreasonably restrained competition (86). Second, it is argued that the practices that were deemed to preserve monopoly may not be tying because they may not alter competition in browsers (87).

Then, the District Court must resolve an alleged price-bundling phenomenon. Judge Jackson accepted the free-browser presumption in his Findings of Fact, but his Conclusions of Law talked about an implicit charge. The Circuit Court helpfully relates this to a conflict between Schmalensee's testimony that no separate charge is made for browsers and Fisher's assertion that browserless operating systems are sold at a discount (89-90). The statement (January 6, 1999, p.m., 42) is an assertion that, when asked, other operating system vendors indicated a willingness to discount if asked to supply a browserless operating system. No indication was given about who asked the other suppliers and whether any has actually done so. Reasonability then depends on whether or not Schmalensee is right. The government agreed to drop the tying charge.

The one thing that unites the District Court and Circuit Court treatment of the issues is failure adequately to confront the government's success criterion of a share large enough to prevent emergence of the Netscape/Java platform. To be sure, the goal is mentioned, but its implications for the browser monopoly and tying are ignored. However, the viewpoint is tacit in the decisions. Jackson deems success at thwarting the platform threat equivalent to monopolizing and illegal tying; the Circuit Court denies the equivalence. None of this resolves whether the hypothesis was credible or whether, as both Judge Jackson and the Circuit Court conclude, a reasonable probability of success really existed.

Review of the remedy phase (90-106) finds that the failure to hold hearings and issue satisfactory justification necessitates a retrial. That retrial must consider the implications of the Circuit Court's review of the District Court's Conclusions of Law (100-116). Moreover, the review must evaluate Microsoft's claim it is a unitary company that cannot be easily broken up (103-5). A further requirement is better to establish the connection between anticompetitive behavior and Microsoft's monopoly. It is asserted that stronger proof is needed in the remedy phase than in the appraisal phase.

This is fuzzy economics at least in presentation. The essence is that different punishments have different consequences. Microsoft's guilt might not be great enough to justify break up. In any case, the Justice Department has decided not to pursue divestiture.

The decision seems hobbled by too many restraints. The reluctance to overturn even the more nonsensical charges suggests strong fears about radical precedents. The search for unanimity probably fostered this restraint. The proposed settlement announced in November 2001 imposed restrictions on behavior far milder that those Judge Jackson accepted.

Commentaries

The Salop and Romaine and the Cass and Hylton papers present divergent views of antitrust enforcement suggested by the case. The Salop and Romaine article is composed in roughly equal parts of a description of the charges in the case and proposals of principles for evaluating such charges. Their treatment of the case makes accusations that go beyond the government's assertions and needs no examination here.

Their policy review observes three proposed standards–avoidable conduct, sole purpose and effect, and unnecessarily restrictive (649). As they describe the tests, the avoidable conduct test means that, if elimination is feasible, guilt is found without considering the efficiency effects. Conversely, the sole-purpose criterion allows action only when the practice has only undesirable effects. The unnecessarily restrictive concept allows balancing the benefits and costs of the action. Since they are economists, Salop and Romaine naturally prefer such a balancing and urge its adoption.

Cass and Hylton's article is a response that also deals with the case and proposes legal principles. They begin "Antitrust is a hammer, not a scalpel" (1999, 1). This leads to criticizing Salop and Romaine as part of a "nip-and-tuck school" that believes precise adjustment is possible. Cass and Hylton provide defense of Microsoft, which also can be ignored here.

Cass and Hylton reject Salop and Romaine's legal views as inconsistent with legal practice and unsound. Cass and Hylton (27-30) contend that the sole-purpose test is the closest to current law and that this situation is preferable. Salop and Romaine evoked the symmetry that their standard avoided the false acquittals from sole-purpose approach and the false convictions from a feasible-elimination rule. Cass and Hylton argue that sole purpose is preferable because avoiding false convictions is far more important than avoiding false acquittals. False convictions chill competition; market forces can offset failure to convict (30-33). They add that the information requirements of an unnecessarily restrictive rule are excessive (34).

The use of the sole-purpose test in the Microsoft case should discomfort both pairs of authors. The failure even to establish sole purpose is a warning both about the workability of the sole-purpose criterion and about going further and appraising restrictive effects.

Gilbert and Katz (2001) illustrate the problems of devising a sympathetic economic analysis of the case. They provide a good summary of the 2000 debate between Fisher and Rubinfeld versus Evans and Schmalensee and conclude that Fisher and Rubinfeld are more correct (27-9). This ignores that the government had two other theories. Gilbert and Katz add the essential caution that this does not prove damage to consumers. They describe the Netscape/Java platform threat and Evans and Schmalensee's contention that it is implausible that only one threat matters. Gilbert and Katz disagree (30).

They argue that Microsoft's claim that it was the newcomer in browsers ignores that it might have used its power in operating systems to secure a browser monopoly (32). The treatment of predatory behavior ultimately focuses on Fisher's support of any-good-browser point (35). Gilbert and Katz proceed to conclude from use of air supply and similar things that Microsoft "was mainly concerned with reducing Netscape Navigator's sales" (35). As usual, this omits consideration of whether the elimination was by Internet Explorer or as, Fisher tried to suggest, by reduced browser use. Gilbert and Katz toss in, but attribute to the government, Fisher's concern about an Apple browser. They recognize that Netscape lives (36), but the middleware threat may not (37).

In dealing with harm, they equivocate more. They argue first that the short-run benefits of a cheaper browser existed but are offset by the resulting maintenance of a higher Windows price (37-8, 40). They add the equivalent point that the advent of a Netscape/Java platform was discouraged (38, 40). They note the impossibility of appraising the effects on long-term innovation.

They then argue that while if the record consisted solely of facts about Microsoft actions, Microsoft's case might have been plausible, the documents justify stronger conclusions. Gilbert and Katz admit the ambiguity of the language but claim that the combination of potential damage and the desire to "harm competitors" is one justification. A further rationale is how much effort was exerted to "discourage consumers from using Netscape's browser" (39). The defense of using documents is better than Fisher's but still problematic. The charge of discouraging Netscape has the same ambiguity as their earlier remarks on the subject.

They conclude with one of many arguments that the restructuring plan accepted by Judge Jackson and the alternative restructuring plan proposed by several economists may have undesirable impacts (40-43). They propose stressing some form of monetary penalties.

Liebowitz prepared a criticism of the proposal to break up Microsoft. He postulates high costs from break-up because of the effects on software prices. His starting point is the plausibility of Schmalensee's analysis. Liebowitz sees a shift under separation from restrained to profit-maximizing prices. For Windows, that would be at least $300. A $300 price would raise costs to consumers worldwide by $95 billion over the 2000-2002 period; he shows the effects for other price rises (3-4). He sees the prospects of at least a 50 percent rise in the price of Microsoft Office giving a further three-year worldwide consumer cost of $34 billion (10-16).

He also notes the questionable profitability of a Linux Office and the conflict between the advocacy and the applications barrier to entry argument (16-18). He goes on also to reject the plausibility of Word or Excel becoming a platform (18). His next point is that the separation would undermine the strategy Microsoft devised to compete in the server market (19-21). Microsoft's server operating system, Windows NT, is marketed with a database program. The package challenges both existing operating systems and Oracle's database program. Similar damage would occur to Microsoft's challenge to existing game machines (21-2).

Implicitly following Microsoft arguments in the case, he argues that the remedies would fragment Windows (22-7). He tries to estimate costs and sees a three-year worldwide cost of $27 billion (27-32). He notes further costs that he cannot quantify of a lower quality Windows (32-4) and uncertainty (34). Thus, his best guess is of three-year, worldwide costs of $121 billion dollars with a high-end of $308 billion.

Crandall (2001) prepared a negative review of prior major antitrust divestitures to suggest the problems of application to Microsoft.

Shelanski and Sidak would merit attention even if the Circuit Court had not cited them. They try to establish and apply to the Microsoft case proper rules for antitrust remedies. Their treatment starts with an overview of the case that is noncommittal until ending with a review (14-15) of former antitrust head William Baxter's skepticism about attacking Microsoft.

The article presents a three-criteria basis for remedies and then discusses the relationship to actual practice. A totally descriptive review of Judge Jackson's decisions follows. Then the applicability of the guidelines to the Microsoft case is presented. Warnings about the experience with the break-up of AT&T comprise the final point. A particular concern is evaluating the comparative merits of the three possible types of remedies, divestiture, supervision of conduct, and monetary penalties.

Their three-part process starts with requiring the demonstration of a "static economic efficiency" gain (20-21). The benefits from lower prices must exceed any increases in production costs. Within the discussion is recognition of the difficulty of determining the effects in the Windows case (25-8). The second step is to ensure that no offsetting losses in "dynamic efficiency" (i.e., reduced innovation) occur (28-31). Finally, the costs of enforcement must be considered (31-9). This simply recognizes the issues that modern economics indicates are relevant in appraising efficiency.

Little of what follows needs explicit treatment here. The reviews of both prior practice and proposed Microsoft remedies are, by the nature of what is being discussed, too detailed and too inconclusive. What matters is the conclusion that the government proposals and the other alternatives suggested are inadequately justified (75).

The article can be used in at least two further ways to attack the government. The more obvious critique is that the government does not try implicitly to meet the criteria. It, as often noted here, does not quantify. The second concern relates to why the government did not quantify. Shelanski and Sidak seem unconcerned about the practicality of their criteria and, therefore, of how it might be made more operational. A crying need seems apparent for more recognition of the intrinsic limitations of antitrust than a passing reference to McChesney and Shughart.

Chapter 11 Summary and Conclusions

The case is built on the key premises that Microsoft has an impenetrable operating-system monopoly, that the monopoly was threatened by the Netscape/Java platform, and solely to meet that threat Microsoft engaged in inefficient efforts to develop and promote Internet Explorer. These arguments fail. They are barely consistent with each other, dubious in theory, and untenable in practice.

As Evans and Schmalensee argued, the strong-monopoly and serious-threat hypotheses are difficult to reconcile. Invulnerability or ease of entry are more plausible than that the bravado of a young programmer is the only thing to scare Microsoft. Microsoft is not a conventional monopolist and its strategy for Internet Explorer is not predation as normally defined. Such predation is not a credible strategy particularly towards a company as well financed as Netscape. The government's interpretation of what Gates and Maritz said ignores this backing.

Therefore, unconventional theories are evoked. In particular, the names of the theories are frequently repeated as slogans but never explained or meaningfully explored. Assertions by Fisher and Warren-Boulton are the only support. This conveniently avoids recognizing that the theories have severe defects that preclude application to any case including the Microsoft litigation. The slogan about monopoly is the applications barrier to entry. For promoting Internet Explorer, the key concept is raising rivals' costs. Theory shows that, as Schmalensee argued, the investment needed to promote a promising new operating system will emerge. Cost-raising strategies are at least as hard to implement successfully as a traditional predatory approach. The new theories do not help.

Similarly, the others supposedly victimized by Microsoft include many strong companies. The vision of Microsoft running rampant against such companies as Intel, IBM, Hewlett-Packard, Disney, AT&T, AOL, and Sun is absurd. The idea of multiple threats, moreover, is inconsistent with claims that only the middleware-platform challenge mattered.

Whatever the uncertainties of appraisal, Schmalensee's argument that Microsoft is adopting a low-price competition-forestalling strategy that produces a $50-$65 price is more plausible than either government alternative. The idea that the middleware-platform challenge was the only reason for Internet Explorer is implausible. Whatever the reason, the charge of excessive effort was also not well stated and never substantiated.

The government managed to convince gullible journalists and judges that assertions of the desire to succeed and evidence of vigorous efforts to promote Internet Explorer sufficed to prove inefficient behavior. This is the main manifestation of a fallacy central to the government case. Outcomes that occur with monopoly are taken as evidence even when the result also can arise without monopoly. The behavior would occur under both the government's monopoly-preservation scenario or Microsoft's vigorous-competition defense. The government ignores the problem of determining the motivation and quantifying the impact. This denial allows evasion of stating and implementing a verification process. Again, the claims of the expert economists substitute for proof. Those who doubted the practical relevance of the "new" industrial organization understated the case.

The concern that this was inappropriate government intervention in a commercial rivalry seems amply confirmed. The case is sufficiently defective that it should not have been brought in the first place.

The Microsoft case will live as another perennially controversial antitrust action. The case at a minimum supports Bork's injunction (which he ignored in commentary on the case) that antitrust focus on economic efficiency and particularly on Frank Easterbrook's 1984 warning that policy errors are more dangerous than market problems. The self-correcting aspects of markets are a critical difference from governments. Indeed, the case reinforces the abolitionist case.

More fully, the questionable theoretic and empirical premises that are badly presented and defended are:

1. That Microsoft possessed and benefited from an operating-system monopoly protected by an applications barrier to entry, a variant of a network-effect concept. That effect was postulated from incorrect interpretation of a few choices of technology in a few industries. The alleged "mistakes" in choosing technologies did not occur. This lack of empirical evidence is critical because the efforts to develop a supporting theory produced the familiar result that the outcome depends critically on the circumstances. In this case, the sufficient conditions are unlikely to prevail. Financing is available for attractive concepts.

2. Netscape Navigator using Java to create a middleware platform for applications was a threat to that monopoly greater than any other faced by Microsoft including existing rival operating systems and various existing and emerging alternatives to a personal computer. The case is taking sides in one commercial battle of the many that Microsoft has

waged in its history with variable success. Thus, the widespread concern that antitrust tends to protect competitors, even if competition is undermined, seems applicable.

3. The case ignores that entry into browsers follows a Microsoft pattern of entering all main markets. The entry always improves competition but does not inevitably lead to Microsoft dominance. Microsoft is being punished for competing too much.

4. Reliance is placed on an untested new theory of profitable predation through raising rivals' cost. The government asserts predatory behavior by Microsoft because Fisher and Warren-Boulton see no other explanation. Fisher and Warren-Boulton, in turn, consider only supporting documents and ignore the economics. Neither the economists nor the government explain the theory or its limitations. Nowhere in the prosecution (or defense) is it made clear that the predation aspect of the case depends *only* on whether Fisher and Warren-Boulton are right. The alternative explanations presented by Microsoft merited response, not the neglect that they received.

5. The charge that Microsoft priced Explorer on a predatory basis, moreover, critically involves the questionable and inapplicable deep-pockets concept. Netscape was not capital starved as an independent and now is part of a giant, AOL-Time Warner.

6. The evidence that Netscape was harmed is nonexistent. Selling out at an initial value of $4 billion that rises to $10 billion is an unusual form of ruin.

7. Therefore, the government resorts to speculation about harm to Netscape's platform-creation ambitions. The unobservable ruin of a hypothetical threat is made the center of the case.

8. The government stresses reduced market share as an indicator of injury to Netscape's platform ambitions when the relevant question is the absolute size of the market. Share would have been relevant if the issue had been conventional concerns over competitive position.

9. The government's claim that, although America Online acquired Netscape and continues to improve and market what is now Netscape Communicator, it will not switch to Communicator when its agreement with Microsoft ends is dubious.

10. The case relies upon economic theories whose practical relevance is difficult to determine. Therefore, a detailed, coherent presentation of the analytic basis for the case was essential. That presentation should have reviewed the theory, what the economic literature indicates about the issues, provided overwhelming supporting evidence, and thoroughly subjected Microsoft's defense to careful detailed economic argument. Any desirable use of the antitrust law requires such efforts. None were

provided. Worse, what did appear is indication that such an appraisal was impossible because so little is readily measured. The government successfully obscured these weaknesses by categorical assertions. The case is an effort to employ brute force to undermine economic criticism of antitrust. Thus, the case is further ammunition for those who argue (see Chapter 2) that efficient enforcement of antitrust is impossible and abolition is desirable.

11. The government's case is conjectures supported entirely by Microsoft documents and complaints by companies feeling threatened by Microsoft. The existence of documents is made the test of validity. The government and its economists make no effort to test whether these assertions are plausible. They use the documents carelessly. Accepting this insistence on documentary justification of decisions will chill corporate decision making.

12. The government never presents its models of competition; they must be pieced together from scattered fragments (and relevant literature ignored in the case). Initial stress is on the absence of currently viable competition. The contrary vision of Microsoft proposed by Schmalensee is of facing many competitive threats. The Microsoft competitive response involves such vigorous competition including refraining from monopoly pricing that no successful competitors emerge. The government's alternatives emerge late and elliptically (in a section of gfof criticizing Schmalensee). The government first claims limit pricing is not a plausible strategy because Microsoft can wait until entry occurs. As noted, this ignores that the competition that Schmalensee identified includes existing options and the effects of current prices on future sales. Thus, the government asserts implicitly that only current competition affects pricing. Without concern for consistency, an alternative model is presented in which limit pricing prevails but preserves monopoly profits.

13. The case material is dominated by detailed discussions of the efforts of Microsoft to promote Internet Explorer. However, these details do not demonstrate whether or not a predatory strategy was employed and succeeded.

14. The intervention involves making the technical judgments that a Court of Appeals decided were beyond the competence of a court to evaluate.

15. The government has invalid visions of computers, computer users, and companies in the computer industry.
   a. Computers lack adequate memory and storage.
   b. Users are helpless idiots incapable of coping with basic tasks.
   c. Relationships between Microsoft and other companies make Microsoft omnipotent and the others impotent.

   d. Similarly, the existence of venture capitalists eager to participate is ignored.
16. The effort to discredit witnesses involved clearly false accusations.
17. The government's case is riddled with arguments that are at best difficult to reconcile:
   a. Microsoft dominance of operating systems is undesirable, but Netscape's lead in browsers should be protected.
   b. A broad lock-in theory implies that no upgrade of anything could succeed. No new operating system can take over despite the transition from Apple and other earlier computers to DOS to Windows as a shell over DOS to Windows as a stand-alone system. More than just extensive use, thus, must preclude displacement. By ignoring the problems with the theory, the government evaded demonstrating that Windows had a locked in position.
   c. Others, particularly Apple, are no threat to Microsoft, but efforts to damage Apple are important. What these supposedly radically different operating-system companies do is a model that Microsoft should follow.
   d. Fisher at different times argues that the price of Windows was profit maximizing, was reduced to further other goals including to some degree limit pricing, and had increased but no charge was made for including Explorer.
   e. The government tries to dismiss the profitable sale of Netscape to AOL as reflecting the value of its Web portal but bases its case against Microsoft on the absence of payoffs (such as helping its own portal) other than thwarting the competitive threat to Windows. This also ignores that the value of the Netscape portal comes from access by Netscape Navigator users.
   f. Periodic retreat occurs from the argument that the number of application is critical to recognition that certain applications are critical.
   g. One expert (Shapiro) supporting break-up uses the example of Intel's support for the Linux operating system, which Fisher called a joke, as evidence of how strong firms promote competition. Weakening Microsoft, which undertakes similar activities, weakens rivalry.
   h. The government must argue that even monopolists have incentives to innovate to explain why Microsoft introduces product improvements and even suggests excessive innovation. However, it then argues that Microsoft, nevertheless, retarded innovation. In essence, the case demands trading innovations

from Microsoft that are assured for ones (from a freed industry) that are conjectural.

j. Microsoft's integration of Internet Explorer into Windows is unjustified, but it is undesirable not to have a browser installed at the computer factory. To prove that other providers did not *integrate* a browser, the government demonstrates that they *provide* a browser.

Microsoft's enemies correctly portray it as an arrogant firm seeking advantage. This is no crime. In brief, the case is an effort to criminalize arrogance.

Attackers criticize Microsoft for disrespect of the political process. What the complainers think they mean is disregard of legal requirements. An alternative view is that Microsoft properly feels that legitimate business activities should be free of government interference and refrained from seeking political favors. The case strongly reinforces concerns that political decisions are dominated by interest-group concerns that undermine economic efficiency. Many (e.g., McKenzie 2000b) have observed that the case has increased Microsoft's political consciousness. McKenzie and I do not consider that desirable. The idea that avoidance of antitrust prosecution requires political activity makes Armentano's complaints minor. The problem shifts from inefficiency to government-run extortion.

Bibliography

Note: Downloads in forms different from a PDF of the published version are identified. Lexis/Nexis sources are (LN); the download gives the original pages. Published papers downloaded in manuscript form are denoted as manuscripts.

Adams, Walter (ed.) (1990), *The Structure of American Industry*, 8th edn, New York: Macmillan Publishing Company.

Adelman, M. A. (1948), "Effective Competition and the Antitrust Laws," *Harvard Law Review*, 61:8, 1289-1350.

Adelman, M. A. (1949), "Integration and Antitrust Policy," *Harvard Law Review*, 63:1, 27-77.

Adelman, M. A. (1959), A&P: *A Study in Price-Cost Behavior and Public Policy*, Cambridge, Mass.: Harvard University Press.

Adelman, M. A. (1972), *The World Petroleum Market*, Baltimore: Johns Hopkins University Press for Resources for the Future.

Adelman, M. A. (1993), *The Economics of Petroleum Supply: Papers by M. A. Adelman 1962-1993*, Cambridge, Mass.: The MIT Press.

Adelman, M. A. (1995), *The Genie out of the Bottle: World Oil since 1970*, Cambridge, Mass.: The MIT Press

Areeda, Phillip and Donald F. Turner (1975), "Predatory Pricing and Related Practices under Section 2 of the Sherman Act," *Harvard Law Review*, 88:4, 697-733.

Areeda, Phillip and Donald F. Turner (1976), "Scherer on Predatory Pricing: A Reply," *Harvard Law Review*, 89:5, 891-900.

Areeda, Phillip and Donald F. Turner (1978), "Williamson on Predatory Pricing," *The Yale Law Journal*, 87:7, 1337-52.

Armentano, Dominick T. (1990), *Antitrust and Monopoly: Anatomy of a Policy Failure*, 2nd edn, New York: Homes and Meier for The Independent Institute. Modest revision of book published by Wiley in 1982; this, in turn, was an updating of a 1972 book.

Arthur, W. Brian (1989), "Competing Technologies, Increasing Returns and Lock-in by Historical Small Events," *Economic Journal*, 99, 116-31.

Auletta, Ken (2001), *World War 3.0: Microsoft and Its Enemies*, New York: Random House.

Bain, Joe S. (1949), "A Note on Pricing in Monopoly and Oligopoly," *American Economic Review*, 39:1 (March), 448-64. Reprinted in Heflebower and Stocking (eds) (1958, 220-35).

Bain, Joe S. (1954), "Economies of Scale, Concentration, and the Conditions of Entry in Twenty Manufacturing Industries," *American Economic Review*, 44:1, 15-39. Reprinted in Heflebower and Stocking (eds) (1958, 46-68).

Bain, Joe S. (1956), *Barriers to New Competition: Their Character and Consequences in Manufacturing Industries*, Cambridge, Mass.: Harvard University Press.

Bain, Joe S. (1968), *Industrial Organization*, 2nd edn, New York: John S. Wiley & Sons.

Baumol, William J. (1977), "Quasi-Permanence of Price Reductions: A Policy for Prevention of Predation," *The Yale Law Journal*, 89:1, 1-26.

Baumol, William J. and Janusz A. Ordover (1985), "Use of Antitrust to Subvert Competition," *Journal of Law and Economics*, 28:2, 247-65.

Baumol, William J., John C. Panzer, and Robert D. Willig (1982), *Contestable Markets and the Theory of Industry Structure*, New York: Harcourt Brace and Jovanovich.

Beckner, Paul and Erick R. Gustafson (eds) (2000), *Trial and Error: United States v. Microsoft*, Washington, D.C.: Citizens for a Sound Economy.

Beesen, Stanley M. and Joseph Farrell (1994), "Choosing How to Compete: Strategies and Tactics in Standardization," *Journal of Economic Perspectives*, 8:2 (Spring), 117-31.

Bittlingmayer, George (1999), "U.S. v. Microsoft: Cui Bono?" Cornell *Journal of Law and Public Policy*, 9 (Fall), 9-28.[1] (LN)

Bolton, Patrick, Joseph F. Brodley, and Michael H. Riordan (2000, "Predatory Pricing: Strategic Theory and Legal Policy," *Georgetown Law Review*, 88 (August), 2239-330. (LN)

Bork, Robert H. (1954), "Vertical Integration and the Sherman Act: The Legal History of an Economic Misconception," *The University of Chicago Law Review*, 22:1, 157-201.

Bork, Robert H. (1965), "The Rule of Reason and the per se Concept: Price Fixing and Market Division, Part I," *Yale Law Journal*, 74:5, 775-847.

Bork, Robert H. (1966a), "Legislative Intent and the Policy of the Sherman Act," *Journal of Law and Economics*, 9, 7-48. Reprinted with deletions in Sullivan (1991).

[1] This is one of several articles from the Fall issue of the journal that were located and downloaded from Lexis/Nexis. The article and at least one other cite material obtained in 2000 suggesting that, as sometimes happens, the issue was released long after its nominal publication date.

Bork, Robert H. (1966b), "The Rule of Reason and the per se Concept: Price Fixing and Market Division, Part 2," *Yale Law Journal*, 75:3, 373-475.

Bork, Robert H. (1978), *The Antitrust Paradox, a Policy at War with Itself*, New York: Basic Books.

Boudreaux, Donald J. and Andrew N. Kleit (1966a), "Cleaning Hands in Predation Cases: A Modest Proposal to Improve Predatory-Pricing Suits," Washington, D.C.: Competitive Enterprise Institute.

Boudreaux, Donald J. and Andrew N. Kleit (1966b), "How the Market Self-Polices against Predatory Pricing," Washington, D.C.: Competitive Enterprise Institute.

Brodley, Joseph F. and George A. Hay (1981), "Predatory Pricing: Competing Economic Theories and the Evolution of Legal Standards," *Cornell Law Review*, 66:4, 738-803.

Buchanan, James M. ([1969] 1999), *Cost and Choice: An Inquiry in Economic Theory*, The Collected Works of James M. Buchanan, vol. 6, Indianapolis: Liberty Fund.

Burns, Malcolm R. (1986), "Predatory Mergers and the Acquisition Cost of Competitors," *Journal of Political Economy*, 94:2, 266-99.

Butz, David A. and Andrew N. Kleit (2001), "Are Vertical Restraints Pro- or Anticompetitive? Lessons from Interstate Circuit," *Journal of Law and Economics*, 44:1 (April), 131-59.

Carlton, Dennis W. and Jeffrey M. Perloff (1994), *Modern Industrial Organization*, 2nd edn, New York: Harper Collins.

Carlton, Dennis W. and Michael Waldman (1998, 2000), "The Strategic Use of Tying to Preserve and Create Monopoly Power in Evolving Industries," working paper 6831, Cambridge, Mass.: National Bureau of Economic Research, revised 2000 as Working Paper Chicago: University of Chicago, George J. Stigler Center for the Study of the Economy and the State.

Cass, Ronald A. (1999), "Copyright, Licensing, and the 'First Screen'," *Michigan Telecommunications Technical Law Review*, 5, 35. (LN)

Cass, Ronald A. and Keith N. Hylton (1999), "Preserving Competition: Economic Analysis, Legal Standard and Microsoft," *George Mason Law Review*, 8:1, 1-40.

Cass, Ronald A. and Keith N. Hylton (2001), "Antitrust Intent," *Southern California Law Review*, 74 (March), 657-745. (LN)

Chamberlin, Edward H. (1962), *The Theory of Monopolistic Competition: A Re-orientation of the Theory of Value*, eighth edn, Cambridge, Mass: Harvard University Press.

Cheung, Stephen (1973), "The Fable of the Bees: An Economic Investigation," *Journal of Law and Economics*, 16:1, 11-33.

Church, Jeffrey and Neil Gandal (1992), "Network Effects, Software Provision, and Standardization," *Journal of Industrial Economics*, 40:1 (March), 85-103.

Coase, Ronald H. (1937), "The Nature of the Firm," *Economica*, NS 4:4, 386-405. Reprinted in Stigler and Boulding (eds) (1952, 331-51); Coase (1988); and Williamson and Winter (1991).

Coase, Ronald H. (1960), "The Problem of Social Cost," *Journal of Law and Economics*, 3, 1-44. Reprinted in Coase (1988).

Coase, Ronald H. (1988), *The Firm, the Market and the Law*, Chicago: University of Chicago Press.

Coate, Malcolm B. and Jeffrey H. Fischer (2001), "Can Post-Chicago Economics Survive Daubert?" *Akron Law Review*, 34, 795-52. (LN)

Coate, Malcolm B. and Andrew N. Kleit (1994), "Exclusion, Collusion, or Confusion: The Underpinnings of Raising Rivals' Costs," *Research in Law and Economics*, 16, 73-93.

Crandall, Robert W. (2001), "The Failure of Structural Remedies in Sherman Act Monopolization Cases," Washington, D.C.: AEI-Brookings Joint Center for Regulatory Studies, working paper 01-05.

Crew, Clyde Wayne, Jr. (2001), "The Antitrust Terrible 10: Why the Most Reviled 'Anti-competitive' Business Practices Can Benefit Consumers in the New Economy," Policy Analysis 405, Washington, D.C.: The Cato Institute.

David, Paul A. (1985), "CLIO and the Economics of QWERTY," *American Economic Review, Papers and Proceedings*, 75:2 (May), 332-7.

Demsetz, Harold (1974), "Two Systems of Belief About Monopoly," in Harvey J. Goldschmid, H. Michael Mann, and J. Fred Weston (eds), 164-84. Reprinted in Demsetz (1989, 91-111).

Demsetz, Harold (1988), *Ownership, Control and the Firm, the Organization of Economic Activity*, vol. 1, Cambridge Mass. and Oxford: Blackwell.

Demsetz, Harold (1989), *Efficiency, Competition and Policy, the Organization of Economic Activity*, vol. 2, Cambridge Mass. and Oxford: Blackwell.

Easley, David, Robert T. Masson, and Robert J. Reynolds (1985), "Preying for Time," *Journal of Industrial Economics*, 33:4, 445-60.

Easterbrook, Frank H. (1981), "Predatory Strategies and Counterstrategies," *The University of Chicago Law Review*, 48:2, 263-337.

Easterbrook, Frank H. (1984), "The Limits of Antitrust," *Texas Law Review*, 63:1, 1-40.

Easterbrook, Frank H. (1999), "First Principles: Is There a Role for Antitrust Law? Does Antitrust Have a Comparative Advantage?" *Harvard Journal of Law and Public Policy*, 23 (Fall), 3-10. (LN)

Economides, Nicholas (2001a), "The Microsoft Antitrust Case," *Journal of Industry, Competition and Trade: From Theory to Policy*, (August) (manuscript).

Economides, Nicholas (2001b), "The Microsoft Antitrust Case: Rejoinder," *Journal of Industry, Competition and Trade: From Theory to Policy*, (August). (manuscript)

Economides, Nicholas (2001c), "United States v. Microsoft: A Failure of Antitrust in the New Economy," *UWLA Law Review*, 32, 3-49. (LN)

Economides, Nicholas and Steven C. Salop (1992), "Competition and Integration Among Complements, and Network Market Structures," *Journal of Industrial Economics*, 40:1 (March), 105-23.

Elzinger, Kenneth (1988), "The New International Economics Applied: Japanese Televisions and U.S. Consumers," *Chicago-Kent Law Review*, 64, 941-67. (LN)

Evans, David S. (2000), "All the Facts That Fit: Square Pegs and Round Holes in U.S. v. Microsoft," *Regulation*, 22, 54-63. Reprinted in Beckner and Gustafson (2000, 11-37).

Evans, David S., Franklin M. Fisher, Daniel L. Rubinfeld, and Richard L. Schmalensee (2000), *Did Microsoft Harm Consumer? Two Opposing Views*, Washington, D.C.: AEI-Brookings Joint Center for Regulatory Studies.

Evans, David S., Albert Nichols, and Bernard Reddy (1998), "The Rise and Fall of Leaders in Personal Computer Software," December (prepared with support from Microsoft).

Evans, David S., Albert Nichols, and Richard L. Schmalensee (2001), "An Analysis of the Governments Case in U.S. v. Microsoft," *Antitrust Bulletin* (Summer). (manuscript)

Evans, David S. and Richard L. Schmalensee (2000a), "Be Nice to our Rivals: How the Government Is Selling an Antitrust Case without Consumer Harm in United States v. Microsoft," in David S. Evans, Franklin M. Fisher, Daniel L. Rubinfeld, and Richard L. Schmalensee (2000), 45-86 (notes, 120-30).

Evans, David S. and Richard L. Schmalensee (2000b), "Consumers Lose If Leading Firms Are Smashed for Competing," in David S. Evans, Franklin M. Fisher, Daniel L. Rubinfeld, and Richard L. Schmalensee (2000), 97-106 (notes, 131-2).

Farrell, Joseph and Garth Saloner (1986), "Installed Base and Compatibility: Innovation Product Preannouncements, and Predation," *American Economic Review*, 76:5 (December), 940-55.

Farrell, Joseph and Garth Saloner (1992), "Converters, Compatibility, and the Control of Interfaces," *Journal of Industrial Economics*, 40:1 (March), 9-35.

Fisher, Franklin M. (1979), "Diagnosing Monopoly," *Quarterly Review of Economics and Business*, 19 (Summer), 7-33.

Fisher, Franklin M. (1988), "Matsushita: Myth v. Analysis in the Economics of Predation," *Chicago-Kent Law Review*, 64, 969-77. (LN)

Fisher, Franklin M. (1989), "Games Economists Play: A Noncooperative View," *Rand Journal of Economics*, 20:1, 113-24.

Fisher, Franklin M. (1991), "Organizing Industrial Organization: Reflections on the *Handbook of Industrial Organization*," *Brookings Papers on Economic Activity: Microeconomics*, 201-25 (Comments, 226-38).

Fisher, Franklin M. (2000), "The IBM and Microsoft Cases: What's the Difference?" *American Economic Review, Papers and Proceedings*, 90:2 (May), 180-3.

Fisher, Franklin M., John J. McGowan, and Joen E. Greenwood (1983), *Folded, Spindled, and Mutilated Economic Analysis and U.S. v. IBM*, Cambridge, Mass.: The MIT Press.

Fisher, Franklin M. and Daniel L. Rubinfeld (2000a), "Misconceptions, Misdirections, and Mistakes, in David S. Evans, Franklin M. Fisher, Daniel L. Rubinfeld, and Richard L. Schmalensee (2000), 87-96 (notes 130-1).

Fisher, Franklin M. and Daniel L. Rubinfeld (2000b), "U.S. v Microsoft: An Economic Analysis," in David S. Evans, Franklin M. Fisher, Daniel L. Rubinfeld, and Richard L. Schmalensee (2000), 1-44 (notes 109-20).

Fisher, Franklin M. and Daniel L. Rubinfeld (2000c), "U.S. v Microsoft: An Economic Analysis," *Antitrust Bulletin*, 46:1 (Spring 2001), 1-69. (manuscript)

Fudenberg, Drew and Jean Tirole (1984), "The Fat-Cat Effect, The Puppy-Dog Ploy, and the Lean and Hungry Look," *American Economic Review, Papers and Proceedings*, 74:2, 311-16.

Gifford, Daniel J. (1999), "Java and Microsoft: How Does the Antitrust Story Unfold?" *Villanova Law Review*, 44, 67-123. (LN)

Gilbert, Richard J. (1989), "Mobility Barriers," in Richard Schmalensee and Robert D. Willig (eds), 475-535.

Gilbert, Richard J. (1992), "Symposium on Compatibility: Incentives and Market Structure," *Journal of Industrial Economics*, 40:1 (March), 1-8.

Gilbert, Richard J. and Michael L. Katz (2001), "An Economist's Guide to U.S. v. Microsoft," *Journal of Economic Perspectives*, 15:2 (Spring), 25-44.

Goldschmid, Harvey J., H. Michael Mann, and J. Fred Weston (eds) (1974), *Industrial Concentration: The New Learning*, Boston: Little Brown.

Gordon, Richard L. (1994), *Regulation and Economic Analysis: A Critique over Two Centuries*, Boston: Kluwer Academic Publishers.

Gordon, Richard L. (2000), "Debunking Path Dependence, review of *Winners, Losers & Microsoft* by Stan J. Liebowitz and Stephen E. Margolis," *Regulation*, 23:2 (Spring), 57-8.

Gordon, Richard L. (2001), "Appraising Predation: Review of *Are Predatory Commitments Credible? Who Should the Courts Believe?* By John R. Lott, Jr.," *Regulation*, 24:1 (Spring), 59-60.

Graglia, Lino A. (1999), "Is There a Role for Antitrust Law? Is Antitrust Obsolete?" *Harvard Journal of Law and Public Policy*, 22, (Fall), 11-23. (LN)

Granitz, Elizabeth and Benjamin Klein (1996), "Monopolization by 'Raising Rivals' Costs': The Standard Oil Case," *Journal of Law and Economics*, 21, 1-20.

Hall, Chris E. and Robert E. Hall (1999), "National Policy on Microsoft: A Neutral Perspective: Version 2.0," NetEcon.com.

Harvard Law Review (unsigned) (2001), "Note: Antitrust and the Information Age: Section 2 Monopolization Analyses in the New Economy," 114 (March), 1623-46. (LN)

Hawker, Norman W. (1999), "Open Windows: The Essential Facilities Doctrine and Microsoft," *Ohio Northern University Law Review*, 25, 115-47. (LN)

Hay, George A. (1981), "A Confused Lawyer's Guide to the Predatory Pricing Literature," in Stephen C. Salop (ed.).

Hazlett, Thomas W. (1999), "Microsoft's Internet Exploration: Predatory or Competitive?" *Cornell Journal of Law and Public Policy*, 9 (Fall), 29-59. (LN)

Heflebower, Richard B. and George W. Stocking (eds) (1958), *Readings in Industrial Organization and Public Policy*, Homewood, Ill.: Richard D. Irwin.

Heilemann, John (2000), "The Truth, The Whole Truth, and Nothing but the Truth," *Wired*, 8:11 (November), 260-311.

Houck, Stephen D. (1999), "Antitrust Enforcement in High Tech Industries," *Cornell Journal of Law and Public Policy*, 9 (Fall), 1-8. (LN)

Hovenkamp, Herbert (2001), "Post-Chicago Antitrust: A Review and Critique," *Columbia Business Law Review*, 258-337. (LN)

Hylton, Keith N. and Michael Salinger (2001), "Tying Law and Policy: A Decision Theoretic Approach," Working Paper Series, Law and Economics 01-04, Boston: Boston University School of Law.

Joskow, Paul L. and Alvin K. Klevorick (1979), "A Framework for Analyzing Predatory Pricing Policy," *The Yale Law Journal*, 89:2, 213-70.

Katz, Michael L. (1989), "Vertical Contractual Relations," in Richard Schmalensee and Robert D. Willig (eds).

Katz, Michael L. and Carl Shapiro (1985), "Network Externalities, Competition, and Compatibility," *American Economic Review*, 75:3 (June), 424-40.

Katz, Michael L. and Carl Shapiro (1986), "Technology Adoption in the Presence of Network Externalities," *Journal of Political Economy*, 94:4 (August), 822-41.

Katz, Michael L. and Carl Shapiro (1992), "Product Introduction with Network Externalities," *Journal of Industrial Economics*, 40:1 (March), 55-83.

Katz, Michael L. and Carl Shapiro (1994), "Systems Competition and Network Effects," *Journal of Economic Perspectives*, 8:2 (Spring), 93-115.

Kaysen, Carl and Donald F. Turner (1959), *Antitrust Policy: An Economic and Legal Analysis*, Cambridge, Mass.: Harvard University Press.

Klein, Benjamin (1999), "An Economic Analysis of Microsoft's Conduct," *Antitrust*, (Fall). (manuscript downloaded from NERA.com)

Klein, Benjamin (2001), "The Microsoft Case: What Can a Dominant Firm Do to Defend Its Market Position?" *Journal of Economic Perspectives*, 15:2 (Spring), 45-62.

Kleit, Andrew N. (1992), "Computer Reservations Systems: Competition Misunderstood," *Antitrust Bulletin*, 37:4 (Winter), 833-61.

Kleit, Andrew N. (1993), "Efficiencies without Economists: The Early Years of Retail Price Maintenance," *Southern Economic Journal*, 59: 4 (April), 597-619.

Kleit, Andrew N. and Malcolm B. Coate (1993), "Are Judges Leading Economic Theory?" Sunk Costs, the Threat of Entry and the Competitive Process," *Southern Economic Journal*, 60:1 (July), 103-18.

Kleit, Andrew N. and Robert J. Michaels (1994), "Antitrust, Rent-seeking, and Regulation: the Past and Future of Otter Tail," *The Antitrust Bulletin*, 39:3 (Fall), 659-725.

Klevorick, Alvin K. (1991), "Directions and Trends in Industrial Economics: A Review Essay on the *Handbook of Industrial Organization*," *Brookings Papers on Economic Activity: Microeconomics 1991*, 241-64 (Comments, 265-79).

Koller, Roland H., II (1971), "The Myth of Predatory Pricing–An Empirical Study," *Antitrust Law and Economics Review*, 4, 105-23.

Koopmans, Tjalling Charles (1947), "Measurement without Theory," *Review of Economic Statistics*, 2:39 (August), 161-72.

Krattenmaker, Thomas G. and Steven C. Salop (1986), "Anticompetitive Exclusion: Raising Rivals' Costs to Achieve Power over Price," *Yale Law Journal*, 6:2: 209-93.

Kreps, David M. and Robert Wilson (1982), "Reputation and Imperfect Information," *Journal of Economic Theory*, 27:2, 253-79.

Krouse, Clement G. (1990), *Theory of Industrial Competition*, Cambridge Mass.: Basil Blackwell.

Kuhn, Thomas (1970), *The Structure of Scientific Revolutions*, 2nd edn enlarged, Chicago: University of Chicago Press.

Landes William M. and Richard A. Posner (1981), "Market Power in Antitrust Cases," *Harvard Law Review*, 94:5, 937-86.

Langer, Robert M. (1999), "Symposium Introduction: United States v. Microsoft," *Connecticut Law Review*, 33 (Summer), 1245-50. (LN)

Letwin, William (1965), *Law and Economic Policy in America: The Evolution of the Sherman Antitrust Act*, New York: Random House. (Now University of Chicago Press.)

Levy, Robert A. (1998), "Microsoft and the Browser Wars: Fit to Be Tied," Cato Institute Policy Analysis 296, Washington, D.C.: the Cato Institute. Reprinted *Connecticut Law Review*, 31 (Summer 1999, 1321-60). (LN)

Levy, Robert A. (1999), "Microsoft Redux: Anatomy of a Baseless Lawsuit," Cato Institute Policy Analysis 352, Washington, D.C.: the Cato Institute.

Levy, Robert A. and Alan Reynolds (2000), "Microsoft's Appealing Case," Cato Institute Policy Analysis 385, Washington, D.C.: the Cato Institute.

Liebeler, Wesley J. (1986), "Whither Predatory Pricing? From Areeda and Turner to Matsushita," *Notre Dame Law Review*, 61, 1052-98. (LN)

Liebowitz, S. J. (2000), "An Expensive Pig in a Poke: Estimating the Cost of the District Court's Proposed Breakup of Microsoft," Association for Competitive Technology.

Liebowitz, S. J. and Stephen E. Margolis (1990), "The Fable of the Keys," *Journal of Law and Economics*, 33, 1-26.

Liebowitz, S. J. and Stephen E. Margolis (1994), "Network Externality: An Uncommon Tragedy," *Journal of Economic Perspectives*, 8:2 (Spring), 133-50.

Liebowitz, S. J. and Stephen E. Margolis (1995), "Are Network Externalities A New Source of Market Failure?" *Research in Law and Economics*, 12, 1- 22. (manuscript)

Liebowitz, S. J. and Stephen E. Margolis (1996), "Should Technology Choice Be a Concern of Antitrust?" *Harvard Journal of Law and Technology, 9 (Summer)*, 283-318. (LN)

Liebowitz, S. J. and Stephen E. Margolis (1998), "Dismal Science Fictions: Network Effects, Microsoft, and Antitrust Speculation," Cato Institute Policy Analysis 324, Washington, D.C.: The Cato Institute.

Liebowitz, S. J. and Stephen E. Margolis (1999), *Winners, Losers & Microsoft, Competition and Antitrust in High Technology* (revised edn 2001), Oakland: The Independent Institute.

Lipsey, Richard G. and K. Lancaster (1956), "The General Theory of Second Best," *Review of Economic Studies*, 24:1, 11-32. Reprinted in M. J. Farrell (ed.) (1973), *Readings in Welfare Economics*, London: Macmillan and Company.

Lopatka, John E. and Andrew N. Kleit (1995), "The Mystery of Lorain Journal and the Quest for Foreclosure in Antitrust," *Texas Law Journal*, 73:6 (May), 1255-1306.

Lopatka, John E. and William H. Page (1999), "Antitrust on Internet Time: Microsoft and the Law and Economics of Exclusion," *Supreme Court Economic Review*, 7, 157-231. (LN)

Lott, John R. Jr. (1999), *Are Predatory Commitments Credible? Who Should the Courts Believe?* Chicago: The University of Chicago Press.

McChesney, Fred S. and William F. Shughart II (eds) (1995), *The Causes and Consequences of Antitrust*, Chicago: The University of Chicago Press.

McGee, John S. (1958), "Predatory Price Cutting: The Standard Oil (N.J.) Case," *Journal of Law and Economics*, 1, 137-69.

McGee, John S. (1971), *In Defense of Industrial Concentration*, New York: Praeger Publishers.

McGee, John S. (1974), "Efficiencies and Economies of Size," in Harvey J. Goldschmid, H. Michael Mann, and J. Fred Weston (eds), 55-97.

McGee, John S. (1980), "Predatory Pricing Revisited," *Journal of Law and Economics*, 23:2, 289-329.

McGee, John S. (1988), *Industrial Organization*, Englewood Cliffs: Prentice Hall.

McGee, John S. and Lowell R. Bassett (1976), "Vertical Integration Revisited," *Journal of Law and Economics*, 19:1, 17-38.

McKenzie, Richard B. (2000a), "Microsoft's 'Applications Barrier to Entry' The Missing 70,000 Programs," Cato Institute Policy Analysis 380, Washington, D.C.: The Cato Institute.

McKenzie, Richard B. (2000b), *Trust on Trial: How the Microsoft Case Is Reframing the Rules of Competition*, Cambridge, Mass.: Perseus Publishing.

McKenzie, Richard B. and William F. Shughart II (1998), "Is Microsoft a Monopolist?" *Independent Review*, 3:3 (Fall), 165-97.

Mariger, Randall (1978), "Predatory Price Cutting: The Standard Oil of New Jersey Case Revisited," *Explorations in Economic History*, 15:4, 341-67.

Mariotti, Renato (2000), "Note: Rethinking Software Tying," *Yale Journal on Regulation*, 17 (Summer), 367-406.

Mason, Edward S. (1957), *Economic Concentration and the Monopoly Problem*, Cambridge, Mass.: Harvard University Press.

Mathewson, G. Frank and R. A. Winter (1983a), "The Incentives for Resale Price Maintenance under Imperfect Information," *Economic Inquiry*, 21 (July), 337-48.

Mathewson, G. Frank and R. A. Winter (1983b), "Vertical Integration by Contractual Restraints in Spatial Markets," *Journal of Business*, 56:4, 479-517.

Mathewson, G. Frank and R. A. Winter (1984), "An Economic Theory of Vertical Restraint," *Rand Journal of Economics*, 15:1, (Spring), 27-38.

Means, Gardiner (1939), *The Structure of the American Economy*, Washington, D.C.: National Resources Council.

Milgrom, Paul and John Roberts (1982), "Predation, Reputation and Entry Deterrence," *Journal of Economic Theory*, 27:2, 280-312.

Milgrom, Paul and John Roberts (1987), "Informational Asymmetries, Strategic Behavior, and Industrial Organization," *American Economic Review, Papers and Proceedings*, 7:2, 184-93.

Neale, A. D. and D. G. Goyder (1980), *The Antitrust Laws of the United States of America, A Study of Competition Enforced by Law*, 3rd edn, Cambridge: Cambridge University Press.

Nichols, Albert L. (1999), "U.S. v. Microsoft: Hard Competition is Good for Consumers," Cambridge, Mass.: National Economic Research Associates.

Ordover, Janusz A. and Garth Saloner (1989), "Predation, Monopolization, and Antitrust," in Richard Schmalensee and Robert D. Willig (eds), 537-96.

Ordover, Janusz A. and Robert D. Willig (1981a), "An Economic Definition of Predation: Pricing and Product Innovation," *Yale Law Journal*, 91:8, 8-53.

Ordover, Janusz A. and Robert D. Willig (1981b), "An Economic Definition of Predatory Product Innovation," in Stephen C. Salop (ed.).

Page, William H. and John E. Lopatka (1999), "The Dubious Search for 'Integration' in the Microsoft Trial," *Connecticut Law Review*, 31 (Summer), 1251-74. (LN)

Peltzman, Sam (1991), "*The Handbook of Industrial Organization*: A Review Article," *Journal of Political Economy*, 99, 201-17.

Perry, Martin K. (1989), "Vertical Integration: Determinants and Effects," in Richard Schmalensee and Robert D. Willig (eds), 183-255.

Piraino, Thomas A., Jr. (2000), "Identifying Monopolist's Illegal Conduct under the Sherman Act," *New York University Law Review*, 75 (October), 809-92. (LN)

Posner, Richard A. (1976), *Antitrust Law: An Economic Perspective*, Chicago: University of Chicago Press.

Posner, Richard A. (1979), "The Chicago School of Antitrust," *University of Pennsylvania Law Review*, 27, 925-52. Reprinted with deletions in Sullivan (1991).

Rasmusen, Eric B., J. Mark Ramseyer, and John S. Wiley, Jr. (1991), "Naked Exclusion," *American Economic Review*, 81:5 (December), 1137-45.

Reback, Gary, Susan Creighton, David Killam, and Neil Nathanson with assistance from Garth Saloner and W. Brian Arthur (1994), "Technological, Economic and Legal Perspectives Regarding Microsoft's Business Strategy in Light of the Proposed Acquisition of Intuit, Inc." (downloaded from Upside.com.)

Reddy, Bernard J., David S. Evans, and Albert L. Nichols (1999), "Why Does Microsoft Charge So Little for Windows?" (Downloadable at NERA.com.)

Reiffen, David and Andrew N. Kleit (1990), "Terminal Railroad Revisited: Foreclosure of an Essential Facility of Simple Horizontal Monopoly?" *Journal of Law and Economics*, 33:2 (October), 419-38.

Reynolds, Alan (2001), *The Microsoft Antitrust Appeal: Judge Jackson's "Findings of Fact" Revisited*, Westfield: The Hudson Institute.

Roberts, John (1986), "A Signalling Model of Predatory Pricing," *Oxford Economic Papers*, 38 (Supplement-November), 75-93.

Robinson, Joan (1933), *The Economics of Imperfect Competition*, London: Macmillan and Company.

Rule, Charles F. (1999), "Why Microsoft Hasn't Violated the Antitrust Law," *Connecticut Law Review*, 31 (Summer), 1387-95. (LN)

Salop, Stephen C. (ed.) (1981), *Strategy, Predation, and Antitrust Analysis*, Washington, D.C.: U.S. Federal Trade Commission.

Salop, Steven C. and R. Craig Romaine (1999), "Preserving Monopoly: Economic Analysis, Legal Standards, and Microsoft," *George Mason Law Review*, 7 (Spring), 617-69. (LN)

Salop, Steven C. and David T. Scheffman (1983), "Raising Rivals Costs," *American Economic Review, Papers and Proceedings*, 73:2, 267-71.

Salop, Steven C. and David T. Scheffman (1987), "Cost-Raising Strategies," *Journal of Industrial Economics*, 36, 19-34.

Sappington, David E. M. and J. Gregory Sidak (2000), "Are Public Enterprises the Only Credible Predators?" *University of Chicago Law Review*, 67 (Winter), 271-92. (LN)

Scherer, F. M. (1974), "Economies of Scale as a Determinant," in Harvey J. Goldschmid, H. Michael Mann, and J. Fred Weston (eds), 15-54.

Scherer, F. M. (1976a), "Predatory Pricing and the Sherman Act: A Comment," *Harvard Law Review*, 89:5, 869-90.

Scherer, F. M. (1976b), "Some Last Words on Predatory Pricing," *Harvard Law Review*, 89:5, 901-3.

Scherer, F. M. and David Ross (1990), *Industrial Market Structure and Economic Performance*, 3rd edn, Boston: Houghton-Mifflin Co.

Schmalensee, Richard L. (1982), "Diagnosing Market Power in Antitrust Cases: Another Look at Market Power," *Harvard Law Review*, 95, 1789-1816.

Schmalensee, Richard L. (undated), "Diagnosing Market Power in Antitrust Cases," n/e/r/a topics, New York: National Economic Research Associates. (GX 2335)

Schmalensee, Richard and Robert D. Willig (eds) (1989), *Handbook of Industrial Organization*, 2 vols, Amsterdam: North-Holland.

Schumpeter, Joseph A. (1954), *History of Economic Analysis*, New York: Oxford University Press.

Shelanski, Howard A. and J. Gregory Sidak (2001), "Antitrust Divestiture in Network Industries," *University of Chicago Law Review*, 68 (Winter), 1-99. (LN)

Shenefield, John H. and Irwin M. Stelzer (1998), *The Antitrust Laws A Primer*, 3rd edn, Washington, D.C.: The AEI Press.

Shy, Oz (1995), *Industrial Organization: Theory and Applications*, Cambridge, Mass.: The MIT Press.

Sidak, Joseph Gregory (1983), "Debunking Predatory Innovation," *Columbia Law Review*, 83:5, 1121-81.

Spulber, Daniel F. (1989), *Regulation and Markets*, Cambridge, Mass.: The MIT Press.

Stigler, George J. (1951), "The Division of Labor is Limited by the Extent of the Market," *Journal of Political Economy*, 59:3 (June), 185-93. Reprinted in Stigler (1968, 129-41).

Stigler, George J. (1959), "The Politics of Political Economists," *Quarterly Journal of Economics*, 73:4 (November), 522-32. Reprinted in Stigler (1965, 51-65).

Stigler, George J. (1965), *Essays in the History of Economics*, Chicago: University of Chicago Press.

Stigler, George J. (1966), "The Economic Effects of Antitrust Laws," *Journal of Law and Economics*, 9, 225-58. Reprinted in Stigler (1968, 259-95).

Stigler, George J. (1968), *The Organization of Industry*, Homewood, Ill.: Richard D. Irwin (available as a paperback from the University of Chicago Press).

Stigler, George J. (1987), *The Theory of Price*, 4th edn, New York: Macmillan Publishing Company.

Stigler, George J. (ed.) (1988), *Chicago Studies in Political Economy*, Chicago: University of Chicago Press.

Stigler, George J. and Kenneth E. Boulding (eds) (1952), *Readings in Price Theory*, Homewood, Ill.: Richard D. Irwin.

Sullivan, E. Thomas (ed.) (1991), *The Political Economy of the Sherman Act: The First One Hundred Years*, New York: Oxford University Press.

Telser, L. G. (1960), "Why Should Manufacturers Want Fair Trade?" *Journal of Law and Economics*, 3, 86-105.

Telser, L. G. (1965), "Abusive Trade Practices: An Economic Analysis," *Law and Contemporary Problems*, 30:3, 488-505.

Telser, L. G. (1966), "Cutthroat Competition and the Long Purse," *The Journal of Law and Economics*, 9, 259-77.

Thorelli, Hans B. (1955), *Federal Antitrust Policy: Origination of an American Tradition*, Baltimore: John Hopkins Press.

Tirole, Jean (1988), *The Theory of Industrial Organization*, Cambridge, Mass.: The MIT Press.

U.S. Court of Appeals for the District of Columbia Circuit (1998), United States of America Appellee v. Microsoft Corporation, Appellant (June 23).

Varian, Hal R. (1989), "Price Discrimination," in Richard Schmalensee and Robert D. Willig (eds), 597-654.

Varian, Hal R. (1992), *Microeconomic Analysis*, 3rd edn, New York: W. W. Norton.

Vaughn, Karen I. (1994), *Austrian Economics in America: The Migration of a Tradition*, Cambridge: Cambridge University Press.

Weiss, Leonard W. (1974), "The Concentration-Profits Relationship and Antitrust," in Harvey J. Goldschmid, H. Michael Mann, and J. Fred Weston (eds), 185-233.

Werden, Gregory J. (1992), "The History of Antitrust Market Delineation," *Marquette Law Review*, 76 (Fall), 123-215. (LN)

Whinston, Michael D. (1990), "Tying, Foreclosure, and Exclusion," *American Economic Review*, 80:4 (September), 837-59.

Whinston, Michael D. (2001), "Exclusivity and Tying in U.S v. Microsoft: What We Know, and Don't Know," *Journal of Economic Perspectives*, 15:2 (Spring), 63-80.

Williamson, Oliver E. (1968), "Economies as an Antitrust Defense: The Welfare Tradeoffs," *American Economic Review*, 58, 18-36. Reprinted in Williamson (1987, 3-23).

Williamson, Oliver E. (1975), *Markets and Hierarchies: Analysis and Antitrust Implications*, New York: Free Press.

Williamson, Oliver E. (1977), "Predatory Pricing: A Strategic and Welfare Analysis," *The Yale Law Journal*, 87:2, 284-340.

Williamson, Oliver E. (1979), "Williamson on Predatory Pricing II," *The Yale Law Journal*, 88:6, 1183-1200.

Williamson, Oliver E. (1985), *The Economic Institutions of Capitalism: Firms, Markets, Relational Contracting*, New York: The Free Press.

Williamson, Oliver C. 1987. *Antitrust Economics: Mergers, Contracting, and Strategic Behavior*, Cambridge, Mass.: Basil Blackwell.

Williamson, Oliver E. and Sidney G. Winter (eds) (1991), *The Nature of the Firm: Origins, Evolution and Development*, New York: Oxford University Press. Except for the original Coase article and the introduction by Williamson, the material is taken from the Spring 1988 issue of the *Journal of Law, Economics, and Organization*.

Willig, Robert D. (1976), "Consumer's Surplus Without Apology," *American Economic Review*, 66:4 (September), 589-597.

Yamey, B. S. (1972), "Predatory Price Cutting: Notes and Comments," *Journal of Law and Economics*, 15:1, 129-42.

Zitrain, Jonathan (1999), "The U-Microsoft Un-Remedy: Law Can Prevent the Problem That It Can't Patch Later," *Connecticut Law Review*, 31 (Summer), 1361-74. (LN)

Appendix Case Material Examined

Briefs

Amici Curiae America Online, Inc. Computer and Communications Industry Association, Project to Promote Competition & Innovation in the Digital Age, and Software & Information Industry Association in Support of the United States and State Appellees January 12, 2001.

Brief for Appellees United States and the State Plaintiffs, initial January 12, 2001, Final February 9, 2001.

Complaint May 18, 1998.

Defendant Microsoft Corporation's Revised Proposed Findings of Fact, September 10, 1999.

Defendant Microsoft Corporation's Proposed Conclusions of Law, January 18, 2000.

Defendant Microsoft Corporation's Memorandum in Opposition to the States' Memorandum and Proposed Conclusions of Law, January 8, 2000.

Joint Status Report, September 20, 2001.

Plaintiffs' Joint Proposed Findings of Fact, August 10, 1999.

Plaintiffs' Joint Proposed Conclusions of Law, December 6, 1999.

Plaintiffs' Joint Reply to Microsoft's Proposed Conclusions of Law, January 25, 2000.

Plaintiffs' Proposed Final Judgment, April 28, 2000.

Plaintiffs' Memorandum in Support of Proposed Final Judgment, April 28, 2000.

Remedies Brief of Amici Curiae Robert E. Litan, Roger G. Noll, William D. Nordhaus, and Frederic M. Scherer, April 27, 2000.

Direct Testimony

Allchin, James Edward, no date.[1]
Barksdale, Jim, October 13, 1998.

---

[1] The "no date" designation indicates the absence of a date in the posted document. However, the testimony was issued no later than the appearance in the courtroom. Citations in the text indicate the year of that appearance for undated direct testimony.

Chase, Brad, no date.

Colburn, David Martin, October 27, 1998.

Devlin, Michael T., no date.

Engstrom, Eric, January 1999.

Farber, David J., December 8, 1998.

Felten, Edward W., December 7, 1998.

Fisher, Franklin M., no date.

Gosling, Dr. James A., October 19, 1998 (actually says 1988).

Harris, William H. Jr., October 13, 1998.

Kempin, Joachim, no date.

Maritz, Paul, January 20, 1999.

Muglia, Robert, no date.

Myhrvold, Cameron, no date.

Poole, William, January 6, 1999.

Rosen, Daniel, no date.

Rose, John T., no date.

Schmalensee, Richard L., January 3, 1999.

Soyring, John, November 17, 1998.

Tevanian, Avadis Jr., October 12, 1998.

Warren-Boulton, Frederick R., November 11, 1998.

Weadock, Glen E., November 13, 1998.

Declaration of Franklin M. Fisher, May 12, 1998.

Declaration of David S. Sibley, May 15, 1998.

Statements in Support of the Final Judgment, April 28, 2000.

Greenhill, Robert F. and Jeffrey P. Williams

Henderson, Rebecca M.

Romer, Paul M.

Shapiro, Carl

Statement

Defendant Microsoft Corporation's Pretrial Statement October 6, 1998

Transcripts (dates and principal contents)

October 19, 1998, a.m. (Government's opening arguments)

October 19, 1998, p.m. (Government's opening arguments)

October 20, 1998, a.m. (Microsoft's opening arguments)

October 20, 1998, p.m. (Cross-examination of Jim Barksdale)

October 21, 1998, a.m. (Cross-examination of Jim Barksdale)

October 21, 1998, p.m. (Cross-examination of Jim Barksdale)

October 22, 1998, a.m. (Cross-examination of Jim Barksdale)

October 22, 1998, p.m. (Cross-examination of Jim Barksdale)

October 26, 1998, a.m. (Cross-examination of Jim Barksdale)

October 26, 1998, p.m. (Cross-examination of Jim Barksdale)

October 27, 1998, a.m. (Redirect-examination of Jim Barksdale)

October 27, 1998, p.m. (Redirect- and Recross-examination of Jim Barksdale)

November 2, 1998, a.m. (Discussion of procedural disputes)

November 2, 1998, p.m. (Excerpts of Gates's deposition; also appears as GX 1400)

November 4, 1998, a.m. (Cross-examination of Avadas Tevanian)

November 4, 1998, p.m. (Cross-examination of Avadas Tevanian)

November 5, 1998, a.m. (Cross-examination of Avadas Tevanian)

November 5, 1998, p.m. (Cross-examination of Avadas Tevanian)

November 9, 1998, a.m. (Redirect- and Recross-examination of Avadas Tevanian)

November 9, 1998, p.m. (Direct-Examination of Steven McGeady)

November 10, 1998, a.m. (Direct- and Cross-examination of Steven McGeady)

November 10, 1998, p.m. (Cross-examination of Steven McGeady)

November 12, 1998, a.m. (Cross-examination of Steven McGeady)

November 12, 1998, p.m. (Cross-, Redirect-, and Recross-examination of Steven McGeady)

November 16, 1998, a.m. (Cross-examination of Glen E. Weadock)

November 16, 1998, p.m. (Cross-examination of Glen E. Weadock)

November 17, 1998, a.m. (Cross-, Redirect-, and Recross-examination of Glen E. Weadock)

November 17, 1998, p.m. (Recross- and Redirect-examination of Glen E. Weadock, Cross-examination of John Soyring)

November 18, 1998, a.m. (Cross-examination of John Soyring)

November 18, 1998, p.m. (Cross-, Redirect-, and Recross-examination of John Soyring)

November 19, 1998, a.m. (Cross-examination of Frederick Warren-Boulton)

November 19, 1998, p.m. (Cross-examination of Frederick Warren-Boulton)

November 23, 1998, a.m. (Cross-examination of Frederick Warren-Boulton)

November 23, 1998, p.m. (Cross-examination of Frederick Warren-Boulton)

November 24, 1998, a.m. (Cross-examination of Frederick Warren-Boulton)

November 24, 1998, p.m. (Cross-examination of Frederick Warren-Boulton)

November 30, 1998, a.m. (Cross-examination of Frederick Warren-Boulton)

November 30, 1998, p.m. (Cross-examination of Frederick Warren-Boulton)

December 1, 1998, a.m. (Cross- and Redirect-examination of Frederick Warren-Boulton)

December 1, 1998, p.m. (Redirect- and Recross-examination of Frederick Warren-Boulton)

December 2, 1998, a.m. (Cross-examination of James A Gosling)

December 2, 1998, p.m. (Cross-examination of James A Gosling)

December 3, 1998, a.m. (Cross-examination of James A Gosling)

December 3, 1998, p.m. (Cross-examination of James A Gosling)

December 9, 1998, p.m. (Cross-examination of James A Gosling)

December 10, 1998, a.m. (Cross-examination of James A Gosling)

December 10, 1998, p.m. (Cross-, Redirect-, and Recross-examination of James A Gosling)

December 15, 1998, a.m. (Excerpts of Gates's deposition; Available DOJ as Gates 6; also Steve Wadsworth and Ron Rasmussen)

January 5, 1999, p.m. (Cross-examination of Franklin M. Fisher)

January 6, 1999, a.m. (Cross-examination of Franklin M. Fisher)

January 6, 1999, p.m. (Cross-examination of Franklin M. Fisher)

January 7, 1999, a.m. (Cross-examination of Franklin M. Fisher)

January 7, 1999, p.m. (Cross-examination of Franklin M. Fisher)

January 11, 1999, p.m. (Cross-examination of Franklin M. Fisher)

January 12, 1999, a.m. (Redirect-examination of Franklin M. Fisher)

January 12, 1999, p.m. (Redirect- and Recross-examination of Franklin M. Fisher)

January 13, 1999, a.m. (Redirect- and Recross-examination of Franklin M. Fisher)

January 13, 1999, p.m. (Cross-examination of Richard L. Schmalensee)

January 14, 1999, a.m. (Cross-examination of Richard L. Schmalensee)

January 19, 1999, a.m. (Cross-examination of Richard L. Schmalensee)

January 19, 1999, p.m. (Cross-examination of Richard L. Schmalensee)

January 20, 1999, a.m. (Cross-examination of Richard L. Schmalensee)

January 20, 1999, p.m. (Cross- and Redirect-examination of Richard L. Schmalensee)

January 21, 1999, a.m. (Redirect-examination of Richard L. Schmalensee)

January 21, 1999, p.m. (Redirect- and Recross-examination of Richard L. Schmalensee)

January 25, 1999, a.m. (Redirect- and Recross-examination of Richard L. Schmalensee)

January 25, 1999, p.m. (Cross-examination of Paul Maritz)

January 26, 1999, a.m. (Cross-examination of Paul Maritz)

January 26, 1999, p.m. (Cross-examination of Paul Maritz)

January 27, 1999, a.m. (Cross-examination of Paul Maritz)

January 27, 1999, p.m. (Cross- and Redirect-examination of Paul Maritz)

January 28, 1999, a.m. (Redirect-examination of Paul Maritz)

January 28, 1999, p.m. (Redirect- and Recross-examination of Paul Maritz)

February 1, 1999, a.m. (Direct-examination of James Allchin)

February 1, 1999, p.m. (Direct- and Cross-examination of James Allchin)

February 2, 1999, a.m. (Cross-examination of James Allchin)

February 2, 1999, p.m. (Cross- and Redirect-examination of James Allchin)

February 3, 1999, a.m. (Redirect- and Recross-examination of James Allchin)

February 3, 1999, p.m. (Recross-examination of James Allchin)

February 4, 1999, a.m. (Direct-, Cross-, Redirect-, and Recross-examination of Michael T. Devlin)

February 4, 1999, p.m. (Redirect- and Recross-examination of James Allchin)

February 8, 1999, a.m. (Cross-examination of William Poole)

February 8, 1999, p.m. (Cross-examination of William Poole)

February 9, 1999, a.m. (Cross-, Redirect- and Recross-examination of William Poole)

February 9, 1999, p.m. (Direct- and Cross-examination of Cameron Myhrvold)

February 10, 1999, a.m. (Cross-examination of Cameron Myhrvold)

February 10, 1999, p.m. (Cross-, Redirect-, and Recross-examination of Cameron Myhrvold)

February 11, 1999, a.m. (Direct- and Cross-examination of Brad Chase)

February 11, 1999, p.m. (Cross-examination of Brad Chase)

February 16, 1999, a.m. (Cross-examination of Brad Chase)

February 16, 1999, p.m. (Cross-examination of Brad Chase)

February 17, 1999, a.m. (Cross-examination of Brad Chase)

February 17, 1999, p.m. (Redirect- and Recross-examination of John Rose)

February 18, 1999, a.m. (Cross-examination of John Rose)

February 18, 1999, p.m. (Cross-examination of John Rose)

February 19, 1999, a.m. (Redirect- and Recross-examination of John Rose)

February 22, 1999, a.m. (Cross-examination of Dan Rosen)

February 22, 1999, p.m. (Cross-examination of Dan Rosen)

February 23, 1999, a.m. (Redirect- and Recross-examination of Dan Rosen)

February 23, 1999, p.m. (Cross-examination of Eric Engstrom)

February 24, 1999, a.m. (Cross- and Redirect- examination of Eric Engstrom; Direct-examination (a demonstration) of Joachim Kempin)

February 24, 1999, p.m. (Demonstration and Cross-examination of Joachim Kempin)

February 25, 1999, a.m. (Cross-examination of Joachim Kempin)

February 25, 1999, p.m. (Cross-examination of Joachim Kempin)

February 26, 1999, a.m. (Redirect- and Recross-examination of Joachim Kempin; Direct-examination of Robert Muglia (demonstration))

February 26, 1999, p.m. (Cross- and Redirect-examination of Robert Muglia)

June 1, 1999, a.m. (Direct-examination of Franklin M. Fisher)

June 1, 1999, p.m. (Direct-examination of Franklin M. Fisher)

June 2, 1999, a.m. (Direct and Cross-examination of Franklin M. Fisher)

June 2, 1999, p.m. (Cross-examination of Franklin M. Fisher)

June 3, 1999, a.m. (Cross-examination of Franklin M. Fisher)

June 3, 1999, p.m. (Cross- and Redirect-examination of Franklin M. Fisher)

June 4, 1999, a.m. (Redirect-examination of Franklin M. Fisher)

June 4, 1999, p.m. (Redirect- and Recross-examination of Franklin M. Fisher)

June 7, 1999, a.m. (Direct-examination of Garry Norris)

June 7, 1999, p.m. (Direct-examination of Garry Norris)

June 8, 1999, a.m. (Direct- and Cross-examination of Garry Norris

June 8, 1999, p.m. (Cross-examination of Garry Norris)

June 9, 1999, a.m. (Cross-examination of Garry Norris)

June 9, 1999, p.m. (Cross-, Redirect- and Recross-examination of Garry Norris)

June 10, 1999, a.m. (Direct-examination of Edward Felten)

June 10, 1999, p.m. (Direct-, Cross-, Redirect-, and Recross-examination of Edward Felten)

June 14, 1999, a.m. (Direct-examination of David Colburn)

June 14, 1999, p.m. (Direct-examination of David Colburn)

June 16, 1999, a.m. (Direct-examination of Gordon Eubanks)

June 16, 1999, a.m. (Cross-, Redirect-, and Recross-examination of Gordon Eubanks)

June 21, 1999, a.m. (Direct-examination of Richard L. Schmalensee)

June 21, 1999, p.m. (Direct-examination of Richard L. Schmalensee)

June 22, 1999, p.m. (Direct-examination of Richard L. Schmalensee)

June 23, 1999, a.m. (Direct-examination of Richard L. Schmalensee)

June 23, 1999, p.m. (Direct- and Cross-examination of Richard L. Schmalensee)

June 24, 1999, a.m. (Cross-examination of Richard L. Schmalensee)

June 24, 1999, p.m. (Cross- and Redirect-examination of Richard L. Schmalensee)

September 21, 1999, a.m. (Prosecution Closing Argument)

September 21, 1999, p.m. (Defense Closing Argument and Prosecution Reply)

February 22, 2000, a.m. (Arguments on the conclusions of law)

February 22, 2000, p.m. (Arguments on the conclusions of law)

May 24, 2000, a.m. (Arguments on Remedy)

May 24, 2000, p.m. (Arguments on Remedy)

February 26, 2001 (Circuit Court hearing)

February 27, 2001 (Circuit Court hearing)

Selected Exhibits

GX 1 Actual and Projected Microsoft market share, first introduced in Sibley declaration.

GX 20 Bill Gates, "The Internet Tidal Wave," May 25, 1995.

GX 21 Ben Slivka, "The Web is the Net Platform," May 29, 1995.

GX 22 E-mail chain including Bill Gates, May 31, 1995.

GX 23 GX 24 Thomas Reardon, "working with netscape," June 1, 1995. GX 23 is just the memo; GX 24 adds Maritz's memo forwarding to Gates and the agenda of the June 21, 1995 meeting. The agenda is also GX 32.

GX 33 Marc Andreessen, undated, untitled memo on June 21, 1995 Netscape-Microsoft meeting.

GX 34 David Kaiser (AOL) Report on Microsoft Netscape meeting, June 22, 1995.

GX 39 Brad Chase, "Winning the Internet platform battle," April 4, 1966. (Also GX 465 with appendixes.)

GX 47 Jim Allchin, "concerns for our future," December 20, 1996.

GX 48, GX 49, GX 50 Jim Allchin, "IE and Windows," January 2, 1997; GX 49 adds Maritz's reply; GX 50 adds Allchin's reply.

GX 51 "NC & Java Challenge," (slides) January 6, 1997 with cover from Maritz indicating preparation for Gates's use.

GX 53 Exchange between Maritz and David Cole, about introduction of IE 4, January 7, 1997.

GX 56 A series of e-mails from March 25-6, 1997 on strategy for issuing IE4.

GX 100 Amar Nehru, "Netscape Revenues," November 27, 1996.

GX 113 E-mails from July 10-14, 1997 on browser plans.

GX 128 Ben Slivka, "RE: internet client stuff," October 6, 1994, indicates efforts to secure rights to an existing browser to include in Windows 95.

GX 134 Russell Siegelman, December 12, 1994 indicates licensing of SpyGlass (a browser). Dan Rosen December 9, 1994 on problems of a deal with Netscape, James Allard, December 12, 1994 commenting negatively on a deal with Netscape.

GX 182 Nick Zaharias of Netscape, "Dell/Zenith Data Systems," March 14, 1996.

GX 202 Christian Wildheuer, "Memphis IEU focus groups report (long mail)," February 24, 1997. Reactions to possible features in Windows 98.

GX 204 Kumar Mehta, "FW: ie data," March 27, 1997 on the advantages of integrating Internet Explorer into Windows.

GX 205, GX 204 plus several comments from March 27-8, 1997.

GX 236 Ram Shiram of Netscape, "Re: Dell," undated discussion of competition on browser preference.

GX 259 "VJ98 SKUs and Pricing–Proposal." (undated, unsigned Microsoft "polluted Java" memorandum)

GX 279 Ron Whittier of Intel, "Microsoft Meeting August 2, 1995," August 2, 1995. Deals with assorted issues including Maritz statement "Internet is a platform."

GX 291 Letter from Gary Stimac of Compaq to Steve Ballmer of Microsoft, August 3, 1995 on issues with cooperative agreement with Microsoft.

GX 292 Response to Stimac letter from Don Hardwick of Microsoft to Steve Flannigan of Compaq, August 15, 1995.

GX 295 Bill Gates, "OEMs and the Internet," January 5, 1996. Complaint on greater attention given rival browsers. Urges better features and better promotion.

GX 297 Paul Maritz, "AOL," January 15 1996 on survey of what is loaded on computers from leading companies preceded by Joachim Kempin response. January 16, 1996 including mention of noncompliance by Compaq and HP.

GX 333 Bill Gates "The Use and Misuse of Technology (Q&A 10/24/95)" (distributed by *New York Times* Special Features).

GX 334, GX 485, GX 684 "How to Get to 30% Share in 12 Months," October 25, 1996.

GX 351 Bill Gates, "HTML Openness," January 28, 1997. On the desirability of features in Microsoft programs that encourage use of Windows.

GX 354 Jim Allchin, "'Losing a Franchise–The Microsoft Windows Story' (a new Harvard Case study)" February 18, 1997. (GX 475 has Gates's reply, February 19, 1997, followed by the original memo.)

GX 355 E-mails from March 20-21, 1997 on problems of developing IE4.

GX 365 Joachim Kempin, "DT-OS pricing strategy," December 16, 1997.

GX 401 Joachim Kempin, "Microsoft OEM Sales: FY'96 Midyear Review," January 22, 1996 (Slides).

GX 475, GX 354 plus Gates's reply, February 19, 1997.

GX 480 Jim Allchin, "IE," December 23, 1997. Discusses strategy, wants a more unified approach.

GX 510 Brad Chase, "Preserving the desktop paradise," April 4, 1997 (update of GX 39). (Also GX 512 which adds routing memorandum.)

GX 515 E-mail chain from February 6-7, 1998 on Internet Explorer prospects.

GX 518 E-mail chain from October 24-5, 1996 on limitations of Java. Ben Slivka's "Microsoft Java Strategy" is the main component.

GX 521 E-mail chain from April 13, 1995 on Internet strategy.

GX 623 John Ludwig, "RE: Netscape meeting reality," June 23, 1995. On how fast to introduce Internet Explorer.

GX 655 Carl Stork, "Memphis Plans," September 19, 1996 (Slides).

GX 921 E-mail chain May 10-15, 1995 on NSP.

GX 952 Thomas Reardon, "W3C and Netscape meetings 5/22," May 25, 1995.

GX 994 Nathan Myhrvold, "Telling It Like It Is," dated July 18, 1993, with a July 24, 1993 cover letter but with a May 11, 1994 date at the top of all the later pages.

GX 1259 Gary L. Reback, June 23, 1995, complaint to Department of Justice with Andreessen's notes (GX 33) attached.

GX 1334 E-mail chain from April 20-23, 1997 on Java strategy and ActiveX.

GX 1400 Gates Deposition as Played in Court, November 9, 1998.

GX 1467 Gates Deposition material admitted January 13, 1999 (as transcribed in court; also available as excerpts of original 8a, 8b, 8c, 8d, 8f)

GX 1469 Deposition Excerpts of Christopher Jones from trial transcript January 13, 1999, p.m.

Gates 3 (played in Court November 16, 1998)

Gates 4 (played in Court November 17, 1998)

Gates 5 (played in Court December 2, 1998)

Gates 7 (played in Court January 5, 1999)

DX 1807 E-mail from Jim Clark to McGeady urging testimony, July 13, 1998.

The Gates deposition excerpts are available at various locations on the Internet. The Antitrust Division's deposition section of its site for the case lists seven deposition extracts played and one admitted. Those played also appear in the transcripts.

Decisions

United States Court of Appeals for the District of Columbia Circuit, June 28, 2001.

United States District Court for the District of Columbia, Findings of Fact, November 5, 1999.

United States District Court for the District of Columbia, "Conclusions of Law," April 3, 2000.

United States District Court for the District of Columbia, Final Judgment, June 8, 2000.

Index